Designing
Object-Oriented
C++ Applications

Using the Booch Method

Robert Cecil Martin

Object Mentor Associates

Prentice Hall, Englewood Cliffs, New Jersey 07632

Martin, Robert C.
    Designing object-oriented C++ applications using the Booch method
 / Robert C. Martin.
        p.   cm.
    "An Alan R. Apt Book."
    Includes index.
    ISBN 0-13-203837-4
    1. Object-oriented programming. 2. C++ (Computer program
language) 3. Computer software--Development.   I. Title.
QA76.64.M384 1995
005.13'3--dc20   94-47129
                                                         CIP

Publisher: Alan Apt
Production Editor: Mona Pompili
Cover Designer: Wendy Alling Judy
Copy Editor: Nick Murray
Production Coordinator: Lori Bulwin
Editorial Assistant: Shirley McGuire

 © 1995 by Prentice-Hall, Inc.
A Simon & Schuster Company
Englewood Cliffs, New Jersey 07632

Printed in the United States of America

10 9 8 7 6 5 4 3 2

ISBN   0-13-203837-4

PRENTICE-HALL INTERNATIONAL (UK) Limited, *London*
PRENTICE-HALL OF AUSTRALIA PTY. LIMITED, *Sydney*
PRENTICE-HALL CANADA, INC., *Toronto*
PRENTICE-HALL HISPANOAMERICANA, S.A., *Mexico*
PRENTICE-HALL OF INDIA PRIVATE LIMITED, *New Delhi*
PRENTICE-HALL OF JAPAN, INC., *Tokyo*
SIMON & SCHUSTER ASIA PTE. LTD., *Singapore*
EDITORA PRENTICE-HALL DO BRASIL, LTDA., *Rio de Janeiro*

For Ann Marie, Angela, Micah, Gina and Justin . . .

There is no greater treasure,
Nor any wealthier trove,
Than the company of my family,
And the comfort of their love.

Forward

By Grady Booch

Writing good software is indeed hard work. Moreover, the demand for quality software continues to grow at an insane pace, fueled by the increased connectivity of distributed computing systems and by greater user expectations for better visualization of and access to information. The good news is that this makes for very interesting times for the professional software developer.

Another piece of good news is that, over the past decade or so, developments in abstract data type theory, modularity, information modeling, and software process have evolved to provide the professional developer a sound collection of practices that can be used to attack this growing complexity. In many ways, these practices all come together in the form of object-oriented technology. Most notably, a whole family of object-oriented programming languages, such as C++ and Smalltalk, have emerged. In addition, a variety of object-oriented analysis and design methods have been proposed that exploit these object-oriented languages and help us model complex systems.

Yet, for the developer building real systems under very real schedules and limited resources, all theory is irrelevant if it is not pragmatic. Reality is that languages such as C++ and Smalltalk are not simple, and the applications to which we direct them are even less simple. Just because you are using an object-oriented programming language does not mean that all your projects will automatically be on schedule, under budget, and free of all flaws.

Robert Martin is, first and foremost, a very pragmatic developer. I've had the honor to work with him, and I've learned many things from his experience. This book speaks clearly of that experience. In this work, you will understand how to apply C++ effectively. You will also learn how to apply C++ in the context of the Booch method of object-oriented analysis and design, a method that provides a unification of what we know as the best practices today in object-oriented development.

Enjoy. I know I did in reading Robert's manuscript, and I'm sure you'll gain many useful — and ultimately very practical — insights as well.

Grady Booch
Chief Scientist
Rational Software Corporation

Preface

Software design is hard, and we need all the help we can get.

— Bjarne Stroustrup, 1991

Software design *is* hard. We are now well into the fifth decade since John Von Neumann conceived of the notion of a stored program. And although there have been many advances in both the theory and practice of software engineering, in comparison to our need, those advances have been precious and few. Object-Oriented Design is one of those advances and is the subject of this book.

Let's get one thing straight. Object-Oriented Design is not going to save the software world—it's not even going to come close. Applications designed using OOD will still be difficult to estimate, will still be difficult to implement, will still be difficult to maintain; and will still have bugs. Software design will still be hard. What OOD *will* do is provide some useful new tools that you can employ while designing software applications. Those tools, properly employed, will help you to manage the complexity of designing, implementing and supporting a software design. They will also help you to build your designs in terms of reusable high level components.

OOD is a complex topic. Many books have been written on the topic. Most of them describe OOD in terms of its definitions, notations, and methods. This book looks at the subject from the point of view of its *practice*. It tries to answer the question: "How do I do OOD?" In trying to answer that question I will employ two specific tools: *The Booch Notation*[1] for recording object-oriented designs and the C++[2] programming language, a language that supports object-oriented programming. We will explore how designs can be documented and manipulated using Booch's notation, and how they can be translated into C++. During this exploration we will encounter the important principles of OOD and investigate many ways in which they may be employed.

---

1. Grady Booch, *Object-Oriented Design with Applications,* (Copyright © 1991 by The Benjamin/ Cummings Publishing Company).
2. Bjarne Stroustrup, *The C++ Programming Language, 2d. ed.* (Addison Wesley, 1991).

About This Book

Goals/Purpose

There are many books describing the various practices of object-oriented Design (OOD). There are many other books describing the syntax and usage of C++. This book is a synthesis of these two concepts. C++ is a rich and expressive language. Having C as a subset may encourage software engineers to use it as "a better C." While this is not altogether a bad thing, it falls short of the potential benefits that a true object-oriented approach could yield. This book presents the fundamental concepts of object-oriented design and shows how to apply those concepts using C++. The approach is a practical, problem-solving presentation, written for those who are, or aspire to become, practitioners of object-oriented design. Special attention is given to traps, pitfalls, and techniques in the application of C++ to OOD.

The Booch notation was chosen as the representational vehicle for OOD because of its popularity, scalability, and notational elegance. The notation is explored in detail, and is used to present the concepts of OOD. Where appropriate, the notation is translated into corresponding C++ code. This provides the reader with a "Rosetta stone" describing the linkage between the abstract OOD notation and the syntax of C++.

The practices of software engineering receive special attention, both in the creation of the logical design, and the physical development environment. The methods for designing and developing "big" software are discussed in detail. The goal is to provide the tools needed to deal with large and complex projects.

Audience

This book is for software engineers—specifically for those who are interested in learning how to design applications using object-oriented design techniques, and who want to implement those applications in C++. It is assumed that the reader has a minimal working knowledge of C++.

You should be prepared to work hard while reading this book. Quite a bit of detail is presented, and you will benefit by studying it carefully. You can also browse the book to gain a general notion of OOD, its representation in the Booch notation, and its ultimate expression in C++. However, diligence in learning these techniques, as opposed to just skimming them, will be well worth the effort.

Anatomy and Physiology of Design

OOD is a complex discipline. It has its own vernacular, full of words, diagrams, principles, and concepts. No reasonable discussion about OOD can occur until you have learned this vocabulary. Thus the first five chapters of this book are a step-by-step anatomy and physiology of OOD. They present the concepts, definitions and principles of OOD by exploring a number of relatively simple case studies. These case studies come from a variety of application domains, so that you can learn how to use OOD and C++ to solve diverse sets of problems. Each case study works through a simple object-oriented design, and often shows its implementation in C++.

The first five chapters also present the Booch notation as a vehicle for recording and manipulating object-oriented design decisions. The Booch notation is "large"; it provides many notational conventions for dealing with issues at all levels of the design. Each of the first five chapters explores a different part of the notation and how it applies to OOD and C++.

The next three chapters demonstrate how to apply the practices and principles of OOD to a problem of significant size. They are an expedition through the analysis, high-level design, low-level design, and physical design of a single complex application.

During this expedition, we thoroughly discuss the methods and rationale behind the important design decisions. Also, many false starts and design errors are documented. These errors are real, not contrived examples; I actually made these design errors while writing this book. Furthermore the methods by which these errors are discovered and solved are represented as faithfully as possible.

By reading through these chapters, you will follow the path that I took while doing the design, including the dead ends, cul-de-sacs, and wrong turns. In my opinion, studying design errors is just as educational (if not more educational) as studying "correct" solutions.

Software Is Hard

The real crux of the "software crisis" (and the real reason why books like this are necessary) is that software *is* hard. An application comprises myriads of intricate little details. It is hard to weave all those details into a working program. Why should this be so? Why is a concept as easy to grasp as a word processor, for example, so hideously complex to implement? It is because humans are so good at abstracting away details.

By using the two words "word processor" I have described a broad class of highly complex and intricate applications. I have also abstracted away all the details involved with those applications. Software is hard because we are so good at envisioning abstract applications without thinking about the details. Somewhere in our gut we *know* what we want an application to do. We don't have to describe it in detail, we just *know*. We *know* what a word processor does. It's obvious. The concept is simple, and so we expect the task of writing the software to be simple. Only when we enumerate the enormous amount of details involved with making a real word processor do we begin to get a feeling for the true complexity of the application. However, enumeration is not enough. Those details must be organized, orchestrated, and intermixed with the details and limitations of the language and machine. The result is a daunting task requiring far more time and effort than generally expected. Software is hard because it takes an enormous effort to produce applications that can be so simply conceived of. Software is hard because it takes so much effort to keep pace with users' requirements and expectations. Software is hard because it is so easy to dream up.

On the other hand, computer hardware is far outstripping the lay person's expectations. It used to be that a computer would require hundreds of engineers to design and build. Nowadays, a moderately skilled hardware engineer can tinker a far superior computer together in the basement. Computer memory used to be hideously expensive, large, and power-hungry. Now we buy gigabyte disks the size of pocket radios, and put them in the multimegabyte, multimegahertz computers that we keep in our briefcases.

This creates a double-whammy for the software crisis. Not only are users' expectations growing faster than our ability to produce workable applications, but the computers themselves are improving faster still. Users reasonably expect that more powerful computers should have more powerful applications to run on them. Unfortunately the power of the computer doesn't provide much assistance in managing the complexity of a huge software project.

To be sure, there have been some very powerful improvements in software technology. But it is nothing near the sort of wild expansion that computer hardware has seen. Suppose that two software engineers are separately trying to write the same program. One is using 1990s software-development technology, and the other is using the tools and techniques from the 1950s. Given that the application can be handled by the corresponding hardware technologies, how much more efficient would the modern engineer be? Is she 30% more efficient? Twice as efficient? Could she be ten times as efficient? Whatever the answer, it will in no way compare with the sheer orders of magnitude by which the efficiency of hardware engineers has increased. One hardware engineer in the 1990s can implement what took armies of engineers to implement in the 1950s.

Hardware engineers are so much more efficient today because they have developed a technology that allows them to build upon each other's work. Nobody has to redesign a flip-flop.[3] Nobody has to build a flip-flop. You can buy them by the thousands in little integrated circuits. Engineers don't have to design op-amps, or adders, or CPUs, or any of the other staples of electronic devices. They can just buy the building blocks and tie them together using standard electronic engineering techniques. And every year the building blocks become more powerful and more complex. Every year this encapsulated power and complexity is made directly available for hardware engineers to bring to bear upon their

---

3. An electronic memory device capable of storing 1 bit of information.

designs. It is this encapsulation and mass production of complexity that has so magnified the power of the hardware engineer.

No such revolution has yet taken place in the realm of software engineering. Oh, we might not have to write **sort** functions anymore.[4] And maybe most of our I/O is taken care of for us by an operating system. But nobody is out there selling "Integrated Application Modules" that software engineers can buy and hook together with the kind of efficiency experienced by hardware engineers. As a group, software engineers are not building upon each other's work. We continue to reimplement different variations of the same functions over and over again.

OOD Can Make Software "Softer"

Software may be hard, but OOD can help to soften it a bit. OOD provides the tools and techniques by which we can encapsulate a certain level of functionality and complexity. Using OOD, we can create black-box software modules that hide a great deal of complexity behind a simple interface. Software engineers can tie these black boxes together using standard software techniques.

Booch calls these black boxes *class categories*. Class categories are comprised of entities known as *classes*, which are bound together by *class relationships*. A great deal of complexity can be buried in a class, while its interfaces can remain relatively simple. This takes advantage of the fact that people are so good at abstracting away details. If we can bury all the details away in some class, then we don't have to think about them any more. We can use the class as often as we like, and for as many applications as we see fit, but we never have to consider the details buried inside it again. This is an enormously powerful concept. Such classes allow us to wield great power at relatively low cost.

Class categories organize groups of classes into mechanisms that implement high-level policies, *independent of the details that they control*. Such categories, designed for one application, can be reused in many other applications that require the same kind of policies.

By 1990 there were some class libraries for sale. These libraries provided basic, low-level classes such as queues, linked-lists, sorted-lists, complex numbers, and so on. They provided abstractions that software engineers could readily build upon and incorporate into their own class categories. By 1992 there were some libraries of class categories for sale that encapsulated the policies that managed particular graphic user interfaces. These category libraries, also called "frameworks", made it much simpler to design and implement applications that employed those GUIs. Again, these frameworks can be built upon to ease the job of designing and building software.

Will more libraries of class categories appear on the market, with more and more policies and functionality and complexity buried within simple interfaces? Will it one day be possible to buy a "Word Processor" framework, or a "Spreadsheet" framework? Will soft-

---

4. Although I'd be willing to bet that many of you have within the last year or so.

ware engineers be able to tie such wildly complex entities together with the same ease and efficiency that hardware engineers currently tie CPUs, UARTs, and RAMs together? That would certainly be a worthy goal. It may be that OOD can move us closer to achieving it.

Acknowledgements

Question: How can I get you to read this section? Without the acknowledged individuals, this work would not have been possible. These people deserve to be recognized, and so I want you to read their names. But you won't do that if I simply list their names, so I am going to give you some incentive to get to know these people. Please read on.

I first became interested in object-oriented programming (OOP) in 1985. I read Adele Goldberg's excellent books on Smalltalk-80, and bought a Smalltalk compiler for my Macintosh, which taught me much about OOP. At the same time, I attempted to implement pseudo object-oriented inheritance and message-dispatching mechanisms in C. This turned out to be very difficult, and I eventually abandoned the idea, but not before I had several stimulating conversations with a friend and associate named Jim Newkirk. We spent many hours discussing object-oriented design while attempting to use the "inheritance mechanisms" that I had invented for C.

In 1986 I got a copy of Bjarne Stroustrup's first edition of *The C++ Programming Language*. Its similarity in size and style to Kernighan and Ritchie's wonderful *The C Programming Language* was extremely compelling. I said to myself, "Oh, this must be the next C."

After reading this book, and becoming enthralled by the language, I found myself leading a one-man abortive campaign to get my employer to purchase a C++ compiler. But the cost, at that time, was high, and the interest among my co-workers was low, so I was unable to achieve this goal. It was difficult to convince people even that strong typing would be beneficial, let alone attempt to explain the odd appellation of object-oriented programming.

It was not until 1989 that I was able to get my hands on a real C++ compiler. By that time I had written thousands of lines of object-oriented code, but none in C++. I bought a copy of Dewhurst and Stark's *Programming in C++* and I quickly began exploring the language and getting used to its quirks and features. In this process, I am not even nearing completion.

In 1990 I read Coad's *OOA*, Booch's *Object-Oriented Design with Applications*, and *Designing Object-Oriented Software* by Wirfs-Brock, Wilkerson, and Wiener. I began applying the techniques of OOD that I learned in these books to the applications I was writing for my employer. I also adopted Booch's notation as my prime mechanism for recording design decisions. I was pleasantly surprised that the notation, odd as it may seem at first glance, was actually quite easy to draw by hand and allowed me to record my designs with a density that I had not experienced with other notational methods.

In the middle of 1991, my co-worker, Bill Vogel, got a call from a recruiter looking for object-oriented engineers. After some discussion with the agent on the other end of the phone, he handed the phone over to me and said: "Uncle Bob, I think this is for you." That phone call eventually led me to leave my employer and begin working as a consultant for Rational, where Grady Booch was employed as chief scientist.

At Rational I worked on a product called "Rose." I was fortunate enough to work with Grady on several projects during my months there. I was also fortunate to be working with a group of some of the most astounding engineers that I have ever met. The Rose team was awesome in the sheer brain-power of its members. I learned a great deal from all of them. There were, to mention a few, Paul Rogers, the cool-head; Bob Weissman, the trouble-shooter; Paul Jasper, the sound-man; Dave Stevenson, the rocket scientist; and Mike Higgs, the pragmatist.

While working at Rational, I conceived the idea for this book. I wrote drafts of the first three chapters, and showed them to Grady. He was kind enough to read and review them, and then to guide me into the publishing process.

Grady introduced me to Alan Apt of Prentice Hall, who is the editor of this book. Alan is a diligent and enthusiastic editor. He recruited some of the industry's top people to review my work—names like Steve Buroff, Jim Coplien, Mike Vilot, and Stan Lippman. Of Stan's reviews I will say only that they caused me, at once, the most pain and profit.

Of course this was just the kick-off. Many other people reviewed my work. Brett Schuchert, Bob Weissman, and Mike Higgs deserve special mention. To Jim Newkirk, who became the sounding-board for many of my partially formed ideas, and who made many contributions of his own, I would like to say a heartfelt thank you.

Writing a book takes a great deal of time, and for a man who is supporting a large family, that time must be taken away from that family. This book could never even have been conceived, let alone written, if not for the faithful and loving support provided to me by my wonderful wife Ann Marie, and all my terrific kids: Angela, Micah, Gina, and Justin. Every man should be as lucky as I am.

The production of this book was an arduous task, and would have been beyond my abilities were it not for the unfailing efforts of Jennifer Kohnke and Mona Pompili, Jim Newkirk and Bhama Rao. The harder I worked, the harder they worked. Thanks.

Much of what appears in the pages to come has been significantly influenced by the fluid and incredibly dynamic discussions that appear on the net. Among those "netters" who have had a profound influence on my thinking are Jim Adcock, Steve Clamage, Jamshid Afshar, Mark Terribile, John Skaller, Scott Meyers, Marshall Cline, Paul Lucas, Red Mitchell, and John Goodsen.

Finally, there are several people who deserve mention because they have influenced my thinking concerning software over the last two decades. Of course if they were all enumerated, the list would fill many dozens of pages. So I will constrain myself to mention just these few: Dave Lasker, who helped a would-be consultant achieve his goals; Ken Finder, who taught wisdom to a fool; Jerry Fitzpatrick, who believed the weakling could defeat the giant; and Tim Conrad, who turned impossible dreams into a few week's joyous labor.

Contents

00

1

2

Managing Complexity   106

3

Analysis and Design   **189**

4

Paradigm Crossings   **271**

5

High-Level OOAD: A Case Study   321

7

8

Epilogue 471

Appendix A

C++ Coding Guidelines 475

Appendix B

Multiprocessing: Concepts and Notation 480

I

Figures

3

7

6

Appendix B

C++ Listings

3

4

00

OOverview

The reason for accepting this extra complexity is that it permits a wider range of concepts to be conveniently expressed.

— Ole-Johan Dahl and C. A. R. Hoare

The discipline of object-oriented design is more complex than other software disciplines. This complexity derives partially from variety. Objects, and the classes that describe them, come in many varieties. Also, a large variety of relationships can exist between them. Moreover, each different kind of object, class, or relationship has its own unique semantics. This complexity makes the discipline of OOD harder to learn than others. However, it also creates a richness and expressiveness that does not exist in other software design disciplines. It is in this expressiveness that we find some of the benefits of OOD. When we describe a software application in terms of interrelated objects, we find that the resulting design is clearer, simpler, and more robust, and that its pieces enjoy a higher percentage of reuse. Thus we are willing to endure the complexity of the discipline to achieve simplicity and elegance in the design.

Introduction

This chapter is divided into two parts. The first part is presented in a question and answer style. In it I discuss why OOD is important, what benefits the engineer is likely to derive from it, and how it differs from other design disciplines. I also talk about C++ and why it is a good choice for implementing object-oriented designs.

1

The second part of this chapter a tutorial format. It can be considered either an intro-duction to or a review of the fundamental concepts of OOD. It is intended to familiarize the reader with the vocabulary and concepts discussed in the later chapters, and to relate some of those concepts with C++ structures.

In the second part we discuss just the *first principles* of object-oriented design. We talk about objects, what they are, what they do, and how they relate to each other. We discuss the various forms of classes, some of which define objects, and some of which do not. We describe the various relationships that can exist between classes, and the ways access to those relationships.

Part 1: Some Common Questions about OOD

Before we get into subject of what OOD is, I would like to address a number of questions that are commonly asked by people who are considering the transition into OOD.

What is object-oriented design?

Object-oriented design is an engineering discipline. The goal of that discipline is to *man-age dependencies* within a program. It achieves this goal by dividing the program into chunks of a manageable size, and then hiding those chunks behind interfaces and rerouting the dependencies between the chunks to the interfaces. Thus, given a client in one chunk and a server in another, no part of the client has a dependency upon the server. Instead the client depends upon the interface that hides the server. Moreover, and most importantly, the interface does not depend upon the server. Instead *the dependency has been inverted so that the server depends upon the interface*. Thus, there are no transitive dependencies between the client and the server.

This *inversion* of dependencies means that we can reuse both clients and servers in other contexts. A client that has no dependencies upon specific servers does not require those servers to be brought along when the client is reused in other programs. The client simply requires that the interfaces that it uses be fully implemented (i.e., some kind of server is behind those interfaces). The reusers may implement those interfaces by any means that they choose.

The inversion of dependencies also means that changes made to one part of a program need not ripple throughout the rest of the program. Such changes will be contained within a particular client or server, but since there are no dependencies upon the client or server, those changes will be irrelevant to the other software modules in the system.

Object-oriented design is a paradigm in which to frame solutions to software prob-lems. It is a paradigm of abstraction that allows us to represent entities from the problem domain as software objects with particular states and behaviors. Such objects may be dealt with at many levels of abstraction, from the very general to the very specific. OOD provides an easy way to stereotype a set of different but related objects beneath a single abstraction. As far as the similarities of those objects allow, they can be treated as objects of the same type.

The ability to create stereotypes is very powerful. It allows designers to define boundaries that hide details. For example, though an application may deal with several different modems, we can generalize the interface to those modems so that their differences are not seen by the rest of the application, which simply deals with the abstract concept of a *modem*. Thus, code that manages those modem abstractions depends only upon the modem interface, not upon the code that implements that interface. Thus we can reuse the code that manages the modem abstraction for many different kinds of modems. Also, when new kinds of modems are added to the system, they can be incorporated into the abstraction. The rest of the application will be unaware that it is dealing with a new type of modem.

Is OOD better than previous software-design disciplines? If so, why?

In one of his reviews of this chapter, Jim Coplien likened this question to asking if a drill is better than a saw. He has a point. In many ways OOD is simply another tool that software engineers can apply to the problems that they are solving. However, it is also true that solving certain software problems without OOD is rather like trying to saw a sheet of plywood by using a drill.

Yes, OOD is an improvement in the way that we model certain complex tasks. Using OOD, we describe a computer application in terms of interfaces rather than implementations. Those interfaces become software entities in their own right, and depend neither upon the software that uses them, nor the software that implements them. Therefore, those interfaces represent stereotypes, general umbrellas under which we can group many different implementations. The ability to create stereotypes, and the functions that manipulate those stereotypes without knowing the exact implementation they are manipulating, supports more flexible and robust designs.

For example, consider operating systems that provide device independence. Device independence provides interfaces or stereotypes called **files** that can represent many different kinds of I/O devices. Programs usually do not need to know which kind of I/O device they are manipulating; they manipulate the **file** interface instead. This provides for a great deal of flexibility and robustness in the designs of the software applications that use it. If those programs had to handle the differences between I/O devices intrinsically, then they would be less flexible and less robust. OOD provides a simple way to expand this kind of stereotyping beyond I/O devices to objects within the application domain.

Is OOD a revolution, or has it evolved from "older" design methods?

There is a lot of discussion (i.e., argument) about this point. The revolutionaries want to throw away all the old techniques and do OOD from now on. The evolutionists believe that OOD is an extension of structured analysis and design (SA/SD), that SA/SD should still be practiced, but with an object layer on top of it.

SA/SD and OOD can trace their roots back to about the same time, circa 1967. The seeds of both concepts were discussed in papers[1] whose overall concern was to explore various ways to structure data and algorithms. One set of papers, primarily written by Dijkstra and Hoare, talked about the proper structure of program control. They spoke about the harmfulness of **goto** statements and how programs should be structured in terms of loops, decisions, and sequences. This concept came to be known as *structured programming*. The other set of papers, written by Ole-Johan Dahl, discussed block structure in languages. One such block was known as a *class*, and it had most of the characteristics that we now identify with object-oriented programming.

These two concepts diverged almost instantly. Structured programming became all the rage in the late 1960s and especially throughout the 1970s. The industry was initially in turmoil about the proscription of **goto**. It was a huge conceptual leap for most of us. Many of us had been happily glorying in the "clever" control structures that we could build into our programs. When, **goto**s were suddenly considered to be harmful, many of us felt that doing without **goto** was like doing without an arm. Eventually, of course, most of us realized the wisdom of using a regular set of control structures. To this simple idea were added the ideas behind *structured analysis* and *structured design* (SA/SD). Men like Constantine, Yourdon, DeMarco, and Page-Jones wove together an elegant methodology whereby software could be analyzed, designed, and implemented. These became known as the *structured techniques*.

In the meantime, object-oriented programming was finding its way into research labs and educational institutions. While the precepts of structured programming could be practiced on any computer and in any computer language, object-oriented programming was very difficult without special language features that allowed the declaration of classes and the instantiation of objects, and that provided the semantics for the relationships between classes. In the late 1960s, there was only one such language: Simula-67. During the 70's Alan Kay et al. at the Xerox Palo Alto Research Center (PARC) created a new language based on the object-oriented approach. It was called Smalltalk. Smalltalk and several other object-oriented programming languages (OOPLs) remained isolated as special-purpose or "research" languages until the mid 1980s. During this time of isolation, those research teams discovered many of the principles of OOD. Thus, even though OOD and SA/SD had a common birth, they evolved separately.

---

1. O.-J. Dahl, E. W. Dijkstra, and C.A.R. Hoare, *Structured Programming,* (London and New York: Academic Press, 1972).

OOD approaches software design from a perspective that is entirely different from SA/SD. SA/SD focuses upon and exposes the structure of data, and the processes that manipulate it. In OOD processes and data structures are hidden and nearly irrelevant; they are subordinate to objects, their interfaces, and their responsibilities.[2]

The sudden popularity of OOD in the 1990s is indeed a revolution, but this does not mean that the older design methods are obsolete or useless. As with all successful revolutions, the foundation of the new regime must be laid upon the best aspects of what went before—and much of what went before was very, very good. The design methodologies of the 1970s and 1980s revealed many valuable concepts. We daren't ignore them. Many of these concepts will be discussed and integrated into OOD in the chapters that follow.

How is OOD different from more traditional software methods?

Consider a structured design, which consists of a set of modules arranged in a tree. The root of the tree is the main module. The leaves of the tree are the utility modules and low-est-level functions.   The tree represents the calling hierarchy. Each module calls those modules that are directly below it, and is called by those modules directly above it.

Which of these modules captures the policies that are of primary importance to the application? Those that are close to the top, of course. The modules at the bottom simply implement the smallest of details. The modules at the top are concerned with the bigger problems, and implement the bigger solutions.

Thus, the higher one goes in this hierarchy, the more abstract the concepts are, the more germane they are to the problem domain of the application, and the less germane they are to the solution domain of the application. The farther down one goes, the more detailed the concepts become, the less relevant they are to the problem domain, and the more relevant they are to the solution domain.

However, since the modules on top call the modules beneath them, those higher-order modules *depend* upon the details beneath them. To say this another way, *the modules that contain the relevant abstractions depend upon the modules that contain the irrelevant details!* This means that when changes are made to the details, the abstractions are affected. Moreover, if we attempt to reuse one of those abstractions, we must drag along all the details that it depends upon.

In OOD, we attempt to invert these dependencies. We create abstractions that are independent of any details. And we create details that depend heavily upon those abstractions. This *inversion of dependencies* is the prime difference between OOD and the more traditional techniques — it is what OOD is really all about.

---

2. Wirfs-Brock, *Designing Object-Oriented Software,* (Englewood Cliffs, NJ: Prentice Hall, 1990), Chapter 4.

Software is software. Isn't OOD just a new face painted on an old canvas?

No! It is a new way to paint. This is not to say that designers must throw away everything they know about design and start from scratch. It *is* to say that designers must learn a new technique and integrate it with their experience and talent.

As Booch says, "Let there be no doubt that object-oriented design is fundamentally different from traditional structured design approaches."[3] The structured approach puts a great deal of emphasis on separating the definition of the data from the definition of the processes. It models an application as a set of processes with data passing among them. Object-oriented design uses a completely different perspective. It hides the data and processes within objects that have interfaces and responsibilities. It models an application as a set of objects collaborating with one another to fulfill their responsibilities.

Will OOD solve all my design problems?

OOD is not the silver bullet with which we will eliminate the software crisis. Nor is it the prelude to the software millennium. It is simply a technique. However, it is a *good* technique, and it will affect many of the problems that currently plague this industry. It will also, undoubtedly, call forth a whole set of new problems.

The real problem in this industry is this: The complexity of the problems we are trying to solve is increasing more rapidly than the ability of our technology to cope with it. OOD gives us some very important tools for dealing with complex applications. However, if the current trend continues, the problems we face today will appear trivial when compared with the problems ten years from now. Will OOD be able to handle the problems of the third millennium? I can't say. All I will venture is that it will be an important step on the way.

What can I really expect from OOD?

You can expect headaches; OOD is complex both to learn, and then to master. You can expect disappointment; OOD is immature, and there are several unsolved problems. You can expect to learn the appreciation of a new technique; OOD is *fun* after you get the hang of it. You can expect to be a better designer; OOD will provide you with tools for creating more robust, maintainable, and reusable designs.

Tools are what OOD provides us. Talent and experience are important, but they are also impotent without good tools to give them the means of expression. The better the

---

3. Interview with Grady Booch, *The C++ Journal,* vol. 2., no. 1 (1992).

tools, the more effectively the designer will be able to express his talents. OOD provides a set of superior tools with which software engineers will be better able to design complex applications.

Is C++ a "true" object-oriented programming language?

This is a matter of some controversy. Many software engineers feel that C++ lacks some essential features of a "true" OOPL—features like garbage collection, multiple-dispatch, or covariant function arguments. However, the lack of these controversial features hardly impairs an engineer's ability to implement an object-oriented design in C++. C++ is fully capable of implementing object-oriented designs for a wide variety of applications, elegantly and efficiently.

In my view, any language that *directly* supports the implementation of object-oriented designs, is as "true" an OOPL as is necessary. C++ is well suited to this task. It *directly* supports inheritance, polymorphism, encapsulation, and abstraction, which are the essentials of OOD. Furthermore, its compatibility with C makes it an ideal transition language for those engineers who know C and want to learn an OOPL. Lastly, C++ can support industrial-strength software. It sacrifices little if any efficiency in order to support the OO paradigm. Megaline programs can be written in C++, and the full range of C development tools can be used in the effort.

Why was the Booch notation chosen for this book?

Design notations for OOD are appearing everywhere. There are more OOD notations than there are notations for the more traditional approaches. Why? Because OOD has such a rich fund of relationships, objects, and class types. Because of this richness, OOD really *needs* a notational shorthand.

Is any one notation better than the others? A notation is simply a way to represent design decisions in a concise and comprehensible form. To be useful, a notation must capture as many kinds of design decisions as possible, and represent them in semantically meaningful ways. These are the only true criteria. Religious factions may be engaged in battle over the shape of class icons or the direction of inheritance arrows, but these issues are hardly relevant.   The shape of an icon has little meaning as long as it is easy to draw, easy to recognize, and nicely represents the intended concept.

Beyond usability, there is one other consideration that influences on the choice of notation. The Latin language is certainly a usable language. It was used by the government of one of the largest and most long-lived empires that the world has known, but it would be a poor choice as the language for a modern detective novel, because nobody speaks it anymore. Not only must the design notation we choose be useful, it must also be well known, so that we can communicate our design decisions as easily as possible.

The Booch notation is both usable and well known. Of all the notations I have seen, it contains the most expressive power, because it contains the largest repertoire of icons and symbols for the expression of relationships, objects, class types, and their modifiers. It is also quite well known in the OO industry. Thus, I consider it to be an excellent choice for recording design decisions.

Part 2: Tutorial

This tutorial presents the fundamental concepts of OOD. The goal is to provide basic familiarity with these concepts and the terms and vocabulary that prevail in the OO community. To achieve this goal, I describe the concepts and vocabulary in terms of simple examples.

The examples used in this section are purposely simplistic and generally unrelated to software concepts. I use examples such as cars and books instead of examples from real software problems, because I want to describe the OO concepts as clearly as possible without pollution from other software sources. I don't want you to be trying to solve a software problem when I want you to be learning a fundamental concept. The chapters that follow this one will present many very challenging software problems; fear not. This chapter is not the place for them.

Vocabulary is something of a problem. There are two diverse OO vocabularies in concurrent use. One is used in books that are written about Smalltalk, and the other is used in books that are written about C++. Both vocabularies use completely different words to describe precisely the same concepts.

In my opinion, OOD is OOD. There is not a C++ variety and a Smalltalk variety. Certainly some of the strategies may differ depending upon the target language, but the primary principles and motivations are the same. The division of vocabulary is arbitrary, and serves only to limit communications; thus, the serious student of OOD must learn both vocabularies. Therefore, when I present a concept, I present it in terms of both vocabularies. I usually describe the concept by its Smalltalk name first, and then provide examples in C++, using the appropriate synonyms from the C++ vocabulary.

Objects

What are objects? Booch[4] defines an object as "something you can do things to." To paraphrase, objects are things that can be manipulated. Manipulation implies change. An object should somehow be in a different *state* after it has been manipulated. Also, manipulation must occur according to a specific protocol. So objects must have *interfaces* through

---

4. Grady Booch, *Object-Oriented Design with Applications* (Copyright © 1991 by The Benjamin/ Cummings Publishing Company).

which they are manipulated. When an object is manipulated through its interface, it must do something useful. It must express a desired *behavior*. Thus, an object is something that has *state*, *behavior*, and an *interface*.

We do not have to understand an object in order to manipulate it. The interface of the object makes it unnecessary for us to know anything about its inner workings. Few people understand the inner workings of a telephone or a VCR, but they are still able to use them. We can manipulate objects in complete ignorance of their internal machinery. In fact, for most people, this is the essential norm. Who has the time to study how a VCR really works? We just buy one, perhaps read a few pages of the instruction manual, and then start pushing buttons until the machine does something reasonable.

We manipulate an object through its interface. The interface of an object is the set of controls that the object supplies for the use of its clients. The interface of a telephone is composed of the dial, hook switch, mouthpiece, and earphone. The interface for a room light is the switch on the wall. The interface for a bathtub is the faucet controls and the drain plug. Nothing can be done to an object unless it is done through its interface. The interface of an object is the only way that we can manipulate its internal mechanisms, and the interface hides the details of those mechanisms.

In fact, the internal workings are a nuisance to most of us because they change so much from object to object. Take cars for example. All cars have very similar interfaces, yet they have very different internal mechanisms. While driving a car we use, among other things, the steering wheel, gear selector, accelerator, and brake. These items make up the standard interface for nearly all cars. The type of engine in the car is irrelevant to this interface; it may be 4-cylinder, 6-cylinder, V8, slant-6, diesel, or even rotary. These differences are hidden by the interface. As long as we know the standard interface, we can drive the car. Thus, the internal workings of an object are irrelevant to the interface. There may be many different kinds of objects, each with different internal machinery, that share the same interface. The clients of these objects can use them interchangeably.

This ability to use different objects interchangeably through a common interface is one of the most important advantages of OOD. Object-oriented programs are written not to manipulate objects, but to manipulate interfaces. The kind of object being manipulated is irrelevant, as long as the interface is compatible.

Abstraction

Abstraction is *the elimination of the irrelevant and the amplification of the essential.* Consider again the car object. What is essential about a car? For most of us, the essential things about a car are that it accelerates when we push the accelerator, stops when we push the brake, and turns when we turn the steering wheel. The mechanisms that perform these jobs are irrelevant. When we apply abstraction to a car, we amplify the essential part, which is its interface, and we eliminate the irrelevant mechanisms. What we are left with is an abstract interface for *all* cars.

When we are taught how to drive a car, we are taught this abstract interface. Although our lessons may be given in a particular kind of vehicle, it is not just that particular vehicle that we are learning how to drive. Through the abstract interface we are learning how to drive *all* cars. This is a very powerful technique; by learning just one car, we have learned them all. This gives us a tremendous advantage. When we decide to buy a car; we can search for the one that meets our particular needs. We consider price, efficiency, space, hauling power, aesthetics, reputation, and so on. Then we choose. We seldom, if ever, consider the interface of the car. Thus, we can select the car that is right for us, without having to think about learning how to drive it.

Think of how many different types of automobiles there are in the world. What horrible chaos would prevail if every car in the world had a different interface! The only cars you could buy would be those that you had been trained in. Others would be useless to you. Even though they were still "cars," and they might have specifications that were more appropriate to your needs, you would be unable to drive them.

Such a state of chaos exists today in the software industry. The same software functions are provided by dozens of modules, all containing incompatible interfaces. Although we would like to reuse this code in new software systems, it is very difficult. The interfaces of the modules are not standard, and are too difficult to connect together. So we wind up reimplementing the same functionality over and over again.

Object-oriented design allows us to use the power of the abstract interface in the building of software systems. Object-oriented software systems manipulate abstract interfaces as opposed to specific modules. Many different implementations can be represented by a single abstract interface. This allows the user to choose from among the modules that conform to an interface. Some may be fast but use lots of memory; others may be slow but very memory-efficient. Some may be thread-safe, allowing them to run in concurrent environments. Some may use special memory-management techniques. As long as each of these different implementations conforms to the user's interface, the user is free to choose the one with the characteristics that best match the application.

 This is not a new concept. Operating systems have been providing abstract interfaces for I/O devices for three decades. In such operating systems, `files` are objects that can be manipulated through the abstract interfaces `open()`, `close()`, `read()`, and `write()`. Users of these `files` have a great deal of latitude to choose the particular kind of `files` that will work best for their application. Perhaps it represents a line-printer, or a display, or a disk file. These choices can be made at any time, and changed later when circumstances require it. The use of abstract interfaces is a common experience for most software engineers, but providing such abstract interfaces without object-oriented programming languages (OOPLs) is hard. The difficulty could be justified in the case of heavily used operating system resources, but for normal procedural programming, the concept is very rarely applied. With the advent of OOPLs, abstract interfaces have become much simpler to implement. We can now use abstraction to design interfaces at every level of a project. OOD is the discipline that describes the techniques of abstraction and aids the designer in creating abstract interfaces.

Abstraction of State

If an object is "something we can do things to," then the things that we do must affect the object. When we manipulate an object through its interface, we intend to make desired changes in the state of that object. Thus, objects must be able to remember their state. The form that the state memory takes is completely irrelevant. The state of the object could be remembered in binary integers or ASCII strings; this detail is abstracted out of the interface. The users of an object have no need to know just how the state information is actually stored.

For example, take the simple example of an object that represents a date. We would like to ask this object questions like "What is your month?", "What is your year?" and so on. In C++ such an interface might look like this:

```
class Date
{
 public:
      enum Month {jan, feb, mar, apr, may, jun
                  jul, aug, sep, oct, nov, dec};
      Month GetMonth() const;
      int   GetYear()  const;
      int   GetDayOfMonth() const;
};
```

This interface reveals nothing about the implementation of the state variables. The state variables of class Date might be stored as follows:

```
private:
      Month itsMonth;
      int   itsYear;
      int   itsDayOfMonth;
```

Or perhaps like this:

```
private:
      int itsYear;
      int itsJulianDate;
```

Or maybe like this:

```
private:
      int itsDays;// Days since 1/1/70;
```

The implementation of the state information is irrelevant to the interface. Although users know that **Date** objects have state, and although they can access that state through the public interface, the interface hides the implemented form of that state information. What shows through the public interface is an abstraction of the state information.

Abstraction of Behavior

In object-oriented design, objects are manipulated by *sending messages* to them. In C++ we send messages to objects by calling their member functions. For example, given a **pump** object, we might send it a message telling it to start pumping at a rate of 3 gallons per minute.

```
class Pump
{
  public:
    void StartPumping(int theRate);
    ...
};

Pump thePump;
thePump.StartPumping(3);
```

In general terms, a message is a verb phrase accompanied by optional modifiers. In the example of the pump, **StartPumping** is the verb phrase, and **3** is the modifier.

The interface of an object describes the name and form of all the messages that the object can accept. In C++ we see this in the member-function prototypes within a class definition. The implementation of the object describes how the object behaves when messages are received. The behavior of an object is coded into an algorithm called a *method*. In C++ a method is simply the body of a member function. When a message is received at the interface of an object, the appropriate method is invoked.

However, the behavior of an object in response to a message is abstract. Users of an object cannot predict exactly what the object will do when they send it a message. Two factors make this determination impossible: the object's state, and its type.

The behavior that a message evokes in an object often depends upon the state of the object. As the object changes from state to state, the behaviors of its methods can change. For example, sending the **off** method to a **LightSwitch** object evokes a completely different behavior when it is on than when it is off. Thus, if you don't know the state of an object, you cannot predict its response to a message.

Also the *type* of an object plays an important part in determining its behavior in response to a message. The way that a **Corvette** object responds to the **Accelerate** message will differ substantially from the way that a **Yugo** object responds. It is possible and desirable that the client of these objects not know their type; thus, the client cannot predict their behavior.

Abstraction of behavior means that clients of an object don't care what the object does when they send it a message, so long as it does what is appropriate based upon its state and its type. As clients of **Car** objects, when we tell the car to accelerate, we expect it to start moving. We do not care how it achieves that goal. Thus, when we send a message to an object, we are asking it to do whatever is necessary to achieve the desired abstract behavior.

Collaboration Among Objects

We may reasonably define an object-oriented application as *a set of objects working together to support a common purpose.* Objects are complex devices that expose their functionality through relatively simple interfaces. The methods of one object will send messages to other objects. When one object manipulates another, it is called a *collaboration.*

Objects collaborate in order to fulfill their responsibilities to their users. For example, a toaster object may collaborate with a timer object, a heater object, and a carriage object. The carriage holds the bread, while the heater toasts the bread, and the timer keeps track of how long the bread has been cooking. When the timer expires, the heater must turn off, and the carriage must pop up. The toaster object carries the responsibility of monitoring the timer and telling the heater and the carriage how to behave.

The objects in the tiny application shown in Listing 00-1, collaborate with each other. No particular object has all the intelligence. Each one takes care of its own responsibilities, and leaves the others to deal with theirs. Although I have shown the implementation of **Toaster::Run()** in detail, I have not shown any of the implementations of the other classes. In fact, they have none; they are pure virtual functions. New classes must be derived from **Heater**, **Carriage**, and **Timer** that specify the implementations for those functions. Those implementations may be very simple or very complex. **Heater** derivatives, for example, may monitor their temperature and employ complex feedback mechanisms to achieve "even toasting" of the bread. None of this complexity will show up in the **Toaster** class, because the **Toaster** collaborates with the abstract interface of **Heater** and expects it to take care of its own concerns. Thus, collaboration is a manipulation of interfaces, and need not depend upon any particular implementation.

Listing 00-1

Toaster program
```
class Heater
{
  public:
    virtual void TurnOn() = 0;
    virtual void TurnOff() = 0;
};

class Timer
{
  public:
    virtual void SetTime(int) = 0;
    virtual int  IsRunning() const = 0;
};
```

Listing 00-1 (Continued)

Toaster program

```
class Carriage
{
  public:
    virtual int IsDown() const = 0;
    virtual void PopUp() = 0;
};

class Toaster
{
  public:
    Toaster(Timer& t, Carriage& c, Heater& h);
    void Run();

  private:
    Timer&    itsTimer;
    Carriage& itsCarriage;
    Heater&   itsHeater;
};

void Toaster::Run()
{
    for(;;)
    {
        while (!itsCarriage.IsDown())
        ;
        itsHeater.TurnOn();
        itsTimer.SetTime(120); // two minutes
        while (itsCarriage.IsDown() &&
               itsTimer.IsRunning())
        ;
        itsCarriage.PopUp();
        itsHeater.TurnOff();
    }
}

void main()
{
    Toaster t(someTimer, someCarriage, someHeater);
    t.Run();
}
```

Polymorphism

The word polymorphism means "many forms." Two or more objects are said to be polymorphic if they have identical interfaces and different behaviors. From the client's point of view, such objects are indistinguishable. Their common interface provides a stereotype through which clients may use them without knowing their true form. Thus, "many forms" of objects can be used by the same clients.

In C++, polymorphism is usually achieved when one class inherits the interface of another. Objects of the two classes share a common interface, and so can be used interchangeably.

```
class ChargeCard {...};
class DinersClubCard : public ChargeCard {...};

void BuyDinner(ChargeCard&);

main()
{
    DinersClubCard myCard;
    BuyDinner(myCard);   // DinersClubCard used
                         // polymorphically as a
                         // credit card.
}
```

Classes

A *class* is the specification of an object; it is the "blueprint" from which an object can be created. A class describes an object's interface, the structure of its state information, and the details of its methods. We can create many objects of the same kind according to the specifications within a single class. Each such object is called an *instance* of that class. The process of creating an object from a class is called *instantiation*.

For example, suppose we have an application for managing a library. We will certainly have many **book** objects in this system. But there need only be one **book** class from which all the **book** objects are instantiated. This "book" class describes the external interface and internal structure common to each **book** object.

There may be other classes of objects in the library application besides **book**. There could be the class of all **periodicals**, the class of all **authors**, the class of all **shelves**, and so on. Each of these is a single class that may have many instances.

Specifying State

Classes describe how state information is stored within their instances. The class declares variables that contain the state information. These variables may contain primitive types such as integers or characters, or they may contain instances of other objects. The types of variables within a class fall into two broad categories: **instance variables** and **class variables.**

Instance Variables

Instance variables appear in every instance of an object. Each object has its own private copy, which it is free to manipulate without affecting the other objects. For example, the **Book** object from the library application might have instance variables for keeping the title, the number of pages, the date of publication, the author, the publisher, the ISBN, and so on.

```
class Book
{
  public:
    Book(const String& theTitle, int thePages, int thePubDate,
Author*,
          Publisher*, const String& theISBN);

  private:
    String      itsTitle;
    int         itsPageCount;
    int         itsPublicationYear;
    Author*     itsAuthor;
    Publisher*  itsPublisher;
    String      itsISBN;
};
```

Each instance of the class **book** has the same kinds of variables; the structure of the data is the same. However, the contents of the variables are quite different; each instance contains the data that pertains to one specific book.

```
Book b1("Object-Oriented Design with Applications",
        580, 1991, gradyBooch, benjaminCummings,
        "0-8053-0091-0");

Book b2("C++ Primer (2nd Edition)", 614, 1991,
        stanLippman, addisonWesley, "0-201-54848-8");

Book b3("The C++ Programming Language (2nd Edition)",
        669, 1991, bjarneStroustrup, addisonWesley,
        "0-201-53992-6");
```

The three **Book** objects shown above represent three different books. They all have the same instance variables, but the values that those instance variables contain differ from one object to the next.

Class Variables

Class variables contain data that is relevant to the class itself, and not to any particular instance of the class. A class variable is *shared* by all the objects of the class, but it is not contained by, nor is it part of, any object. It belongs to the class as a whole.

For example, suppose we have a class that describes a person. Each instance of class **Person** will have an instance variable containing the weight of that particular person. We could then use a class variable to maintain the average weight of all the instances. Certainly the average weight of all people is a quantity that we should associate with class **Person**, but just as certainly, this quantity does not belong to any particular instance of class **Person**. It describes the class itself; thus, it is a class variable.

In C++ we can implement class variables as static member variables. We might write the **Person** class as follows:

```
class Person
{
  public:
    Person(int theWeight);

  private:
    int itsWeight;
    static int     theirPopulation;
    static double theirAverageWeight;
};

int Person::theirPopulation = 0;
int Person::theirAverageWeight = 0;

Person::Person(int theWeight)
{
    itsWeight = theWeight;
    double totalWeight = theirAverageWeight * theirPopulation;
    totalWeight += theWeight;
    theirPopulation++;
    theirAverageWeight = totalWeight/theirPopulation;
}
```

Specifying Behavior

The algorithms that define the behavior of an object are specified by the object's class. The class specifies the method interfaces and the algorithms behind those interfaces. As with variables, there are two broad categories into which methods can be categorized: **instance methods** and **class methods**.

Instance Methods

Instance methods are functions that manipulate the state of an object in some way. When invoked, they operate on a particular object. To invoke an instance method, we must send the appropriate message to the object upon which the method is to operate. For example, we can send the **Accelerate** method to instances of class **Car**.

In C++ an instance method can be written as a nonstatic member function:

```
class Car
{
  public:
    void Accelerate();
}
```

Class Methods

Class methods are functions that are relevant to a class, but do not operate on any particular instance of that class. They may be used to create new instances, or to provide utility functions to the instance methods.

```
class Person
{
  public:
    Person(int theWeight);
    static int GetAverageWeight(); // class method

  private:
    int itsWeight;
    static int theirPopulation;
    static int theirAverageWeight;
};

int Person::GetAverageWeight()
{
    return theirAverageWeight;
}

void f() // an example function...
{
    int avg = Person::GetAverageWeight();
}
```

Class Relationships

The relationships that can exist between classes are diverse and rich with semantic meaning. Much of the real design power of OOD is expressed in these relationships. A large portion of the design task lies in inventing structures of collaborating classes that are bound together with the appropriate relationships.

The "Contains" Relationship

A class can contain another class. Typically, this means that an instance of the contained class is held in one of the instance variables of the containing class. Such classes are related with a "contains" or "has" relationship; we say that class A "contains" or "has" class B. Containment is used to build classes that are composites of other classes. For example, a class describing a home stereo system might contain classes for speakers, a tuner, a turntable, a CD player, perhaps a cassette player, maybe an equalizer, an amp, and so on.

```
class HomeStereoSystem
{
  private:
    Speaker      itsSpeakers[2];
    Tuner        itsTuner;
```

```
TurnTable      itsTurnTable;
CDPlayer       itsCDPlayer;
CassetteDeck itsCassetteDeck;
Equalizer      itsEqualizer;
Amplifier      itsAmplifier;
};
```

By using composition, a class can build a simple abstraction for a highly complex grouping of subordinate classes. Yet that complexity can be hidden by the containing class, just as the tangled interconnections behind a home stereo system are hidden. The user of the stereo does not have to deal with them.

The "contains" relationship also implies that the containing object has *intrinsic access* to the contained object. The container knows where the contained objects are, and can use them whenever necessary. In C++ this relationship is commonly expressed by holding the contained object, or a pointer or reference to the contained object, within an instance variable of the container.

The "Uses" Relationship

Classes can also have relationships with classes that they don't contain. Sometimes one class must make use of another class, but need not incorporate that class into its own structure. Such relationships are called "uses" relationships. Typically a "uses" relationship means that the *using* class sends messages to the *used* class, but the *used* class is not stored in one of the instance variables of the *using* class. Instead, the *used* class is passed into the *using class* by some third party, as an argument of one of the methods of the using class.

For example, since our **Stereo** class contains a **CDPlayer** and **Cassette Deck**, it uses the class of all **CD** objects and the class of all **Cassette** objects. The **Stereo** does not contain any individual CDs or cassettes; they are passed into the **Stereo** class through its interface. The **Stereo** class has methods that operate on objects of the **CD** and **Cassette** classes.

```
class HomeStereoSystem
{
  public:
    PlayCD(const CD& theCD);// uses CD objects.
};
```

The "Inheritance" Relationship

A class can *inherit* the instance variables, interfaces, and instance methods of another class. This means that the inheriting class has those variables, interfaces, and methods almost as though they were defined within it. For example, consider the following class:

```
class File
{
  public:
    File (const String& theName)
    virtual int  Open();
```

```
    virtual void Close();
    virtual int  Read(void* theBuffer, int theLength);
    virtual int  Write(void* theBuffer, int theLength);
  private:
    String itsFileName;
};
```

This class has a single instance variable and the interface and implementation for four instance methods. Now consider class **BinaryFile**, which inherits from **File**:

```
class BinaryFile : public File
{
  public:
    BinaryFile(const String& theName);
  ...
};
```

BinaryFile inherits the interfaces and the implementation of the four instance methods, and it inherits the instance variable. We call **File** the *base class* or *superclass,* and we call **BinaryFile** the *derived class* or *subclass.*

Normally, **BinaryFile** can be used wherever **File** can be used. For example,

```
void f(File&);
BinaryFile b;
f(b); // function f thinks it is dealing with a File object.
```

We say that **BinaryFile** *ISA* **File** because it can be used wherever a **File** is used. However, **BinaryFile** can be extended. We can add new instance variables and instance methods to it, and override the behavior of the existing instance methods.

```
class BinaryFile : public File
{
  public:
    BinaryFile(const String& theName);
    virtual int Read(void* theBuffer, int theLength);
    virtual int Write(void* theBuffer, int theLength);
    unsigned long GetSeekPosition() const;
    void Seek(unsigned long theSeekPosition);
  private:
    unsigned long itsSeekPosition;
};
```

Now **BinaryFile** inherits the implementation of only the **Open** and **Close** instance methods. The *interfaces* for all four instance methods are inherited, but the implementations for **Read** and **Write** are overridden—presumably to manage the seek position. Also, two new instance methods and one new instance variable have been added.

These changes make **BinaryFile** quite different from **File**. However, **Binary-File** objects still inherit their interface from **File**. Thus, we can still use them in any function or context that expects a **File**. Our changes have added functionality, but have not taken any away, so it is still true to say that **BinaryFile** *ISA* **File**.

Multiple Inheritance

Sometimes classes need to inherit the methods and interfaces of more than one base class. This is called *multiple inheritance*. In Figure 00-1, we have two kinds of vehicle: an **OffRoadVehicle**, and a **LuxuryVehicle**. The two vehicles contain the attributes that one would expect. Among other things, the **LuxuryVehicle** has an **IncredibleSoundSystem**, whereas the **OffRoadVehicle** has a **RollBar**. By using multiple inheritance, we create a **LuxuryOffRoadVehicle** that inherits the attributes of both the **LuxuryVehicle** and the **OffRoadVehicle**.

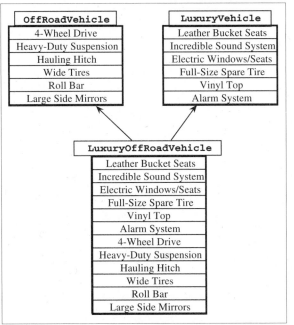

Figure 00-1
Multiple Inheritance Example

Not only does the **LuxuryOffRoadVehicle** inherit all the components of the two base classes, but all of their methods and interfaces too. Thus, the new derived class *ISA* **OffRoadVehicle** and *ISA* **LuxuryVehicle**. It can safely be used in any context that expects either one or the other.

In C++ we describe multiple inheritance by adding multiple base classes onto a class declaration.

```
Class LuxuryOffRoadVehicle : public LuxuryVehicle
                           , public OffRoadVehicle
{
    ...
};
```

Abstract Classes

An *abstract class* is a class that only partially describes an object. Typically, some of the interfaces of an abstract class are without implementation. For example, consider some of the objects within a program that manipulates geometric shapes:

```
class Shape
{
  public:
    Shape(const Box& theBoundingBox)
    : itsBoundingBox(theBoundingBox) {}

    const Box& GetBoundingBox() const
    {return itsBoundingBox;}

    virtual double Area() = 0;

  private:
    Box itsBoundingBox;
};
```

The class **Shape** is described by a bounding box: a rectangle that surrounds the entire shape. All instances of classes *derived* from **Shape** know how to compute their area, but there can be no instances of class **Shape** because the class provides no implementation for the **Area** interface. Within the class **Shape**, **Area** is a *pure interface*, known in C++ as a pure virtual function.

```
class Circle : public Shape
{
  public:
    Circle(const Point& theCenter, double theRadius)
    : itsCenter(theCenter)
    , itsRadius(theRadius)
    , Shape(
          Box(
              Point(theCenter.GetX() - theRadius,
                    theCenter.GetY() + theRadius),
              Point(theCenter.GetX() + theRadius,
                    theCenter.GetY() - theRadius))
    {}

    virtual double Area() const {return pi * itsRadius * itsRadius;}
  private:
    Point  itsCenter;
    double itsRadius;
};
```

This class represents a circle as a subclass of **Shape**. It is a concrete class, meaning that it can be instantiated, because none of its interfaces are pure. The **Area** interface has been given an implementation.

The usefulness of abstract classes is that we can use any object of a class derived from **Shape** in any context that expects a shape. For example,

```
// Scan the set of shapes and compute the total
// area of all the elements contained within.

double TotalArea(const Set<Shape*>& theShapeSet)
{
  double totalArea = 0;
  for(Iterator<Shape*> si(theShapeSet); si; si++)
  {
    totalArea += (*si)->Area();
  }
  return totalArea;
}
```

The wonderful benefit of this function is that it will continue to work, *unchanged*, even when new subclasses of **Shape** are written into the program. Any kind of **Shape**, even shapes that have not been written yet, will be handled correctly. This function *anticipates* program maintenance and changes in requirements—a powerful benefit indeed!

This example gives us our first real look at *dependency inversion*. Imagine that what we pass into the **TotalArea** function is a **Set<Shape*>** that contains nothing but instances of class **Circle**. Then **TotalArea** is acting as the client, and **Circle** is acting as the server. Note that both **TotalArea** and **Circle** depend upon the abstract class **Shape**, which represents the interface for **Circle**. Thus, **TotalArea** does not depend upon **Circle**, and **Circle** does not depend upon **TotalArea**. The dependencies have been inverted. If changes are made to **Circle**, **TotalArea** will remain unaffected. Or if we want to use **TotalArea** in an application that does not have **Circle** objects, that will pose no problem.

Summary

This chapter has provided a quick overview of the major concepts of object-oriented design and how they relate to C++. Its purpose has been to refresh the memory of those who have already learned OOD, and to provide simple definitions for those who have not. The chapters that follow examine each of these concepts in greater detail, and show how to use them in real designs.

Exercises

1. Connect the C++ vocabulary words to their corresponding Smalltalk synonyms.

C++	Smalltalk
class	send a message
Object	subclass
member function	class variable
static member function	instance method
member variable	instance
static member variable	class
base class	superclass
derived class	class method
call a member function	instance variable

2. Which of the following two classes better represents a "contains" relationship? Which better represents a uses relationship?

a. ```
class A
{
   public:
     B* itsB;
};
```

b.```
class A
{
   public:
     B* GetB();
};
```

c. ```
class A
{
   public:
     void f(B*);
};
```

3.  The term "Dependency Inversion" means:

a. Clients depend upon servers.

b. Abstractions depend upon clients.

c. Servers and clients depend upon interfaces.

d. Servers do not depend upon clients.

4.  What can you expect from OOD?

a. Programs that are bug free.

b. Programs that are self-documenting.
```

    c. Programs that describe the real world.

    e. Headaches.

    f. To be a better designer.

1

Static and Dynamic Design

*Sooner or later the OOPL community will have to realize
[that] if you can't draw a precise picture of the pattern,
it doesn't exist.*

—Edward Yourdon, 1992

*"See what things are in themselves,
dividing them into matter, form and purpose."*

*"Examine into the quality of the form of an object,
and detach it altogether from its material part..."*

—Marcus Aurelius, circa A.D. 170

This chapter takes us on a tour through the object-oriented design of three simple applications. These applications are simple, because we wish to reconnoiter the tools and processes of OOD, rather than fully expose them. Our aim is to become familiar with these tools and processes in preparation for later chapters.

The design tools we will be using include C++ and some elements of Booch's notation. Those elements will be described as we encounter them. Our primary focus, however, will be upon the separation and interplay of the static and dynamic structure of an object-oriented design. There is a tension between these two faces of design, and we will exploit that tension to help us create a practical and accurate software design.

Introduction

Consider the blueprints for a piston from an automobile engine. Such a document would be very detailed. It would tell you the shape and structure of the piston. It would tell you what kind of materials it was made from, how its components were assembled, where holes had to be drilled and grooves had to be milled. If you followed these instructions carefully, you could produce a piston, but the blueprints would not tell you *what the piston does.*

All designs, whether software, electronic, or mechanical, can be separated into static and dynamic components. The static component describes how the elements of the design are constructed and also describes the relationships and attributes of those elements. On the other hand, the dynamic component describes what the elements of the design do: what functions they perform and how they work together to achieve those functions.

In the early history of software design, the need for static design was not clearly recognized. Designers used tools such as flow charts and finite state machines to help them model what the program did, but generally did not spend much time thinking about how the algorithms and data should be structured. In the late 1970s and early 1980s this trend reversed itself. Flow charts fell into disfavor through association with past failures. Dynamic modeling, as a whole, took a back seat to static modeling techniques. The early incarnations of structured analysis and design (SA/SD), for example, discouraged dynamic modeling. Data flow diagrams (DFDs), the primary tool of SA, were static. They showed how the functionality of an application was partitioned, and described the data that flowed between those partitions, but they provided no information regarding sequence or the conditions under which that data flowed. Moreover, analysts and designers were discouraged from attempting to show dynamic information on DFDs. To be sure, dynamic modeling techniques were not completely shunned during this time, but they were overshadowed by the enthusiasm invested in static modeling.

Object-oriented design, as described by Booch,[1] Rumbaugh,[2] and many others, has put dynamic modeling on an equal footing with static modeling. A tension exists between the static and dynamic models of a program. The static model provides the framework and facilities that allow the dynamic model to operate, just as the shape and size of a piston allow it to operate within an engine. The dynamic model specifies the behavioral requirements that the static model must support, just as the behavioral specifications for a piston constrain its shape and composition. This tension allows us to connect the static structure of an application with its required behavior.

---

1. Grady Booch, *Object-Oriented Design with Applications* (Copyright © 1991 by The Benjamin/Cummings Publishing Company), Section 1.3, p. 14 ff.
2. James Rumbaugh et al., *Object-Oriented Modeling and Design* (Prentice Hall, 1991), Section 2.2, p. 16 ff.

Connecting Requirements to the Design

A computer program is written in order to achieve a certain set of behaviors. Behavior is the essence of a computer program. Computer programs are not usually written for aesthetic purposes; they are written to make a computer do something. The document that describes the requirements of a computer application describes the set of behaviors that the program must exhibit, so a requirements document is, at least in part, a list of the required behaviors of the program.

Dynamic models express behavior; they show the method by which behaviors are achieved. When you create a dynamic model of a computer program, you are designing how that program achieves its behaviors. In OOD, we create dynamic models that express the behaviors specified by the requirements. Each required behavior generates one or more scenarios that can be described by a dynamic model.

These dynamic models must be consistent with the static models of the design. The static models must provide the facilities that the dynamic models require. Inspection of the static and dynamic models may reveal discrepancies between them. Such discrepancies must be corrected, either by changing the static structure, or by employing a different dynamic strategy.

This tension, or interdependence, between the requirements, dynamic models, and static models connects the design to the requirements. The static models must support the behaviors demanded by the requirements and expressed in the dynamic models.

Static and Dynamic Models in OOD

An object-oriented design specifies a set of collaborations between objects. Booch considers these collaborations as "strategic architectural decisions."[3] The connection of the requirements to the design is well supported by OOD because collaborations depend upon both the static and dynamic models. The dynamic model describes the sequence of messages that flow between collaborating objects, and the static model describes the pathways that those messages use.

Consider, for example, a railway network. The required behavior of the network is to deliver cargoes to specific locations according to a particular schedule. We can describe the tracks, switches, and yards of the railway network by a static model that supplies the facilities needed by the trains in order to make their deliveries on time.

However, just having the tracks in place is not enough. The movement of engines and railroad cars must be coordinated. Semaphores and switches must be thrown at the proper times. Cars need to be uncoupled and switched between different trains. The cargoes must

---

3. Interview with Grady Booch, *The C++ Journal*, vol. 2, no. 1 (1992).

be inventoried and tracked from pickup to delivery. This is the dynamic model, which employs the facilities of the static model.

The static models in an object-oriented design specify the classes within the application and the relationships that exist among those classes. The classes specify objects that are the repositories and processors of data. The relationships specify the channels over which messages are sent between those objects.

The dynamic models in an object-oriented design describe the messages that are passed between objects. Dynamic models specify the order in which messages are sent, the types of messages that are sent, and the data that the messages carry. The objects described by the dynamic models are instances of the classes from the static models. The channels over which messages are sent correspond to relationships among the appropriate classes in the static design.

A Bill-of-Materials Case Study, in C++

In the following sections we will look at a C++ program and reverse-engineer the static and dynamic models. This approach allows us to begin in a familiar environment, C++ code, and extrapolate backwards to the two models. We will use the Booch notation to describe the models, and will briefly digress to explain the notational conventions when necessary.

A C++ Example of a Static Model

In C++ terms, the static models represent the C++ classes with their member variables and compiler dependencies. The dynamic models represent the instances of the classes and the interfaces and bodies of their member functions.

Listing 1-1 shows partial definitions of three classes from a Bill-of-Materials application, in which we model the parts and assemblies in a manufacturing environment. A **Part** may be a low-level component like a spring, a nut, or a bolt. Such parts are called *piece parts*; a part may also be an assembly of other parts.

In our model, each **Part** contains a **PartNumber** and a descriptive string. **Piece-Parts** also have a specific cost associated with them. **Assembly** objects contain sets of **Part** objects, which are actually **Assembly** or **PiecePart** objects. Thus an **Assembly** is an *n*-way tree with other **Assembly** objects at the nodes and **PiecePart** objects at the leaves.

This static model can be described by the Booch notation in a diagram called a *class diagram*. Class diagrams are used to represent static models; they depict the classes and relationships within the application. Figure 1-1 shows a class diagram that represents the Bill-of-Materials application.

Listing 1-1

Partial listing of BOM classes (Static model only)

```cpp
#include "string.h"
#include "set.h"

class PartNumber;

class Part
{
  public:
    virtual double Cost() const = 0;

  private:
    const PartNumber& itsPartNumber;
    String            itsDescription;
};

class Assembly : public Part
{
  public:
    virtual double Cost() const;

  private:
    Set<Part*> itsParts;
};

class PiecePart : public Part
{
  public:
    virtual double Cost() const;

  private:
    double itsCost;
};
```

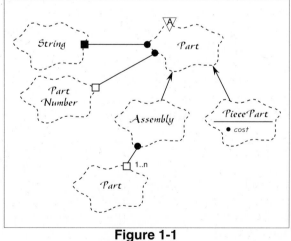

Figure 1-1
A Class Diagram

Let's dissect this diagram carefully, so that we understand what each component represents. The most prominent icon in the diagram is the class icon, the dotted cloud. The cloud shape is a reminder that the internal structure of a class is hidden from the outside world. The dotted outline denotes that it is an abstraction of something physical, and not physical itself. The name inside the icon is the name of the class. Simple names are best, and nouns or noun phrases are the most appropriate. In our case, the names correspond to the names of the C++ classes in our Bill-of-Materials application.

Dotted lines and convoluted shapes may be easy for a computer to draw, but drawing them by hand can be a problem. If you are drawing these diagrams by hand, then you may draw a rectangle with a solid outline instead of a dotted cloud.[4]

Notice that the diagram shows the **Part** class icon twice. Both of these icons represent the same class. I simply used the icon twice to keep the diagram clear.

The triangular adornment in the upper left portion of one of the **Part** class icons indicates that the **Part** class is an abstract class. We briefly discussed abstract classes in Chapter 00, and we discuss them again, in more depth, in Chapter 2. For now, it is sufficient to know that there can be no instances of class **Part**, because it does not represent a complete concept.

Containment by Value

Containment relationships are drawn as shown in Figure 1-2. The black ball touches the *containing* class, a line connects the black ball to the *contained* class. Thus, each instance of **Part** contains an instance of **String**. Inspection of the C++ code in Listing 1-2 reveals the intent of this diagram.

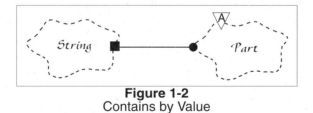

Figure 1-2
Contains by Value

Part (the containing class) has a member variable whose type is **String** (the contained class). Most often, this is what containment boils down to. The containing class has the contained class in a *private* member variable. (Assume that it is private unless specifically noted otherwise.)

The black box on the *contained* side of the relationship denotes that the containment is "by value." This means that the lifetime of the contained object is controlled by the containing object; that is, the containing object *owns* the contained object. This is consistent

---

4. Grady Booch, *Object-Oriented Analysis and Design with Applications*, 2d ed. (Copyright © 1994 by The Benjamin/Cummings Publishing Company), Section 5.2, footnote.

Listing 1-2

Part contains Description

```
class Part
{
  private:
    String itsDescription;
};
```

with the C++ view of a member variable. In the above code the lifetime of the **String** is identical to the lifetime of the **Part**.[5] The member variable **itsDescription** is constructed when **Part** is constructed, and is destroyed when **Part** is destroyed. Thus, containment by value is often implemented in C++ through member variables that are the instances of the contained objects.

However, another interpretation is possible. Objects contained by value may be implemented in C++ by using pointers or references, as in Listing 1-3.

Listing 1-3

Part contains description as pointer.

```
class Part
{
  private:
    String* itsDescription;
};
```

Since containment by value implies ownership, however, we would expect the destructor of **Part** to destroy the contained objects, as in Listing 1-4.

Listing 1-4

Part destructor deletes description

```
Part::~Part()
{
    delete itsDescription;
}
```

We might also expect the constructor to create these objects; however, that is not necessarily implied. The part number and description may be set by member functions of **Part**, as in **SetDescription** in Listing 1-5.

---

5. Within the limits of construction and destruction. Actually, in C++, the lifetimes of the two objects are just slightly out of phase. The contained object is constructed just before the containing object, and it is destroyed just after the containing object.

Listing 1-5
Part::`SetDescription`

```
void Part::SetDescription(const String* theDescription)
{
    delete itsDescription;
    itsDescription = theDescription;
}
```

Notice that this function deletes the old description. This is important for any object contained by value and implemented as a pointer. Objects that *own* other objects through containment by value are always responsible for destroying those objects, even though they may not be responsible for creating them. Of course this can lead to trouble, since there is no way for the containing object to know how the contained object was created. Using **delete** is risky, because the object might have been allocated on the stack or be a static object. Therefore, it is better, where possible, to allow the container to do both the creating and destroying.

Why did we choose containment by value as the relationship between a **Part** and its **Description**? We did so because it makes no sense for a description to exist in the absence of a **Part**; what would the description describe if there were no **Part** object? Generally we choose **containment by value** when the contained object depends upon the containing object to justify its existence.

Containment by Reference

The open box in Figure 1-3 denotes "containment by reference." **Part** objects contain **PartNumber** objects *by reference*. This form of containment does not imply ownership; thus, the containing object is not responsible for the lifetime of the contained object. The lifetimes of the two objects are independent, with the restriction that the contained object must exist as long as it is being contained.[6]

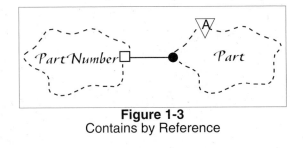

Figure 1-3
Contains by Reference

---

6. This restriction only applies because the default cardinality of the containment is 1. Later we will see other forms of cardinality that put no restrictions at all on the lifetimes of the contained objects.

We choose this form of containment for **PartNumber** objects, because they can exist without referring to an object. Part numbers are often pre-allocated for a particular project. Such part numbers are placeholders waiting for real parts to refer to. Thus, it is possible for a part number to exist *before* any part has been assigned to it. Part numbers also must exist *after* the part that they refer to has been destroyed, in order to prevent reuse of the part number by another part. Part numbers thus have a completely different lifetime than the parts that they represent.

Physically, containment by reference usually means that the containing class has a member variable that holds a pointer or a reference to the contained class. Again, private access should be assumed unless otherwise noted.

The code in Listing 1-6 uses a reference member variable to represent containment by reference. Reference member variables *must* be initialized by the constructor(s) of the class, and they can never be changed to refer to anything else.

Listing 1-6

Initialization of reference member variables

```
class Part
{
  public:
    Part(const PartNumber& thePartNumber)
      : itsPartNumber(thePartNumber) {}
  private:
    const PartNumber& itsPartNumber;
};
```

Reference member variables represent a permanent relationship between the container and the contained. The containment lasts as long as the lifetime of the container, which is why we chose to make **PartNumber** a reference variable. We wanted to permanently attach the **PartNumber** to the **Part**. However, this technique is not without its problems. Assignment operators cannot change what a reference variable refers to. If we were to create the function **Part& Part::operator=(const Part&)**, it could not change what the reference variable **itsPartNumber** referred to.

When we use pointer member variables, we can change the pointer at will, and we can also set it to 0, indicating that nothing is currently being contained. We usually use pointer member variables only when the containment relationship is transient and may refer to many different objects over time, or to no object at all.

We could have written the **Part** class to contain its part number by using a pointer as in Listing 1-7.

However, this would have opened the possibility that **itsPartNumber** could be changed during the lifetime of the **Part**, or that the **Part** could exist without any **PartNumber** at all. That situation violates the model we had in mind. so we chose to use a reference variable instead.

Listing 1-7

Part contains pointer to **PartNumber**

```
class Part
{
  private:
    PartNumber* itsPartNumber;
};
```

Inheritance

Inheritance relationships are depicted with arrows that point to the base class. In the diagram in Figure 1-4, **Assembly** and **PiecePart** both inherit from the abstract base class **Part**. In C++ we describe these relationships as public inheritance, as in Listing 1-8.

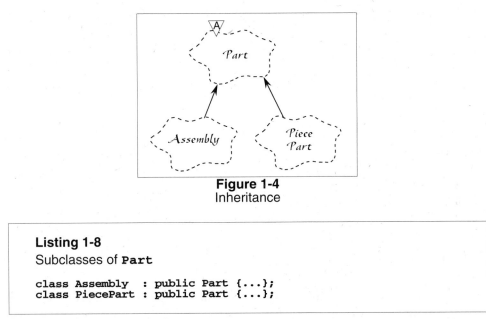

Figure 1-4
Inheritance

Listing 1-8

Subclasses of **Part**

```
class Assembly  : public Part {...};
class PiecePart : public Part {...};
```

On Booch diagrams, like the one in Figure 1-4, inheritance relationships should be considered public unless otherwise specified.

Why do **Assembly** and **PiecePart** inherit from **Part**? The easy answer is that they are both different kinds of a **Part**; they both require descriptions and part numbers. The more complex answer is that we made a strategic decision to isolate the knowledge of **Assembly** and **PiecePart** from the rest of the program. The code that manipulates these objects does so through the generic interface supplied by the **Part** class. It performs this manipulation without knowing the actual type of the objects it manipulates. Thus, we can use **Assembly** and **PiecePart** objects in any context that expects a **Part**. This invokes a principle called the Liskov Substitution Principle[7] which we will return to many times during the course of this book.

Containment with Cardinality

The diagram in Figure 1-5 shows that instances of the **Assembly** class contain *one or more* instances of the **Part** class. The *cardinality* of the containment is depicted by the "**1..n**" icon next to the containment relationship. There are many ways to code this in C++; we could have used an array, as shown in Listing 1-9.

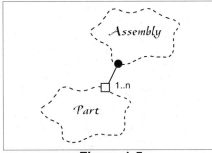

Figure 1-5
Containment with Cardinality

Listing 1-9
Containment with cardinality implemented with an array

```
class Assembly : public Part
{
  public:
    enum {maxParts=100;}
  private:
    Part* itsParts[maxParts];
};
```

However, this has many disadvantages. It is inefficient if the **Assembly** contains only a few **Part** objects; it is restrictive when the **Assembly** needs to contain more than **maxParts Part** objects; and it is dangerous, since arrays in C++ have no bounds checking.

Listing 1-10 shows a safer, less restrictive, and more generic method, using a template container.

7. Barbara Liskov, "Data Abstraction and Hierarchy," *SIGPLAN Notices* (May 1988);
    James O. Coplien, *Advanced C++ Programming Styles and Idioms* (Addison Wesley, 1992).

Listing 1-10

Containment with cardinality, using a template container

```
class Assembly : public Part
{
  private:
    Bag<Part*> itsParts;
};
```

Instances of **Assembly** contain a **Bag** of pointers to **Part** objects. We are using the class **Bag** from a standard class library. **Bag**s are simple container classes that can contain an unspecified number of items. No order is implied, and duplicates are allowed.

Figure 1-6 illustrates another way in which we might have depicted the **Bag**. The dotted cloud with the solid rectangle is called an *instantiated class*. In C++ this translates to the use of a template, where **Bag** is the template class, and **Part*** is the argument of the template.

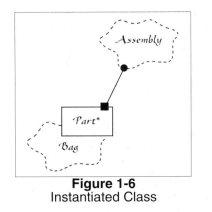

Figure 1-6
Instantiated Class

During the early stages of analysis and design, cardinality is often shown with adornments such as **1..n**. Later, as the design matures, more explicit icons such as the *instantiated class* above are not unusual.

Polymorphic Containment

The diagram in Figure 1-7 shows that an **Assembly** can contain two kinds of **Part**; however, **Assembly** does not know the difference between them. It manipulates both kinds of **Part** through the generic **Part** interface. This is *polymorphic containment*.

Polymorphism is achieved in C++ through the use of a pointer or reference to a base class. Thus, if we want to manipulate **Assembly** and **PiecePart** objects through the generic **Part** interface, we must do so through a pointer or reference to the **Part** class. This is why the **itsParts** member of the **Assembly** class is declared as

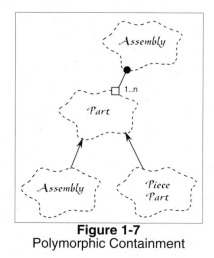

Figure 1-7
Polymorphic Containment

Bag<Part*>. The **Bag** contains *pointers* to the base class **Part**, so that the **Part** objects it contains can be manipulated polymorphically.

A C++ Example of a Dynamic Model

Listing 1-11 shows the implementations for the **Cost** functions of **PiecePart** and **Assembly**. The implementation for **PiecePart** is trivial. The implementation for **Assembly** is a little more interesting. It uses an *iterator* to access each of the **Part** objects contained by the **Assembly** and total up their costs. The iterator is manipulated through **operator++** and **operator*** functions. Note that the **Cost** function treats the **Part** objects polymorphically. Some may be **PiecePart** objects, and others may be **Assembly** objects, but this function does not know the difference.

Listing 1-11
Cost methods for **PiecePart** and **Assembly**

```
double PiecePart::Cost() const
{
    return itsCost;
}

double Assembly::Cost() const
{
    double total=0;

    for(Iterator<Part*> i(itsParts); i; i++) // for each part.
    {
        total += (*i)->Cost();
    }
    return total;
}
```

The dynamic model for this implementation is shown in the object diagrams in Figures 1–8 through 1-11. We will examine these diagrams in detail, looking at each minor aspect to see what it means.

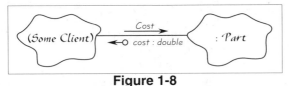

Figure 1-8
Object Diagram: "Cost of Part"

The diagram in Figure 1-8 shows two objects, which we draw as clouds with solid outlines. The solid outline represents the physical reality of an object within the computer. When drawing objects by hand, you can use rounded rectangles instead of clouds.[8]

The object on the left is named **(Some Client)**. It is a placeholder, not a real object, and it represents all the users of the **Part** class. I use parenthesis to represent placeholder objects. The object on the right is an instance of the **Part** class. This object has no name, as indicated by the absence of an identifier before the colon. The identifier after the colon represents the class from which the object is instantiated.

The line that connects the two objects is called an *object relationship* or *link*. Note that it is not an arrow; no directionality is implied. An object relationship is a channel through which messages can be sent. It roughly corresponds to a class relationship on a class diagram. Wherever an object relationship exists between two objects, a class relationship between the two corresponding classes must also exist.

The arrow pointing towards the **Part** object is a *message*, and its label is **Cost**. In this diagram, the message indicates that arbitrary clients **(Some Client)** can send **Cost** messages to instances of the **Part** class. In C++ terms, **Cost** is a public member function of **Part** that can be called by all the clients of the **Part** class.

The arrow with the open circle is a *data couple*. It indicates that the **Cost** message returns a value to the client. The name of that value is **cost**, and its type is **double**. As we will see in later diagrams, we can associate many data couples with a message, and they can point in either direction, showing that data travels in both directions during the sending of a message.

The C++ declaration of the **Part::Cost** member function is **double Cost()** **const**; other than **const**, we can see the various components of this declaration in the object diagram.

Figure 1-9 is nearly identical to Figure 1-8. It shows that instances of **PiecePart** conform to the **Part** interface, and that their behavior is simple. The C++ implementation of **PiecePart::Cost** verifies this.

---

8. Booch, *Object-Oriented Analysis and Design with Applications*, 2d ed(Copyright © 1994 by The Benjamin/Cummings Publishing Company), Section 5.2, footnote.

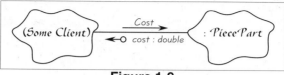

Figure 1-9
Object Diagram: "Cost of PiecePart"

Figure 1-10 shows what happens when the **Cost** message is sent to an **Assembly** object. First note that **Assembly** conforms to the **Part** interface for **Cost**. Next note that **Assembly** must collaborate with other instances of **Part** to get the job done. A quick glance at the C++ code for **Assembly::Cost** shows that the **Assembly** must iterate through all the contained **Part** objects and total up their costs. This is the behavior that the diagram in Figure 1-10 depicts.

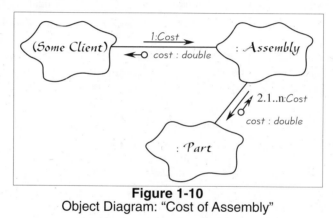

Figure 1-10
Object Diagram: "Cost of Assembly"

Note that sequence numbers precede each message to show the order in which the messages are being sent. Note also that the **Cost** message has the sequence number **2.1..n**; indicating that this message is issued many times in some kind of loop. This loop might be more faithfully represented as in Figure 1-11.

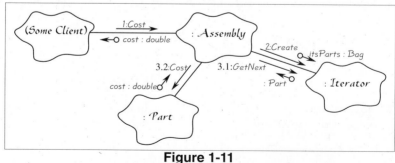

Figure 1-11
Iteration in an Object Diagram

This diagram shows the role of the **Bag** and the **Iterator**. I have taken some license with the message names. I have used the **Create** message to depict construction of the iterator, and the **GetNext** message to depict the access of the **Part** objects through the iterator. I have implied the presence of a loop by using sequence numbers with more than one component.

Message 1 kicks the collaboration off by asking the **Assembly** to calculate its cost. Message 2 creates the iterator and passes **itsParts** (the **Bag**) to it. Message number 3.1 begins a loop; it shows the **Assembly** extracting a **Part** from the iterator. That **Part** is then queried in Message 3.2 to ascertain its cost.

Whether to use the first or second type of diagram depends upon the level of detail you wish to depict. Often a designer is interested in higher-level abstractions, and so does not dive into the depths of detail shown in the second diagram. However, sometimes expressing the detail is the only way to make certain concepts clear. We will see examples of this type of decision throughout the book.

Iteration Between the Models

The dynamic model in Figure 1-11 contradicts the static model to some extent. The static model shows nothing about the iterator that figures so prominently in the **Assembly** class—so let's go back and change the static model.

In Figure 1-12, we have added the **Bag** and **Iterator** to the static model. We have shown that **Assembly** contains the **Bag** by value, and *uses* the **Iterator** and **Part** classes. The open circle with the line represents a *uses relationship*. It indicates that the used class is somehow known to the using class, but that instances of the used class are not intrinsically known to (contained by) the using class. The used instances may be created by the using object, passed to the using object through its interface, or exist in the same lexical scope (i.e., static or global objects) as the using object.

The differences between *uses relationships* and *contains relationships* bears repeating. When one class *contains* another, instances of the container have intrinsic knowledge of the location of the instances of the contained class; that is, they know where they are. However, when one class *uses* another, the using instance does not intrinsically know where the used instance is, so it must be told. Sometimes a pointer or reference to the used instance is passed to the using instance through a member-function argument. At other times the using instance will access the used instance as a static or global variable.

The uses relationship between **Assembly** and **Part** is public. This means that clients of **Assembly** must know about the class **Part**. This is justified by the C++ code within the **Assembly** class that mentions **Part**:

```
Bag<Part*> itsParts;
```

Actually, this particular uses relationship may seem redundant, since **Assembly** *inherits* from **Part**. However, the uses relationship shows that **Assembly** is a client as well as a subclass of **Part**. Code within **Assembly** uses other objects that derive from **Part**.

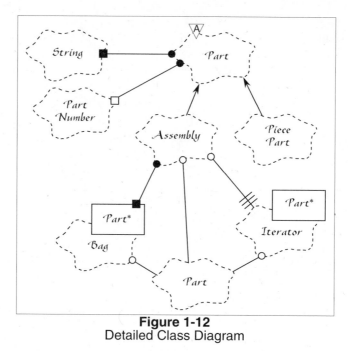

Figure 1-12
Detailed Class Diagram

There are also public uses relationships between **Bag<Part>** and **Part**, and **Iterator<Part>** and **Part**. In C++ terms, this means that **Part** shows up in the interfaces of **Bag<Part*>** and **Iterator<Part*>**, perhaps as shown by the template instantiations in Listing 1-12.

Listing 1-12

Template instantiations of **Bag** and **Iterator**

```
void Bag<Part*>::Add(const Part*);
Part* Iterator<Part*>::operator*() const;
```

These two snippets are part of the code that might have been generated when the **Bag<Part*>** and **Iterator<Part*>** template instantiations were created. They show how the **Part** class appears either as a function argument or as a return value of one of the member functions.

The three strokes on the uses relationship between **Assembly** and **Iterator** indicate that the usage was "in the implementation" and not part of the interface of the **Assembly** class. This means that the clients of **Assembly** do not need to know anything at all about **Iterator**. In C++ terms, this means that **Iterator** was used in the implementation file (**assembly.cc**), and that the header file (**assembly.h**) does not need to **#include** the header file for **Iterator**, nor does it need to forward-declare

Iterator. This, in turn, means that clients of **Assembly** can be compiled without any knowledge of **Iterator**.

Why Is This Better Than Writing Code?

Why should you go to all the trouble of drawing these diagrams, when the code explains things just as well, if not better? For problems as simple as the one above, you shouldn't. Diagramming such simple models is an exercise in futility and pedantry. I have done it here only to demonstrate the mechanics of the diagrams, not their intended use.

The advantage to using the diagrams will become more apparent as we go on to study more and more complex examples. The diagrams allow us to visualize, on one page, concepts that might take dozens of pages of C++ code to express. They also allow us to quickly play with these concepts and communicate them to others.

Moreover, as we just saw in the discussion of the uses relationships, these diagrams allow us to visualize physical compiler dependencies as well as logical and algorithmic concepts, so that we can make a full spectrum of decisions about the static and dynamic structure of an application. Not only can we examine the logical consistency of the design, but we can also probe how well the design will fit into our development environment.

XRef: An Example of Object-Oriented Analysis and Design

Let's look at a slightly more complicated example that we can analyze and design: a program for generating C++ cross-reference listings. The program reads in a C++ program line by line. It must recognize identifiers (i.e., variable, function, and type names) and associate each identifier with the scope that it belongs to. It must remember the file name and line number where each identifier is defined, and all of the file names and line numbers where the identifiers are used. Finally, it must print a report that lists each identifier in alphabetical order, first by name, then by scope. The report must identify where the identifier was defined and where it was used. The result should look something like *Figure 1-13*.

```
Definition       Identifier            Usages
----------       ----------            ------------------------
car.hh:32        itsWheels (Car::)     car.cc:     14,   39,   74,   98,
                                                   152,  387,  432
                                       garage.cc:  59
                                       road.cc:    38,   47
train.hh:59      itsWheels (Train::)   track.cc:   99,   432
                                       train.cc:   38,   39,   57
```

Figure 1-13
Cross-Reference Report

The previous paragraph amounts to a very crude requirements document. We can make use of this document by looking at each of the nouns and seeing which seem to make sense as objects in the application.

- **C++ Program**

  Perhaps. Although the specification does not say so, we will probably want to maintain the name of the program and a list of the files that compose it in some kind of data structure.

- **Line**

  At the high level, the only thing of interest about a line is the file that contains it and its ordinal position within that file (its line number). Moreover, only certain lines are of interest: lines that contain definitions or references to identifiers. So let's skip *line* for the moment.

- **Identifier**

  Yes, this is a good object. We need to remember all the names, and where those names are defined and used. An **Identifier** object seems like a good place to do this.

- **Variable, Function, Type**

  No, I don't think the program will need to know about these entities. It is concerned with names, but not with what the names mean.

- **Scope**

  Yes. We will have to know something about scopes. Every identifier is declared within a certain scope. Rather than copy the name and all the relevant information concerning a scope into every identifier, it might be better to encapsulate that information in a **Scope** object and have each **Identifier** object contain a **Scope** object by reference.

- **Name**

  Yes and no. Names will be objects, but they probably won't be any more complex than a string. I am assuming that we will have a decent **String** class, so we will use that in lieu of the **Name** object.

- **File name**

  Yes, A file name has two components: a path and a name. We learn about the name from **#include** statements. We learn about the path by searching the specified directories and finding the names. It seems wise to me to bind these two components together in a single **File** object.

- **Line number**

  Yes. A line number is meaningless unless associated with a file, so some object should associate them. This could be a **LineNumber** object, but I think that **Reference** is a better name.

- **Report**.

  Yes. We might want to generate many possible types of reports from the accumulated data. The cross-reference report is just one of them, so an abstract base class **Report** might be a good idea. It could encapsulate all the common elements of all reports, and provide tools that all reports could use.

Now that we have this nice set of preliminary objects, what do we do with it? How do we begin to provide static and dynamic models? Getting started is sometimes quite difficult; a blank piece of paper can be a daunting obstacle. This is especially true when we constrain ourselves to a strictly top-down approach or a strictly bottom-up approach. At this point it may not be clear just where the top and bottom really are! A better approach is recommended by Booch when he quotes Robert Heinlein: "When faced with a problem you do not understand, do any part of it you do understand, then look at it again."[9]

For each of us, the "part of it you do understand" could be different. I find myself drawn to figuring out just what a **Reference** object really is, so I will begin there.

XRef References: A Static Model

What is a reference? This is the question that Figure 1-14 tries to answer. A reference is a triplet of information; an identifier, a file, and the line number within the file where the identifier is referenced. This is shown in the figure by the **Reference** class, which contains both an **Identifier** and a **File** by reference and has a line-number attribute. This attribute is written inside the cloud icon for **Reference**, just below the separator line.

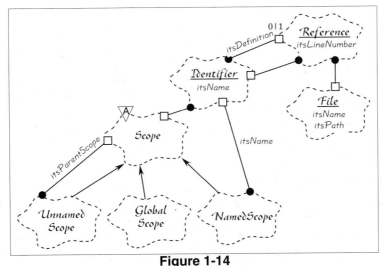

Figure 1-14
Class Diagram depicting the static model of a Reference

Many identifiers within a program will have definitions; others may not. A *definition* is the location in the program where the identifier is defined instead of simply used or

9. Robert Heinlein, *The Moon is a Harsh Mistress* (Berkeley Publishing Group, 1966), p. 290. Quoted in *Object-Oriented Design with Applications* (Benjamin/Cummings, 1991), p. 189.

declared. This is indicated on the diagram by the contains relationship labeled **itsDefinition**. The cardinality of this containment is **0|1**, which indicates that there may or may not be a single defining **Reference** for the **Identifier**.

All identifiers are declared within a scope, which may be the global scope, a named scope such as a class or a function, or an unnamed scope such as the body of an **if** or **while** statement enclosed in braces. This is shown by having the **Identifier** class contain the abstract **Scope** class, and by the inheritance relationships that allow an **Identifier** to polymorphically contain a **NamedScope**, an **UnnamedScope**, or a **GlobalScope**.

The name of a named scope is an identifier. The diagram shows this by having the **NamedScope** class contain an **Identifier**. Since the name of a **NamedScope** is an **Identifier**, and since **Identifiers** can be declared within a **NamedScope**, this model supports unbounded nesting of **Scopes**. Similarly, unnamed scopes must have a parent scope. The model shows this by having the class **UnnamedScope** contain a **Scope** by reference.

A great deal of information has been captured in this small diagram. It represents a lot of decisions and a lot of work, yet it takes up only part of a page. This "density of expression" is an important advantage. It allows us to see a significant portion of the design all at once.

Dynamic Scenario: Printing the Cross-Reference Report

How do reports get printed? The cross-reference report is a list of identifiers and their references. The identifiers should be printed in alphabetical order, with their scope as a secondary key. Thus, **::a** is printed before **A::a**, which is printed before **B::a**, which is printed before **::b**. Unnamed scopes should be printed immediately following the named scope that contains them.

We would like the print operation to be reasonably simple—something like the diagram in Figure 1-15. This diagram shows that some object, which we have temporarily called **(ReportWriter)** should create an iterator for a set called **identifierSet** and iterate over it, telling each of the **Identifier** objects to print their references. The iterator must support iteration in alphabetical order, with the scope of each identifier as the secondary key.

When an **Identifier** object is sent the **PrintReferences** message, it must print the location of its definition, if any; its name, including its scope; and then all the other references, in numeric order by line number. All the references within one file should be printed before the references of the next, and the files should be printed in alphabetical order.

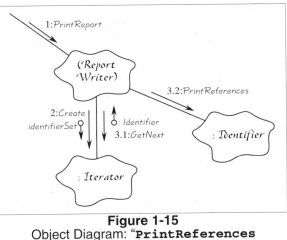

Figure 1-15
Object Diagram: "**PrintReferences**
to an **Identifier**"

Rethinking the Static Model in Light of the Dynamic Requirements

The dynamic analysis above implies that our initial concept of the **Reference** and **Identifier** objects was a bit skewed. To support the ordering of references that is required to print the cross-reference report, **Identifier** objects should maintain an ordered set of the referencing files, and the referencing files should, in turn, contain an ordered set of the referencing line numbers. This allows us to print the references in the correct order.

Figure 1-16 shows the necessary changes. **Identifier** objects contain an **OrderedSet** of **FileReferenceList** objects. A **FileReferenceList** object represents a file that contains references to its containing **Identifier**. The set is kept in alphabetical order by file name. Each **FileReferenceList** object contains a reference to a **File** and an **OrderedSet** of integers that represents the line numbers within that file that contain references to the identifier.

Figure 1-17 shows how an **Identifier** object responds to the **PrintReferences** message. Message number 1 is the **PrintReferences** message that is sent to the **Identifier**. The **Identifier** responds by telling its **Definition** to **Print**, and the **Definition** then prints the associated file name. Then the **Identifier** creates an **Iterator** for iterating over the set of **FileReferenceList** objects. Message 5.1 begins the iteration loop over the references. A **FileReferenceList** object is retrieved from the set, and in 5.2 it is told to **Print**. The **FileReferenceList** prints its associated file name in 5.3 and then in 5.4 builds its own **Iterator** for iterating over the set of line numbers. Message 5.5.1 begins the inner loop, which gets all the integers from the set. We can infer that these integers are then printed by the **FileReferenceList** object.

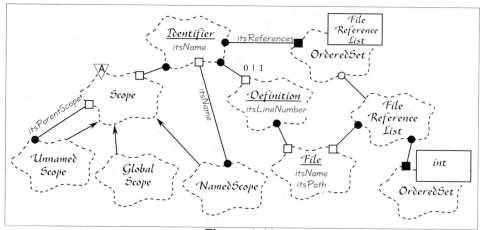

Figure 1-16
Class Diagram supporting ordering of **References** within **Identifiers**

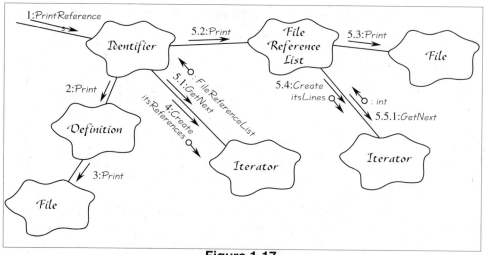

Figure 1-17
Object Diagram: "PrintReferences for an Identifier"

This behavioral model is consistent with the static model in Figure 1-16, but would not have been supported by the original static model shown in Figure 1-14. This is a good example of the effect that behavioral considerations can have on the static model. There didn't appear to be anything wrong with that first static model when I initially drew it; however, when I started thinking about the dynamics of how references should be printed, the weakness of the model became apparent.

Dynamic Scenario: Finding and Adding References

How does the cross-reference program find the references, and what does it do with them once they are found? We must presume that there is some kind of C++ parser that reads in a C++ program, locates the identifiers, and then communicates them to the rest of the program. **Identifiers**, their references and definitions must be added to some kind of list that keeps track of them all. As previously stated, this list should be kept in alphabetical order by identifier name, with the name of the containing scope as a secondary key. Figure 1-18 shows a possible dynamic model.

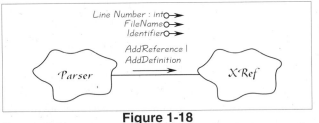

Figure 1-18
Object Diagram: "Finding and Adding References"

Parsers are interesting beasts, to say the least, but for the sake of this example, I am going to ignore this parser's inner workings. Suffice it to say that it hunts through the C++ code, finds identifiers, and determines whether each appearance is a reference or a definition.

What does the **XRef** object do when the **Parser** sends it one of the above messages? Figure 1-19 shows what happens when the **Parser** finds a reference to an identifier that has not yet been added to the cross-reference list. The **XRef** object sends the **IsIn** message to the **IdentifierSet** to see if the identifier already exists. The message returns **NO**, indicating that this is a new identifier, so **XRef** adds the identifier to the list. **XRef** then informs the newly added **Identifier** about the reference that the **Parser** found by sending it the **AddReference** message.

Note the black circle used in the data couple that returns **NO**. I use the black circle to signify a value that is specific to this particular object diagram. The **IsIn** message can return **YES**, but this object diagram only explores what happens when **IsIn** returns **NO**. By the same token, I use open couples to signify that the value of the data couple has no impact upon the object diagram; regardless of the value that an open couple may take, the flow of messages on the object diagram will not deviate.

This is just simple notational convenience. When I see a closed couple, I know that the value is specific to this object diagram, and that there should be other diagrams showing the other possible values of the couple (see Figure 1-20). When I see an open couple, I know that the flow of control is not directly affected by the value of the couple.

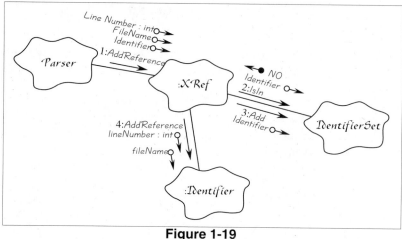

Figure 1-19
Object Diagram: "Adding `Reference` to a new `Identifier`"

Figure 1-20 shows how **XRef** copes with a reference to an identifier that is already in the list. In this case, it uses the `Identifier` passed in from the **Parser** to access the `Identifier` object that is in the `IdentifierSet`. For convenience, we name the `Identifier` that was in the set **X**. We then add the newly found reference to this `Identifier`.

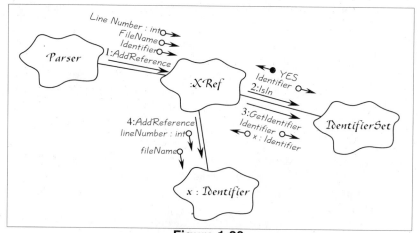

Figure 1-20
Object Diagram: "Adding `Reference` to a known `Identifier`"

Making the Parser Reusable

The static model that supports the preceding object diagrams is shown in Figure 1-21, which shows that **Parser** objects use **Identifier** objects and **XRef** objects. It also shows **XRef** containing an **OrderedSet** of **Identifiers**, which corresponds to the **IdentifierSet** object.

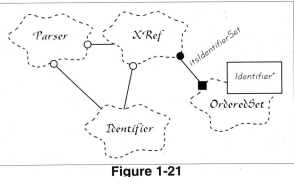

Figure 1-21
Parser and **XRef** High-Level Static Model

There is something that I don't like about this static model: **Parser** is coupled to **XRef**. There ought to be many interesting uses for a C++ parser, but if the **Parser** has intimate knowledge of **XRef**, then we cannot easily reuse it in contexts that do not involve **XRef**.

We can easily solve this problem by using inheritance to separate the interface of a generic client of **Parser** from the implementation of an **XRef**. Figure 1-22 shows that the **Parser** uses an abstract class called a **ParserClient**, and that **XRef** derives from **ParserClient**. This keeps **Parser** from knowing anything at all about **XRef**. We can now reuse **Parser** in any other program simply by creating a new derivative of **ParserClient**.

Using inheritance in this manner is sometimes called building a compiler fire wall, because **Parser** can be compiled without any knowledge of the implementation of the class that it will be calling. No part of the **XRef** code need be included when compiling the **Parser**.

The use of such fire walls is a fundamental requirement for software reuse. Reusable components must not have explicit knowledge of their clients; otherwise they are bound to those clients and cannot be easily disentangled from them.

Depicting Reusability with Class Categories

Compiler fire walls are easier to see (and to plan for) by depicting them in class category diagrams like the one shown in Figure 1-23.

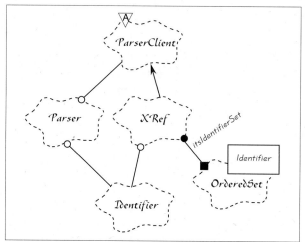

Figure 1-22
Parser and **ParserClient** compiler fire wall

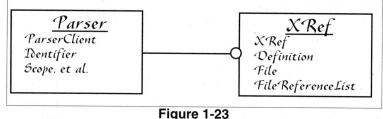

Figure 1-23
Parser and XRef Categories

Simply stated, a class category is a logical grouping of classes. We will see in later chapters that categories are used for more than simply grouping classes together, but for now this definition will suffice. Categories are depicted as rectangles. The name of the category is at the top of the rectangle. Below this name, and below a separator line, is a list of the classes in the category. This list does not need to be complete; in fact it is seldom practical to make it complete. Its purpose is to show a few of the main classes in the category.

In Figure 1-23 we see that the **XRef** category contains the classes that are specific to the problem of creating a cross-reference listing, for example, the **FileReferenceList** that maintains the list of references in file and line-number sequence. This class has nothing to do with parsing the C++ program; it is only used for collecting references and printing them in a certain order.

On the other hand, the classes within the **Parser** category are generic to the problem of parsing a C++ program. No matter what use we make of the **Parser** category, its clients will need to use **Identifiers** and **Scopes**.

Figure 1-23 shows the **XRef** category using the **Parser** category. This means that some of the classes in **XRef** have relationships with some of the classes within **Parser**. For example, the class **XRef** inherits from **ParserClient**. The fact that **Parser** does not depend on any other category means that the Parser category is reusable by other contexts, independent of **XRef**.

It may seem strange that **ParserClient** is part of the **Parser** category. After all, this class describes a user of the category rather than anything inside the category. However, **ParserClient** is the interface that the **Parser** category makes available to those who wish to use it. If **ParserClient** were not within the **Parser** category, then the **Parser** category would be dependent upon whatever category *did* contain it.

Reuse of the **Identifier** Class

Our category diagram shows that the **Parser** category cannot use the **XRef** category. However, Figure 1-16 shows that the **Identifier** class contains a **Definition** object and an **OrderedSet** of **FileReferenceList** objects. Since **Identifier** belongs to the **Parser** category, and the other two classes belong to the **XRef** category, the **Parser** category is still dependent upon the **XRef** category. To fix this, we need to isolate **Identifier** from the other classes. Figure 1-24 shows how we would like the **Parser** category to look after **Identifier** has been isolated.

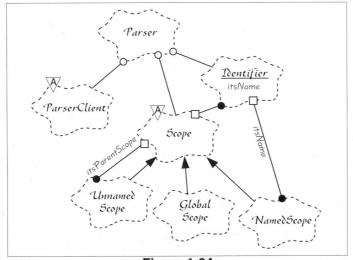

Figure 1-24
Parser category after **Identifier** has been isolated

Figure 1-25 shows the **XRef** category after **Identifier** has been isolated. Note that a new class, **IdentifierReferenceList**, has been created. This class contains the **Identifier** from the **Parser** category, and associates it with the set of

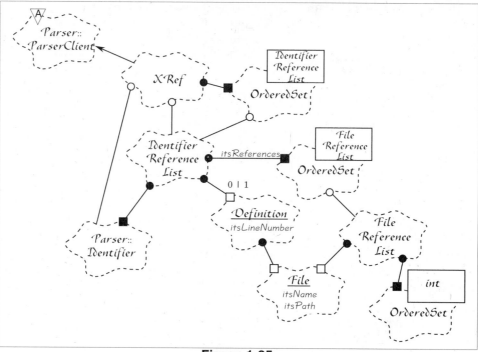

Figure 1-25
XRef category after **Identifier** has been isolated

FileReferenceList objects. Note also that the inheritance relationship between **XRef** and **ParserClient** is shown. Both of the classes imported from the **Parser** category are written with qualified names.

These changes complete the isolation of the two categories. The **Parser** category is now completely disconnected from the **XRef** category, and can be reused for any other purpose.

The **XRef** Application

How are the **XRef** and **Parser** categories tied together into a cross-reference program? Presumably the **main** program will create an instance of a **Parser** and an instance of an **XRef** and will then somehow pass the **XRef** object to the **Parser**, as a **ParserClient**. The C++ code is pretty easy to write. Listing 1-13 shows what it might look like.

Listing 1-13

The **XRef** main program

```
#include <iostream.h>
#include "parser/parser.h"
#include "xref/xref.h"

main(int argc, char** argv)
{
    if (argc != 2)
    {
        cerr << "Usage: xref file" << endl;
        exit(1);
    }

    XRef x;
    Parser p;
    p.Parse(argv[1], x);
    x.PrintReport(cout);
}
```

Converting the **XRef** Design into C++

Now let's look at some of the C++ code implied by the above models. Listing 1-14 shows the definition of the ParserClient class. Note that it implements the messages from Figure 1-18 as pure virtual functions. This allows other users to derive classes from ParserClient and to provide their own implementation for these functions.

The forward declaration of **Identifier** is of special interest. I could have mentioned **identifier.h** in a **#include** statement, but since none of the interface of **Identifier** is used by this module, there is no need. It is a good rule of thumb to limit the number of **#include** statements within a header file.

Another interesting feature of this listing is the conditional compilation surrounding the header file. This is essential in many C++ implementations to prevent multiple compilation of the same code. It may be that many header files will #include parserClient.h. If two or more of these headers are included within any compilation unit, then parserClient.h will be read by the compiler more than once. The conditional compilation prevents the compiler from actually compiling the code more than once.

The name that I selected for the conditional compilation symbol is a conglomeration of the name of the file and the category or subsystem to which the class belongs. This useful convention helps me to organize my code.

Listing 1-15 shows the code for the **XRef** class. As shown in Figure 1-25, **XRef** derives from **ParserClient** and contains an **OrderedSet** of **IdentifierReferenceList** objects. Note the use of directory paths in the **#include** statements. I prefer to place header files into directories based upon the category or subsystem that they

Listing 1-14

```
Parser/parserClient.h

#ifndef PARSER_PARSER_CLIENT_H
#define PARSER_PARSER_CLIENT_H

//------------------------------------------------
// Name
//   ParserClient
//
// Description
//   This class provides an interface for the clients
//   of the Parser.  Whenever the Parser encounters an identifier,
//   it calls one of the two virtual functions.  It calls
//   AddDefinition if the identifier is being defined.  It calls
//   AddReference if the identifier is simply being used.
//
class Identfier;

class ParserClient
{
  public:
    virtual void
    AddReference(Identifier*  theIdentifier,
                 char*        theFileName,
                 int          theLineNumber
                ) = 0;

    virtual void
    AddDefinition(Identifier*  theIdentifier,
                  char*        theFileName,
                  int          theLineNumber
                 ) = 0;
};
#endif
```

belong to. This helps to prevent file-name clashes, as well as giving the category or subsystem structure some physical reality.

Notice the function **PrintReport**, which was first mentioned in Listing 1-13. Its purpose is to iterate over **itsIdentifierSet** and print the references to the identifiers, as in the report in Figure 1-13.

Listings 1-16 through 1-18 show the definitions of the **Identifier**, **Scope**, and **NamedScope** classes. These listings describe the decisions made in Figure 1-24. Notice the use of reference member variable **itsScope** in Listing 1-16 and **itsName** in Listing 1-18. The **Identifier** class contains a reference to a **Scope**. Figure 1-24 shows this as contains-by-reference, and this is clearly the right choice, since many **Identifier**s must share a single **Scope**. Why didn't I use a pointer instead of a reference variable in Listing 1-16? I used the reference variable because the **Scope** *always* predates the **Identifier**, and an **Identifier** can *never* change its **Scope**. This is exactly the semantics of a reference member variable. A reference member variable must be initialized when the object is created, and cannot thereafter be redirected to refer to some other object. Thus, the association between an **Identifier** and its **Scope** is permanent and invariable. The same semantics apply to a **NamedScope** and **itsName** in

---

Listing 1-15

```
XRef/xref.h

#ifndef XREF_XREF_H
#define XREF_XREF_H

#include "Containers/orderedSet.h"
#include "XRef/identifierReferenceList.h"
#include "Parser/parserClient.h"

class ostream;

//----------------------------------------------
// Name
//   XRef
//
// Description
//   This class implements the ParserClient interface by
//   accumulating the references and definitions into a list of
//   references to identifiers.  This is used to print cross-
//   reference reports.

class XRef : public ParserClient
{
  public:
    virtual void
    AddReference(Identifier* theIdentifier,
                 char*       theFileName,
                 int         theLineNumber);

    virtual void
    AddDefinition(Identifier* theIdentifier,
                  char*       theFileName,
                  int         theLineNumber);

    void PrintReport(ostream&);

  private:
    OrderedSet<IdentifierReferenceList*> itsIdentifierSet;
};
#endif
```

Listing 1-18. The **Identifier** that names the **Scope** must predate the **Scope**, and cannot be changed thereafter.

Summary of the **XRef** Example

In the BOM example, we started with C++ code and worked backwards to derive the corresponding design diagrams. In the **XRef** example we reversed this to a more normal flow, beginning with requirements and proceeding through analysis, design, and some implementation. The example is far from complete, but is has shown a great deal of the processes involved with OOA and OOD.

Listing 1-16

`Parser/identifier.h`

```
#ifndef PARSER_IDENTIFIER_H
#define PARSER_IDENTIFIER_H

#include "Parser/Scope.h"
#include "Tools/String.h"

//------------------------------------------------------------
// Name
//   Identifier
//
// Description
//   This class represents an identifier in a C++ program.  It
//   contains its name and the scope that it belongs to.
//
class Identifier
{
  public:
    Identifier(Scope& theScope, const String& theName);

  private::
    Scope& itsScope;
    String itsName;
};
#endif
```

Listing 1-17

`Parser/scope.h`

```
#ifndef PARSER_SCOPE_H
#define PARSER_SCOPE_H

//------------------------------------------------------------
// Name
//   Scope
//
// Description
//   This class is the abstract base for all the different kinds
//   of scopes.  You can query any scope for its parent scope.
//
class Scope
{
  public:
    virtual Scope* GetParentScope() = 0;
        // returns 0 if no parent (i.e. 'this' is global)
};
#endif
```

We began by analyzing the requirements to find a candidate list of objects. If you look over this list, you will find that many of these candidates did indeed make it into the design model. Some other candidate objects did not, which is typical. The objects that belong in a design model are rarely so obvious that they can be predicted before any design work is done.

```
Listing 1-18
Parser/namedScope.h

#ifndef PARSER_NAMED_SCOPE
#define PARSER_NAMED_SCOPE

#include "Parser/scope.h"
class Identifier;

//-----------------------------------------------------------
// Name
//   NamedScope
//
// Description
//   This class represents a named scope.  A named scope is a scope
//   which is created within a class or a function.  The scope carries
//   the name of the class or function.  Thus a named scope has an
//   identifier which specifies its name.
//
//   The parent Scope of a NamedScope is the Scope of itsName;
//

class NamedScope : public Scope
{
  public:
    NamedScope(Identifier& theName);
    virtual Scope* GetParentScope();

  private:
    Identifier& itsName;
};
#endif
```

One interesting case is the **Reference** object. Although it was not in our initial list, I implied its existence in the discussion about the **Line-number** object. I was so intrigued by the **Reference** object that I decided to design a static model that encompassed it. Later, when I considered the dynamics of printing the cross-reference report, I eliminated the **Reference** object from the model. Again, this is typical. We often begin our design models with notions that seem compelling and obvious, only to discard them once we study the problem in more detail.

Once I had considered a few dynamic scenarios and had created a static model that I felt supported them, I started looking at issues of reuse. I was disappointed that the parsing portion of the model was coupled to the cross-reference portion. I wanted to reuse the **Parser** in other contexts, so I decoupled the two by separating them into separate categories and building compiler fire walls around them. This inspired some changes to the static model that might not have otherwise been obvious.

It is interesting to note that all of these manipulations were achieved through the use of class and object diagrams. Not a stitch of code was written until all these decisions had been made and the model had settled down a bit. While this illustrates the power of using diagrams, it is hardly typical. It is far more normal to engage in some coding while the design is in progress. Some important aspects of design can only be recorded while coding. As a case in point, the entire discussion regarding reference member variables could not have arisen in the absence of code to support it.

It is not evil to start coding before completing a design. In many ways it is essential. Design can be viewed as an exploration into the domain of possible solutions. A design is an approximation, not a solution itself. Designs almost always have errors and raise issues that must be worked out in the code. Working code based upon the design is the real solution. If design gets too far ahead of implementation, then the approximations can add up to significant design errors.

I like to design a little, to explore the solution domain, and then code those solutions to lay down some reality to the solution. Then I go back to design to push the exploration a little farther, and then back again to implementation to prove my concepts. This iterative approach leads to a certain amount of rework. Sometimes subsequent design activities reveal that previous implementations should be modified. This is to be expected, and should not be viewed as a waste. It is simply a way of evolving the solution to fit the problem.

In the **XRef** example, I did not employ this iterative approach for two reasons. First, I wanted to demonstrate that the vast majority of design decisions can be dealt with at the level of a Booch diagram. Secondly, the problem was too small for me to feel the need to iterate it.

The Mark IV Special Coffee Maker

Now let's try a slightly larger and more complete example: a coffee maker. Below is a specification of the Mark IV Special Coffee Maker. Our task is to design the software that must run inside this machine to control its various functions. We want the design to be object-oriented, and we want the implementation to be in C++.

Is C++ an appropriate language for a small, embedded, real-time system like a coffee maker? Is OOD an appropriate methodology for designing such a system? Or are the run-time and storage constraints in such a small system too limited to use such "heavyweight" tools and methodologies?

Although the main goal of this chapter is to teach the first principles of OOD in C++, an ancillary goal of the rest of this chapter will be to make a case, by example, supporting the notion that OOD and C++ are viable in the embedded, real-time environment. By the time we are done, we will have a working design and a fair amount of C++ code. I will supply a few benchmarks of that code, and then leave you to judge whether those numbers could be supported in a real-time embedded environment.

Specification

The Mark IV Special Coffee Maker:
A Functional Specification

The Mark IV special makes up to 12 cups of coffee at a time. The user places a filter in the filter holder, fills the filter with coffee grounds, and slides the filter holder into its receptacle. The user then pours up to 12 cups of water into the water strainer and presses the "Brew" button. The water is heated until boiling. The pressure of the evolving steam forces the water to be sprayed over the coffee grounds, and coffee drips through the filter into the pot. The pot is kept warm for extended periods by a warmer plate, which only turns on if there is coffee in the pot. If the pot is removed from the warmer plate while coffee is being sprayed over the grounds, the flow of water is stopped, so that brewed coffee does not spill on the warmer plate. The following hardware needs to be monitored or controlled:

- The heating element for the boiler. It can be turned on or off.
- The heating element for the warmer plate. It can be turned on or off.
- The sensor for the warmer plate. It has three states: **warmerEmpty**, **potEmpty**, **potNotEmpty**.
- A sensor for the boiler, which determines if there is water present or not. It has two states: **boilerEmpty** or **boilerNotEmpty**.
- The brew button. This is a momentary button that starts the brewing cycle. It has an indicator that lights up when the brewing cycle is over and the coffee is ready.
- A pressure-relief valve that opens to reduce the pressure in the boiler. The drop in pressure stops the flow of water to the filter. It can be opened or closed.

Specification of the Mark IV Hardware Interface Functions

The hardware for the Mark IV is already complete. The hardware engineers have even provided a low-level C function call interface for us to use, so we don't have to write any bit-twiddling I/O driver code. The **man** pages for these interface functions follow:

NAME
  GetWarmerStatus

SYNOPSIS
```
enum WarmerPlateStatus {potNotEmpty, potEmpty, warmerEmpty};
WarmerPlateStatus GetWarmerPlateStatus()
```

DESCRIPTION
This function returns the status of the warmer-plate switch.

The switch on the warmer plate, which detects the presence of the pot and whether it has coffee in it, is a pressure transducer. It has 2 thresholds that behave as follows:

```
Pressure             Output
p < T1               warmerEmpty
p >T1 && p < T2      potEmpty
p > T2               potNotEmpty
```

NAME
GetBoilerStatus

SYNOPSIS
```
enum BoilerStatus {boilerEmpty, boilerNotEmpty};
BoilerStatus GetBoilerStatus();
```

DESCRIPTION
This function returns the status of the boiler switch. The boiler switch is a float switch that detects if there is more than 1/2 cup of water in the boiler.

NAME
GetBrewButtonStatus

SYNOPSIS
```
enum BrewButtonStatus {brewButtonPushed, brewButtonNotPushed};
BrewButtonStatus GetBrewButtonStatus();
```

DESCRIPTION
This function returns the status of the brew button. The brew button is a momentary switch that remembers its state. Each call to this function returns the remembered state and then resets that state to brewButtonNotPushed.

Thus, even if this function is polled at a very slow rate, it will still detect when the brew button is pushed.

NAME
SetBoilerState

SYNOPSIS
```
enum BoilerHeaterState {boilerOn, boilerOff};
void SetBoilerState(BoilerHeaterState);
```

DESCRIPTION
This function turns the heating element in the boiler on or off.

NAME
SetWarmerState

SYNOPSIS
```
enum WarmerState {warmerOn, warmerOff};
void SetWarmerState(WarmerState);
```

DESCRIPTION
This function turns the heating element in the warmer plate on or off.

NAME
SetIndicatorState

SYNOPSIS
```
enum IndicatorState {indicatorOn, indicatorOff};
void SetIndicatorState(IndicatorState);
```

DESCRIPTION
This function turns the indicator light on or off. The indicator light should be turned on at the end of the brewing cycle. It should be turned off when the user presses the brew button.

NAME
SetReliefValveState

SYNOPSIS
```
enum ReliefValveState {valveOpen, valveClosed};
void SetReliefValveState(ReliefValveState);
```

DESCRIPTION
This function opens and closes the pressure-relief valve. When this valve is closed, steam pressure in the boiler will force hot water to spray out over the coffee filter. When the valve is open, the steam in the boiler escapes into the environment, and the water in the boiler will not spray out over the filter.

Designing the Mark IV Software

Once again we are faced with the blank sheet of paper. How should we begin the design process? One useful method is to attempt to describe the sequence of events leading from a particular stimulus. This is similar to creating a dynamic model, but without concentrating on objects and messages. Jacobson[10] calls this a *use-case*. So, what happens when the user presses the brew button? Lets see if we can map the use-case out.

- The brewing cycle can't begin until there is water in the boiler, an empty pot on the warmer, and the Brew button is pressed;[11] that is, **GetBoilerStatus** returns **boilerNotEmpty**, **GetWarmerStatus** returns **potEmpty**, and

---

10. Ivar Jacobson, *Object-Oriented Software Engineering* (Addison Wesley, 1992).
11. These constraints are debatable. Should we allow the brewing cycle to start if the pot is not empty? That might cause horrible spills, but it might also prevent the user from warming up an old pot with hot new coffee. In this model, I opt for preventing the spills.

GetBrewButtonStatus returns **brewButtonPushed**.

- The brewing cycle starts by turning on the boiler element. We probably ought to make sure that the pressure-relief valve is closed, too, since if left open it will prevent the water from spraying on the coffee grounds. We also have to turn off the indicator lamp. So we will make three calls:
  ```
  SetIndicatorState(indicatorOff);
  SetReliefValveState(valveClosed);
  SetBoilerState(boilerOn);
  ```

- As water sprays out over the grounds, the pot begins to fill, and the warming plate sensor indicates **potNotEmpty**. So we should probably turn on the heating element for the warming plate; that is, when **GetWarmerStatus** returns **potNotEmpty**, we should call

  ```
  SetWarmerState(warmerOn);
  ```

- When the boiler is nearly empty, **GetBoilerStatus** will return **boilerEmpty**. We should then turn off the boiler heating element and turn on the indicator lamp, indicating that the coffee is ready. We do this by calling
  ```
  SetBoilerState(boilerOff);
  SetIndicatorState(indicatorOn);
  ```

The Control Model: A Finite State Machine for the Coffee Maker

Although far from complete, we recognize the above analysis as a system that moves from state to state based on a set of external events. With each new event, the system changes state and must perform some corresponding action. This is clearly a finite state machine (FSM). The state transition diagram (STD) for this FSM is depicted in Figure 1-26.

As you can see, even simple problems can have complications. Notice that we have covered some pretty weird cases here. The system will behave itself nicely should the user decide to empty the pot halfway through brewing, or add water to the pot to weaken the coffee. It will shut off the warmer if all the coffee in the pot evaporates.

The notation for this STD is Harel's, as described by Booch.[12] The round rectangles represent states. The arrows between the states are called *transitions*. Each transition is labeled with the name of an event and the set of actions that are performed when the event occurs. In this particular diagram, I have prefixed the actions with a bullet for the sake of clarity.

The large round rectangle surrounding the two states on the left of the diagram is a *super state*; and the states nested within it are called *substates*. Transitions from super-states to other states in the model are shared by all the substates within that superstate. Thus, from either of the two nested states, **EmptyPotRemoved** or **FullPotRemoved**,

---

12. Booch, *Object-Oriented Analysis and Design with Applications, 2d ed.* (Copyright © 1994 by The Benjamin/Cummings Publishing Company)

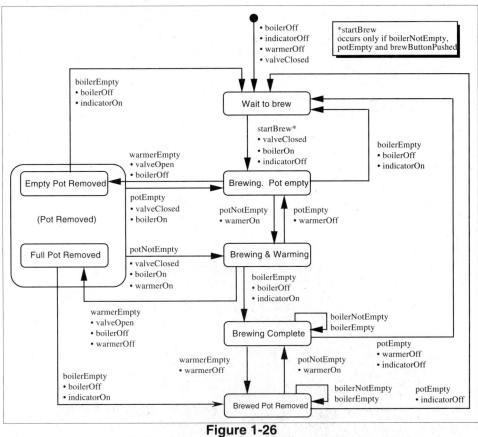

Figure 1-26
Coffee Maker State Transition Diagram

the `potNotEmpty` event will cause a transition to the `Brewing & Warming` state, and will close the valve, turn on the boiler, and turn on the warmer.

Finding the Objects

As we saw from the `XRef` example, one of the first and biggest problems facing the designer is to discover the objects, the primary abstractions, of the problem. Finding these objects can be a very challenging task.[13] In this case, however, the objects seem obvious. They appear to be `Boiler`, `Warmer`, `BrewButton`, `ReliefValve`, and `Indicator`. Listing 1-19 shows how a few of these objects might be implemented as classes.

---

13. As Stroustrup says, "The translation of a concept in the application area into a class in a design is not a simple mechanical operation. It is often a task that requires significant insights." *The C++ Programming Language, 2d ed.*, 1991.

Listing 1-19
Possible implementation of Coffee Maker objects

```
class BrewButton
{
  public:
    static int IsPushed()
    {return GetBrewButtonStatus() == brewButtonPushed;}
};

class Indicator
{
  public:
    static void TurnOn()  {SetIndicatorState(indicatorOn);}
    static void TurnOff() {SetIndicatorState(indicatorOff);}
};

class Boiler
{
  public:
    static int  IsEmpty() {return GetBoilerStatus() == boilerEmpty;}
    static void TurnOn()   {SetBoilerState(boilerOn);}
    static void TurnOff()  {SetBoilerState(boilerOff);}
};
```

We could continue the implementation in this vein, but to what purpose? What good are a lot of static inline functions? You may ask why I made these member functions static? Because the run-time system we have been given by the hardware engineers disallows more than one boiler, indicator, brew button, and so on. Thus, there is no point in instantiating the above classes since there could never be more than one instance of each of them. We might as well make all their member functions static, and simply call them directly: **Boiler::TurnOn()**. But what is the difference between that and simply saying: **SetBoilerState(boilerOn)**? Not much.

Perhaps we have failed to find the true abstractions. Compelling as the previous list of objects is, perhaps it is the wrong list. Perhaps we should look deeper into the problem and try to find the *underlying abstractions*.

Object-Oriented Analysis: Finding the Underlying Abstractions

Our job is to brew coffee. This is not in dispute; but what does it take to brew coffee? Our hardware engineers have given us a nice run-time system that will allow us to accomplish the task.[14]   However, that run-time system is hopelessly tied to their *solution* to the problem, and not to the actual task of brewing coffee. For example, they have the concept of the pressure-relief valve. Its purpose is to relieve the pressure in the boiler, so that water stops spraying out over the coffee grounds, but the underlying abstraction has nothing to do with valves, boilers, or pressure! The underlying abstraction is simply to control the

---

14. In fact, right now, those hardware engineers are thinking, "Oh, oh, those crazy software engineers are at it again. They are wondering how they can take this simple problem and make it much more complicated."

spray of hot water over coffee grounds. Let's name this abstraction **Sprayer**. The **Sprayer** abstraction remains valid, regardless of the hardware solution. The hardware engineers could remove the valve and add a hot water pump, but this would not change the abstraction. We would still be controlling hot water spraying over coffee grounds.

The implementation of the **Sprayer**, in the current run-time environment, has a few complications. In order to spray hot water, the boiler must be on, and the valve must be closed. To stop spraying, the valve must be open, and we probably want to turn the boiler off, since we probably don't want the Mark IV to continuously exude a huge plume of steam.[15] When complications like this can be hidden by a simpler abstraction, then we have gained ground on the complexity of the problem. We have not eliminated that complexity, but we have managed it! We have sequestered it within the **Sprayer** abstraction, from which it cannot escape to pollute the rest of the application.

What underlying abstraction does the warmer plate represent? It represents the need to keep the brewed coffee warm. What complications does the **Warmer** abstraction hide? It hides the complications of empty and absent pots, and warmer-heating elements.

Another underlying abstraction is the **User Interface (UI)**. It hides the complications involving the brew button and the indicator.

What about the boiler? Does it represent an abstraction separate from the **Sprayer**? I don't think so. It is irrelevant that a coffee maker has a boiler, as long as the **Sprayer** delivers hot water. However, the boiler may well appear again as a second-level abstraction within the **Sprayer**.

Assigning Responsibilities to the Abstractions

Assigning responsibilities to the chosen abstractions is often as difficult as finding the objects.[16] I would very much like to decouple these abstractions from each other, dividing their responsibilities and keeping them separate. However, this may be a challenge. For example, I would love to isolate the **Warmer** from the rest of the model. Figure 1-27 shows a potential control model for the **Warmer**.

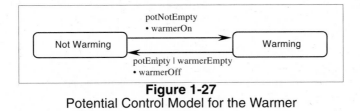

Figure 1-27
Potential Control Model for the Warmer

---

15. Unless, of course, you wanted it to double as a humidifier.
16. Or perhaps even more difficult. As Booch points out, "This step is much harder than the first and takes much longer. This is the phase in which there may be fierce debates, wailing and gnashing of teeth, and general name-calling during design reviews. Finding classes and objects is the easy part; deciding upon the protocol of each object is hard." *Object-Oriented Design with Applications*, by Grady Booch, (Copyright © 1991, by the Benjamin / Cummings Publishing Company).

This model is compelling in its simplicity, but it has some flaws. What happens if the user decides to soak the pot in soapy water overnight. If the pot is placed on the warmer, it will be heated. This is probably not desired. More than likely, we would only like the warmer to be active if the brew button has been pushed, and there is coffee in the pot. Figure 1-28 shows an updated model.

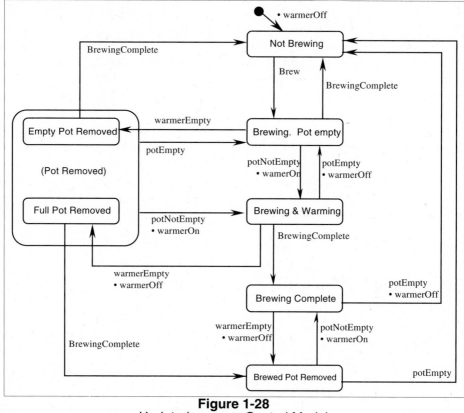

Figure 1-28
Updated **Warmer** Control Model

The structure of this model is remarkably similar to the STD, which represented the entire coffee maker. Does this mean that most of the complexity of that STD was simply to control the heating element of the warmer plate? Examination of the other control models will tell. If they are much simpler, then the answer to the above question must be affirmative. In that case, it is a good thing we are segregating the abstractions, since we don't want the complications of one to pollute the others. So, let's look at the other control models to see how complex they are.

The control model for the **Sprayer** is shown in Figure 1-29. It's pretty simple. The **Sprayer** simply turns on the flow of hot water when the brew cycle begins, interrupts it when the pot is removed, and terminates it when the brew cycle completes. It is pretty clear that this model is expecting some other mechanisms to tell it when to begin the brew cycle, and it is depending upon that mechanism to ensure that conditions are right. For example, the **Sprayer** control model will happily spray hot water into a full pot if told to do so. We will have to handle this at a higher level.

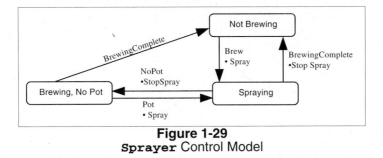

Figure 1-29
Sprayer Control Model

Notice that the **Sprayer** model is completely dissociated from the **Warmer** model. This **Sprayer** will be happy to function in any environment that can supply it with **Brew**, **Pot**, **NoPot**, and **BrewingComplete** events.

Finally, lets look at the **UI** control model shown in Figure 1-30.

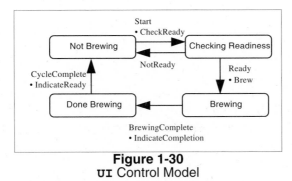

Figure 1-30
UI Control Model

The **UI** ensures that the brewing cycle cannot begin unless everything is ready. Just how it does that is unknown at this point. If the system is ready to brew, the FSM transitions to the **Brewing** state and invokes the **Brew** action. When brewing is complete, the **UI** indicates that to the user. In our case, this means turning on the indicator. **CycleComplete** is an event that signals that we are ready to begin another brew cycle if necessary. In our implementation, it will occur when the pot becomes empty after having been brewed.

Clearly these three models communicate with each other. But how? One possibility is that the **Sprayer**, **Warmer**, and **UI** objects simply send messages to each other. Figure 1-31 shows an object diagram that explores this possibility.

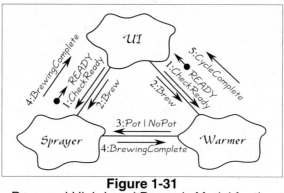

Figure 1-31
Proposed High-Level Dynamic Model for the
Coffee Maker

The **UI** queries the **Sprayer** and the **Warmer** whether or not they are ready to brew. In this scenario, they both reply that they are. Then the **UI** tells the **Sprayer** and the **Warmer** that brewing has begun. During the course of brewing, the **Warmer** tells the **Sprayer** if the pot is present or not. When the **Sprayer** decides that enough water has been sprayed, it tells the **UI** and the **Warmer** that brewing is complete. When the warmer finally detects that the pot has gone empty, it tells the **UI** that the cycle is complete.

This is a relatively simple model, and it looks like it will work. The control models need to be changed a bit to note the fact that they must send external messages like **Pot**, **NoPot**, and **CycleComplete**. Figure 1-32 and Figure 1-33 show the updated models.

The advantage we have gained by separating these abstractions is that they have very little knowledge of one another. If the mechanisms of the **Warmer** change drastically, it will have no effect upon the **UI** or **Sprayer**, as long as the **Warmer** can continue to accept and send the expected messages. Also, all three components are reusable in other contexts. For example, the high-level portions of the **Sprayer** and possibly the entire **Warmer** could be used in a coffee maker with multiple pots.

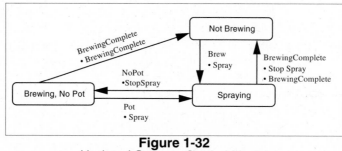

Figure 1-32
Updated Sprayer Control Model

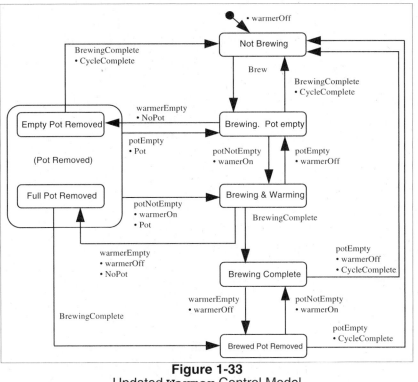

Figure 1-33
Updated `Warmer` Control Model

Reusing the Abstractions

The object relationships and the direction of the messages in Figure 1-31 show that each of the three classes must know that the other two exist. For example, in order for the **UI** to send the **CheckReady** message to **Warmer**, it must know that **Warmer** exists, and it must know where **Warmer** is. It would be better, from the point of view of reusability, if the three major abstractions had no knowledge of each other at all. We can achieve this by using the technique that we employed in the **XRef** example, and by creating a new mediator object. Figure 1-34 shows a likely static model.

This static model shows perfect isolation of the three major abstractions. Each uses an abstract client to "advertise" its interface to prospective users. The **CoffeeMaker** is a very highly coupled class that inherits from all three clients, knows about all three abstractions, and mediates the communications among them.

The **CoffeeMaker** contains the **UI**, **Sprayer**, and **Warmer** by value. I have tentatively chosen this mode because I believe that the **UI**, **Sprayer**, and **Warmer** should not stand alone. They should be created and destroyed by **CoffeeMaker** (or one of its derivatives).

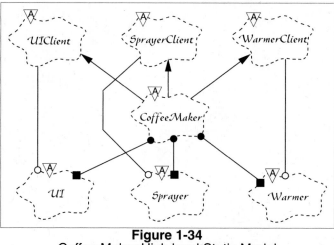

Figure 1-34
Coffee Maker High level Static Model

Note that all these classes are abstract. None, as yet, know anything at all about the implementation of the Mark IV Special Coffee Maker. We are still designing a generic coffee maker!

Figure 1-35 shows a dynamic model using the **CoffeeMaker** object. It is not complete, but shows the concept that **CoffeeMaker** is the nexus of communication among the other abstractions. **CoffeeMaker** knows where to dispatch the **CheckReady** messages, how to combine the responses and return the required result to **UI**, and where to send the **Pot** and **NoPot** messages.

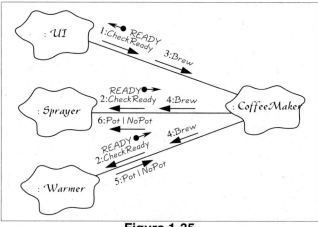

Figure 1-35
CoffeeMaker Dynamic Model

At this point, I would like to see some code. I think I have a few good ideas cooking here, but I want to see how they appear in the light of reality. Listings 1-20 through 1-22 show the implementation of the **UI** class.

Listing 1-20

ui.h

```
#ifndef COFFEE_MAKER_UI_H
#define COFFEE_MAKER_UI_H

class UIClient;

class UI
{
  public:
    UI(UIClient& theClient);
    virtual ~UI();

    // FSM Events.
    void Start();
    void Ready();
    void NotReady();
    void BrewingComplete();
    void CycleComplete();

    // Gain control from main program
    void Poll();

  private:
    // Actions from FSM
    void CheckReady();
    void Brew();
    virtual void IndicateCompletion() = 0;
    virtual void IndicateReady() = 0;

    // Check implementation to see if user wants to brew;
    virtual int CheckStart() = 0;

    UIClient& itsClient;
    enum {notBrewing, checkingReadiness,
          brewing, doneBrewing} itsState;
};
#endif
```

Listing 1-21

uiClient.h

```
#ifndef COFFEE_MAKER_UI_CLIENT_H
#define COFFEE_MAKER_UI_CLIENT_H

class UIClient
{
  public:
```

Listing 1-21 (Continued)

uiClient.h
```
    virtual void Brew() = 0;
    virtual int CheckReady() = 0;
};
#endif
```

Listing 1-22

ui.cc
```
#include "ui.h"
#include "uiClient.h"

UI::UI(UIClient& theClient)
: itsClient(theClient)
, itsState(notBrewing)
{}

UI::~UI() {}

void UI::Start()
{
    switch (itsState)
    {
    case notBrewing: itsState=checkingReadiness; CheckReady();
break;
    case checkingReadiness: /* ignore */ break;
    case brewing: /* ignore */ break;
    case doneBrewing: /* ignore */ break;
    };
}

void UI::Ready()
{
    switch (itsState)
    {
    case notBrewing: /* ignore */ break;
    case checkingReadiness: itsState = brewing; Brew(); break;
    case brewing: /* ignore */ break;
    case doneBrewing: /* ignore */ break;
    };
}

void UI::NotReady()
{
    switch (itsState)
    {
    case notBrewing: /* ignore */ break;
    case checkingReadiness: itsState = notBrewing; break;
    case brewing: /* ignore */ break;
    case doneBrewing: /* ignore */ break;
    };
}
```

Listing 1-22 (Continued)

```
ui.cc
void UI::BrewingComplete()
{
    switch (itsState)
    {
    case notBrewing: /* ignore */ break;
    case checkingReadiness: itsState = notBrewing; break;
    case brewing: itsState = doneBrewing; IndicateCompletion();
break;
    case doneBrewing: /* ignore */ break;
    };
}
void UI::CycleComplete()
{
    switch(itsState)
    {
    case notBrewing: /* ignore */ break;
    case checkingReadiness: itsState = notBrewing; break;
    case brewing: itsState = notBrewing; break;
    case doneBrewing: itsState = notBrewing; IndicateReady(); break;
    }
}

void UI::Poll()
{
    if (itsState == notBrewing && CheckStart()) // user has started
    {
        Start();
    }
}

void UI::CheckReady()
{
    if (itsClient.CheckReady())
    {
        Ready();
    }
    else
    {
        NotReady();
    }
}

void UI::Brew()
{
    itsClient.Brew();
}
```

This code is a bit sketchy. It is meant to be an experiment, not production-quality code. I am writing it to get a feeling for what the real needs of these classes are. For example, one issue is the representation of the finite state machines (FSM). In the code, I have chosen to represent the FSM in a traditional manner. FSM events are modeled as public member functions, so that clients can issue them. The actions of the FSM are private member functions, since only the code within the FSM calls these explicitly. The FSM itself is implemented with a state variable and a set of switch statements within the event functions.

The **Poll** function represents the notion that this class must somehow gain control of the processor in order to detect the Start event. Something, probably the main program, will have to repeatedly call **UI::Poll** so that the **UI** can check to see if the user has started a brewing cycle.

There are several pure virtual functions. Each represents something that this class knows should be done, but doesn't know how to achieve. All of them must be overridden in a derived class that understands the run-time and hardware environment. The **IndicateCompletion** function tells the user that there is a brewed pot of coffee ready for him. The **IndicateReady** function tells the user that all the coffee is gone and he can brew another pot if he would like. The **CheckStart** function determines if the user has decided to brew another pot.

The hardware and run-time environment of the Mark IV has given us the facilities to implement each of the three pure virtual functions of **UI**. Listings 1-23 and 1-24 show a possible implementation.

```
Listing 1-23
MarkIV/MarkIV_UI.h

#ifndef MARKIV_MARKIV_UI
#define MARKIV_MARKIV_UI

#include "UI/ui.h"

class MarkIV_UI : public UI
{
  public:
    virtual void IndicateCompletion();
    virtual void IndicateReady();
    virtual int  CheckStart();
};
#endif
```

This excursion into the code has led us to a static model that looks something like Figure 1-36. This is a typical "ladder" or "dual hierarchy." The concrete classes implement the pure virtual functions within the abstract classes. The using relationships between the **MarkIVCoffeeMaker** and the three concrete classes are purely for the purpose of instantiating those objects. The constructor of **MarkIVCoffeeMaker** probably instantiates the three concrete classes and then hands them to the base **CoffeeMaker** class.

There is something about this structure that I don't like very much. The finite state machines (control models) and the abstract base classes are tightly coupled—but what justification do we have for this? Are we sure that the control models are immutable? for every different kind of coffee maker?

For example, let's assume that the *Mark V* coffee maker has the same warmer hardware, but it makes more sense for the warmer to turn on only *after* all the coffee has been

Listing 1-24

```
MarkIV/MarkIV_UI.cc

#include "MarkIV/markIV_UI.h"
#include "MarkIV/runtime.h"

void MarkIV_UI::IndicateCompletion()
{
    SetIndicatorState(indicatorOn);
}

void MarkIV_UI::IndicateReady()
{
    SetIndicatorState(indicatorOff);
}

int MarkIV_UI::CheckStart()
{
    return (GetBrewButtonStatus() ==  brewButtonPushed);
}
```

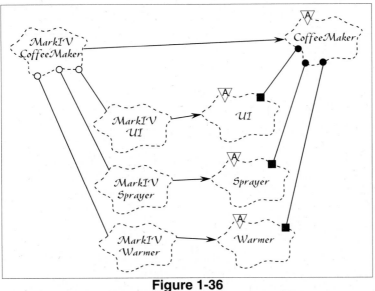

Figure 1-36
Potential Static Model for MarkIV Implementation

brewed. Since this is incompatible with the control model of the **Warmer** class, we will not be able to reuse it. And since **MarkIVWarmer** derives from **Warmer**, we will not be able to reuse it, even though it directly supports the appropriate hardware. Instead, we will have to write a new special variety of the **Warmer** class, simply to change its control model, and then derive a new **MarkVWarmer** from it, which virtually duplicates the code from **MarkIVWarmer**.

We can solve this problem by isolating the control models from the abstract base classes, as shown in Figure 1-37. This structure allows us to specify the interface that drives the hardware separately from the specification of the control model. Thus, what had been the private member functions in the **UI** class of Listing 1-20 now become public pure virtual functions in a **UIDriver** class. The FSMs for the control models are coded in the classes derived from **UI**, **Warmer**, and **Sprayer**. Their base classes provide access to the abstract interface of a corresponding hardware driver class. Each abstract driver must be implemented by a derived class.

Thus, we can use the same hardware driver with many different control models. Likewise, we can use the same control model with many different hardware drivers. This gives us a very nice separation of concerns, and promotes the reusability of the components.

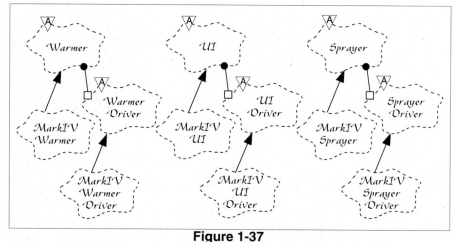

Figure 1-37
Separation of Hardware Driver from the Control Model

CoffeeMaker Categories

Figure 1-38 shows the category structure of the coffee-maker project. This structure separates the reusable components from the components that are tied to the Mark IV.

This diagram shows that the primary abstractions, the **Sprayer**, **UI**, and **Warmer** are independent of each other, which means that they can be reused independently. For example, the **Sprayer** and **UI** could be reused for an iced-tea maker, which does not require a warmer. If those categories were tightly coupled to the **Warmer**, such reuse would be much harder to achieve.

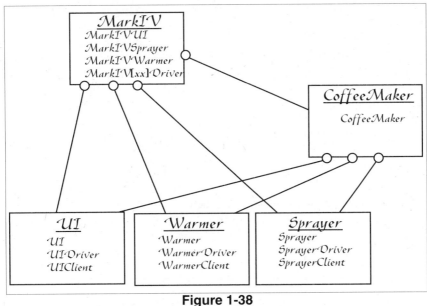

Figure 1-38
`CoffeeMaker` Categories

Implementation of the Mark IV Coffee Maker

If this were a larger project, I would not yet be ready for full-scale implementation. In a larger model I would want to do a lot more dynamic modeling to insure that my static structures were correct. However, in this case I am ready to code. The full implementation of the Mark IV coffee maker is shown in Listings 1-25 through 1-52 at the end of this chapter. We have achieved a good design, well suited for the Mark IV and reusable in many different kinds of coffee makers. More design is certainly possible, but I think we have crossed over the "knee" of the curve, and any further design/analysis would be inefficient at best.

Have we already over-designed this coffee maker? Have we spent so much time designing and fiddling that we have built a monster, when all we needed was a couple of hundred lines of code? Have we added more structure than we will ever use? These are legitimate questions. The answers depend upon our goals for this design.

If this is a one-shot deal, and we will *never* produce another coffee maker, then we have spent far too much time designing it. We should have stopped with the first finite state machine and coded it up in C, or C++ without objects. But if our company is going to make other coffee makers, then our strategy has probably been correct. By investing a little extra time in the design, we have begun to create a library of reusable components that will facilitate the creation of similar products.

Has the use of C++ and OOD been appropriate for such a small embedded system? The code for the coffee maker amounts to 635 non-commented source lines (NCSL). It requires approximately 8K of program space on a 486 computer. A coffee maker would probably not have a 486 chip in it, but we might suppose that it would have an 8088. The machine code for the two is similar enough that no significant increase in memory usage ought to occur. The 8K requirement seems within the limits of even a very stringent embedded environment.

The Design and the Code Aren't a Perfect Match

The careful reader will have noticed that some subtle differences exist between the design and the structure of the source code. For example, the using relationships in Figure 1-34 were promoted to member variables (containment) in the code. Also, the **MarkIVCof-feeMaker** class in Figure 1-36 was never actually created; the main program took its place. Such "design jitter" is to be expected. It is unrealistic to think that we will not find flaws or oversights in the design during the implementation. The code will always inject a little reality into the design.

Summary

Design is mostly hard work. The creative part (the fun part) is only a small part of the process. The rest is simply diligence and a fair amount of rework. As a design evolves, what appear at first to be good ideas must often be (painfully) discarded, and those that appear unlikely sometimes become fundamental. If you are a good designer, you plod through your design looking for ways to use the static and dynamic models to test the integrity of the design. You rarely, if ever, accept a static or dynamic model at face value. Instead, you test it by showing that the static models support the dynamic models, and that the dynamic models implement the required behaviors. If you are a good designer, you look for opportunities to create reusable components. You manipulate your design, creating categories and compiler fire walls that separate the concerns of the application and support independent reuse of its components. If you are a good designer, you weigh the cost of over-design against the cost of under-design. You attempt to trade these costs off against the goals of your project and your company.

In this chapter we have seen three small examples of object-oriented designs and their implementation in C++. The first was simply a portion of a manufacturing system that we reverse-engineered from C++ to design documents. This example got us familiar with the design notation and vocabulary.

The second example was the representational model for a C++ cross-reference program. This example taught us that static models that seem appropriate at first often collapse when forced to support the appropriate dynamic models. We showed that design does not have to begin at the top or the bottom, but can begin at any convenient point. We also showed how to create compiler fire walls and why a separation of concerns supports the reuse of components.

In the final example, the coffee maker, we took a sketchy requirements document and transformed it into working C++ code. This example taught us something about the iterative approach to design. We learned that coding can be a useful design tool, helping us inject reality into our designs. We learned that designs can change a lot during their evolution from simple beginnings. And we learned that OOD takes time. Normally, it is time well spent, but for quick and dirty projects, the investment may be inappropriate.

The introduction of this chapter talked about the blueprints of a piston. We made the point that those blueprints might give you all the information you needed to build a piston, but would not tell you what the piston did. We have seen that this separation of form and function exists in software designs as well. The static portion of a software design is the superstructure used to implement the required dynamics. We have shown that static models that do not support the required dynamics are flawed, regardless of their realism or elegance. Good dynamic models describe the behaviors demanded by the requirements. Good static models support those dynamics while separating the design into reusable components. Good designs comprise both good dynamic models and good static models.

Exercises

1. Consider the diagram below. Should the containment be by reference, or by value?

    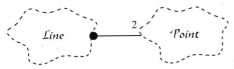

2. Again, for the figure above, write corresponding C++ code.

3. Draw the appropriate Booch Diagram for the following code.

    ```
    class Circle: public GeographicObject
    {
      private:
        Point itsCenter;
        double itsRadius;
    };
    ```

4. Draw a class diagram that corresponds to the object diagram shown below.

    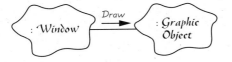

5.   What is the name of the object shown in the diagram below?

6.   What is the name of the class of the object from Exercise 5?

7.   Which of the two diagrams below represent Polymorphic Containment?

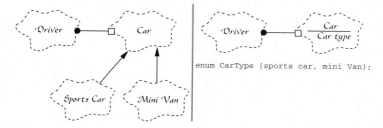

8.   There is a major inconsistency between the two diagrams below. Find it.

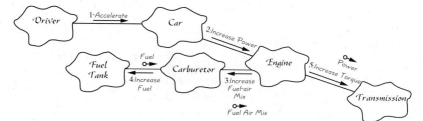

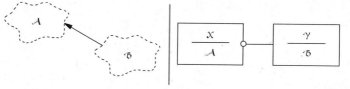

9.   What is wrong with this picture?

10. Design a Multiple Pot Coffee Maker. Reuse as many categories from Figure 1-38 as possible. If necessary, rearrange those categories to enhance their reusability. Write the code.

Mark IV Coffee Maker Implementation

The UI Category

```
Listing 1-25
UI/ui.h

#ifndef UI_UI_H
#define UI_UI_H

class UIClient;
class UIDriver;

//---------------------------------------------------------
// Name
//   UI
//
// Description
//   This class is the abstract interface for the Coffee
//   Maker user interface.  It knows about UI Clients and
//   the driver for the UI hardware.  It allows external
//   classes to inform it of the status of the brewing
//   cycle.
//
class UI
{
  public:
    UI(UIDriver& theDriver, UIClient& theClient);
    virtual ~UI();

    // External Stimuli.
    virtual void BrewingComplete() = 0;
    virtual void CycleComplete() = 0;

  protected:
    UIDriver& GetDriver() {return itsDriver;}
    UIClient& GetClient() {return itsClient;}

  private:
    UIDriver& itsDriver;
    UIClient& itsClient;
};
#endif
```

Listing 1-26

`UI/ui.cc`

```
#include "UI/ui.h"
#include "UI/uiClient.h"
#include "UI/uiDriver.h"

UI::UI(UIDriver& theDriver, UIClient& theClient)
: itsClient(theClient)
, itsDriver(theDriver)
{}

UI::~UI() {}
```

Listing 1-27

`UI/uiDriver.h`

```
#ifndef UI_UI_DRIVER
#define UI_UI_DRIVER

//-----------------------------------------------------
// Name
//   UIDriver
//
// Description
//   This class presents the interface for all UI Hardware
//   drivers.  The UI hardware can be told to tell the user
//   that brewing is complete or that the coffee
//   maker is ready to brew.  It can also poll the user to see if
//   he started a brewing cycle.
//
class UIDriver
{
  public:
    virtual void IndicateCompletion() = 0;
    virtual void IndicateReady()      = 0;
    virtual int  CheckStart()         = 0;
};
#endif
```

Listing 1-28

`UI/uiClient.h`

```
#ifndef UI_UI_CLIENT_H
#define UI_UI_CLIENT_H

class UIClient
{
  public:
    virtual void Brew() = 0;
    virtual int CheckReady() = 0;
};
#endif
```

The Warmer Category

Listing 1-29

```
Warmer/warmer.h

#ifndef WARMER_WARMER_H
#define WARMER_WARMER_H

class WarmerClient;
class WarmerDriver;

//-------------------------------------------------
// Name
//   Warmer
//
// Description
//   This class presents the interface for the Warmer of
//   a coffee maker.  It can be asked if it is ready to start
//   brewing, and it can be told that brewing is complete.
//
class Warmer
{
  public:
    Warmer(WarmerDriver& theDriver, WarmerClient& theClient);
    virtual ~Warmer();

    // External Stimuli
    virtual void Brew() = 0;
    virtual void BrewingComplete() = 0;
    virtual int  CheckReady() = 0;

  protected:
    WarmerDriver& GetDriver() {return itsDriver;}
    WarmerClient& GetClient() {return itsClient;}

  private:
    WarmerDriver& itsDriver;
    WarmerClient& itsClient;
};
#endif
```

Listing 1-30

```
Warmer/warmer.cc


#include "Warmer/warmer.h"
#include "Warmer/warmerClient.h"
#include "Warmer/warmerDriver.h"

Warmer::Warmer(WarmerDriver& theDriver, WarmerClient& theClient)
: itsDriver(theDriver)
, itsClient(theClient)
{}

Warmer::~Warmer() {}
```

Listing 1-31

`Warmer/warmerDriver.h`

```
#ifndef WARMER_WARMER_DRIVER_H
#define WARMER_WARMER_DRIVER_H

//------------------------------------------
// Name
//   WarmerDriver
//
// Description
//   This class presents the generic interface
//   for the hardware dirver of a warmer plate.
//
//   A warmer plate can be turned on or off.  It can
//   also be queried as to the presence and status
//   of a pot.
//
class WarmerDriver
{
  public:
    virtual void WarmerOn() = 0;
    virtual void WarmerOff() = 0;
    virtual void WarmerStatus GetWarmerStatus() = 0;
};
#endif
```

Listing 1-32

`Warmer/warmerClient.h`

```
#ifndef WARMER_WARMER_CLIENT_H
#define WARMER_WARMER_CLIENT_H

//------------------------------------------
// Name
//   WarmerClient
//
// Description
//   This class presents the interface for all clients of
//   a coffee maker warmer.  WarmerClients can be told of the
//   presence or absence of a pot, and whether or not the
//   cycle has completed.  CycleComplete means that an empty pot
//   has been put on the warmer after coffee has been brewed.
//
class WarmerClient
{
  public:
    virtual void Pot() = 0;
    virtual void NoPot() = 0;
    virtual void CycleComplete() = 0;
};
#endif
```

The Sprayer Category

Listing 1-33

`Sprayer/sprayer.h`

```cpp
#ifndef SPRAYER_SPRAYER_H
#define SPRAYER_SPRAYER_H
class SprayerClient;
class SprayerDriver;

class Sprayer
{
  public:
    Sprayer(SprayerDriver&, SprayerClient&);
    virtual ~Sprayer();

    virtual int CheckReady() = 0;

    // External Stimuli
    virtual void Pot() = 0;
    virtual void NoPot() = 0;
    virtual void Brew() = 0;

  protected:
    SprayerDriver& GetDriver() {return itsDriver;}
    SprayerClient& GetClient() {return itsClient;}

  private:
    SprayerDriver& itsDriver;
    SprayerClient& itsClient;
};
#endif
```

Listing 1-34

`Sprayer/sprayer.cc`

```cpp
#include "Sprayer/sprayer.h"

Sprayer::Sprayer(SprayerDriver& theDriver, SprayerClient& theClient)
: itsDriver(theDriver)
, itsClient(theClient)
{}

Sprayer::~Sprayer() {}
```

Listing 1-35

`Sprayer/sprayerDriver.h`

```
#ifndef SPRAYER_SPRAYER_DRIVER_H
#define SPRAYER_SPRAYER_DRIVER_H

//----------------------------------------
// Name
//   SprayerDriver
//
// Description
//   This class presents the interface for the device
//   which sprays hot water over the coffee grounds in
//   a coffee maker.  A sprayer can be told to do two things:
//   to start spraying, and to stop spraying.
//   A sprayer driver can also be asked if water is available
//   for spraying.
//
class SprayerDriver
{
  public:
    virtual void Spray() = 0;
    virtual void StopSpray() = 0;
    virtual int  HasWater() = 0;
};
#endif
```

Listing 1-36

`Sprayer/sprayerClient.h`

```
#ifndef SPRAYER_SPRAYER_CLIENT_H
#define SPRAYER_SPRAYER_CLIENT_H

//----------------------------------------------------
// Name
//   SprayerClient
//
// Description
//   This class presents the interface for a generic
//   client of a coffee-maker sprayer.  There is only one
//   thing a sprayer can say to its clients.  It can tell them
//   that brewing is complete.
//
class SprayerClient
{
  public:
    virtual void BrewingComplete() = 0;
};
#endif
```

The `CoffeeMaker` Category

Listing 1-37

`CoffeeMaker/coffeeMaker.h`

```
#ifndef COFFEEMAKER_COFFEEMAKER_H
#define COFFEEMAKER_COFFEEMAKER_H

class UI;
class Sprayer;
class Warmer;

#include "Sprayer/sprayerClient.h"
#include "UI/uiClient.h"
#include "Warmer/warmerClient.h"

//------------------------------------------------------
// Name
//   CoffeeMaker
//
// Description
//   This class is the nexus of communication between the
//   Warmer, Sprayer, and UI.  It derives from all three of the
//   "client" interfaces and routes the messages among the
//   abstractions.
//
class CoffeeMaker : public SprayerClient,
        public WarmerClient,
                      public UIClient
{
  public:
    CoffeeMaker();
    virtual ~CoffeeMaker();

    // UIClient
    virtual int CheckReady();
    virtual void Brew();

    // SprayerClient
    virtual void BrewingComplete();

    // WarmerClient
    virtual void Pot();
    virtual void NoPot();
    virtual void CycleComplete();

    void SetUI(UI& theUI)                  {itsUI = &theUI;}
    void SetSprayer(Sprayer& theSprayer)   {itsSprayer = &theSprayer;}
    void SetWarmer(Warmer& theWarmer)      {itsWarmer = &theWarmer;}

  private:
    UI*      itsUI;
    Warmer*  itsWarmer;
    Sprayer* itsSprayer;
};
#endif
```

Listing 1-38

`CoffeeMaker/coffeeMaker.cc`

```
#include "CoffeeMaker/coffeeMaker.h"
#include "Sprayer/sprayer.h"
#include "Warmer/warmer.h"
#include "UI/ui.h"

CoffeeMaker::CoffeeMaker()
: itsSprayer(0)
, itsWarmer(0)
, itsUI(0)
{}

CoffeeMaker::~CoffeeMaker() {}

int CoffeeMaker::CheckReady()
{
    return itsWarmer->CheckReady() && itsSprayer->CheckReady();
}

void CoffeeMaker::Brew()
{
    itsWarmer->Brew();
    itsSprayer->Brew();
}

void CoffeeMaker::BrewingComplete()
{
    itsUI->BrewingComplete();
    itsWarmer->BrewingComplete();
}

void CoffeeMaker::Pot()
{
    itsSprayer->Pot();
}

void CoffeeMaker::NoPot()
{
    itsSprayer->NoPot();
}

void CoffeeMaker::CycleComplete()
{
    itsUI->CycleComplete();
}
```

The MarkIV Category

Listing 1-39

MarkIV/m4Warmer.h

```
#ifndef MARKIV_M4WARMER_H
#define MARKIV_M4WARMER_H

#include "Warmer/warmer.h"

//---------------------------------------------------
// Name
//   MarkIV_Warmer
//
// Description
//   This class implements the control model for the
//   Warmer system of the MarkIV Coffee Maker.
//
class MarkIV_Warmer : public Warmer
{
  public:
    MarkIV_Warmer(WarmerDriver&, WarmerClient&);
    virtual ~MarkIV_Warmer();

    // External Stimuli
    virtual void Brew();
    virtual void BrewingComplete();
    virtual int  CheckReady();

    // FSM Events
    void PotEmpty();
    void PotNotEmpty();
    void WarmerEmpty();

    // Couple to main program
    void Poll();

  private:
    enum M4WarmerState
    {
        notBrewing,        brewingPotEmpty, brewingWarming,
        emptyPotRemoved, fullPotRemoved,  brewingComplete,
        brewedPotRemoved
    } itsState;
};
#endif
```

Listing 1-40

`MarkIV/m4Warmer.cc`

```cpp
#include "MarkIV/m4Warmer.h"
#include "Warmer/warmerDriver.h"
#include "Warmer/warmerClient.h"

MarkIV_Warmer::MarkIV_Warmer(WarmerDriver& theDriver,
                             WarmerClient& theClient)
: Warmer(theDriver, theClient)
, itsState(notBrewing)
{GetDriver().WarmerOff();}

MarkIV_Warmer::~MarkIV_Warmer() {}

void MarkIV_Warmer::Brew()
{
    switch (itsState)
    {
    case notBrewing:        itsState=brewingPotEmpty; break;
    case brewingPotEmpty:  /* ignore */ break;
    case brewingWarming:   /* ignore */ break;
    case emptyPotRemoved:  /* ignore */ break;
    case fullPotRemoved:   /* ignore */ break;
    case brewingComplete:  /* ignore */ break;
    case brewedPotRemoved: /* ignore */ break;
    }
}

void MarkIV_Warmer::BrewingComplete()
{
    switch (itsState)
    {
    case notBrewing:        /* ignore */ break;
    case brewingPotEmpty:   itsState=notBrewing;
                            GetClient().CycleComplete(); break;
    case brewingWarming:    itsState=brewingComplete; break;
    case emptyPotRemoved:   itsState=notBrewing;
                            GetClient().CycleComplete(); break;
    case fullPotRemoved:    itsState=brewedPotRemoved; break;
    case brewingComplete:   /* ignore */ break;
    case brewedPotRemoved:  /* ignore */ break;
    }
}

void MarkIV_Warmer::PotEmpty()
{
    switch (itsState)
    {
    case notBrewing:        /* ignore */ break;
    case brewingPotEmpty:   /* ignore */ break;
    case brewingWarming:    itsState=brewingPotEmpty;
                            GetDriver().WarmerOff(); break;
    case emptyPotRemoved:
    case fullPotRemoved :   itsState=brewingPotEmpty;
                            GetClient().Pot(); break;
    case brewingComplete:   itsState=notBrewing;
                            GetDriver().WarmerOff();
                            GetClient().CycleComplete(); break;
    case brewedPotRemoved:  itsState=notBrewing;
                            GetClient().CycleComplete(); break;
    }
}
```

Listing 1-40 (continued)

`MarkIV/m4Warmer.cc`

```
void MarkIV_Warmer::PotNotEmpty()
{
    switch (itsState)
    {
    case notBrewing:         /* ignore */ break;
    case brewingPotEmpty:    itsState=brewingWarming;
                             GetDriver().WarmerOn(); break;
    case brewingWarming:     /* ignore */ break;
    case emptyPotRemoved:
    case fullPotRemoved:     itsState=brewingWarming;
                             GetDriver().WarmerOn();
                             GetClient().Pot(); break;
    case brewingComplete:    /* ignore */ break;
    case brewedPotRemoved:   itsState=brewingComplete;
                             GetDriver().WarmerOn(); break;

    }
}

void MarkIV_Warmer::WarmerEmpty()
{
    switch (itsState)
    {
    case notBrewing:         /* ignore */ break;
    case brewingPotEmpty:    itsState=emptyPotRemoved;
                             GetClient().NoPot(); break;
    case brewingWarming:     itsState=fullPotRemoved;
                             GetClient().NoPot();
                             GetDriver().WarmerOff(); break;
    case emptyPotRemoved:    /* ignore */ break;
    case fullPotRemoved:     /* ignore */ break;
    case brewingComplete:    itsState=brewedPotRemoved;
                             GetDriver().WarmerOff(); break;
    case brewedPotRemoved:   /* ignore */ break;
    }
}

void MarkIV_Warmer::Poll()
{
    switch (GetDriver().GetWarmerStatus())
    {
    case WarmerDriver::noPot:        WarmerEmpty(); break;
    case WarmerDriver::potEmpty:     PotEmpty();    break;
    case WarmerDriver::potNotEmpty:  PotNotEmpty(); break;
    }
}

int MarkIV_Warmer::CheckReady()
{
    return GetDriver().GetWarmerStatus() == WarmerDriver::potEmpty;
}
```

Listing 1-41

`MarkIV/m4WmDriver.h`

```cpp
#include "Warmer/warmerDriver.h"
#include "MarkIV/runtime.h"

//--------------------------------------------------------------
// Name
//   MarkIV_WarmerDriver
//
// Description
//   This class implements the WarmerDriver interface using the
//   MarkIV run-time environment.
//
class MarkIV_WarmerDriver : public WarmerDriver
{
  public:
    virtual void WarmerOn();
    virtual void WarmerOff();
    virtual WarmerStatus GetWarmerStatus();
};
```

Listing 1-42

`MarkIV/m4WmDriver.cc`

```cpp
#include "MarkIV/m4WmDriver.h"

void MarkIV_WarmerDriver::WarmerOn()
{
    SetWarmerState(warmerOn);
}

void MarkIV_WarmerDriver::WarmerOff()
{
    SetWarmerState(warmerOff);
}

WarmerDriver::WarmerStatus  MarkIV_WarmerDriver::GetWarmerStatus()
{
    WarmerStatus status = noPot;
    switch(GetWarmerPlateStatus())
    {
    case (::potEmpty):    status = potEmpty;    break;
    case (::potNotEmpty): status = potNotEmpty; break;
    case (::warmerEmpty): status = noPot; break;
    }
    return status;
}
```

Listing 1-43

`MarkIV/m4Sprayer.h`

```
#ifndef MARKIV_M4SPRAYER_H
#define MARKIV_M4SPRAYER_H

#include "Sprayer/sprayer.h"

//---------------------------------------------------------
// Name
//   MarkIV_Sprayer
//
// Description
//   This class implements the control model for the MarkIV
//   Sprayer.
//
class MarkIV_Sprayer : public Sprayer
{
  public:
    MarkIV_Sprayer(SprayerDriver&, SprayerClient&);
    virtual ~MarkIV_Sprayer();

    virtual int CheckReady();
    void Poll();

    // External Stimuli
    virtual void Pot();
    virtual void NoPot();
    virtual void Brew();

    // FSM Events
    void BrewingComplete();

  private:
    enum SprayerState {notBrewing, spraying, brewingNoPot} itsState;
};
#endif
```

Listing 1-44

`MarkIV/m4Sprayer.cc`

```cpp
#include "MarkIV/m4Sprayer.h"
#include "Sprayer/sprayerClient.h"
#include "Sprayer/sprayerDriver.h"

MarkIV_Sprayer::MarkIV_Sprayer(SprayerDriver& theDriver,
                                SprayerClient& theClient)
: Sprayer(theDriver, theClient)
, itsState(notBrewing)
{GetDriver().StopSpray();}

MarkIV_Sprayer::~MarkIV_Sprayer() {}

int MarkIV_Sprayer::CheckReady()
{
    return GetDriver().HasWater();
}

void MarkIV_Sprayer::Poll()
{
    if (!GetDriver().HasWater())
    {
        BrewingComplete();
    }
}

void MarkIV_Sprayer::Pot()
{
    switch (itsState)
    {
    case notBrewing:    /* ignore */ break;
    case spraying:      /* ignore */ break;
    case brewingNoPot: itsState=spraying;
                        GetDriver().Spray(); break;
    }
}

void MarkIV_Sprayer::NoPot()
{
    switch (itsState)
    {
    case notBrewing:    /* ignore */ break;
    case spraying:      itsState=brewingNoPot;
                        GetDriver().StopSpray(); break;
    case brewingNoPot: /* ignore */ break;
    }
}

void MarkIV_Sprayer::Brew()
{
    switch (itsState)
    {
    case notBrewing:    itsState=spraying;
                        GetDriver().Spray(); break;
    case spraying:      /* ignore */ break;
    case brewingNoPot: /* ignore */ break;
    }
}
```

Listing 1-44 *(continued)*

`MarkIV/m4Sprayer.cc`

```
void MarkIV_Sprayer::BrewingComplete()
{
    switch (itsState)
    {
    case notBrewing:     /* ignore */ break;
    case spraying:       itsState=notBrewing;
                         GetDriver().StopSpray();
                         GetClient().BrewingComplete(); break;
    case brewingNoPot:   itsState=notBrewing;
                         GetClient().BrewingComplete(); break;
    }
}
```

Listing 1-45

`MarkIV/m4SpDriver.h`

```
#ifndef MARKIV_SPDRIVER_H
#define MARKIV_SPDRIVER_H

#include "Sprayer/sprayerDriver.h"

//---------------------------------------------------------
// Name
//   MarkIV_SprayerDriver
//
// Description
//   This class implements the SprayerDriver interface for the
//   MarkIV run-time system.
//

class MarkIV_SprayerDriver : public SprayerDriver
{
  public:
    virtual void Spray();
    virtual void StopSpray();
    virtual int  HasWater();
};
#endif
```

Listing 1-46

`MarkIV/m4SpDriver.cc`

```
#include "MarkIV/m4SpDriver.h"
#include "MarkIV/runtime.h"

void MarkIV_SprayerDriver::Spray()
{
    SetBoilerState(boilerOn);
    SetReliefValveState(valveClosed);
}

void MarkIV_SprayerDriver::StopSpray()
{
    SetBoilerState(boilerOff);
    SetReliefValveState(valveOpen);
}

MarkIV_SprayerDriver::HasWater()
{
    return GetBoilerStatus() == boilerNotEmpty;
}
```

Listing 1-47

`MarkIV/markIV_UI.h`

```
#ifndef MARKIV_MARKVI_UI_H
#define MARKIV_MARKIV_UI_H

#include "UI/ui.h"

//-------------------------------------------------------------
// Name
//   MarkIV_UI
//
// Description
//   This class implements the control model of the User Interface
//   for the MarkIV coffee maker.
//
class MarkIV_UI : public UI
{
  public:
    MarkIV_UI(UIDriver& theDriver, UIClient& theClient);
    virtual ~MarkIV_UI();

    // External Stimuli
    virtual void BrewingComplete();
    virtual void CycleComplete();

    // FSM Events
    void Start();
    void Ready();
    void NotReady();

    // Gain control from main program
    void Poll();

  private:
    // Utility functions
    void CheckReady();

    enum {notBrewing, checkingReadiness,
          brewing, doneBrewing} itsState;
};
#endif
```

Listing 1-48

`MarkIV/markIV_UI.cc`

```cpp
#include "MarkIV/markIV_UI.h"
#include "UI/uiClient.h"
#include "UI/uiDriver.h"

MarkIV_UI::MarkIV_UI(UIDriver& theDriver, UIClient& theClient)
: UI(theDriver, theClient)
, itsState(notBrewing)
{GetDriver().IndicateReady();}

MarkIV_UI::~MarkIV_UI() {}

void MarkIV_UI::Start()
{
    switch (itsState)
    {
    case notBrewing:            itsState=checkingReadiness;
                                CheckReady(); break;
    case checkingReadiness: /* ignore */ break;
    case brewing:               /* ignore */ break;
    case doneBrewing:           /* ignore */ break;
    };
}

void MarkIV_UI::Ready()
{
    switch (itsState)
    {
    case notBrewing:            /* ignore */ break;
    case checkingReadiness: itsState = brewing;
                                GetClient().Brew(); break;
    case brewing:               /* ignore */ break;
    case doneBrewing:           /* ignore */ break;
    };
}

void MarkIV_UI::NotReady()
{
    switch (itsState)
    {
    case notBrewing:            /* ignore */ break;
    case checkingReadiness: itsState = notBrewing; break;
    case brewing:               /* ignore */ break;
    case doneBrewing:           /* ignore */ break;
    };
}

void MarkIV_UI::BrewingComplete()
{
    switch (itsState)
    {
    case notBrewing:            /* ignore */ break;
    case checkingReadiness: itsState = notBrewing; break;
    case brewing:               itsState = doneBrewing;
                                GetDriver().IndicateCompletion(); break;
    case doneBrewing:           /* ignore */ break;
    };
}
```

Listing 1-48 (*continued*)

`MarkIV/markIV_UI.cc`

```
void MarkIV_UI::CycleComplete()
{
    switch(itsState)
    {
    case notBrewing:         /* ignore */ break;
    case checkingReadiness: itsState = notBrewing; break;
    case brewing:            itsState = notBrewing; break;
    case doneBrewing:        itsState = notBrewing;
                             GetDriver().IndicateReady(); break;
    }
}

void MarkIV_UI::CheckReady()
{
    if (GetClient().CheckReady())
    {
        Ready();
    }
    else
    {
        NotReady();
    }
}

void MarkIV_UI::Poll()
{
    if (itsState == notBrewing && GetDriver().CheckStart())
    {
        Start();
    }
}
```

Listing 1-49

`MarkIV/m4UIDriver.h`

```
#ifndef MARKIV_MARKIV_UI_DRIVER
#define MARKIV_MARKIV_UI_DRIVER

#include "UI/uiDriver.h"

//----------------------------------------
// Name
//   MarkIV_UIDriver
//
// Description
//   This class implements the UIDriver interface
//   using the MarkIV run-time environment.
//
class MarkIV_UIDriver : public UIDriver
{
  public:
    virtual void IndicateCompletion();
    virtual void IndicateReady();
    virtual int  CheckStart();
};
#endif
```

Listing 1-50

`MarkIV/m4UIDriver.cc`

```
#include "MarkIV/m4UIDriver.h"
#include "MarkIV/runtime.h"

void MarkIV_UIDriver::IndicateCompletion()
{
    SetIndicatorState(indicatorOn);
}

void MarkIV_UIDriver::IndicateReady()
{
    SetIndicatorState(indicatorOff);
}

int MarkIV_UIDriver::CheckStart()
{
    return GetBrewButtonStatus() == brewButtonPushed;
}
```

Listing 1-51

`MarkIV/runtime.h`

```
//----------------------------
// Name
//   runtime.h
//
// Description
//   This file contains the prototypes for the run-time interface
//   to the MarkIV hardware
//

extern "C"
{
    enum WarmerPlateStatus {potNotEmpty, potEmpty, warmerEmpty};
    WarmerPlateStatus GetWarmerPlateStatus();

    enum BoilerStatus {boilerEmpty, boilerNotEmpty};
    BoilerStatus GetBoilerStatus();

    enum BrewButtonStatus {brewButtonPushed, brewButtonNotPushed};
    BrewButtonStatus GetBrewButtonStatus();

    enum BoilerHeaterState {boilerOn, boilerOff};
    void SetBoilerState(BoilerHeaterState);

    enum WarmerState {warmerOn, warmerOff};
    void SetWarmerState(WarmerState);

    enum IndicatorState {indicatorOn, indicatorOff};
    void SetIndicatorState(IndicatorState);

    enum ReliefValveState {valveOpen, valveClosed};
    void SetReliefValveState(ReliefValveState);
}
```

Listing 1-52

`MarkIV/markIVmain.cc`

```
#include "CoffeeMaker/coffeeMaker.h"
#include "MarkIV/m4Sprayer.h"
#include "MarkIV/m4Warmer.h"
#include "MarkIV/markIV_UI.h"
#include "MarkIV/m4UIDriver.h"
#include "MarkIV/m4SpDriver.h"
#include "MarkIV/m4WmDriver.h"

main()
{
    CoffeeMaker cm;
    MarkIV_WarmerDriver   warmerDriver;
    MarkIV_SprayerDriver  sprayerDriver;
    MarkIV_UIDriver       uiDriver;
    MarkIV_Sprayer        sprayer(sprayerDriver, cm);
    MarkIV_Warmer         warmer(warmerDriver, cm);
    MarkIV_UI             ui(uiDriver, cm);

    cm.SetUI(ui);
    cm.SetSprayer(sprayer);
    cm.SetWarmer(warmer);

    for(;;)
    {
        ui.Poll();
        sprayer.Poll();
        warmer.Poll();
    }
}
```

2

Managing Complexity

In the development of our understanding of complex phenomena,
the most powerful tool available to the human intellect is abstraction.

— C. A. R. Hoare

The art of programming is the art of organizing complexity.

With processing power increased by a factor of a thousand over the last ten to fifteen
years, Man has become considerably more ambitious in selecting problems that now
should be "technically feasible." Size, complexity and sophistication of programs one
should like to make have exploded and over the past years it has become patently clear
that on the whole our programming ability has not kept pace with these exploding
demands made on it.

— Edsger W. Dijkstra, circa 1972

Two decades later, Dijkstra's complaint about how our ambition and
demands outstrip our programming ability remains true. Concern regarding
software complexity and software reliability have reached the highest levels in
our society. Experts are seriously considering avoiding the use of software in
situations that are mission-critical or that involve significant public safety issues.[1]
Yet people have been managing complexity for thousands of years, with
considerable success. Imagine the problem of building the pyramids, or
assembling Stonehenge. How complex must it have been to rule the Roman
Empire without mass communication or air travel? We software engineers are
only the latest in the vast army of engineers to face the dilemma of geometrically
increasing complexity and we will also solve the problem. This chapter discusses

---

1. Bev Littlewood and Lorenzo Strigini, "The Risks of Software," *Scientific American*, November
1992.

the contributions that OOD has made to the issue of complexity management.

Introduction

Managing software complexity is a major issue. Software engineers are being asked to produce products of immense complexity, and they are having a hard time rising to the challenge. Each of the last several decades has seen an increase of an order of magnitude in software complexity. In the 1960s, a 10,000-line program was a *big* program,[2] and running it required a big and expensive computer. In the 1990s programs aren't really *big* until they approach 1,000,000 lines of code. This trend continues unabated. Each year brings increased expectations from the user community, increased demands for compatibility and interoperability, increased demands for standardization, and increased demands for functionality. Unfortunately, the progress made in the science of software engineering has not kept pace with these demands. The complexity of our projects has grown a hundredfold in the last 20 years; but we are not a hundred times better at producing them.

The last few decades have brought several advances in the art of managing software complexity: structured programming, in the late 1960s, functional decomposition in the 1970s, abstract data types and data modeling in the 1980s, to mention just a few. The object-oriented paradigm is another such advance. It provides new tools and new ways to apply old tools to the problem of managing complexity.

Managing vs. Reducing Complexity

The complexity of an application is the sum of two major components: the complexity of the problem, and the complexity of the solution. This can be expressed by the following equation:

$$C_{app} = C_{prb} + C_{sol}$$

C_{prb} cannot be reduced except by reducing the list of requirements, but we can take steps to minimize C_{sol}. For example, writing the solution in assembly language would almost certainly be many times more complicated than writing it in C++. Also, some design solutions are more complex than others. Much of the work of design involves the search for a simpler approach.

Still, even after C_{sol} has been reduced as much as possible, if C_{prb} is big then C_{app} will be big, and it is C_{app} that we must eventually implement. Since we cannot reduce C_{app}, we must manage it. To quote Stroustrup : "The most fundamental problem in soft-

---

2. A 10,000-line program required five full boxes of cards. It was too big for one person to carry down the hall to the card reader.

ware development is complexity. There is only one basic way of dealing with complexity: Divide and conquer."[3]

To manage complexity, we must find a way to reduce it locally; that is, we divide the problem into pieces that are less complex than the whole. In Structured Analysis and Design, (SA/SD) we divide the application into separate functions, and each one does a small piece of the job. Each function is simple, but together they make a complex whole.

In object-oriented analysis and design, we still use a form of functional decomposition, but in a very different way. Rather than dividing the application into a set of functions, we divide it into a set of abstractions. Each abstraction represents a set of functions, but does not specify their implementations. The abstractions can therefore represent many different objects that have similar functions but different implementations.

Abstraction: "The Most Powerful Tool"

Abstraction is *the elimination of the irrelevant and the amplification of the essential.* According to Hoare it is the most powerful tool for managing complexity. When we divide an application into a set of separate abstractions, we form *groups* of objects. The members of these groups may be of different types, but because they all conform to the same abstraction, we can ignore the differences between them. When we create an abstraction, we hide the details that are irrelevant to the rest of the world, so that no other object will grow to depend upon them.

Grouping and hiding are like the Yin and Yang of abstraction. They both have to do with the amplification of the essential and the elimination of the irrelevant, but the motivations behind them are quite different. Grouping is permissive. When we gather a number of disparate objects together in a group under a single abstraction, we are allowing them to be viewed as objects with identical interfaces. Hiding, however, is restrictive. When we hide the details of an object, we restrict access to them. We are reserving the right to change those details with impunity by making sure that no other object becomes dependent upon them.

Abstraction is not an innovation of OO or C++. Software engineers have been using the abstraction techniques of grouping and hiding for years. However, OO and C++ interact to greatly enhance the number of ways that grouping and hiding can be employed. It is therefore much easier to manage the complexity of an OO/C++ project than that of a conventional project.

---

3. Bjarne Stroustrup, *The C++ Programming Language,* 2d ed. (Addison-Wesley, 1991), p. 364.

Product Costing Policy: Case Study.

Grouping

To group objects together is to ignore the differences between them and to deal with the group as a single entity. It is much easier to talk about the population of the world as a group than it is to attempt to deal with the 5×10^9 individuals that the group represents.

In order for a grouping to be useful, it must be possible to perform operations upon a set of objects from the group. When operations are performed on sets, they are performed equally upon each member of the set. Even though the members of the set may be individuals of different types, their differences are ignored. This reduces the complexity of an application, because functions can manipulate the set of objects without having to know that the set may include many different types. Listing 2-1 shows an example that uses the **Part** class from Chapter 1.

Listing 2-1

Computing the total cost of a set of parts

```
double TotalCost(const Set<Part*>& theParts)
{
    double totalCost = 0;

    for (Iterator<Part*> i(theParts); i; i++)
    {
        totalCost += (*i)->Cost();
    }

    return totalCost;
}
```

Listing 2-1 shows that we can group **Part** objects together in a set and treat them identically, as if there were no other different kinds of **Part**. This is a powerful benefit. It allows the **TotalCost** function to remain stable even when we create new and different kinds of **Part** objects. The complexities involved with the different kinds of **Part** objects are irrelevant to this function.

The Open-Closed Principle

The **TotalCost** function demonstrates an application of the open-closed principle.[4] The function is *closed* for modification. As long as its job is simply to total the cost of a set of parts, then this function will never have to be changed, or even recompiled. On the other

---

4. Bertrand Meyer, *Object-Oriented Software Construction,* (Prentice Hall, 1988), p. 23, section 2.3.

hand, the function is *open* for extension. We can extend the capabilities of **TotalCost** by creating new classes that are derived from **Part**.

This ability to close a function against modification, and yet allow it to be extended is quite remarkable. Functions can be written that invoke the virtual member functions of other objects, without knowing (or caring) which actual function will be called. Indeed, the calling function may have been written at a time before the called function was even conceived of.

This idea is not particularly new. Many operating systems have put "hooks" in place so that new functions can be called in place of old ones. These hooks amount to pointers to functions; the operating system calls the functions through their pointers. If a user wants to replace an old function with a new one, he overwrites the appropriate pointer. Thus, the user does not have to modify the operating system in order to extend it.

What makes this ability remarkable in C++ is the convenience of its expression. By using inheritance and virtual functions, we can easily create functions and classes that have the same open-closed attributes. A set of classes that inherits the same virtual functions from a common base can be grouped in such a way that the functions that manipulate them do not need to know their actual types. Instead, those functions can deal with them through the interface declared in the base class. We can close these functions to modification, because we can extend their behaviors by creating new derivatives of the base class that supply different implementations of the virtual functions.

Why is this important? Why should we want to close functions against modification? Clearly, if we can really close a function, then we will never have to modify it! This is quite a goal. If we close all the functions in a system, then we can extend and enhance that system without making changes to existing *working* code. Instead, all changes will be made by adding new code. If you don't have to change a function in order to enhance it, then you don't have to read it either. You don't have to understand how the function works. All you have to understand is what it expects from the virtual functions that it calls. Ideally, then, extending an existing software system in which all functions are closed involves no changes to existing *working* code, and no reading of that code either.

Idealism is great—but can we really close functions against all modifications? Unfortunately, we can't; however we *can* close them against many kinds of changes, and we can design them to be closed for the kinds of changes that we expect to be highly likely.

For example, Figure 2-1 shows a possible static model for an inventory system. Inventories contain sets of products that contain sets of parts. It seems likely that **Inventory** will want to be able to ask **Product** for its cost. Listings 2-2 and 2-3 show a partial implementation for **Product**.

The function in Listing 2-3 is just **TotalCost** from Listing 2-1, rephrased as a member function of **Product**. We know that this function is closed with respect to **Part**. **TotalCost** will never have to be changed to support changes in **Part** or any of its derivatives, existing or otherwise.

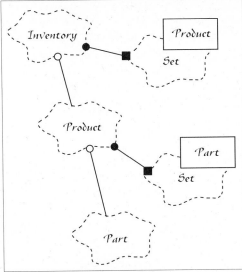

Figure 2-1
Inventory Class Diagram

Listing 2-2

Product.h

```
class Product
{
    public:
        double TotalCost();

    private:
        Set<Part*> itsParts;
{;
```

Listing 2-3

Product.cc

```
#include "product.h"

double Product::TotalCost()
{
    double totalCost = 0;

    for (Iterator<Part*> i(itsParts); i; i++)
    {
        totalCost += (*i)->Cost();
    }

    return totalCost;
}
```

However, other kinds of changes *can* affect **TotalCost**. For example, suppose that the accounting department decides that the cost of a product is really 167% of the cost of its parts.[5] We could solve this problem by modifying **TotalCost** as in Listing 2-4.

Listing 2-4

```
Product.cc (modified)
#include "product.h"

double Product::TotalCost()
{
    double totalCost = 0;

    for (Iterator<Part*> i(itsParts); i; i++)
    {
        totalCost += (*i)->Cost();
    }

    return totalCost * 1.67;
}
```

There are reasons why this might not be a good solution, and we will look at them presently. For many situations, however, this would be exactly the right thing to do. It is an easy change, with very low risk. By making this change, we are asserting that **Total-Cost** is not closed against changes in accounting policy; when accounting policy changes, so might **TotalCost**.[6] If accounting policy does not change often, this is probably a good trade-off, since the benefit of leaving **TotalCost** open is that it is a simple piece of code that can easily support a low level of maintenance.

However, what if we suspect that accounting policy will change frequently and in complex ways? For example, what if several different multipliers were used for different kinds of products? We might categorize products as "simple" or "difficult" to assemble, or we might want to differentiate between the costs of products assembled in our factory and products assembled elsewhere. If we knew that modeling the cost of a product could be complex and variable, then we would want to close **TotalCost**. If you are unconvinced of this, then consider Listing 2-5 and 2-6 as the result of leaving the function open.

These listings describe a **TotalCost** function that implements many accounting policies. There are three manufacturing sites, each with its own cost multiplier.[7] Parts made locally are multiplied by 1.67, as before, but manufacturing in Taiwan is cheaper so the multiplier for parts made there is only 1.43. Furthermore, there is a plant in Kentucky that uses a multiplier of 1.53.

---

5. Such models are frequently used as a means for estimating manufactured cost.
6. The observant reader might object that **TotalCost** need not change if a constant variable is used instead of the literal 1.67. Certainly this is true, but the net result is the same, since a piece of existing and working source code (albeit not **TotalCost**) would have to change.
7. The multipliers in the following section are utterly fictitious. They do not reflect or imply anything at all about the author's or publisher's opinions about Taiwan or Kentucky. So there.

Listing 2-5

product.h with **TotalCost** left open

```
#ifndef PRODUCT_H
#define PRODUCT_H
#include "componen/u_set.h"
class Part;
class Product
{
 public:
    enum LaborCode {simple, complex};
    enum AssemblyLocation {local, taiwan, kentucky};
    enum ProductType {mechanical, electronic};

    double TotalCost();

  private:
    UnboundedSet<Part*> itsParts;
    LaborCode            itsCode;
    AssemblyLocation     itsLocation;
    ProductType          itsType;
};
#endif
```

Listing 2-6

product.cc with **TotalCost** left open

```
double Product::TotalCost()
{
    double totalCost = 0;
    Iterator<Part*> i(itsParts);
    for(; i; i++)
    {
        totalCost += (*i)->Cost();
    }

    switch (itsLocation)
    {
    case local:
        totalCost *= 1.67;
         switch (itsType)
         {
         case mechanical: totalCost *= 1.14; break;
         case electronic: totalCost *= 1.10; break;
         default:         assert(0);         break;
         }
    break;

    case taiwan:
        totalCost *= 1.43;
        switch (itsType)
        {
        case mechanical: /* no change */    break;
        case electronic: totalCost *= 1.13; break;
        default:         assert(0);         break;
```

Listing 2-6 (Continued)

`product.cc` with `TotalCost` left open

```
        }
    break;

    case kentucky:
        totalCost *= 1.53;
        switch (itsType)
        {
        case mechanical: totalCost *= 1.16; break;
        case electronic: totalCost *= 1.18; break;
        default:              assert(0);              break;
        }
    break;

    default: assert(0); break;
    }

    switch (itsCode)
    {
    case simple:  /* no change */   break;
    case complex: totalCost *= 1.2; break;
    default:         assert(0);         break;
    }

    return totalCost;
}
```

It turns out that each plant is more or less efficient, depending upon the type of product it is making. For electronic products, Taiwanese manufacturing gets multiplied by an extra 1.1, whereas a 1.13 multiplier is used locally, and in Kentucky a 1.18 multiplier is used. On the other hand, mechanical products are cheapest locally, so no penalty is paid, but in Taiwan we suffer an extra 1.14 multiplier, and in Kentucky a 1.16 multiplier.

Finally, the accounting department has identified several products that are much more complicated than the rest. They have decided to assign an extra 1.2 multiplier to these products.

The result of these policies in a function that is completely open to policy changes is not pretty. It is rather large, and somewhat difficult to understand. Consider how much more cluttered this function would be if there were dozens of manufacturing sites and classifications. However, these philosophical observations are not the real issue. This function must change every time the accounting policy changes. The result is a module that is very sensitive to change, and very error-prone. It is possible, even likely, that a policy change regarding electronics could introduce bugs for all products made in Kentucky, for example.

Because this function embodies the *whole* policy, it is going to be changed a lot, and with each change comes the possibility that bugs will be inadvertently added. Moreover, because all policies come together in a single function, *every* policy must be retested every time *any* policy is changed. Clearly, leaving this function open to any and all changes to accounting policy is a problem if those policies are complex and variable.

Using Grouping Strategies to Close a Function

How can we close the **TotalCost** function against changes in policy? Figures 2-2 and 2-3 show one possible scheme. Figure 2-2 shows that **Product** is a virtual base for five abstract derivatives. The inverted triangle with the *V* inside represents virtual inheritance. Virtual inheritance allows the concrete classes to inherit from more than one of the abstract derivatives without inheriting more than a single instance of **Product**.

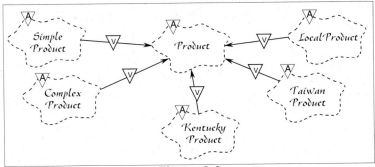

Figure 2-2
First-Level Product-Inheritance Hierarchy

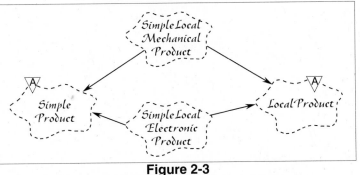

Figure 2-3
Second-Level Product-Inheritance Hierarchy

Figure 2-3 shows just two of the twelve concrete classes. Others would include **ComplexMechanicalKentuckyProduct** and **SimpleMechanicalTaiwanProduct**. The benefit of this kind of separation is that each policy can be contained within its own class. The manufacturing modifier for Taiwan, for example, is contained within the **TaiwanProduct** class. The Simple vs. Complex modifiers are contained within the **SimpleProduct** and **ComplexProduct** classes, respectively. Whenever a policy changes, only one of these classes will need to be changed; the others remain closed. Thus, we can close the classes with respect to all but their own policies.

Figure 2-4 is an object diagram that shows how the concrete objects in this model send messages to the base classes to handle the different parts of the costing policy. When a **TotalCost** message is sent to **SimpleLocalMechanicalProduct**, it gets deferred to the **TotalCost** method of **Product.** This function then invokes the **ModifyForLocation** method of **LocalProduct**, the **ModifyForProductType** method of **SimpleLocalMechanicalProduct** and the **ModifyForComplexity** method of **SimpleProduct**. Although each of these calls appears to be routed to a different class, they are really deployed as virtual functions of the **Product** class. Thus, **Product::TotalCost** does not know which functions it is really calling. The C++ code that supports this arrangement is shown in Listings 2-7 through 2-11.

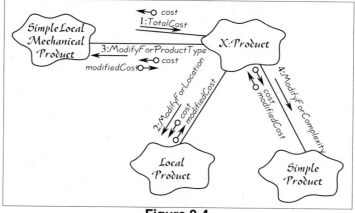

Figure 2-4
Product Hierarchy Object Diagram

Listing 2-7

product.h

```
#ifndef PRODUCT_H
#define PRODUCT_H
#include "componen/u_set.h"

class Part;

class Product
{
  public:
    double          TotalCost()                      const;
    virtual double ModifyForComplexity(double) const = 0;
```

Listing 2-7 (Continued)

product.h

```
    virtual double ModifyForLocation(double)    const = 0;
    virtual double ModifyForProductType(double) const = 0;
    double         CalculateBaseCost()           const;

  private:
    UnboundedSet<Part*> itsParts;
};
#endif
```

Listing 2-8

product.cc

```
#include "product.h"
#include "part.h"
#include <assert.h>
#include "componen/set.h"

double Product::TotalCost() const
{
    double base =     CalculateBaseCost();
    double mlCost =   ModifyForLocation(base);
    double typeCost = ModifyForProductType(mlCost);
    double cost =     ModifyForComplexity(typeCost);
    return cost;
}

double Product::CalculateBaseCost() const
{
    double basecost = 0;
    Iterator<Part*> i(itsParts);
    for (; i; i++)
    {
        baseCost += (*i)->Cost();
    }
    return baseCost;
}
```

Listing 2-9

simpleprod.h

```
#ifndef SIMPLE_PRODUCT_H
#define SIMPLE_PRODUCT_H
#include "product.h"

class SimpleProduct : public virtual Product
{
  public:
    virtual double ModifyForComplexity(double cost) const
```

Listing 2-9 (Continued)

---

simpleprod.h

```
      {return cost * 1.0;} // Simple multiplier
};

#endif
```

Listing 2-10

---

localprod.h

```
#ifndef LOCAL_PRODUCT_H
#define LOCAL_PRODUCT_H
#include "product.h"

class LocalProduct : public virtual Product
{
  public:
    virtual double ModifyForLocation(double cost) const
    {return cost * 1.67;} // Local multiplier
};

#endif
```

Listing 2-11

---

slmproduct.h

```
#ifndef SIMPLE_LOCAL_MECHANICAL_PRODUCT
#define SIMPLE_LOCAL_MECHANICAL_PRODUCT
#include "simpleprod.h"
#include "localprod.h"
class SimpleLocalMechanicalProduct : public SimpleProduct
                                   , public LocalProduct
{
  public:
    virtual double ModifyForComplexity(double d) const
    {return SimpleProduct::ModifyForComplexity(d);}
    virtual double ModifyForLocation(double d) const
    {return LocalProduct::ModifyForLocation(d);}
};
#endif
```

By grouping the different policies under the umbrella of the **Product** class, we have managed to close the **Product** class and its derivatives against many policy changes. We have also managed to close each of the different policies against changes in any other policy. Yet, in spite of all this closure, the **Product** class is still extensible. New policies can be added without changing any of the old policy algorithms. Moreover, users of class **Product** and indeed, class **Product** itself, do not need to know what policies there are, or even that different policies exist.

Although **Product** and its derivatives enjoy a high degree of closure, they are not immune to all policy changes. For example, if we create a policy for estimating the cost of import duty, then we must give **Product** a new pure virtual function: **Calculate-ImportDuty**. **Product::TotalCost** must be modified to call this function, and the derivatives of **Product** that represent locations (i.e., **Local**, Taiwan, **Kentucky**) will have to add implementations for the new virtual function. We would like to achieve closure against even this kind of change if possible—and that brings us to the topic of hiding.

Hiding (Restricting Visibility)

Whereas grouping allows us ignore certain details, hiding actually prevents us from seeing them. The practice of hiding information about one part of a design from the other parts of the design is critical to the management of complexity. Grouping stategies appear to be elegant and obvious methods for managing a complex system, while hiding stragegies are often counterintuitive.

It seems absurd that we should reduce or manage complexity by putting intentional limits on what we are able to do and see. Our minds often view the restrictions as *complexities* rather than simplifications. Indeed, if you narrow your focus sufficiently, limitations *are* complexities. For example, a traffic light presents a restriction and a complication to individual vehicles. To avoid these complexities, we often select the routes with the fewest traffic lights. Yet, it would be very hard to argue that traffic would be simpler without traffic lights. The limitations imposed by the traffic lights help to manage the complexity of all the traffic, at the expense of the individual driver. Each driver accepts the complexities imposed by the traffic lights, because they make the overall problem of moving traffic tractable.

The same is true in software design. We impose limitations on our designs because they help to manage the overall complexity. These limitations may make certain tasks more difficult, but we accept this in order to manage the complexity of the overall task. Carefully placed restrictions upon the accessibility of entities within a software project can lead to a reduction in or, at least, better management of the complexity within that project.

Of course, individual programmers sometimes take it upon themselves to violate the restrictions imposed by the designers. This may make the programmer's job simpler, but like the person who runs red lights, he has made the system less robust and is risking a disaster that he did not foresee. If such practices are common, then over time the carefully constructed hiding rules of well-designed systems can crumble into chaos, and the result is disaster.

The Problem of Too Much Visibility

A software project can be thought of as a set of components that work together to get a job done. In order to work together they must be able to communicate with each other. Whenever one component communicates with another, an interface is formed. The number of such interfaces can be very large. To understand this, consider a program with 1,000 software components. Now, in your mind, draw a large circle and lay out all the software components along its circumference. If the components are evenly spaced, they will represent the vertices of a regular, 1,000-sided polygon. Now begin to connect these vertices with straight lines, not just the neighbors around the circumference of the circle, but every component to every other component. Each line represents one of the diagonals of the polygon. Given a polygon with n vertices, the number of diagonals is $(n^2 - n)/2$. If you had a thousand software components, you could have 499,500 possible interfaces.

Clearly this is unacceptable. A big software project will require many more than 1,000 software components, but the spectre of half a million interfaces is unthinkable. Certainly no project ever starts out with every possible interface represented. Few if any of the components of a software system need to communicate with all of the others or even a majority of the others. As a product grows and evolves, however, more and more interfaces will be needed. More diagonals will be filled in, and more complicated interfaces will be developed. Without a *designed* approach to visibility, the number of interfaces can increase until they overwhelm the programmers and destroy the integrity of the software.

How can the number of interfaces destroy the integrity of a project? One way is by sheer volume. The more interfaces that exist, the more that must be remembered. Moreover, most of those interfaces are not going to be formally documented. Instead they will be created when one programmer decides to cheat a little and sneak into the data structures or utility functions of another. Many of these interfaces will be hidden, and most programmers won't know that they exist. This exacerbates another problem, which is that each interface represents a dependency. If Module A has an interface with Module B, then A depends upon B. When B is changed, A may need to be changed as well, or at least recompiled. The more modules that depend upon B, the harder B is to change, because each of the dependent modules may, as a result, need to be changed. Eventually, if the number of interfaces to a module continues to increase, it will become virtually impossible to change that module.

As the number of interfaces in a software project increases, the amount of interdependency among the modules also increases. As the number of interfaces increases, the ramifications of even the most simple changes become hard to determine, and modification and maintenance of the project become very difficult. Each bug fix can introduce new bugs in dependent modules. Each of those fixes can introduce yet other bugs in their dependents. The more interfaces that exist, the more likely it is that such bugs will be created, and the longer the chain of bug fixes becomes. This situation can get so severe that a project becomes virtually impossible to maintain. It is not uncommon, in such projects, for even simple bug fixes to require man-months of work and for such repair work to create more problems than it solves.

Hiding and Closure

Consider the diagram in Figure 2-5. In this diagram **SalesOrder** uses **Product**, which privately contains **ProductCostingPolicy**. The privacy is denoted by the two hash marks near the containing class. Notice that no matter what happens to **ProductCostingPolicy**, **SalesOrder** remains unaffected. Thus, **SalesOrder** is closed with respect to **ProductCostingPolicy**. By making the containment private, we have "hidden" **ProductCostingPolicy** from **SalesOrder** and prevented a dependency between the two classes. In fact, as long as **ProductCostingPolicy** is known only to **Product**, we have closed all the clients of **Product** against changes to **Product-CostingPolicy**.

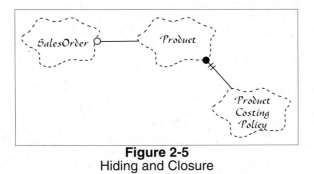

Figure 2-5
Hiding and Closure

Thus, we can increase the overall closure within a design by using private containment to hide unrelated classes from one another. The hiding prevents the formation of spurious interfaces, and the closure reduces the dependency between the modules.

Listing 2-12 shows how this might be coded in C++. In C++, private containment restricts access; that is, the compiler will complain if a client of **Product** attempts to access **itsProductCostingPolicy**. Thus, users who are tempted to create interfaces with **ProductCostingPolicy** will be forced to change the **Product** class first. While this is not impossible, the privacy of the containment is a "strong hint" that the original designer wanted to hide the **ProductCostingPolicy** from clients of **Product**, and that communication with the **ProductCostingPolicy** should be performed in an abstract way through **Product**.

Abstraction and Hiding

As noted, the privacy of the containment restricts outside access to **ProductCosting-Policy**; however, privacy in C++ does not restrict *visibility*. The users of **Product**

Listing 2-12

`product.h` — Private containment of `ProductCostingPolicy`

```
class ProductCostingPolicy;
class Product
{
 private:
    ProductCostingPolicy* itsProductCostingPolicy;
};
```

---

must `#include "product.h"`, and they will therefore have visibility of the names
`ProductCostingPolicy` and `itsProductCostingPolicy`.

This may not seem like a big problem, but it does have its costs. For example, if we
merely wanted to change the name of the `ProductCostingPolicy` class, we would
have to change the `product.h` header file, and this could force us to recompile every
module that depended upon `product.h`![8]

A more likely scenario involves the redesign of the policy mechanism. We may
decide that `Product` should not contain a `ProductCostingPolicy`, but should
instead contain a `LocationPolicy`, a `ComplexityPolicy`, and a `DutyPolicy`.
Changes like this should be invisible to `SalesOrder`. But if `salesOrder.cc`
includes `product.h`, then these changes could force `salesOrder.cc` to be recompiled.

Figure 2-6 shows how to remedy this problem of visibility by creating an abstract
class to represent a product that is ignorant of the way in which policies are implemented.

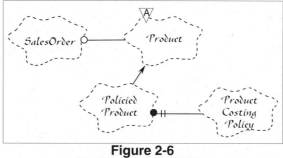

Figure 2-6
Abstraction and Hiding

We have separated `Product` into an abstract base class that knows nothing about
`ProductCostingPolicy`, and a derived class that does. Now, changes in the design
of policy management will affect only `PoliciedProduct`; they cannot affect `Sales-
Order`.

Listings 2-13 and 2-14 show the C++ representation of Figure 2-6.

---

8. Some compiler environments may be smart enough to ignore irrelevant changes; most are not.

Listing 2-13

```
product.h : abstract class
class Product
{
  public:
    virtual double GetCost() const = 0;
};
```

Listing 2-14

```
policiedProduct.h : derived class

class ProductCostingPolicy;
class PoliciedProduct : public Product
{
  public:
    virtual double GetCost() const; // employ policy to get cost.

  private:
    ProductCostingPolicy* itsProductCostingPolicy;
};
```

Now **ProductCostingPolicy** is entirely hidden from all the clients of **Product**. Changes to **ProductCostingPolicy**, or to **PoliciedProduct** will not force clients of **Product** to be recompiled.

Note that **PoliciedProduct** is the only subclass that we currently anticipate for **Product**. We did not create the **Product** abstraction in order to group many dissimilar types of product under a single interface; we created it so that it could hide the details of the implementation of **PoliciedProduct**. It is possible (even likely) that new subclasses of **Product** will appear as the design proceeds, but this was not the motivation for creating the abstraction.

Completing the Product / Policy Design

Another benefit of the design in Figure 2-6 is that **Product** objects can change their **ProductCostingPolicy** objects. This was not true in the design in Figures 2-2 and 2-3, in which a particular product was inseparable from its policy.

Figures 2-7 through 2-10 continue the design that was started in Figure 2-6, showing how we can employ abstraction to hide details, increase closure, expose similarities, and maintain an openness for extension.

This design employs abstraction to hide **PoliciedProduct** from the clients of **Product**, and to hide **CTLPolicy** from **PoliciedProduct**. This means that clients of **Product** are immune to changes in product policy, and that **PoliciedProduct** is immune to changes in the strategy for implementing policy. Thus, **Product** and all its

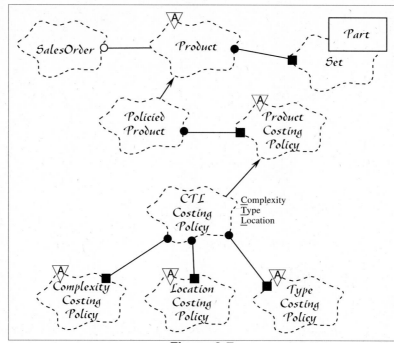

Figure 2-7
ProductPolicy Abstractions

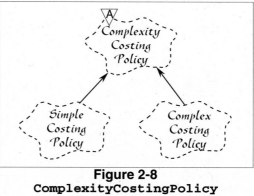

Figure 2-8
ComplexityCostingPolicy

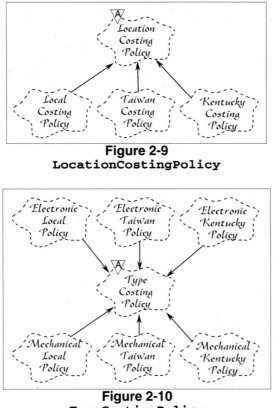

Figure 2-9
LocationCostingPolicy

Figure 2-10
TypeCostingPolicy

clients are closed to changes in **PoliciedProduct** and its derivatives and minions. Also, **PoliciedProduct** and **ProductCostingPolicy** are closed to changes in the specific policy implementations.

Abstraction is also employed to create several groupings. **SimpleCosting-Policy** and **ComplexCostingPolicy** are grouped beneath **Complexity-CostingPolicy**. Similarly, there is a grouping for **LocationCostingPolicy** and **TypeCostingPolicy**. Each of these groupings allows the client of the grouping, **CTLCostingPolicy**, to be closed to any changes that take place below them, while remaining open to working with policies that are not yet defined.

The benefit of this design is that changes are very isolated. We accept the fact that product policy is variable, and that the program must be maintained to stay in sync with policy changes. However, most policy changes will require modification of only one class. Each of the policy classes, at the bottom of the inheritance hierarchy, are closed to changes in any of the others, so there is no chance that a change in one of those policies can introduce a bug anywhere else. Moreover, the change will not even force recompilation of any other code.

Changes to the algorithm of the policy would either cause changes to **CTLCosting-Policy**, or cause a new class to be derived from **ProductCostingPolicy**. In either case, such changes cannot introduce bugs in the code of **PoliciedProduct**, **Product**, or **SalesOrder**. Moreover, if a new policy class is derived from **ProductCostingPolicy**, then no bugs can be introduced into **CTLCostingPolicy** or its minions.

Thus, the system is well isolated from the kinds of changes that we expect might occur. We would expect that maintenance of the system would be straightforward in most cases, and that the chances of introducing new bugs while maintaining the code would be small.

Figures 2-11 through 2-13 show the dynamic models for computing the cost of a product.

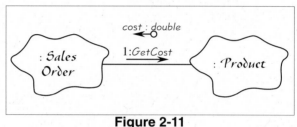

Figure 2-11
Abstract GetCost

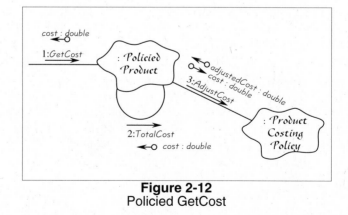

Figure 2-12
Policied GetCost

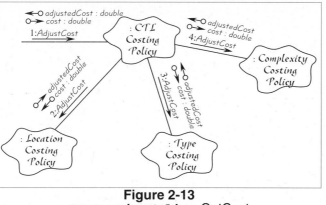

Figure 2-13
CTLCostingPolicy GetCost

The Cost of Complexity Management

Listings 2-15 through 2-46 show the complete implementation of this design in C++. The entire program comes to 32 files and 339 lines of code. Consider again Listings 2-5 and 2-6, which solved the entire problem in 2 files and 74 lines of code. What is wrong with this picture? These two programs do exactly the same thing. Yet there is nearly a 5:1 difference in line count! Which would you rather maintain? Which is more complex?

It seems that all our hiding and grouping and closing has made this program much more complex. The result seems horribly over-designed. The code that we thought was "managing complexity" increased the size of the program by almost a factor of 5, and created a massive jumble of files.

The lesson in all of this is that it requires complexity to manage complexity. You must judge carefully the complexity of the problem to see if the extra complexity involved with grouping, hiding, and closing will produce a net gain. In our case, the actual costing policies were so trivial that the code we put in place to manage complexity greatly outweighed them. However, what if each policy had required 20 or more lines of code. There are 11 policies altogether. If each averaged 20 lines of code, then Listings 2-5 and 2-6 would have amounted to $74 - 11 + (20 \times 11) = 283$ lines of code, most of which would have been invested in the **TotalCost** function in Listing 2-6. This function would be much more difficult to maintain and would probably become a pile of spaghetti.

On the other hand, Listings 2-15 through 2-46 would amount to $339 - 11 + 220 = 548$. In this case the overhead of the complexity management code amounts to $(548 - 283) \div 283 = 94\%$ more lines: a 2:1 difference. This may not be too great a penalty to pay, especially since many of those extra lines are taken up with non-executable, boilerplate code, and the benefits provided by those 265 extra lines of code are significant. Each policy is isolated from all the others, to the extent that we can change a single policy without affecting or even recompiling the rest. In fact, we can rewrite or replace the entire policy mechanism without affecting **Product** or any of its clients. Also, modifications to a single policy will not mandate the retesting of all policies, as they would if all the policies were contained in a single function.

Another way of describing this benefit is that as the code grows, there will be places for it to grow into. What we have built is a framework that can support a complex set of policies. As those policies change, grow, and become more complex, there will be places to put those changes that are well protected from the rest of the code. Many strange and crazy things can be done in the policies, without affecting the framework, so the complexity is managed.

The Efficiency of the Diagrams

Note that to represent the code contained in 32 source files, we used only seven simple diagrams: Figures 2-7 through 2-13. This is a clear demonstration of the expressive power of using a diagramming notation. The Booch notation can represent complex designs with a few expressive diagrams—another form of complexity management. We can design our programs in a medium that is simultaneously dense, expressive, and easy to manipulate. We shall see even more effective demonstrations of this later in this chapter, and in those that follow.

The Product Costing Code

Listing 2-15

```
product.h

#ifndef PRODUCT_H
#define PRODUCT_H
#include "componen/u_set.h"
class Part;

class Product
{
  public:
    double TotalCost() const;
    virtual double GetCost() const = 0;

  private:
    UnboundedSet<Part*> itsParts;
};
#endif
```

Listing 2-16

`product.cc`

```
#include "product.h"
#include "part.h"
#include <assert.h>
#include "componen/set.h"

double Product::TotalCost() const
{
    double totalCost = 0;
    Iterator<Part*> i(itsParts);
    for (; i; i++)
    {
        totalCost += (*i)->Cost();
    }
    return totalCost;
}
```

Listing 2-17

`plcyprod.h`

```
#ifndef POLICIED_PRODUCT
#define POLICIED_PRODUCT
#include "product.h"
class ProductCostingPolicy;

class PoliciedProduct : public Product
{
  public:
    PoliciedProduct(ProductCostingPolicy& thePolicy);
    virtual double GetCost() const;

  private:
    ProductCostingPolicy* itsPolicy;
};
#endif
```

Listing 2-18

`plcyprod.cc`

```
#include "plcyprod.h"
#include "pcostpolicy.h"
PoliciedProduct::PoliciedProduct(ProductCostingPolicy& thePolicy)
: itsPolicy(&thePolicy)
{}

double PoliciedProduct::GetCost() const
{
    double cost = TotalCost();
    return itsPolicy->AdjustCost(cost);
}
```

Listing 2-19

```
pcostpolicy.h

#ifndef PRODUCT_COSTING_POLICY
#define PRODUCT_COSTING_POLICY
class ProductCostingPolicy
{
  public:
    virtual double AdjustCost(double theCost) const = 0;
};
#endif
```

Listing 2-20

```
ctlpolicy.h

#ifndef CTL_COSTING_POLICY
#define CTL_COSTING_POLICY
#include "pcostpolicy.h"
class ComplexityCostingPolicy;
class LocationCostingPolicy;
class TypeCostingPolicy;

class CTLCostingPolicy : public ProductCostingPolicy
{
  public:
    CTLCostingPolicy(ComplexityCostingPolicy&,
                     LocationCostingPolicy&,
                     TypeCostingPolicy&);

    virtual double AdjustCost(double theCost) const;

  private:
    ComplexityCostingPolicy*  itsComplexityPolicy;
    LocationCostingPolicy*    itsLocationPolicy;
    TypeCostingPolicy*        itsTypePolicy;
};
#endif
```

Listing 2-21

```
ctlpolicy.cc

#include "ctlpolicy.h"
#include "cmplxtyplcy.h"
#include "typepolicy.h"
#include "locpolicy.h"
CTLCostingPolicy::CTLCostingPolicy(ComplexityCostingPolicy& c,
                                   LocationCostingPolicy& l,
                                   TypeCostingPolicy& t)
: itsComplexityPolicy(&c), itsLocationPolicy(&l), itsTypePolicy(&t)
{}

double CTLCostingPolicy::AdjustCost(double theCost) const
{
    double locationAdjustment =
        itsLocationPolicy->AdjustCost(theCost);
    double typeAdjustment =
        itsTypePolicy->AdjustCost(locationAdjustment);
    return itsComplexityPolicy->AdjustCost(typeAdjustment);
}
```

Listing 2-22

```
cmplxtyplcy.h

#ifndef COMPLEXITY_COSTING_POLICY
#define COMPLEXITY_COSTING_POLICY

class ComplexityCostingPolicy
{
  public:
    virtual double AdjustCost(double theCost) const = 0;
};

#endif
```

Listing 2-23

```
locpolicy.h

#ifndef LOCATION_COSTING_POLICY
#define LOCATION_COSTING_POLICY

class LocationCostingPolicy
{
  public:
    virtual double AdjustCost(double theCost) const = 0;
};
#endif
```

Listing 2-24

```
typepolicy.h

#ifndef TYPE_COSTING_POLICY
#define TYPE_COSTING_POLICY

class TypeCostingPolicy
{
  public:
    virtual double AdjustCost(double theCost) const = 0;
};
#endif
```

Listing 2-25

```
cmplxpolicy.h

#ifndef COMPLEX_CONSTING_POLICY
#define COMPLEX_CONSTING_POLICY

#include "cmplxtyplcy.h"

class ComplexCostingPolicy : public ComplexityCostingPolicy
{
  public:
    virtual double AdjustCost(double theCost) const;
};
#endif
```

Listing 2-26

`cmplxpolicy.cc`

```
#include "cmplxpolicy.h"

double ComplexCostingPolicy::AdjustCost(double theCost) const
{
    return theCost * 1.2;
}
```

Listing 2-27

`smplepolicy.h`

```
#ifndef SIMPLE_COSTING_POLICY
#define SIMPLE_COSTING_POLICY
#include "cmplxtyplcy.h"

class SimpleCostingPolicy : public ComplexityCostingPolicy
{
  public:
    virtual double AdjustCost(double theCost) const;
};
#endif
```

Listing 2-28

`smplepolicy.cc`

```
#include "smplepolicy.h"
double SimpleCostingPolicy::AdjustCost(double theCost) const
{
    return theCost * 1.0;
}
```

Listing 2-29

`localpolicy.h`

```
#ifndef LOCAL_COSTING_POLICY
#define LOCAL_COSTING_POLICY
#include "locpolicy.h"

class LocalCostingPolicy : public LocationCostingPolicy
{
  public:
    virtual double AdjustCost(double theCost);
};
#endif
```

Listing 2-30

`localpolicy.cc`

```
#include "localpolicy.h"
double LocalCostingPolicy::AdjustCost(double theCost)
{
    return theCost * 1.67;
}
```

Listing 2-31

`taiwanpolicy.h`

```
#ifndef TAIWAN_COSTING_POLICY
#define TAIWAN_COSTING_POLICY
#include "locpolicy.h"

class TaiwanCostingPolicy : public LocationCostingPolicy
{
  public:
    virtual double AdjustCost(double theCost);
};
#endif
```

Listing 2-32

`taiwanpolicy.cc`

```
#include "taiwanpolicy.h"
double TaiwanCostingPolicy::AdjustCost(double theCost)
{
    return theCost * 1.43;
}
```

Listing 2-33

`kntkypolicy.h`

```
#ifndef KENTUCKY_COSTING_POLICY
#define KENTUCKY_COSTING_POLICY
#include "locpolicy.h"

class KentuckyCostingPolicy : public LocationCostingPolicy
{
  public:
    virtual double AdjustCost(double theCost);
};
#endif
```

Listing 2-34

`kntkypolicy.cc`

```
#include "kntkypolicy.h"
double KentuckyCostingPolicy::AdjustCost(double theCost)
{
    return theCost * 1.53;
}
```

Listing 2-35

`ek_policy.h`

```
#ifndef ELECTRONIC_KENTUCKY_POLICY
#define ELECTRONIC_KENTUCKY_POLICY
#include "typepolicy.h"

class ElectronicKentuckyPolicy : public TypeCostingPolicy
{
  public:
    virtual double AdjustCost(double theCost) const;
};
#endif
```

Listing 2-36

`ek_policy.cc`

```
#include "el_policy.h"

double ElectronicKentuckyPolicy::AdjustCost(double theCost) const
{
    return theCost * 1.18;
}
```

Listing 2-37

`el_policy.h`

```
#ifndef ELECTRONIC_LOCAL_POLICY
#define ELECTRONIC_LOCAL_POLICY
#include "typepolicy.h"

class ElectronicLocalPolicy : public TypeCostingPolicy
{
  public:
    virtual double AdjustCost(double theCost) const;
};
#endif
```

Listing 2-38

`el_policy.cc`

```
#include "el_policy.h"

double ElectronicLocalPolicy::AdjustCost(double theCost) const
{
    return theCost * 1.10;
}
```

Listing 2-39

`et_policy.h`

```
#ifndef ELECTRONIC_TAIWAN_POLICY
#define ELECTRONIC_TAIWAN_POLICY
#include "typepolicy.h"

class ElectronicTaiwanPolicy : public TypeCostingPolicy
{
  public:
    virtual double AdjustCost(double theCost) const;
};
#endif
```

Listing 2-40

`et_policy.cc`

```
#include "et_policy.h"

double ElectronicTaiwanPolicy::AdjustCost(double theCost) const
{
    return theCost * 1.13;
}
```

Listing 2-41

`mk_policy.h`

```
#ifndef MECHANICAL_KENTUCKY_POLICY
#define MECHANICAL_KENTUCKY_POLICY
#include "typepolicy.h"

class MechanicalKentuckyPolicy : public TypeCostingPolicy
{
  public:
    virtual double AdjustCost(double theCost) const;
};
#endif
```

Listing 2-42

`mk_policy.cc`

```
#include "mk_policy.h"

double MechanicalKentuckyPolicy::AdjustCost(double theCost) const
{
    return theCost * 1.16;
}
```

Listing 2-43

`ml_policy.h`

```
#ifndef MECHANICAL_LOCAL_POLICY
#define MECHANICAL_LOCAL_POLICY
#include "typepolicy.h"

class MechanicalLocalPolicy : public TypeCostingPolicy
{
  public:
    virtual double AdjustCost(double theCost) const;
};
#endif
```

Listing 2-44

`ml_policy.cc`

```
#include "ml_policy.h"

double MechanicalLocalPolicy::AdjustCost(double theCost) const
{
    return theCost * 1.14;
}
```

Listing 2-45

`mt_policy.h`

```
#ifndef MECHANICAL_TAIWAN_POLICY
#define MECHANICAL_TAIWAN_POLICY
#include "typepolicy.h"

class MechanicalTaiwanPolicy : public TypeCostingPolicy
{
  public:
    virtual double AdjustCost(double theCost) const;
};
#endif
```

Listing 2-46

`mt_policy.cc`

```
#include "mt_policy.h"

double MechanicalTaiwanPolicy::AdjustCost(double theCost) const
{
    return theCost * 1.00;
}
```

Managing Complexity with Abstraction

As we saw in the previous section, abstraction can be a powerful tool for managing complexity. We saw how it can be used to group similar objects under a common interface, and to hide one class from another. In the following sections we examine this idea more closely.

Polymorphism

Polymorphism allows us to treat a group of objects of different types as though they belonged to the same type. The user of the objects does not know or care about their differences. This helps us manage complexity because the complexity of their differences is made irrelevant to the user.

Polymorphism comes in several varieties. It can be total or partial, and it can be typed or untyped. Object A is totally polymorphic to Object B if anything that can be done to Object B can also be done to Object A. Thus, A can replace B in any of its contexts. Partial polymorphism, on the other hand, occurs when some contexts allow A to substitute for B, but others do not. This happens because A can only reasonably perform a subset of the operations that can be requested of B.

Typed polymorphism is based upon the declared types of the classes of the objects. In C++, if A derives from B via inheritance, then A will have typed polymorphism with B. Untyped polymorphism occurs when A and B are related only because their interfaces are similar. This kind of polymorphism can be achieved by using C++ templates. Let's consider a few examples.

Total Typed Polymorphism

Figure 2-14 shows a typical case for polymorphism that is both total and typed. The three specific shapes, **Circle**, **Rectangle**, and **Polygon**, have been grouped under the abstraction **DisplayItem**. The class definition of **DisplayItem** shows a pure virtual function named **Draw**. Listing 2-47 demonstrates that a set of **DisplayItem** objects containing any mix of **Circle**, **Rectangle**, and **Polygon** objects can be dealt with in a manner that ignores the differences among them.

It doesn't matter what mix of shapes is stored in **theSet**, the **DisplayAllItems** function will draw them. If we add other shape types to the code at a later date, this function will still draw them. This represents a tremendous collapsing of states. The complexity of drawing a list of diverse shapes is managed by relegating the knowledge of how to draw the shapes to the derived classes. **DisplayItem** represents the abstract group of all shapes that can be displayed.

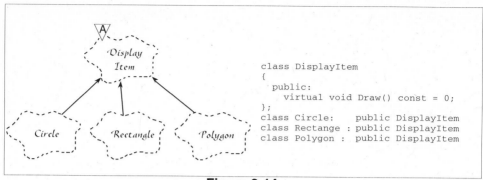

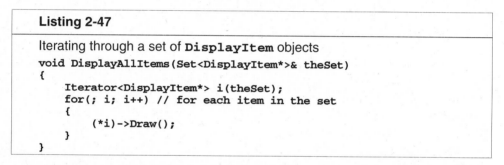

```
class DisplayItem
{
  public:
    virtual void Draw() const = 0;
};
class Circle:    public DisplayItem
class Rectange : public DisplayItem
class Polygon :  public DisplayItem
```

Figure 2-14
`DisplayItem` Abstraction

Listing 2-47

Iterating through a set of **`DisplayItem`** objects

```
void DisplayAllItems(Set<DisplayItem*>& theSet)
{
    Iterator<DisplayItem*> i(theSet);
    for(; i; i++) // for each item in the set
    {
        (*i)->Draw();
    }
}
```

This is another way of saying that **`DisplayAllItems`** is closed against the further addition of new kinds of **`DisplayItem`**. Total polymorphism is one of the main mechanisms for closing a function or a class. A function can be closed as long as every object passed into it is totally polymorphic with the objects it expects as its arguments. Thus, as long as the derivatives of **`DisplayItem`** are totally polymorphic with **`DisplayItem`**, **`DisplayAllItems`** will work with them as expected.

In C++, total polymorphism is usually typed. **`DisplayAllItems`** is a good example. It will accept as an argument only those objects whose type is derived from **`DisplayItem`**. While such typing is not a guarantee of total polymorphism, it is a strong indication of it. Indeed, my favorite style of C++ programming dictates that public inheritance be used for nothing less than total polymorphism.

Partial, Untyped Polymorphism

Listing 2-48 demonstrates a simple variety of partial, untyped polymorphism. It contains the standard **min** and **max** template functions.

To be used as an argument of these functions, an object must conform to a certain minimum interface. It must understand what **<** or **>** means. That is, it must either be a primitive type, or **operator<** and **operator>** must be overloaded, either as member

---

Listing 2-48

`min` and `max` template functions.
```
template <class T>
T min(const T& a, const T& b) {return a<b ? a : b;}

template <class T>
T max(const T& a, const T& b) {return a>b ? a : b;}
```

functions or as global functions. It must also be copyable like a primitive type, or have a copy constructor, so that it can be returned. Those are the only requirements. The arguments do not have to be derived from a certain type, and they do not have to be totally polymorphic with any other kind of object. They simply need that minimum interface, regardless of how they get it.

This form of polymorphism manages complexity by allowing the `min` and `max` functions to be closed. Regardless of what new types may be applied to them in the future, these functions will not require changing. They are closed by virtue of their demands on the interface of their arguments.

ISA and the Liskov Substitution Principle

> *What is wanted here is something like the following substitution property: If for each object o_1 of type S there is an object o_2 of type T such that for all programs P defined in terms of T, the behavior of P is unchanged when o_1 is substituted for o_2 then S is a subtype of T.*[9]

The Liskov Substitution principle describes total polymorphism. We use this principle in conjunction with public inheritance in C++ in a style of programming called the *ISA* style. In *ISA* programming, every time you use public inheritance, you are guaranteeing that the subclasses being defined will be true subtypes according to the Liskov Substitution principle (i.e., totally polymorphic). Less formally, and in C++, we express this guarantee as follows: *You can always pass a pointer or reference to a derived class to a function that expects a pointer or reference to a base class.*

Think about this rule carefully. Think about what it means to a programmer confronted with a function that takes a pointer or reference to a public base. If he has been given the *ISA* guarantee, then he does not have to worry about special cases for any derivatives of that public base. He can use the public base without fear that some subclass of that base will eventually foul him up. This is a big boon, and powerful management of complexity.

---

9. Barbara Liskov, "Data Abstraction and Hierarchy," *SIGPLAN Notices,* 23,5 (May, 1988).

Mathematical vs. Polymorphic Relationships

It is easy to become confused about how to use inheritance in an *ISA* style. One common mistake is to confuse mathematical relationships with polymorphic relationships. For example, mathematically, a square *is* a rectangle. This is true because every rule or constraint that applies to a rectangle applies equally to a square. A square is *more* constrained than a rectangle, since all its sides must be equal. This mathematical equivalence often tempts programmers to try to derive the class **Square** from the class **Rectangle**; yet this sometimes leads to problems in programs that have adopted an *ISA* style. See Listings 2-49 and 2-50.

Listing 2-49

```
rect.h
#ifndef RECTANGLE_H
#define RECTANGLE_H

class Rectangle
{
  public:
    Rectangle(double width, double height)
    : itsWidth(width), itsHeight(height)
    {}

    double        GetWidth()  const          {return itsWidth;}
    double        GetHeight() const          {return itsHeight;}
    virtual void  SetWidth(double width)     {itsWidth = width;}
    virtual void  SetHeight(double height)   {itsHeight = height;}

  private:
    double itsWidth;
    double itsHeight;
};
#endif
```

Listing 2-50

```
square.h
#ifndef SQUARE_H
#define SQUARE_H
#include "rect.h"

class Square : public Rectangle
{
  public:
    Square(double side)
    : Rectangle(side, side)
    {}

    virtual void SetWidth(double width)
    {
        Rectangle::SetWidth(width);
```

Listing 2-50 (Continued)

```
square.h
        Rectangle::SetHeight(width);
    }

    virtual void SetHeight(double height)
    {
        Rectangle::SetWidth(height);
        Rectangle::SetHeight(height);
    }
};
#endif
```

There are several problems with **Square**. First, it is a little wasteful for a **Square** to have both a width and a height where a single side will do. However, in most circumstances this problem is relatively minor. Of more importance to the *ISA* style is that some functions will accept a **Rectangle** but will be confused by a **Square**. These functions make the reasonable assumption that changing the height of a **Rectangle** will not change its width. Consider, for example, Listing 2-51.

Listing 2-51

SetAspectRatio

```
void SetAspectRatio(Rectangle& r, double theRatio)
{
    double width = r.GetHeight() * theRatio;
    r.SetWidth(width);
}
```

This function will happily set the aspect ratio of every **Rectangle** that is passed to it to its argument **theRatio**. It does so by modifying the width of that **Rectangle**. It seems reasonable for the function to assume that changing the width of a **Rectangle** will not alter its height! Yet if a **Square** is passed into this function, its aspect ratio will remain 1:1 and both its height and width will be changed to meaningless values.

Since **Square** cannot be meaningfully passed into **SetAspectRatio**, it is not totally polymorphic with **Rectangle** and is not a valid subtype according to the Liskov Substitution principle. Mathematically, a square is a rectangle because a square has all the constraints of a rectangle, plus a few more. However, *in OOD a subtype must have no more constraints than its base type*. This is because it must be usable anywhere the base is usable. If the subtype had more constraints than its base, there would exist uses that would be valid for the base but would violate one of the extra constraints of the subtype. Thus, the criterion for the mathematical relationship is nearly the opposite of the criterion for the polymorphic relationship.

This realization sometimes leads to the notion that a **Rectangle** should derive from a **Square**. Certainly a **Rectangle** has fewer constraints than a **Square**, so perhaps the inheritance relationship should be turned upside down, so that **Rectangle** inherits from **Square**. This reasoning runs into the same problem as the previous example. Users of a **Square** have a right to expect that changing its width will change its height as well. Such a user would be confused if it were passed a **Rectangle** whose width and height could be different.

Thus, even though there is a mathematical relationship between a **Square** and a **Rectangle**, it appears that there is no polymorphic relationship. A **Square** cannot always be used as a subtype of a **Rectangle**, and a **Rectangle** cannot always be used as a subtype of a **Square**. Although mathematical relationships are often tempting to express as *ISA* relationships in OOD via public inheritance, it is seldom wise to do so. The criteria for the two relationships are almost opposites.

Factoring Instead of Deriving

Another interesting and puzzling case of inheritance is the case of the **Line** and the **LineSegment**. Consider Listings 2-52 and 2-53. These two classes appear, at first, to be natural candidates for public inheritance. **LineSegment** needs every member variable and every member function declared in **Line**. Moreover, **LineSegment** adds a new member function of its own, **GetLength**, and overrides the meaning of the **IsOn** function. Yet these two classes violate the *ISA* style in a subtle way.

Listing 2-52

```
geometry/line.h
#ifndef GEOMETRY_LINE_H
#define GEOMETRY_LINE_H
#include "geometry/point.h"

class Line
{
  public:
    Line(const Point& p1, const Point& p2);

    double      GetSlope()          const;
    double      GetIntercept()      const; // Y Intercept
    Point       GetP1()             const {return itsP1;};
    Point       GetP2()             const {return itsP2;};
    virtual bool IsOn(const Point&) const; // true if point on line

  private:
    Point itsP1;
    Point itsP2;
};
#endif
```

A user of **Line** has a right to expect that all points that are collinear with it are on it. For example, the point returned by the **Intercept** function is the point at which the line intersects the Y-axis. Since this point is collinear with the line, users of **Line** have a right

---

Listing 2-53

```
geometry/lineseg.h
#ifndef GEOMETRY_LINESEGMENT_H
#define GEOMETRY_LINESEGMENT_H
#include "geometry/line.h"

class LineSegment : public Line
{
  public:
    LineSegment(const Point& p1, const Point& p2);

    double       GetLength()          const;
    virtual bool IsOn(const Point&) const; // true if on segment
};
#endif
```

---

to expect that `IsOn(Intercept()) == true`. In many instances of `LineSegment`, however, this statement will fail.

Why is this an important issue? Why not simply derive `LineSegment` from `Line` and live with the subtle problems? This is a judgment call. There are *rare* occasions when it is more expedient to accept a subtle flaw in polymorphic behavior than to attempt to manipulate the design until all the *ISA* relationships are perfect. Accepting compromise instead of pursuing perfection is an engineering trade-off. A good engineer learns when compromise is more *profitable* than perfection. However, the simplification of total polymorphism *should not be surrendered lightly*. The guarantee that a subclass will always work where its base classes are used is a powerful way to manage complexity. Once it is forsaken, we must consider each subclass individually.

In the case of the `Line` and `LineSegment`, there is a simple solution that illustrates an important tool of OOD. If we have access to both the `Line` and `LineSegment` classes, and if those classes can be opened for modification, then we can *factor* the common elements of both into an abstract base class. Listings 2-53.5 through 2-55 show the factoring of `Line` and `LineSegment` into the base class `LinearObject`.

Listing 2-53.5

```
geometry/linearobj.h
#ifndef GEOMETRY_LINEAR_OBJECT_H
#define GEOMETRY_LINEAR_OBJECT_H

#include "geometry/point.h"

class LinearObject
{
  public:
    LinearObject(const Point& p1, const Point& p2);

    double   GetSlope() const;
    double   GetIntercept() const;
```

Listing 2-53.5 (Continued)

```
geometry/linearobj.h

    Point GetP1() const {return itsP1;};
    Point GetP2() const {return itsP2;};
    virtual int    IsOn(const Point&) const = 0; // abstract.

  private:
    Point itsP1;
    Point itsP2;
};
#endif
```

Listing 2-54

```
geometry/line.h
#ifndef GEOMETRY_LINE_H
#define GEOMETRY_LINE_H
#include "geometry/linearobj.h"

class Line : public LinearObject
{
  public:
    Line(const Point& p1, const Point& p2);
    virtual bool IsOn(const Point&) const;
};
#endif
```

Listing 2-55

```
geometry/lineseg.h
#ifndef GEOMETRY_LINESEGMENT_H
#define GEOMETRY_LINESEGMENT_H
#include "geometry/linearobj.h"

class LineSegment : public LinearObject
{
  public:
    LineSegment(const Point& p1, const Point& p2);

    double       GetLength()        const;
    virtual bool IsOn(const Point&) const;
};
#endif
```

LinearObject represents both **Line** and **LineSegment**. It provides most of the functionality and data members for both subclasses, with the exception of the **IsOn** method, which is pure virtual. Users of **LinearObject** are not allowed to assume that they understand the extent of the object they are using. Thus, they can accept either a **Line** or a **LineSegment** with no problem. Moreover, users of **Line** will never have to deal with a **LineSegment**.

Factoring is a design tool. It is most effectively applied before there is much code written. Certainly if there were dozens of clients of the **Line** class shown in Listing 2-52, we would not have had the luxury of factoring out the **LinearObject** class. When factoring is possible, however, it is a powerful tool. If qualities can be factored out of two subclasses, there is the distinct possibility that other classes will show up later that need those qualities too. Thus, the employment of factoring during the design phase is a way of anticipating reuse. Of factoring, Rebecca Wirfs-Brock, Brian Wilkerson, and Lauren Wiener say,

> *We can state that if a set of classes all support a common responsibility, they should inherit that responsibility from a common superclass.*
>
> *If a common superclass does not already exist, create one, and move the common responsibilities to it. After all, such a class is demonstrably useful – you have already shown that the responsibilities will be inherited by some classes. Isn't it conceivable that a later extension of your system might add a new subclass that will support those same responsibilities in a new way? This new superclass will probably be an abstract class.*[10]

Listing 2-56 shows how the attributes of **LinearObject** can be used by an unanticipated class, **Ray**. A **Ray** is totally polymorphic to **LinearObject**, and no user of **LinearObject** would have any trouble dealing with it.

Listing 2-56

```
geometry/ray.h
#ifndef GEOMETRY_RAY_H
#define GEOMETRY_RAY_H

class Ray : public LinearObject
{
  public:
    Ray(const Point& p1, const Point& p2);
    virtual bool IsOn(const Point&) const;
};
#endif
```

Managing Complexity with Aggregation

Another very common grouping strategy is to build a single class from a collection of disparate component classes. In the example in Figure 2-15, the **MoonRocket** class is composed of a hierarchy of more detailed components.

MoonRocket is a complicated class. It sits at the top of a complex composition hierarchy, and it probably has a number of complex methods for administering this hierarchy.

---

10. Rebecca Wirfs-Brock et al., *Designing Object-Oriented Software* (Prentice Hall, 1990), p. 113.

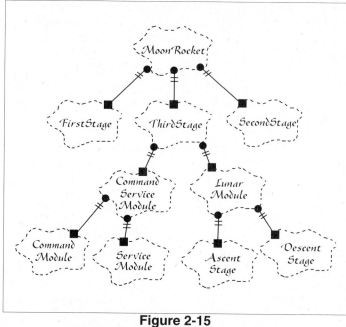

Figure 2-15
MoonRocket Composition Hierarchy

However, if the rest of the application deals only with the **MoonRocket**, and not with its components, then the complexity of this structure has been managed. If **MoonRocket** has the responsibility of orchestrating and managing its components to ensure that they work together as a team, then the complexity can be ignored by the rest of the application; it has been sequestered and managed.

For example, assume that **MoonRocket** has a method called **Launch**. This method controls the complex process of getting the vehicle into orbit. Many places within the overall **MoonMission** application may invoke this **Launch** method, but none of these places need to worry about the details of how the launch is controlled. Moreover, if the visibility of the components of the **MoonRocket** is restricted to the **MoonRocket** class, then the application is protected against illicit or inadvertent manipulation by classes or functions outside of **MoonRocket** (e.g., nobody could tell the second stage to ignite while the vehicle was still on the pad).

Well-formed composition structures hide their details beneath a veneer of useful manipulation functions that drive the structure through its legal states and operations and avoid illegal states and operations. The components of such structures are meant to be used in unison. The changes that are applied to them through the methods of the containing class are carefully choreographed by the designer. To expose these components to individual manipulation by external users can sometimes be a grave design flaw.

Consider the following example:

```
class NuclearReactor
{
  public:
    void SetPowerOutput(double watts);

    Pump& GetPump() {return itsCoolantPump;}

  private:
    ControlRod itsControlRods[nControlRods];
    FuelRod itsFuelRods[nFuelRods];
    Pump itsCoolantPump;
};
```

The whimsical example illustrates the usefulness of hiding the components of a composition structure. The **SetPowerOutput** function of the **NuclearReactor** class is the only function that manipulates the components of the reactor appropriately. It ensures that the fuel and control rods are set for the proper power output, and that the flow of coolant through the reactor is sufficient to drain off the excess heat that would otherwise melt the fuel rods. But the programmer thought it would be useful to expose the coolant pump through the reactor's public interface via the **GetPump** method. Unfortunately, a terrorist from the RPLA[11] infiltrated the software engineering organization of the primary contractor for the reactor software and wrote the following function:

```
void JanesNightmare(NuclearReactor& theReactor)
{
    theReactor.SetPowerOutput(1.2e9);      // 1.2 gigawatts!
    theReactor.GetPump().SetFlowRate(0); // "I can feel it."
}
```

Clearly, it is not malicious abuse that we are usually concerned with; rather, it is the inadvertent or careless misuse of an object by someone who is unfamiliar with the design. We want, as much as possible, to ensure that objects are only manipulated by other objects that, *by design*, are competent to do so. To help us achieve this goal, we use private containment where possible, and resist the temptation to expose a privately contained object through a public **get** method.

This point is critical to the management of complexity. Conventions are often adopted about the manner in which certain objects should be used. Other design decisions are then based upon the conviction that those conventions will not be violated. If the designer does not enforce these conventions by restricting access and visibility, then the design can be subverted by engineers who ignore them, either through ignorance, laziness, or desperation. As time passes and the original designers go on to bigger and better things,[12] the violations will increase until the design falters and collapses.

---

11. RPG Programmer's Liberation Army
12. I knew one engineer who took up chicken farming.

Restricting Visibility by the use of Friendship

In the example above, what motivated the programmer to make the **Pump** visible through the public interface of the **NuclearReactor**? Probably some other agency had a legitimate use for the **Pump** object. For example, assume that there is a class called **PumpInspector** that needs to access the **Pump** object on a regular basis.

Figure 2-16 shows a typical scenario. A **PumpInspector** object queries the **NuclearReactor** for its **Pump** so that it can go about the business of inspecting it. The *P* adornment signifies that the **PumpInspector** has access to the **Pump** *parametrically*, that is, via the return value of the **GetPump** method. To support this access, the **GetPump** method must either be public, or **PumpInspector** must be a **friend** of **NuclearReactor**.

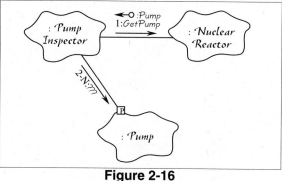

Figure 2-16
PumpInspector Object Diagram

In this scenario, we only want the **Pump** to be used by those who are competent to manipulate it. Thus, the friendship option seems appropriate. By making **PumpInspector** a **friend** of **NuclearReactor**, we can keep the **Pump** out of the public interface of **NuclearReactor** (see Figure 2-17).

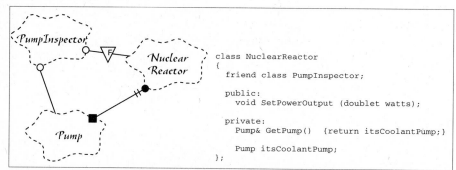

```
class NuclearReactor
{
    friend class PumpInspector;

    public:
        void SetPowerOutput (doublet watts);

    private:
        Pump& GetPump()    {return itsCoolantPump;}

        Pump itsCoolantPump;
};
```

Figure 2-17
Friendship Used to Restrict Public Access

Used in this manner, friendship is an indispensable tool for maintaining encapsulation and controlling access. It allows the encapsulation barriers of a class to be widened and thrown around several other classes, without generally compromising those barriers.

Case Study: The Design of a Container Library

In this section, we explore the issue of complexity management by looking at a reasonably significant example. We will examine the development of a family of classes that represent containers. There are many kinds of container classes: **Sets**, **Bags**, **Queues**, **Stacks**, **Dequeues**, **Trees**, **Lists**, and so on. Each of these classes specifies an object that can contain other objects. They differ only in the details of the containment. Some containers keep the objects in a certain order; others restrict the order in which the objects can be entered or removed. Some allow duplicates; others maintain complex relationships among the contained objects. In this example, we will examine two specific kinds of container: **Bags** and **Sets**.

A **Bag** contains an unordered collection of objects and allows duplicates. Objects can be entered and removed in any order, and can be tested for membership in the **Bag**. A **Set** is like a **Bag** in that objects can be entered or removed in any order, and we can test them for membership. However, duplicates are not allowed in a **Set**; a **Set** ignores an attempt to add an object that is already present. This probably makes **Sets** a little slower than **Bags**, at least for adding objects.

Both **Bags** and **Sets** support an ancillary object called an "iterator," which allows sequential access to each of the contained objects. No order is guaranteed by the iterator; that is, the objects are not guaranteed to be accessed in the same order that they were added, or even in the same order of a previous iteration. Nothing can be assumed about their order at all.

Listing 2-57 shows a possible scenario for the declaration and use of a **Set** of integers. It is a variation on the Sieve of Eratosthenes, which finds all the prime numbers between 2 and 100. It works by creating four sets of integers. The first set contains all the multiples of 2 between 2 and 100, the second contains the multiples of 3, the third contains the multiples of 5, and the fourth contains the multiples of 7. These sets are then subtracted from a fifth set, which contains all the integers from 2 to 100. After the subtractions, the result will contain all the primes between 2 and 100. The four sets are also added to a sixth set, which starts out empty. After the additions, this set will contain all the non-prime integers between 2 and 100.

This algorithm is not at all efficient. Even if the implementation of **Set** is very fast, there are algorithms that are *much* faster. However, the algorithm is very easy to understand, and it is an adequate demonstration of a **Set**.

Listing 2-57

The usage of a set of integers

```
// Create set of primes and non-primes between 2 and 100.

Set<int> fSets[4]; // store the multiples of 2,3,5 and 7
                   // (primes < sqrt(100))
int i;

for (i=4; i<100; i+=2) fSets[0].Add(i);
for (i=6; i<100; i+=3) fSets[1].Add(i);
for (i=10; i<100; i+=5) fSets[2].Add(i);
for (i=14; i<100; i+=7) fSets[3].Add(i);

Set<int> primes;
for (i=2; i<100; i++) primes.Add(i); // create set of integers < 100
for (i=0; i<4; i++) primes -= fSets[i]; // subtract non-prime
multiples.

Set<int> nonPrimes;
for (i=0; i<4; i++) nonPrimes += fSets[i]; // add all multiples
                                           // to non-primes

cout << "Primes:" << endl;
for (Iterator<int> psi(primes); psi; psi++) cout << *psi << endl;
cout << "Non Primes:" << endl;
for (Iterator<int> npi(nonPrimes); npi; npi++) cout << *npi << endl;
```

Notice that all the **Set** objects in Listing 2-57 could be replaced with **Bag** objects, except for **nonPrimes**. The **nonPrimes** object depends upon the fact that duplicates are ignored since **fSet[0]** and **fSet[1]** will both contain the integer 6. Changing most of the **Set** objects into **Bag** objects might speed the algorithm up a little, since **Bags** are probably faster at adding members than **Sets** are, but making this change would cloud the algorithm. All of these containers are logically sets, in that they should not contain duplicates. Clearly, if speed is a big issue, then we should use a faster algorithm. If **Bags** increase the speed to an acceptable level, then their use is justified. But if speed is not a big issue, then the clarity of the algorithm outweighs the efficiency issue.

Listing 2-58 and 2-59 show an approximation of the class declarations of **Set** and **Bag**.

Listing 2-58

Set class declaration

```
template <class T>
class Set
{
 public:
    void      Add(const T& t);
    int       Remove(const T& t);
    void      Clear();
    int       IsMember(const T& t) const;
```

Listing 2-58 (Continued)

Set class declaration

```
    Set<T>& operator+= (const Set<T>&); // union
    Set<T>& operator-= (const Set<T>&); // difference
    Set<T>& operator&= (const Set<T>&); // intersection

    Set<T>  operator+ (const Set<T>&) const;
    Set<T>  operator- (const Set<T>&) const;
    Set<T>  operator& (const Set<T>&) const;
};
```

Listing 2-59

Bag class declaration

```
template <class T>
class Bag
{
  public:
    void    Add(const T& t);
    int     Remove(const T& t);
    void    Clear();
    int     IsMember(const T& t) const;

    Bag<T>& operator+= (const Bag<T>&); // union
    Bag<T>& operator-= (const Bag<T>&); // difference
    Bag<T>& operator&= (const Bag<T>&); // intersection

    Bag<T>  operator+ (const Bag<T>&) const;
    Bag<T>  operator- (const Bag<T>&) const;
    Bag<T>  operator& (const Bag<T>&) const;
};
```

These two classes are very similar. Should we factor their common attributes into an abstract class from which they both inherit? If we did this, we would be able to share the code that the two classes had in common. In this case it appears that this would be everything but the **Add** function.

Perhaps, however, we should inherit **Set** from **Bag**. Then we could simply override the **Add** function, and we could reuse the **Add** function from **Bag**, as follows:

```
void Set::Add(const T& item)
{
    if (!IsMember(item))
        Bag::Add(item);
}
```

Publicly inheriting **Set** from **Bag** would be a violation of the Liskov Substitution Principle, because clients of **Bag** expect to be able to add duplicates. Such clients could get confused if they were given **Set**s. We could remedy this by *privately* inheriting **Set** from **Bag** and then forcing the functions of **Bag** that were appropriate to **Set** to be public, as shown in Listing 2-60.

Listing 2-60

Private inheritance of `Set` from `Bag`

```
class Set : private Bag
{
 public:
     void      Add(const T& t);
     Bag::Remove;
     Bag::Clear;
     Bag::IsMember;

     Bag::operator+=; // union
     Bag::operator-=; // difference
     Bag::operator&=; // intersection
     Bag::operator+;
     Bag::operator-;
     Bag::operator&;
};
```

A third option would be to have a **Set** privately contain a **Bag** and simply pass most of the member function calls through to its contained **Bag**, filtering the **Add** function so that duplicates were ignored.

Without further information, it is difficult to determine which alternative is best. Each will work, and each avoids the duplication of code. It would be a shame to make an arbitrary decision; perhaps more investigation will make the choice easier.

Consider the **Iterator** class. Listing 2-61 shows a potential class definition.

Listing 2-61

Potential **Iterator** definition

```
template <class T>
class Iterator
{
 public:
     operator void*() const; // used in conditionals.  returns 0 if at
end.
     void operator++(int);    // postincrement; bump to next object
     T operator*() const;     // access the current object.
};
```

The **Iterator** is tested for completion by using the **void*** operator. This is similar in concept to the **void*** operator used in **iostreams**. It allows us to mention the **Iterator** object in a conditional context, as follows:

```
void PrintSet(const Set<int>& theSet)
{
    Iterator<int> i(s);
    while (i) // uses void* operator
    {
        cout << *i << endl;
        i++;
    }
}
```

The above example also demonstrates how the **++** operator moves the iterator to the next item in the list, and how the ***** operator accesses the object referred to by the iterator.

Note the absence of a constructor—I did not know how to define it. For **Iterator** to work with a **Set**, I would have to declare **Iterator(Set&);**. To make it work with a **Bag**, I would need **Iterator(Bag&);**. I could certainly have both constructors in the class, but that implies that every time I invent a new type of container that can be iterated, I am going to have to modify the **Iterator**. This violates the open-closed principle. I would like to have **Iterator** closed for modification, regardless of how many new types of containers I create.

Another option would be to create separate iterators for each kind of container. I could have **SetIterator** for **Set**s, and **BagIterator** for **Bag**s. Then each could have its own constructor, which would take the correct kind of argument. However, it seems to me that clients of **Iterator** may not be interested in the type of container they are iterating. For example, I might like to write a function that accepts two **Iterator**s and creates a set of ordered pairs (see Listing 2-62). This function does not care whether the **Iterator**s were created from **Bag**s, **Set**s, **Stack**s or **Queue**s; it simply uses them to gain sequential access to each item and build a **Set** of ordered pairs.

Listing 2-62

Create **Pairs** from **Iterators**

```
template <class A, class B>
struct Pair
{
    Pair(A& theA, B& theB) : a(theA), b(theB) {}
    A a;
    B b;
};

template<class A, class B>
Set<Pair<A,B> > MakePairs(Iterator<A>& ia, Iterator<B>& ib)
{
    Set<Pair<A,B> > pairs;
    Iterator<B> bStart = ib; // save starting B iterator

    for (; ia; ia++)
    {
        for(; ib; ib++)
        {
            pairs.Add(Pair(*ia, *ib));
        }
        ib = bStart; // reset the B iterator.
    }
    return pairs;
}
```

There are at least two ways to have an iterator that can act polymorphically, as in Listing 2-62. Figure 2-18 shows them. The first way is to have **Iterator** use an abstract base, like **IterableContainer**, from which **Set** and **Bag** derive. The second is to have **Iterator** be the abstract base of derived iterators, such as **BagIterator** and **Iterator**, which know how to use their respective containers. Either of these techniques is workable, so deciding between them would be arbitrary. Rather than make an arbitrary decision at this point, we should probably continue to explore the problem. Perhaps we will stumble upon something that will force our hand one way or the other.

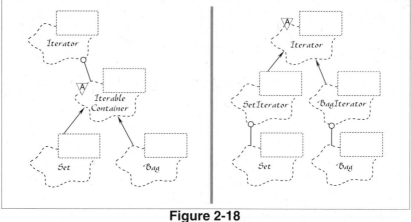

Figure 2-18
Possible Scenarios for a Polymorphic **Iterator**

Figure 2-18 uses a class icon with a dotted box in the upper right corner. These represent *parameterized classes*: classes that are templates whose parameters are, for the purposes of the diagram, irrelevant. We use these icons to show the relationships that must exist for all instantiations of the templates.

How should **Bag** and **Set** be implemented? We can choose from many different algorithms, each with its own advantages and disadvantages. We could use a linked list, allocating nodes from the heap and linking them together inside the container whenever we added a new item. This would allow the container to grow without bound, but might be a bit slow, and it runs the risk of exhausting memory. We could use a fixed-size array of items. This would probably be faster than allocating and deallocating individual nodes. Also the user could control exactly how much memory was to be used by the container. Once the container was successfully built, using it would not risk exhausting system memory.

Both of these approaches have merit, and both have disadvantages. For certain applications, the unbounded nature of a linked list would be appropriate. For others, the speed and safety of a vector would be more appropriate. It would be a shame to restrict our users to one form or the other. We would like to make both forms available, and allow users to choose between them according to their needs. Thus we can create four classes: **BoundedSet** and **BoundedBag**, which make use of a fixed-size vector of items, and **UnboundedSet** and **UnboundedBag**, which make use of a linked list.[13]

Some clients, however, will want to use our **Set**s and **Bag**s without caring if they are bounded or unbounded. Listing 2-63 shows an example of such a client. We do not want to force these clients to use particular kinds of **Sets** or **Bags**, nor do we want to force them to duplicate their code for each different kind. Therefore, we should make the **Set**s and **Bag**s polymorphic, as shown in Figure 2-19

Listing 2-63

Polymorphic use of **Set**

```
void DrawSet(Set<DisplayItem*> theSet)
{
    for (Iterator<DisplayItem*> di(theSet); di; di++)
        (*di)->Draw();
}
```

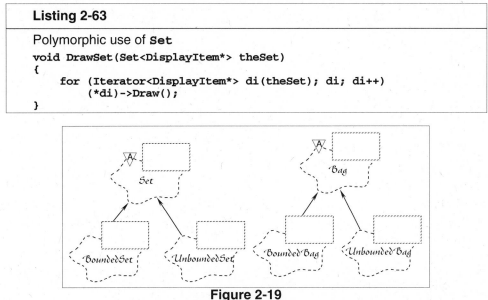

Figure 2-19
Polymorphic Structure of **Set** and **Bag**

What effect does this structure have on the **Iterator**? The details involved in iterating through a linked list are probably different from the details involved in iterating through a vector, so different implementations of **Iterator** will almost certainly be necessary. This tends to support the model that has **Iterator** as an abstract base, and variations of iterators are derived from it, as shown in Figure 2-20.

This structure also allows us to create new kinds of iterators when we invent new kinds of containers. Since we can expect containers such as **Stacks**, **Queues**, **Dequeues**, and **Trees** to be created over time, it seems most sensible to choose this model.

However, there is a problem with this approach: generic iterators cannot be created. You must create the kind of iterator that corresponds to the kind of container you are using. This is not a big problem if you *know* the kind of container you are using, but many clients will not want to deal with that knowledge. Listing 2-63 shows such a client. The

---

13. This partitioning is very similar to that used in the "Booch Components" Class Library.

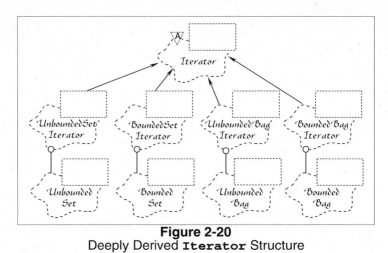

Figure 2-20
Deeply Derived **Iterator** Structure

function in this listing does not know what kind of **Set** it is using, nor does it care—but it does want to create an iterator for the set.

We can address this problem by putting a **MakeIterator** method in each of the container classes, and declaring it as pure in the abstract container classes **Set** and **Bag**. Each concrete container class implements this function to return a newly created iterator of the appropriate sort. Listing 2-64 is an example of how this function would be implemented in the **BoundedBag** container.

Listing 2-64

```
BoundedBag::MakeIterator
Iterator* BoundedBag::MakeIterator() const
{
    Iterator* ip = new BoundedBagIterator(*this);
    return ip;
}
```

Listing 2-65 shows how the clients of a container can use this function to make iterators, even when they don't know what kind of iterators they are making.

Listing 2-65

Polymorphic use of **Set** with **MakeIterator**
```
void DrawSet(Set<DisplayItem*> theSet)
{
    Iterator* dip = theSet.MakeIterator();
    Iterator& di = *dip;
    for (; di; di++)
        (*di)->Draw();
    delete dip;
}
```

The code in Listing 2-65 is too complex. The risk for memory leaks is large. We have placed a memory-management burden upon the user, even though memory management has nothing to do with the abstract nature of an **Iterator**. We would prefer that the user be able to write code such as Listing 2-63 while still being able to create **Iterator**s without knowing the kind of container that they are being created for.

We can achieve this goal by employing a hybrid of the two models shown in Figure 2-18, and combining it with the **MakeIterator** idea. Figures 2-21 and 2-22 show this scheme. **Iterator** becomes a concrete class that contains an **IteratorMechanism** by value, so it is responsible for managing its memory. **IteratorMechanism** is an abstract class whose derivatives know how to iterate over their corresponding concrete container classes. All container classes must derive from the abstract base class **IterableContainer**, into which we have factored the pure virtual **Make-IteratorMechanism** function. When an **Iterator** is created, it automatically creates an **IteratorMechanism** from the **IterableContainer** that was passed in. **Iterator** then delegates the standard iterator functions to that **Iterator-Mechanism**. This scheme makes the code in Listing 2-63 valid.

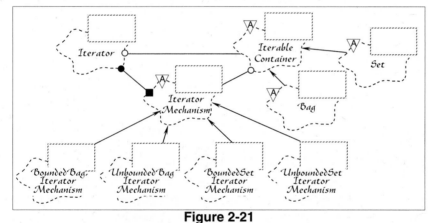

Figure 2-21
IteratorMechanism Class Diagram

This model also settles our dilemma regarding whether **Bag** should be a private base of **Set** or not. Since **IterableContainer** must be a *public* base of both **Bag** and **Set**, and since the private inheritance of **Bag** into **Set** would not make **Iterable-Container** a public base of **Set**, then **Set** would have to multiply inherit directly from **IterableContainer**. **Set** would derive from **IterableContainer** twice, and thus **IterableContainer** would have to be a virtual base of **Bag** and **Set** (see Figure 2-23). This seems like a needless complication. Virtual inheritance adds a small time and space overhead, and in many compilers (as of this writing), it disallows downcasting.[14] Since there are no factors compelling us to use this model, and since it has these disadvantages, we will opt for the model that gives **Bag** and **Set** a common base that supplies their interfaces.

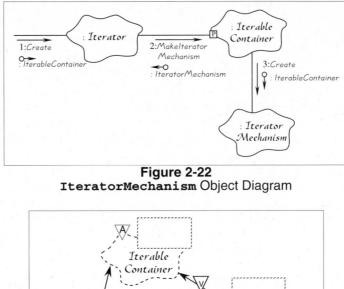

Figure 2-22
IteratorMechanism Object Diagram

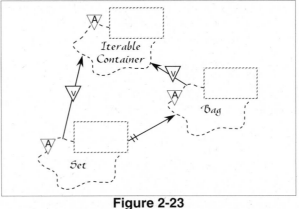

Figure 2-23
Private inheritance of **Bag** into **Set** forces virtual
inheritance of **IterableContainer**

The model in Figure 2-24 allows users to accept **MemberContainers** instead of simply **Bag**s or **Set**s. Thus, they can write code that can use a container without knowing whether it is a **Bag**, or a **Set**, or some other kind of **MemberContainer**. In fact, we can change the intersection, union, and difference operators so that they take **MemberContainers** instead of **Set**s or **Bag**s. This means that we can take the union or intersection between a **Set** and a **Bag**.

The code for **BoundedSet** and **BoundedBag** will be very similar: It will be a vector implementation. The same is true for the code of **UnboundedBag** and **UnboundedSet**, except that it will be a linked-list implementation. We would prefer not to write the vector and linked-list code twice. The most obvious solution might be to create subclasses of **MemberContainer**, one bounded and one unbounded (see Figure 2-25).

---

14. The time and space overhead is very small. Implementations may vary, but space for an extra pointer, and time to dereference that pointer for each member access is a reasonable guess. Downcasting from virtual base classes is possible in those compilers that support **dynamic_cast**

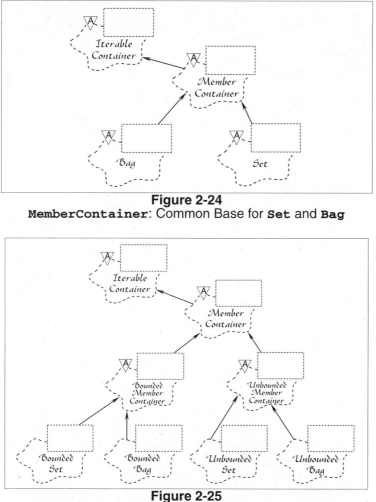

Figure 2-24
MemberContainer: Common Base for **Set** and **Bag**

Figure 2-25
MemberContainer: Common Base for **Set** and **Bag**

This neatly separates the bounded from the unbounded forms. It also allows the linked-list code to be kept in **UnboundedMemberContainer**, and the vector code to be contained in **BoundedMemberContainer**. However, there is no abstract **Set** or **Bag** class in this hierarchy. This is a problem, because we would like our clients to be able to use **Set** or **Bag** without knowing that they are bounded or unbounded.

We could solve this by multiply inheriting **BoundedSet** from **Set** and **BoundedMemberContainer**, but this means that **MemberContainer** would be inherited twice: once through **BoundedMemberContainer** and once through **Set**. Thus, **MemberContainer** would have to be a virtual base.

If this were the only solution, we would accept it, but there is another solution that does not involve virtual inheritance. We can create *implementation classes* that will supply a vector implementation for **BoundedSet** and **BoundedBag**, and a linked-list implementation for **UnboundedBag** and **UnboundedSet**. Let's call the set supplying the "bounded" implementation **Vector**, and the set supplying the "unbounded" implementation **List**. Figure 2-26 shows how we can use private inheritance to provide these implementations to the **Bag** and derivatives.

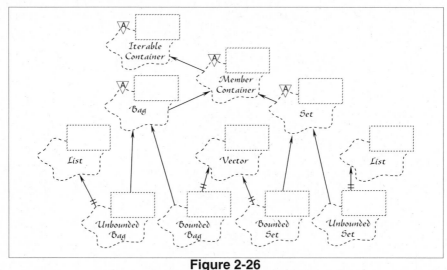

Figure 2-26
Private Inheritance of **List** and **Vector** into the **Bag** and **Set** classes

We have used private inheritance so that users of **UnboundedSet** don't see the interface for **List**. **UnboundedSet** simply uses the methods of **List** to implement the functionality of a **Set**. The same is true for **UnboundedBag**. The functionalities of **UnboundedBag** and **UnboundedSet** are different, even though they share the same basic implementation. The small differences are coded into the "glue" code within the methods of **UnboundedSet** and **UnboundedBag**.

Anonymous Containers

We now have a flexible hierarchy of containers. Users can choose the most appropriate kind of container for their work, while preserving for their clients the flexibility of not knowing the kind of containers chosen. Clients can write functions that deal with **Set**, or **Bag**, or even **MemberContainer**, and these functions will happily accept any of the appropriate concrete forms. Also, we can build **Iterator** objects without regard to the type of container upon which they are iterating. Users can build an **Iterator** for any container that derives from **IterableContainer**.

However, there is still a problem with this design. Consider Listing 2-66, which shows a function **f** that takes two **Set**s as input and returns an output **Set**.

Listing 2-66

Using an anonymous **Set**

```
Set<int> f(const Set<int>& s1, const Set<int>& s2)
{
    Set<int> x = s1+s2;
...
    return x;
}

UnboundedSet<int> ui1;
UnboundedSet<int> ui2;
set<int> y = f(ui1, ui2);
```

What kind of **Set** does **f** return? Is it bounded or unbounded? From the code at the bottom of Listing 2-66 we might think that it ought to be an **UnboundedSet**, since that's what its arguments were. However, as written, this code is illegal. **Set** is abstract, and no instance can be created. Clearly we would like to be able to return a **Set** without having to know what kind of **Set** it is. We would also like to operate on two or more **Set**s, producing resultant **Set**s whose type depends upon the arguments. Is there a way to do this?

There is a way. It is an adaptation of Coplien's "envelope/letter" idiom.[15] (See Figure 2-27). In this scheme, **MemberContainer** is not abstract; it is a concrete class that contains a pointer to a different instance of a **MemberContainer**. Presumably this other instance will be one of the concrete bounded or unbounded sets or bags. Any calls made to a containing **MemberContainer** are delegated to the contained **MemberContainer**. Both **Set** and **Bag** will inherit this ability, so they also lose their abstract nature and become concrete classes that can act as surrogates for a real concrete object.

Consider Listing 2-67. Note that **MemberContainer** has only one public constructor, the copy constructor. This constructor makes a copy of its argument by invoking the virtual **Clone** function and then assigning that copy to **itsRep**. Virtual **Clone** functions are written to return a copy of their object, typically by invoking the copy constructor on **this**. Nearly all other functions of **MemberContainer** simply delegate themselves through the contained **MemberContainer** in **itsRep**. The three binary operators return values that are **MemberContainer** objects. These values will be copy-constructed from some concrete derivative of **MemberContainer**, so the returned value will be a surrogate for the copied container.

Now consider the implementation for **operator+** at the bottom of Listing 2-67. This function creates a temporary copy of **this** using the **MemberContainer** copy constructor. Thus, this temporary object will act as a surrogate for the type of **this**. Then the function invokes **operator+=** and returns the result. Thus, the result of the operator

---

15. James O. Coplien, *Advanced C++ Programming Styles and Idioms* (Addison Wesley, 1992), section 5.5, p. 133.

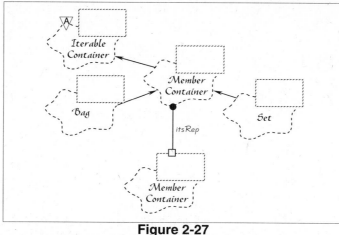

Figure 2-27
Envelope/Letter Configuration of `MemberContainer`

is a **MemberContainer** object that delegates its operations to an object of the same type as **this**.

These changes make the code in Listing 2-66 perfectly legal. Functions can now create containers without knowing their type, and return them as function values.

Listing 2-67

```
membcont
template <class T>
class MemberContainer : public IterableContainer<T>
{
  public:
    MemberContainer(const MemberContainer<T>& t);
    virtual ~MemberContainer() {delete itsRep;};
    MemberContainer<T>& operator=(const MemberContainer<T>&);

    // Primary Methods
    virtual void     Add(const T& t)      {itsRep->Add(t);}
    virtual int      Remove(const T& t)   {return itsRep->Remove(t);}
    virtual void     Clear()              {itsRep->Clear();}

    virtual int IsMember(const T& t) const
    {return itsRep->IsMember(t);}

    virtual int Cardinality() const
    {return itsRep->Cardinality();}

    virtual MemberContainer<T>* Clone()  const
    {return new MemberContainer<T>(*this);}

    // Operators
    MemberContainer<T>& operator+= (const MemberContainer<T>&);
        //union
```

```
Listing 2-67  (Continued)
```

```
membcont
    MemberContainer<T>& operator-= (const MemberContainer<T>&);
        //difference

    MemberContainer<T>& operator&= (const MemberContainer<T>&);
        //intersect

    MemberContainer<T>  operator+ (const MemberContainer<T>&) const;
    MemberContainer<T>  operator- (const MemberContainer<T>&) const;
    MemberContainer<T>  operator& (const MemberContainer<T>&) const;

  protected:
    MemberContainer() : itsRep(0) {};
    void CopyItems(const MemberContainer&);

  private:
    virtual IteratorMechanism<T>* MakeIteratorMechanism() const
            {return itsRep->MakeIteratorMechanism();}
    MemberContainer<T>* itsRep;
}

template <class T>
MemberContainer<T> MemberContainer<T>::operator+(const
MemberContainer<T>&
theMemberContainer) const
{
    MemberContainer<T> x = *this; // invoke copy constructor
    x += theMemberContainer;
    return x;
}
```

Summary of the Container Case Study

By exploiting the techniques described in this chapter and paying special attention to clo-sure, abstract interfaces, hiding of details, polymorphism, and factoring, we have created a group of container classes that are easy and natural to use. Clients of the containers can choose the type of container they need, without constraining those functions that don't want to know about the details of the containment.

Applying the Liskov Substitution Principle makes all the variations of the abstract base classes well behaved. No client that accepts arguments belonging to an abstract type will be confused by the behavior of any of the concrete derivatives.

Finally, the functions, classes, and modules that form this hierarchy are closed. We can add new types of containers to the structure without having to modify any existing code. We can fix bugs in individual modules without creating effects that ripple through the rest of the structure.

The complete listings for these classes appear at the end of this chapter.

Summary

In this chapter we have discussed some of the techniques of OOD that help us manage the complexity of our designs. The most important of these techniques is abstraction. To support abstraction, we discussed grouping, hiding, polymorphism, and the Liskov Substitution Principle.

We also discussed the benefits of the open-closed principle: By using abstraction, grouping, and hiding appropriately, we can close whole functions and classes against maintenance and modifications while allowing them to be extended through inheritance.

We saw many designs expressed in both C++ code and in Booch notation. We saw how the Booch notation provided a dense and efficient medium for the expression and manipulation of OOD concepts. We also saw how those concepts could be directly translated into C++ code.

The most important thing we learned in this chapter was that complexity management comes at a cost. It is not free, *and it does not arise naturally out of OOD or C++.* An effort to manage complexity will cost you in lines of code, size of executables, and the time it takes to complete a design. It requires planning, forethought, and the willingness to explore the problem domain. It requires the willingness to throw out ideas that may have seemed good at the start, but later proved to be inappropriate. It requires the willingness to spend time up front on issues that will not pay back until later in the project—but pay back they will, in lines of code, bytes of executables, and time for implementation and maintenance. *The costs of managing complexity are recoverable many times over.*

These costs are independent of OOD. The management of complexity incurs these costs regardless of the methodology used to achieve it. OOD helps to minimize these costs, however, and provides what may be the most effective tools for managing complexity to date.

In the 1960s there was little, if any, software engineering: "Every man did what was right in his own eyes."[16]   In the 1970s the problems due to software complexity had increased to the point that we were searching for a solution. Modular programming and structured programming were hot topics. Programmers argued endlessly about whether or not they should use `goto` statements, and how many bytes of object code should be in a module. In the 1980s the true magnitude of software complexity was becoming apparent. Many of us began to search for a more formal and all-encompassing methodology. The structured analysis and design methodologies became popular, and everyone was drawing data flow diagrams, structure charts, and entity-relationship diagrams. Now it is the 1990s and we are all chitter-chattering about object-oriented toasters and bedwarmers. There is nothing wrong with this; it's good, and it shows that we are making progress. It shows that we are dealing with the issues of complexity management.

---

16. Judges 17:6, New American Standard Bible.

But it also shows something else: No single methodology or technique will be enough. As time passes, we will need better and better tools to help us manage the geometric increase in software complexity. So I wonder, What will be grabbing our attention in the coming decades (other than fixing all the programs that are going to break when the century turns, of course)?[17]

Exercises

1. What is the definition of abstraction?

2. What is the open-closed principle?

3. Modify the program in Listing 2-15 through Listing 2-46 so that product complexity is calculated as a function of the number of components contained in the product. If the product has 1–20 components, then the price multiplier is 1.00. From 21–100 components the modifier is 1.10. From 101 and up yields a 1.20 multiplier.

4. Which of the following statements is equivalent to the Liskov Substitution Principle:
    a. Base classes should do no less than derived classes.
    b. Base classes should be usable where derived classes are used.
    c. Derived classes should be able to do everything a base class is able to do.
    d. Derived classes should be usable wherever base classes are used.

5. Given the classes **RealNumber** and **ComplexNumber**, which statement ought to be true?
    a. **ComplexNumber** derives from **RealNumber**.
    b. **RealNumber** derives from **ComplexNumber**.
    c. **ComplexNumber** contains **RealNumber**.
    d. **ComplexNumber** and **RealNumber** are unrelated.

6. Consider the following class diagram. Factor the classes and employ the Liskov Substitution Principle.

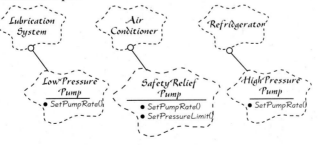

---

17. Arthur C. Clarke, *The Ghost from the Grand Banks* (Bantam, 1990), Chapter 4, "The Century Syndrome."

7. Justify the use of friendship in the following diagram.

8. Use the **UnboundedSet** class from the listings at the end of the chapter to write the "Sieve of Eratosthenes" algorithm in order to calculate all the prime numbers from 2–1000.
    - Load the integers 2-1000 into set P.
    - For each element E of P, (E<$\sqrt{1000}$)
    - Remove all multiples of E from P.

Container Class Listings

The complete source files for the container classes follow. I have successfully used these classes in many projects, and I find them quite useful. Although I cannot guarantee that they are free from bugs, and must stipulate that you use them at your own risk, I can say that it has been quite awhile since I have found any problems with them.

I often mix these classes with third-party class libraries. For example, for one project I needed the object-persistence mechanisms of the Rogue Wave Tools++ library. I did not want to have to use their **RWSet** directly, since it was neither template-driven, nor did it interface nicely with my iterator and anonymous container type schemes. So I wrapped the implementation of **RWSet** in a derivative of **Set** named **PersistentSet**. **PersistentSet** was Liskov-compatible with **Set**, but had the persistence of **RWSet**.

These files were last compiled with Borland C++ 3.1.

---
itercont.h

```
#ifndef COMPONENTS_ITERABLE_CONAINER_H
#define COMPONENTS_ITERABLE_CONAINER_H
//----------------------------------------------------
// Name
//   IterableContainer
//
// Description
//   This class is an Absract class which describes the interface of a
//   IterableContainer which is a container which can be iterated over
```

```
//   with an IteratorMechanism.
//
template <class T> class Iterator;
template <class T> class IteratorMechanism;

template <class T>
class IterableContainer
{
  public:
    // Cannonicals
    virtual ~IterableContainer() {};

  private:
    virtual IteratorMechanism<T>* MakeIteratorMechanism() const = 0;

  friend Iterator<T>;
};

//---------------------------------------------------------
// Name
//   IteratorMechanism
//
// Description
//   This is a private class used by IterableContainer and
//   Iterator.  It represents the mechanism by which
//   Iterators are operated.  IterableContainers provide a
//   private method which returns a pointer to an appropriate
//   derivative of IteratorMechanism.  Iterator calls this
//   method on its IterableContainer and then employs it to iterate
//   over the IterableContainer.
//
//   This allows the Iterator to be unaware of the type of
//   IterableContainer it is iterating over.
//
template <class T>
class IteratorMechanism
{
  private:
    virtual void* IsNotEmpty() const = 0;
    virtual void  Next() = 0;
    virtual T     Item() = 0;

    virtual IteratorMechanism<T>* Clone() const = 0;

    // Assignment semantics are private and degenerate.
    IteratorMechanism<T>& operator= (const IteratorMechanism<T>&);

  friend IterableContainer<T>;
  friend Iterator<T>;
};

template <class T>
class Iterator
{
  public:
    Iterator(const IterableContainer<T>& theIterableContainer)
    {itsMechanism = theIterableContainer.MakeIteratorMechanism();}

    virtual ~Iterator() {delete itsMechanism;}

    Iterator(const Iterator<T>& theIterator)
    {itsMechanism = theIterator.itsMechanism->Clone();}

    Iterator& operator= (const Iterator<T>& theIterator)
    {
```

```
            delete itsMechanism;
            itsMechanism=theIterator.itsMechanism->Clone()
            return *this;
        }

        virtual operator void*() const
        {return itsMechanism->IsNotEmpty();}

        virtual void operator++(int)    {itsMechanism->Next();}
        virtual T    operator*()        {return itsMechanism->Item();}

    private:
        IteratorMechanism<T> *itsMechanism;
};
#endif
```

membcont.h

```
#ifndef COMPONENTS_MEMBER_CONTAINER_H
#define COMPONENTS_MEMBER_CONTAINER_H
#include "componen/itercont.h"
//-------------------------------------------------
// Name
//  MemberContainer
//
// Description
//  This class is an ADT which describes the interface of a
//  MemberContainer.  A MemberContainer is a container which allows
//  members to be added and removed and tested for membership.
//  Members can be added in any order and removed in any order.
//  MemberContainers can be anonymously copy constructed.
//  This means that you can say:
//
//      void f(MemberContainer<T>& s)
//      {
//         MemberContainer<T> copy = s; // anonymous copy
//      }
//
//  An anonymous membcont maintains a pointer (itsRep) to the
//  MemberContainer of the appropriate type, and delegates all calls
//  to it.  This allows the operators to returns anonymous
//  MemberContainers.
//
//  What is an anonymous MemberContainer?  Remember, MemberContainer
//  is a class without an implementation.  It does not know how to
//  store elements, it simply provides an interface that other
//  classes can inherit.
//
//  Let us say that we have a derivative of MemberContainer called
//  UnboundedSet.  This class uses a linked list to hold its
//  elements.  Now we can say:
//
//      UnboundedSet<int> x;
//      MemberContainer<int> copy = x;
//
//  The membcont "copy" is an anonymous membcont which refers to
//  (itsRep points to) a copy of x...
//
template <class T>
class MemberContainer : public IterableContainer<T>
{
  public:
    MemberContainer(const MemberContainer<T>& t);
```

```
            // copy constructor.  MUST NOT BE CALLED FROM DERIVED
            // COPY CONSTRUCTORS!!!  Infinite recursion will be the
            // result....
        virtual ~MemberContainer() {delete itsRep;};
        MemberContainer<T>& operator=(const MemberContainer<T>&);

        virtual void     Add(const T& t)      {itsRep->Add(t);}
        virtual int      Remove(const T& t) {return itsRep->Remove(t);}
        virtual void     Clear()              {itsRep->Clear();}

        virtual int IsMember(const T& t) const
        {return itsRep->IsMember(t);}

        virtual int Cardinality() const
        {return itsRep->Cardinality();}

        virtual MemberContainer<T>* Clone()  const
        {return new MemberContainer<T>(*this);}

        MemberContainer<T>& operator+= (const MemberContainer<T>&);
            //union

        MemberContainer<T>& operator-= (const MemberContainer<T>&);
            //difference

        MemberContainer<T>& operator&= (const MemberContainer<T>&);
            //intersection

        MemberContainer<T>  operator+  (const MemberContainer<T>&) const;
        MemberContainer<T>  operator-  (const MemberContainer<T>&) const;
        MemberContainer<T>  operator&  (const MemberContainer<T>&) const;

    protected:
        // copy constructor is protected and degenerate.
        MemberContainer() : itsRep(0) {};
        void CopyItems(const MemberContainer&);

    private:
        virtual IteratorMechanism<T>* MakeIteratorMechanism() const
        {return itsRep->MakeIteratorMechanism();}
            // makes an iterator mechanism for use in a Iterator.

        MemberContainer<T>* itsRep;
};
#include "componen/membcont.cpp"
#endif
```

membcont.cpp

```
#include "components/membcont.h"
template <class T>
MemberContainer<T>::MemberContainer(const MemberContainer<T>& t)
: itsRep(0)
{
    if (t.itsRep)
    {
        itsRep = t.itsRep->Clone();
    }
    else
    {
        itsRep = t.Clone();
    }
}
```

```
template <class T>
MemberContainer<T>& MemberContainer<T>::
operator=(const MemberContainer<T>& theMemberContainer)
{
    if (this != &theMemberContainer)
    {
        Clear();
        CopyItems(theMemberContainer);
    }
    return *this;
}

template <class T>
void MemberContainer<T>::
CopyItems(const MemberContainer<T>& theMemberContainer)
{
    Iterator<T> i(theMemberContainer);
    for (; i; i++)
    {
        Add(*i);
    }
}

template <class T>
MemberContainer<T>& MemberContainer<T>::
operator+= (const MemberContainer<T>& theMemberContainer)
{
    Iterator<T> i(theMemberContainer);
    for (; i; i++)
    {
        Add(*i);
    }
    return *this;
}

template <class T>
MemberContainer<T>& MemberContainer<T>::
operator-= (const MemberContainer<T>& theMemberContainer)
{
    Iterator<T> i(theMemberContainer);
    for (; i; i++)
    {
        Remove(*i);
    }
    return *this;
}

template <class T>
MemberContainer<T>& MemberContainer<T>::
operator&= (const MemberContainer<T>& theMemberContainer)
{
    MemberContainer<T>& difference = *Clone();
    difference -= theMemberContainer;
    operator-=(difference);
    return *this;
}

template <class T>
MemberContainer<T> MemberContainer<T>::
operator+(const MemberContainer<T>& theMemberContainer) const
{
    MemberContainer<T> x = *this;
    x += theMemberContainer;
    return x;
}
```

```
}

template <class T>
MemberContainer<T> MemberContainer<T>::
operator-(const MemberContainer<T>& theMemberContainer) const
{
    MemberContainer<T> x = *this;
    x -= theMemberContainer;
    return x;
}

template <class T>
MemberContainer<T> MemberContainer<T>::
operator&(const MemberContainer<T>& theMemberContainer) const
{
    MemberContainer<T> x = *this;
    x &= theMemberContainer;
    return x;
}
```

---

set.h

```
#ifndef COMPONENTS_SET_H
#define COMPONENTS_SET_H
#include "componen/membcont.h"
//-----------------------------------------------
// Name
//    Set
//
// Description
//    This class is an ADT which describes the interface of a Set.  A
//    Set is a container which does not allow duplicates, and which
//    does not keep the contained objects in any particular order.
//
//    Sets can be anonymously copy constructed.  This means that you
//    can say:
//        void f(Set<T>& s)
//        {
//            Set<T> copy = s; // anonymous copy
//        }
//
//    An anonymous set maintains a pointer (itsRep) to the Set of
//    the appropriate type, and delegates all calls to it.  This allows
//    the operators to returns anonymous sets.
//
//    What is an anonymous set?  Remember, Set is a class without
//    an implementation.  It does not know how to store elements, it
//    simply provides an interface that other classes can inherit.
//    Let us say that we have a derivative of Set called UnboundedSet.
//    This set uses a linked list to hold its elements.
//    Now we can say:
//
//        UnboundedSet<int> x;
//        Set<int> copy = x;
//
//    The set "copy" is an anonymous set which refers to (itsRep points
//    to) a copy of x...
//
template <class T>
class Set : public MemberContainer<T>
{
  public:
    Set(const Set<T>& t);
```

```cpp
        // copy constructor.  MUST NOT BE CALLED FROM DERIVED
        // COPY CONSTRUCTORS!!!  Infinite recursion will be the
        // result....
    Set(const MemberContainer<T>&);
    virtual ~Set() {};
    Set<T>& operator=(const MemberContainer<T>&);

    virtual MemberContainer<T>* Clone() const
    {return new Set<T>(*this);}

  protected:
    // copy constructor is protected and degenerate.
    Set() {};

  private:
};
#include "componen/set.cpp"
#endif
```

set.cpp

```cpp
#include "components/set.h"
template <class T>
Set<T>::Set(const Set<T>& t)
: MemberContainer<T>(t)
{}

template <class T>
Set<T>::Set(const MemberContainer<T>& t)
: MemberContainer<T>(t)
{}

template <class T>
Set<T>& Set<T>::operator=(const MemberContainer<T>& theSet)
{
    MemberContainer<T>::operator=(theSet);
    return *this;
}
```

bag.h

```cpp
#ifndef COMPONENTS_BAG_H
#define COMPONENTS_BAG_H
#include "componen/membcont.h"
//-------------------------------------------------
// Name
//   Bag
//
// Description
//   This class is an ADT which describes the interface of a Bag.  A /
//   Bag is a container which allows duplicates, and which does not
//   keep the contained objects in any particular order.
//
//   Bags can be anonymously copy constructed.  This means that you
//   can say:
//      void f(Bag<T>& s)
//      {
//        Bag<T> copy = s; // anonymous copy
//      }
//
//   An anonymous bag maintains a pointer (itsRep) to the Bag of
//   the appropriate type, and delegates all calls to it.  This allows
```

```
//    the operators to returns anonymous bags.
//
//    What is an anonymous bag?  Remember, Bag is a class without
//    an implementation.  It does not know how to store elements, it
//    simply provides an interface that other classes can inherit.
//    Let us say that we have a derivative of Bag called UnboundedBag.
//    This bag uses a linked list to hold its elements.
//    Now we can say:
//
//        UnboundedBag<int> x;
//        Bag<int> copy = x;
//
//    The bag "copy" is an anonymous set which refers to (itsRep points
//    to) a copy of x...
//
template <class T>
class Bag : public MemberContainer<T>
{
  public:
    Bag(const Bag<T>& t);
        // copy constructor.  MUST NOT BE CALLED FROM DERIVED
        // COPY CONSTRUCTORS!!!  Infinite recursion will be the
        // result....
    Bag(const MemberContainer<T>&);
    virtual ~Bag() {};
    Bag<T>& operator=(const MemberContainer<T>&);

    virtual MemberContainer<T>* Clone()const
    {return new Bag<T>(*this);}

  protected:
    // copy constructor is protected and degenerate.
    Bag() {};

  private:
};
#include "componen/bag.cpp"
#endif
```

bag.cpp

```
#include "components/bag.h"
template <class T>
Bag<T>::Bag(const Bag<T>& t)
: MemberContainer<T>(t)
{}

template <class T>
Bag<T>::Bag(const MemberContainer<T>& t)
: MemberContainer<T>(t)
{}

template <class T>
Bag<T>& Bag<T>::operator=(const MemberContainer<T>& theBag)
{
    MemberContainer<T>::operator=(theBag);
    return *this;
}
```

list.h

```
#ifndef CONTAINER_LIST_H
#define CONTAINER_LIST_H
template <class T> class Node
{
  public:
    Node(T theValue, Node<T>* theForwardLink,
                     Node<T>* theBackwardLink)
    : itsValue(theValue)
    , itsForwardLink(theForwardLink)
    , itsBackwardLink(theBackwardLink)
    {}
    Node<T>* itsForwardLink;
    Node<T>* itsBackwardLink;
    T itsValue;
};

template <class T> class List
{
    friend class ListIterator<T>;

  public:
    List() : itsFirstNode(0), itsLastNode(0), itsCardinality(0) {}
    ~List();

    void        AddFront(const T&);
    void        AddBack(const T&);
    Node<T>*    Find(const T&) const;
    void        Delete(Node<T>*);
    Node<T>*    GetLastNode() const {return itsLastNode;}
    Node<T>*    GetFirstNode() const {return itsFirstNode;}
    int         GetCardinality() const {return itsCardinality;}
    virtual void Clear();

  private:
    Node<T>* itsFirstNode;
    Node<T>* itsLastNode;
    int itsCardinality;

    // Copy semantics are private and degenerate
    List(const List<T>&);
    List<T>& operator=(const List<T>&);
};

template <class T> class ListIterator
{
  public:
    ListIterator(const List<T>& l) {itsCurrentNode=l.itsFirstNode;}
    ListIterator(const ListIterator<T>& li)
    : itsCurrentNode(li.itsCurrentNode)
    {}

    ~ListIterator() {}
    ListIterator<T> operator= (const ListIterator<T>& li)
    {itsCurrentNode = li.itsCurrentNode; return *this;}

    void* IsNotEmpty() const {return itsCurrentNode;}
    void Next()
    {
        if (itsCurrentNode)
            itsCurrentNode = itsCurrentNode->itsForwardLink;
    }
```

```
        Node<T>* Item() {return itsCurrentNode;}

    private:
        Node<T>* itsCurrentNode;
};
#include "componen/list.cpp"
#endif
```

list.cpp

```
template <class T>
List<T>::~List()
{
    Node<T>*p = itsFirstNode;
    Node<T>*n = 0;
    for (; p; p=n)
    {
        n = p->itsForwardLink;
        delete p;
    }
}

template <class T>
void List<T>::AddFront(const T& theValue)
{
    Node<T>* p = new Node<T>(theValue, itsFirstNode, 0);
    if (itsFirstNode != 0)
        itsFirstNode->itsBackwardLink = p;
    else
        itsLastNode = p;
    itsFirstNode = p;
    itsCardinality++;
}

template <class T>
void List<T>::AddBack(const T& theValue)
{
    Node<T>* p = new Node<T>(theValue, 0, itsLastNode);
    if (itsLastNode != 0)
        itsLastNode->itsForwardLink = p;
    else
        itsFirstNode = p;
    itsLastNode = p;
    itsCardinality++;
}

template <class T>
Node<T>* List<T>::Find(const T& theValue) const
{
    Node<T>* p = itsFirstNode;
    Node<T>* found = 0;
    for (; !found && p; p=p->itsForwardLink)
    {
        if (p->itsValue == theValue)
            found = p;
    }
    return found;
}

template <class T>
void List<T>::Clear()
{
    Node<T>*p = itsFirstNode;
```

```
        Node<T>*n = 0;
        for (; p; p=n)
        {
            n = p->itsForwardLink;
             delete p;
        }
        itsFirstNode = itsLastNode = 0;
        itsCardinality = 0;
}

template <class T>
void List<T>::Delete(Node<T>* theNode)
{
    if (theNode->itsForwardLink == 0)
         itsLastNode = theNode->itsBackwardLink;
    else
          theNode->itsForwardLink->itsBackwardLink =
              theNode->itsBackwardLink;

    if (theNode->itsBackwardLink == 0)
         itsFirstNode = theNode->itsForwardLink;
    else
         theNode->itsBackwardLink->itsForwardLink =
              theNode->itsForwardLink;
    itsCardinality--;
    delete theNode;
}
```

vector.h

```
#ifndef COMPONENTS_VECTOR_H
#define COMPONENTS_VECTOR_H
//------------------------------------------------------------
// Name
//   Vector
//
// Description
//   A doubly linked list with a fixed number of elements.
//
template <class T, int S> class VectorIterator;
template <class T, int S>
class Vector
{
  friend VectorIterator<T,S>;
  public:
    Vector();

    void AddFront(const T& theValue);
    void AddBack(const T& theValue);
    int  Find(const T& theValue) const;
    void Delete(int);
    int  GetCardinality() const {return itsCardinality;};
    int  GetFront() const {return itsFront;}
    int  GetBack() const {return itsBack;}

    void    Clear();

  private:
    T    itsVector[S];
    int itsForwardLinks[S];
    int itsBackwardLinks[S];
    int itsFreeList;
    int itsFront;
```

```
      int itsBack;
      int itsCardinality;
};

template <class T, int S>
class VectorIterator
{
  public:
    VectorIterator(const Vector<T, S>&);
    ~VectorIterator();
    VectorIterator(const VectorIterator<T, S>&);
    VectorIterator<T, S>& operator=(const VectorIterator<T,S>&);
    void* IsNotEmpty() const;
    void Next();
    T Item();

  private:
    const Vector<T,S>* itsVector;
    int itsCurrentSlot;
};
#include "componen/vector.cpp"
#endif
```

vector.cpp

```
#include "componen/vector.h"
#include <assert.h>
template <class T, int S>
Vector<T,S>::Vector()
{
    Clear();
}

template <class T, int S>
void Vector<T,S>::AddFront(const T& theValue)
{
    assert(itsFreeList != S);
    int freeSlot = itsFreeList;
    itsFreeList = itsForwardLinks[freeSlot];
    itsVector[freeSlot] = theValue;
    itsForwardLinks[freeSlot] = itsFront;
    itsBackwardLinks[freeSlot] = S;
    if (itsFront != S)
        itsBackwardLinks[itsFront] = freeSlot;
    itsFront = freeSlot;
    if (itsBack == S)
        itsBack = freeSlot;
    itsCardinality++;
}

template <class T, int S>
void Vector<T,S>::AddBack(const T& theValue)
{
    assert(itsFreeList != S);
    int freeSlot = itsFreeList;
    itsFreeList = itsForwardLinks[freeSlot];
    itsVector[freeSlot] = theValue;
    itsBackwardLinks[freeSlot] = itsBack;
    itsForwardLinks[freeSlot] = S;
    if (itsBack != S)
        itsForwardLinks[itsBack] = freeSlot;
    itsBack = freeSlot;
    if (itsFront == S)
```

```
            itsFront = freeSlot;
        itsCardinality++;
    }

    template <class T, int S>
    int Vector<T,S>::Find(const T& theValue) const
    {
        for (int p=itsFront;
                itsVector[p] != theValue && p != S;
                p=itsForwardLinks[p])
            {}
        return p;
    }

    template <class T, int S>
    void Vector<T,S>::Delete(int theNode)
    {
        assert(theNode < S);
        assert(theNode >= 0);
        int b = itsBackwardLinks[theNode];

        if (b == S)
            itsFront = itsForwardLinks[theNode];
        else
            itsForwardLinks[b] = itsForwardLinks[theNode];

        int f = itsForwardLinks[theNode];

        if (f == S)
            itsBack = itsBackwardLinks[theNode];
        else
            itsBackwardLinks[f] = itsBackwardLinks[theNode];

        itsForwardLinks[theNode] = itsFreeList;
        itsFreeList = theNode;
        itsCardinality--;
    }

    template <class T, int S>
    void Vector<T,S>::Clear()
    {
        itsCardinality = 0;
        itsFront = S;
        itsBack = S;
        itsFreeList = 0;
        for (int i=0; i<S; i++)
        {
            itsForwardLinks[i] = i+1;
            itsBackwardLinks[i] = i ? i-1 : S;
        }
    }

    template <class T, int S>
    VectorIterator<T,S>::
    VectorIterator(const Vector<T, S>& theVector)
    : itsVector(&theVector)
    , itsCurrentSlot(theVector.itsFront)
    {}

    template <class T, int S>
    VectorIterator<T,S>::
    ~VectorIterator()
    {}

    template <class T, int S>
```

```
VectorIterator<T,S>::
VectorIterator(const VectorIterator<T, S>& i)
: itsVector(i.itsVector)
, itsCurrentSlot(i.itsCurrentSlot)
{}

template <class T, int S>
VectorIterator<T,S>&
VectorIterator<T,S>::operator=(const VectorIterator<T,S>& i)
{
    itsVector = i.itsVector;
    itsCurrentSlot = i.itsCurrentSlot;
    return *this;
}

template <class T, int S>
void* VectorIterator<T,S>::IsNotEmpty() const
{
    return (itsCurrentSlot != S) ? (void*)1 : 0;
}

template <class T, int S>
void VectorIterator<T,S>:: Next()
{
    if (itsCurrentSlot != S)
        itsCurrentSlot = itsVector->itsForwardLinks[itsCurrentSlot];
}

template <class T, int S>
T VectorIterator<T,S>::Item()
{
    return itsVector->itsVector[itsCurrentSlot];
}
```

---

u_bag.h

```
#ifndef COMPONENTS_UNBOUNDED_BAG_H
#define COMPONENTS_UNBOUNDED_BAG_H
#include "componen/bag.h"
#include "componen/list.h"
//-------------------------------------------------------------
// Name
//   UnboundedBag
//
// Description
//   A Bag which has no limit on the number of members it can
//   contain.  This particular implementation is based upon the
//   List class.
//
// Bugs
//   The implementation is not particularily fast.  It uses a
//   a linked list and linear search.
//
template <class T> class UnboundedBagIteratorMechanism;
template <class T>
class UnboundedBag : public Bag<T>, private List<T>
{
    friend UnboundedBagIteratorMechanism<T>;
    public:
        UnboundedBag() : itsLastFound(0) {}
        virtual ~UnboundedBag() {}
        UnboundedBag(const UnboundedBag<T>&);
        UnboundedBag(const MemberContainer<T>&);
```

```cpp
    UnboundedBag& operator= (const UnboundedBag<T>&);
    UnboundedBag& operator= (const MemberContainer<T>&);

    virtual void     Add(const T& theValue)
        {AddFront(theValue);}
    virtual int      IsMember(const T& theValue) const
        {return ((Node<T>*)itsLastFound = Find(theValue)) != 0;}
    virtual int      Remove(const T&);

    virtual int      Cardinality() const
    {return List<T>::GetCardinality();}

    virtual void     Clear() {List<T>::Clear();}
    virtual MemberContainer<T>* Clone() const;

 private:
   IteratorMechanism<T>* MakeIteratorMechanism() const;
   Node<T>* itsLastFound;
};

template <class T>
class UnboundedBagIteratorMechanism : public IteratorMechanism<T>
                                    , private ListIterator<T>
{
 public:
   UnboundedBagIteratorMechanism(const UnboundedBag<T>& theBag)
   : ListIterator<T>(theBag) {}
   ~UnboundedBagIteratorMechanism() {}
   UnboundedBagIteratorMechanism(
       const UnboundedBagIteratorMechanism<T>& theIterator)
   : ListIterator<T>(theIterator)
   {}

   UnboundedBagIteratorMechanism<T>&
   operator=(const UnboundedBagIteratorMechanism& theIterator)
     {ListIterator<T>::operator=(theIterator); return *this;}

   void* IsNotEmpty() const {return ListIterator<T>::IsNotEmpty();}
   void  Next()                  {ListIterator<T>::Next();}
   T     Item();

   virtual IteratorMechanism<T>* Clone() const
   {
       return new UnboundedBagIteratorMechanism<T>(*this);
   }
};
#include "componen/u_bag.cpp"
#endif
```

u_bag.cpp

```cpp
#include "componen/u_bag.h"
#include <assert.h>
template <class T>
UnboundedBag<T>::UnboundedBag(const UnboundedBag<T>& theBag)
: itsLastFound(0)
{
    CopyItems(theBag);
}

template <class T>
UnboundedBag<T>::UnboundedBag(const MemberContainer<T>& theBag)
: itsLastFound(0)
```

```
{
    CopyItems(theBag);
}

template <class T>
UnboundedBag<T>& UnboundedBag<T>::operator= (const UnboundedBag<T>&
theBag)
{
    MemberContainer<T>::operator=(theBag);
    return *this;
}

template <class T>
UnboundedBag<T>& UnboundedBag<T>::
operator= (const MemberContainer<T>& theBag)
{
    MemberContainer<T>::operator=(theBag);
    return *this;
}

template <class T>
int UnboundedBag<T>::Remove(const T& theValue)
{
    int retval = 0;
    if (IsMember(theValue))
    {
        Delete(itsLastFound);
        retval=1;
    }
    return retval;
}

template <class T>
MemberContainer<T>* UnboundedBag<T>::Clone() const
{
    return new UnboundedBag<T>(*this);
}

template <class T>
IteratorMechanism<T>* UnboundedBag<T>::MakeIteratorMechanism() const
{
    return new UnboundedBagIteratorMechanism<T>(*this);
}

template <class T>
T UnboundedBagIteratorMechanism<T>::Item()
{
    assert(IsNotEmpty());
    Node<T>* n = ListIterator<T>::Item();
    return n->itsValue;
}
```

u_set.h

```
#ifndef COMPONENTS_UNBOUNDED_SET_H
#define COMPONENTS_UNBOUNDED_SET_H
#include "componen/set.h"
#include "componen/list.h"
//-----------------------------------------------------------
// Name
//   UnboundedSet
//
// Description
```

```
//   A Set which has no limit on the number of members it can
//   contain.  This particular implementation is based upon the
//   List class.
//
// Bugs
//   The implementation is not particularily fast.  It uses a
//   a linked list and linear search.
//
template <class T> class UnboundedIteratorMechanism;
template <class T>
class UnboundedSet : public Set<T>, private List<T>
{
  friend UnboundedIteratorMechanism<T>;
  public:
    UnboundedSet() : itsLastFound(0) {}
    virtual ~UnboundedSet() {}
    UnboundedSet(const UnboundedSet<T>&);
    UnboundedSet(const MemberContainer<T>&);
    UnboundedSet& operator= (const UnboundedSet<T>&);
    UnboundedSet& operator= (const MemberContainer<T>&);

    virtual void     Add(const T& theValue)
    {if (!IsMember(theValue)) AddFront(theValue);}

    virtual int      IsMember(const T& theValue) const
    {return ((Node<T>*)itsLastFound = Find(theValue)) != 0;}

    virtual int      Remove(const T&);

    virtual int      Cardinality() const
    {return List<T>::GetCardinality();}

    virtual void     Clear() {List<T>::Clear();}

    virtual MemberContainer<T>* Clone() const;

  private:
    IteratorMechanism<T>* MakeIteratorMechanism() const;
    Node<T>* itsLastFound;
};

template <class T>
class UnboundedIteratorMechanism : public IteratorMechanism<T>
                                 , private ListIterator<T>
{
  public:
    UnboundedIteratorMechanism(const UnboundedSet<T>& theSet)
    : ListIterator<T>(theSet) {}
    ~UnboundedIteratorMechanism() {}
    UnboundedIteratorMechanism(
        const UnboundedIteratorMechanism<T>& theIterator)
    : ListIterator<T>(theIterator)
    {}

    UnboundedIteratorMechanism<T>&
    operator=(const UnboundedIteratorMechanism& theIterator)
    {ListIterator<T>::operator=(theIterator); return *this;}

    void* IsNotEmpty() const {return ListIterator<T>::IsNotEmpty();}
    void  Next()             {ListIterator<T>::Next();}
    T Item();

    virtual IteratorMechanism<T>* Clone() const
    {
        return new UnboundedIteratorMechanism<T>(*this);
```

```
        }
    };
    #include "componen/u_set.cpp"
    #endif
```

u_set.cpp

```
#include "componen/u_set.h"
#include <assert.h>
template <class T>
UnboundedSet<T>::UnboundedSet(const UnboundedSet<T>& theSet)
: itsLastFound(0)
{
    CopyItems(theSet);
}

template <class T>
UnboundedSet<T>::UnboundedSet(const MemberContainer<T>& theSet)
: itsLastFound(0)
{
    CopyItems(theSet);
}

template <class T>
UnboundedSet<T>& UnboundedSet<T>::
operator= (const UnboundedSet<T>& theSet)
{
    Set<T>::operator=(theSet);
    return *this;
}

template <class T>
UnboundedSet<T>& UnboundedSet<T>::
operator= (const MemberContainer<T>& theSet)
{
    MemberContainer<T>::operator=(theSet);
    return *this;
}

template <class T>
int UnboundedSet<T>::Remove(const T& theValue)
{
    int retval = 0;
    if (IsMember(theValue))
    {
        Delete(itsLastFound);
        retval=1;
    }
    return retval;
}

template <class T>
MemberContainer<T>* UnboundedSet<T>::Clone() const
{
    return new UnboundedSet<T>(*this);
}

template <class T>
IteratorMechanism<T>* UnboundedSet<T>::MakeIteratorMechanism() const
{
    return new UnboundedIteratorMechanism<T>(*this);
}
```

```
template <class T>
T UnboundedIteratorMechanism<T>::Item()
{
    assert(IsNotEmpty());
    Node<T>* n = ListIterator<T>::Item();
    return n->itsValue;
}
```

b_set.h

```
#ifndef COMPONENTS_BOUNDED_SET_H
#define COMPONENTS_BOUNDED_SET_H
#include "componen/set.h"
#include "componen/vector.h"
//------------------------------------------------------------
// Name
//   BoundedSet
//
// Description
//   A Set which has a limit on the number of members it can
//   contain.  This particular implementation is based upon the
//   Vector class.
//
// Bugs
//   Probably a double linked list is a bit of an overkill for
//   the implementation.  It might slow things down a bit.
//
template <class T,int S> class BoundedIteratorMechanism;
template <class T, int S>
class BoundedSet : public Set<T>, private Vector<T, S>
{
    friend BoundedIteratorMechanism<T,S>;
  public:
    BoundedSet() : itsLastFound(0) {}
    virtual ~BoundedSet() {}
    BoundedSet(const BoundedSet<T,S>&);
    BoundedSet(const MemberContainer<T>&);
    BoundedSet& operator= (const BoundedSet<T,S>&);
    BoundedSet& operator= (const MemberContainer<T>&);

    virtual void     Add(const T& theValue)
    {if (!IsMember(theValue)) AddFront(theValue);}

    virtual int      IsMember(const T& theValue) const
    {return ((int)itsLastFound = Find(theValue)) != S;}

    virtual int      Remove(const T&);
    virtual int      Cardinality() const {return GetCardinality();}
    virtual void     Clear() {Vector<T,S>::Clear();}

    virtual MemberContainer<T>* Clone() const;

  private:
    IteratorMechanism<T>* MakeIteratorMechanism() const;
    int itsLastFound;
};

template <class T, int S>
class BoundedIteratorMechanism : public IteratorMechanism<T>
                                  , private VectorIterator<T,S>
{
  public:
    BoundedIteratorMechanism(const BoundedSet<T,S>& theSet)
```

```
        : VectorIterator<T,S>(theSet) {}
        ~BoundedIteratorMechanism() {}
        BoundedIteratorMechanism(
          const BoundedIteratorMechanism<T,S>& theIterator)
        : VectorIterator<T,S>(theIterator)
        {}

        BoundedIteratorMechanism<T,S>&
        operator=(const BoundedIteratorMechanism& theIterator)
        {VectorIterator<T,S>::operator=(theIterator); return *this;}

        void* IsNotEmpty() const
        {return VectorIterator<T,S>::IsNotEmpty();}

        void  Next() {VectorIterator<T,S>::Next();}
        T     Item();

        virtual IteratorMechanism<T>* Clone() const
        {
            return new BoundedIteratorMechanism<T,S>(*this);
        }
};
#include "componen/b_set.cpp"
#endif
```

b_set.cpp

```
#include "componen/b_set.h"
#include <assert.h>
template <class T, int S>
BoundedSet<T,S>::BoundedSet(const BoundedSet<T,S>& theSet)
: itsLastFound(S)
{
    CopyItems(theSet);
}

template <class T, int S>
BoundedSet<T,S>::BoundedSet(const MemberContainer<T>& theSet)
: itsLastFound(S)
{
    CopyItems(theSet);
}

template <class T, int S>
BoundedSet<T,S>& BoundedSet<T,S>::operator= (const BoundedSet<T,S>&
theSet)
{
    Vector<T,S>& v = *this;
    v = theSet;
    return *this;
}

template <class T, int S>
BoundedSet<T,S>& BoundedSet<T,S>::
operator= (const MemberContainer<T>& theSet)
{
    Set<T>::operator=(theSet);
    return *this;
}

template <class T, int S>
int BoundedSet<T,S>::Remove(const T& theValue)
{
```

```
    int retval = 0;
    if (IsMember(theValue))
    {
        Delete(itsLastFound);
        retval=1;
    }
    return retval;
}

template <class T, int S>
MemberContainer<T>* BoundedSet<T,S>::Clone() const
{
    return new BoundedSet<T,S>(*this);
}

template <class T, int S>
IteratorMechanism<T>* BoundedSet<T,S>::MakeIteratorMechanism() const
{
    return new BoundedIteratorMechanism<T,S>(*this);
}

template <class T, int S>
T BoundedIteratorMechanism<T,S>::Item()
{
    assert((VectorIterator<T,S>::IsNotEmpty()));
    return VectorIterator<T,S>::Item();
}
```

---

b_bag.h

```cpp
#ifndef COMPONENTS_BOUNDED_BAG_H
#define COMPONENTS_BOUNDED_BAG_H
#include "componen/bag.h"
#include "componen/vector.h"
//-------------------------------------------------------------
// Name
//   BoundedBag
//
// Description
//   A Bag which has a limit on the number of members it can
//   contain.  This particular implementation is based upon the
//   Vector class.
//
// Bugs
//   Probably a double linked list is a bit of an overkill for
//   the implementation.  It might slow things down a bit.
//
template <class T,int S> class BoundedBagIteratorMechanism;
template <class T, int S>
class BoundedBag : public Bag<T>, private Vector<T, S>
{
  friend BoundedBagIteratorMechanism<T,S>;
  public:
    BoundedBag() : itsLastFound(0) {}
    virtual ~BoundedBag() {}
    BoundedBag(const BoundedBag<T,S>&);
    BoundedBag(const MemberContainer<T>&);
    BoundedBag& operator= (const BoundedBag<T,S>&);
    BoundedBag& operator= (const MemberContainer<T>&);

    virtual void    Add(const T& theValue)
    {AddFront(theValue);}
```

```cpp
      virtual int       IsMember(const T& theValue) const
      {return ((int)itsLastFound = Find(theValue)) != S;}

      virtual int       Remove(const T&);
      virtual int       Cardinality() const {return GetCardinality();}
      virtual void      Clear() {Vector<T,S>::Clear();}

      virtual MemberContainer<T>* Clone() const;

    private:
      IteratorMechanism<T>* MakeIteratorMechanism() const;
      int itsLastFound;
  };

  template <class T, int S>
  class BoundedBagIteratorMechanism : public IteratorMechanism<T>
                                    , private VectorIterator<T,S>
  {
    public:
      BoundedBagIteratorMechanism(const BoundedBag<T,S>& theBag)
      : VectorIterator<T,S>(theBag) {}
      ~BoundedBagIteratorMechanism() {}
      BoundedBagIteratorMechanism(
        const BoundedBagIteratorMechanism<T,S>& theIterator)
      : VectorIterator<T,S>(theIterator)
      {}

      BoundedBagIteratorMechanism<T,S>&
      operator=(const BoundedBagIteratorMechanism& theIterator)
      {VectorIterator<T,S>::operator=(theIterator); return *this;}

      void* IsNotEmpty() const
      {return VectorIterator<T,S>::IsNotEmpty();}

      void  Next()              {VectorIterator<T,S>::Next();}
      T     Item();

      virtual IteratorMechanism<T>* Clone() const
      {
          return new BoundedBagIteratorMechanism<T,S>(*this);
      }
  };
  #include "componen/b_bag.cpp"
  #endif
```

b_bag.cpp

```cpp
  #include "componen/b_bag.h"
  #include <assert.h>
  template <class T, int S>
  BoundedBag<T,S>::BoundedBag(const BoundedBag<T,S>& theBag)
  : itsLastFound(S)
  {
      CopyItems(theBag);
  }

  template <class T, int S>
  BoundedBag<T,S>::BoundedBag(const MemberContainer<T>& theBag)
  : itsLastFound(S)
  {
      CopyItems(theBag);
  }
```

```
template <class T, int S>
BoundedBag<T,S>& BoundedBag<T,S>::operator= (const BoundedBag<T,S>&
theBag)
{
    Vector<T,S>& v = *this;
    v = theBag;
    return *this;
}

template <class T, int S>
BoundedBag<T,S>& BoundedBag<T,S>::
operator= (const MemberContainer<T>& theBag)
{
    MemberContainer<T>::operator=(theBag);
    return *this;
}

template <class T, int S>
int BoundedBag<T,S>::Remove(const T& theValue)
{
    int retval = 0;
    if (IsMember(theValue))
    {
        Delete(itsLastFound);
        retval=1;
    }
    return retval;
}

template <class T, int S>
MemberContainer<T>* BoundedBag<T,S>::Clone() const
{
    return new BoundedBag<T,S>(*this);
}
template <class T, int S>
IteratorMechanism<T>* BoundedBag<T,S>::MakeIteratorMechanism() const
{
    return new BoundedBagIteratorMechanism<T,S>(*this);
}

template <class T, int S>
T BoundedBagIteratorMechanism<T,S>::Item()
{
    assert((VectorIterator<T,S>::IsNotEmpty()));
    return VectorIterator<T,S>::Item();
}
```

3

Analysis and Design

*"Everything which is in any way beautiful is beautiful in itself,
and terminates in itself, not having praise as part of itself."*

—Marcus Aurelius, circa A.D. 170

*"Rule of thumb: if you think something is clever and sophisticated, beware —
it is probably self-indulgence."*

—Donald A. Norman, 1990
(*The Design of Everyday Things,* Donald A. Norman, Doubleday, 1990)

How do you create a "good design"? This chapter examines this question in some detail. To paraphrase Crosby: A good design is a design that conforms to specifications.[1] For software applications, however, the specifications are rarely complete. For example, a specification seldom states that the software must be easy to maintain, have a long lifetime by being able to tolerate a high level of maintenance, or comprise components that can be reused in other applications. Yet these requirements are almost always implied or expected. In this chapter we consider how to satisfy these unspecified requirements.

Introduction

Many traditional software methods separate analysis and design into distinct phases of the software life cycle. Often the notation and method used during analysis are different from the notation and method used for design. At the end of analysis, a translation must take place in order to convert the diagrams of analysis to diagrams suitable for design. This

---

1. Phillip B. Crosby, *Quality IsFree* (McGraw-Hill, 1979)

translation barrier can be difficult to cross. Worse, when problems in the analysis are found during design, we must backtrack from the design to the analysis in order to fix them. In most cases, such backtracking is considered to be too difficult, so the analysis model is left in its deficient form. As the design proceeds, more and more problems may be found with the analysis model. Backtracking becomes less and less plausible. Eventually the analysis model is so far out of sync with the design that it is often discarded.

The translation barrier between analysis and design is just one symptom of a larger problem. Methodologies that separate analysis and design presume that designs are based upon analyses—that a design cannot begin until an analysis has been completed. This presumes that the analysis *does not* depend upon the design in any way. In most cases, this is incorrect.

In this chapter we consider the notion that analysis and design are nearly concurrent efforts; knowledge from the analysis flows into design, and knowledge from the design flows into analysis. We will view the analysis and design effort as a continuum of activity, beginning primarily with analysis activities and ending primarily with design activities, but with no clear separation of these activities in any part of the process. By analogy, consider a spectrum. There is definitely red light and definitely yellow light, but no clear separation between them—just a gradual change from red to yellow.

Does this mean that we are discarding domain analysis and enterprise modeling as too separate from design? No, it merely means that we are bringing some design activities to bear on these models. It means that these models must *consider* the computational environment in which they will eventually be implemented. Absence of such consideration may create analyses that are round pegs trying to fit into the square holes of the environment they are supposed to run in.

This may sound heretical. Shouldn't the analysis of an application be independent of the computer platform it is going to run on? In theory, this sounds fine. In practice, it can be misleading. Remember that our goal is to produce computer applications; thus, the computational environment is an intrinsic part of the problem. Attempting to specify an application without knowledge of the computational environment is like trying to specify Newton's laws of motion without mathematics. Imagine attempting to specify a word processor without knowing the characteristics of the user interface hardware. Is there a mouse? Is the screen bitmapped? Or are we using an ASCII terminal with no graphics capability? Clearly the final specification depends significantly upon the answers to these questions.

The best way to understand the synergy between analysis and design is to experience it first-hand. Therefore this chapter includes a single, relatively significant, case study.

Case Study: A Batch Payroll Application

There is a prevalent concern in the industry that object-orientation is inappropriate for certain kinds of applications. The following case study counters this notion, at least as far as batch business applications are concerned. The application is a simple batch payroll system. The following specification is extremely simplistic. It is not intended as an example of an actual payroll system. Instead, it is a simplified model of a payroll system that is complex enough to be interesting, but not so complex as to be daunting.

Specification

A Simple Batch Payroll System

This system consists of a database of the employees in the company, and their associated data, such as timecards. The system must pay each employee. Employees must be paid the correct amount, on time, by the method that they specify. Also, various deductions must be taken from their pay.

- Some employees work by the hour. They are paid an hourly rate that is one of the fields in their employee record. They submit daily time cards that record the date and the number of hours worked. If they work more than 8 hours per day, they are paid 1.5 times their normal rate for those extra hours. They are paid every Friday.

- Some employees are paid a flat salary. They are paid on the last working day of the month. Their monthly salary is one of the fields in their employee record.

- Some of the salaried employees are also paid a commission based on their sales. They submit sales receipts that record the date and the amount of the sale. Their commission rate is a field in their employee record. They are paid every other Friday.

- Employees can select their method of payment. They may have their paychecks mailed to the postal address of their choice; they may have their paychecks held for pickup by the Paymaster; or they can request that their paychecks be directly deposited into the bank account of their choice.

- Some employees belong to the union. Their employee record has a field for the weekly dues rate. Their dues must be deducted from their pay. Also, the union may assess service charges against individual union members from time to time. These service charges are submitted by the union on a weekly basis and must be deducted from the appropriate employee's next pay amount.

- The payroll application will run once each working day and pay the appropriate employees on that day. The system will be told what date the employees are to be paid to, so it will generate payments for records from the last time the employee was paid up to the specified date.

How do we begin? We could begin by generating the database schema. Clearly this problem calls for some kind of relational database, and the requirements give us a very good idea of what the tables and fields should be. It would be easy to design a workable schema and then start building some queries. However, this approach will generate an application for which the database is the central concern.

Databases are *implementation details*; they should be absent from the initial object model. Far too many applications are inextricably tied to their databases because they were designed with the database in mind. Remember the definition of abstraction: "the amplification of the essential and the elimination of the irrelevant." The database is irrelevant at this stage of the model; it is merely a technique used for storing and accessing data, nothing more.

Analysis by Noun Lists

Then how should we begin? Many texts suggest that we consider the nouns in the requirements list as candidates for objects in our model. Figure 3-1 shows the nouns that can be extracted from the requirements.

amount	employee	paycheck
company	hourlyrate	sales
deduction	pay	timecards
hour	salary	commission
month	system	day
postalAddressOfTheirChoice	weeklyDuesRate	field
serviceCharge	commissionRate	methodOfPayment
unionMember	date	paymaster
bankAccountOfTheirChoice	employeeRecord	salesReceipts
database	method	union

Figure 3-1
Noun List from the Payroll System Requirements

Compiling a list of nouns as a first step gives us something to do, which may make us feel "warm and fuzzy." At least we don't have to ask how to begin. Once the list is compiled, however, we are still faced with the question, "What do we do next?" The list in Figure 3-1 does not give us much help; it is reasonably impenetrable. Imagine the list that might accrue from 50 pages of requirements!

Some texts suggest that you prune the list by eliminating anything that does not correspond to a physical thing, role, event, process, and so on. This can be difficult, since the matching criteria are subject to interpretation. One analyst might determine that *paycheck* is a physical thing, and another might determine that it is outside of the model. As an example of the variability of such prunings, take a moment to prune the above list. Remove obvious synonyms and any noun or noun phrase that does not relate to a physical thing, a role, an event, or a process. Then compare your list to the list in Figure 3-2, which shows my own interpretation of how the list might be pruned. The two lists should be somewhat different; perhaps remarkably so. This demonstrates the crudeness of compiling noun lists.

However crude, noun lists have their place. The pruned list in Figure 3-2 is a little easier to come to terms with than the unabridged list from Figure 3-1. Although some of

bankAccountoftheirChoice	methodOfPayment	salesReceipts
hourlyrate	salary	weeklyDuesRate
postalAddressOfTheirChoice	unionMember	employee
timecards	date	paymaster
commissionRate	pay	serviceCharge

Figure 3-2
Pruned Noun List from the Payroll System Requirements

the elements of this list may remain puzzling (e.g., what do we do with *paymaster*), others present some clear relationships. Here are a few:

1. Employees may have time cards or sales receipts.
2. All Employees have a method of payment.
3. Employees have either a salary and/or a commission rate, or they have an hourly rate.
4. Union members have weekly dues rates.
5. Union members also have a list of service charges associated with them.
6. Depending upon the method of payment, an employee may have a bank account or postal address of his choice.

The class diagrams that represent these relationships appear in Figure 3-3.

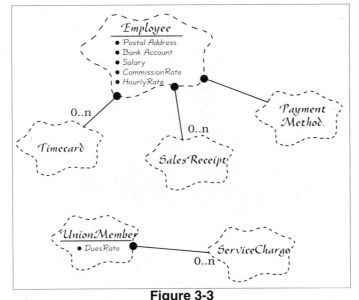

Figure 3-3
Class Diagrams for Initial Payroll Relationships

Many things are missing from these diagrams and relationships. For example, how are **UnionMember** and **Employee** related? How do **Employee** objects know whether they are paid hourly or by salary or by commission? Before we arbitrarily try to determine the answers to these questions, let's use Jacobson's technique of use-cases[2] to see what illumination they may provide.

Analysis by Use-Cases

When we perform use-case analysis, we ask ourselves, "What kind of things can the users of this system do, and how does the system respond?" We then enumerate each of these scenarios and describe them in detail.

For example, what can users of our payroll system do?

1. Add a new employee
2. Delete an employee
3. Post a time card
4. Post a sales receipt
5. Post a union service charge
6. Change employee details (e.g., hourly rate, dues rate, etc.)
7. Run the payroll for today

Let's examine each of these cases in detail.

Adding Employees

Use-Case 1
Add New Employee

A new employee is added by the receipt of an **AddEmp** transaction. This transaction contains the employee's name, address and assigned employee number.   The transaction has three forms:

```
AddEmp <EmpID> "<name>" "<address>" H <hrly-rate>
AddEmp <EmpID> "<name>" "<address>" S <mtly-slry>
AddEmp <EmpID> "<name>" "<address>" C <mtly-slry> <comm-rate>
```

The employee record is created with its fields assigned appropriately.

Alternatives:
An error in the transaction structure

If the transaction structure is inappropriate, it is printed out in an error message, and no action is taken.

Use-case 1 hints at an abstraction. There are three forms of the **AddEmp** transaction, yet all three forms share the **<EmpID>**, **<name>** and **<address>** fields. This leads us to the conclusion that there is an **AddEmployeeTransaction** abstract base class, with three

2.   Ivar Jacobson, *Object Oriented Software Engineering, A Use Case Driven Approach* (Addison Wesley, 1992)

derivatives: **AddHourlyEmployeeTransaction**, **AddSalariedEmployee-Transaction** and **AddCommissionedEmployeeTransaction** (see Figure 3-4).

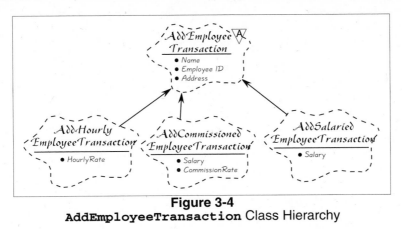

Figure 3-4
AddEmployeeTransaction Class Hierarchy

Use-case 1 specifically talks about an employee record, which implies some sort of database. Again our predisposition to databases may tempt us into thinking about record layouts or the field structure in a relational database table, but we should resist these urges. What the use-case is really asking us to do is to create an employee. What is the object model of an employee? A better question might be: What do the three different transactions create? In my view, they create three different kinds of employee objects, mimicking the three different kinds of **AddEmp** transactions. Figure 3-5 shows a possible structure.

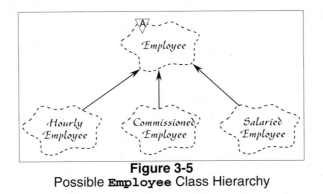

Figure 3-5
Possible **Employee** Class Hierarchy

An astute analyst might have inferred this structure from the requirements, but certainly not from the noun list. Still, it is perhaps too soon to be sure that this structure is the most optimal for the payroll application, so let's continue the analysis.

We Are Already Making Design Decisions

The above analysis suggests that there are some abstract classes in our model. Making a class abstract is a design decision. It pertains to the sharing of code and the closure of the class; it has very little to do with the analysis of the model.

Remember that analysis describes what the application does, but not how it does it. An equally valid description would have been to state that there were three independent classes: **SalariedEmployee**, **HourlyEmployee** and **CommissionedEmployee**. However, the very names of these classes cry out for some kind of unifying relationship, and so we make a design decision to create the abstract class **Employee**. This is just a small example of how design and analysis begin to intermix very early in the analysis of an application.

Deleting Employees

Use-Case 2
Deleting an Employee

Employees are deleted when a **DelEmp** transaction is received. The form of this transaction is as follows:

```
DelEmp <EmpID>
```

When this transaction is received, the appropriate employee record is deleted.

Alternative:
Invalid or unknown **EmpID**

If the <EmpID> field is not structured correctly, or if it does not refer to a valid employee record, then the transaction is printed with an error message, and no other action is taken.

Use-Case 2 implies that every employee object should have a **Delete** operation, as in Figure 3–6.

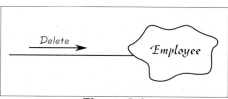

Figure 3-6
Employee **Delete** Operation

Posting Time Cards

Use-Case 3
Post a `TimeCard`

Upon receipt of a **TimeCard** transaction, the system will create a time-card record and associate it with the appropriate employee record.

    TimeCard <empid> <date> <hours>

Alternative 1:
The selected employee is not hourly

The system will print an appropriate error message and take no further action.

Alternative 2:
An error in the transaction structure

The system will print an appropriate error message and take no further action.

This use-case points out that some transactions apply only to certain kinds of employees, strengthening the idea that the different kinds should be represented by different classes. In this case there is also an association implied between time cards and hourly employees. Figure 3-7 shows a possible static model for this association.

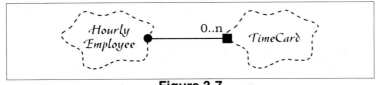

Figure 3-7
Association between **HourlyEmployee** and **TimeCard**

Posting Sales Receipts

Use-Case 4
Posting a `SalesReceipt`

Upon receipt of the **SalesReceipt** transaction, the system will create a new sales-receipt record and associate it with the appropriate commissioned employee.

    SalesReceipt <EmpID> <date> <amount>

Alternative 1:
The selected employee is not commissioned

The system will print an appropriate error message and take no further action.

Alternative 2:
An error in the transaction structure

The system will print an appropriate error message and take no further action.

This use-case is very similar to Use-case 3. It implies the structure shown in Figure 3-8.

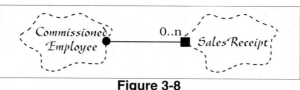

Figure 3-8
Commissioned Employees and Sales Receipts

Posting a Union Service Charge

Use-Case 5
Posting a Union Service Charge

Upon receipt of this transaction, the system will create a service-charge record and associate it with the appropriate union member.

```
ServiceCharge <memberID> <amount>
```

Alternative 1:
Poorly formed transaction

If the transaction is not well formed, or if the **<memberID>** does not refer to an existing union member, then the transaction is printed with an appropriate error message.

This use-case shows that union members are not accessed through employee IDs. The union maintains its own identification numbering scheme for union members. Thus, the system must be able to associate union members and employees. There are many different ways to provide this kind of association, so to avoid being arbitrary, let's defer this decision until later. Perhaps constraints from other parts of the system will force our hand one way or another.

One thing is certain. There is a direct association between union members and their service charges. Figure 3-9 shows a possible static model for this association.

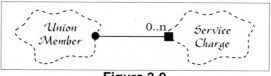

Figure 3-9
Union Members and Service Charges

Changing Employee Details

Use-Case 6
Changing Employee Details

Upon receipt of this transaction, the system will alter one of the details of the appropriate employee record. There are several possible variations to this transaction.

`ChgEmp <EmpID> Name <name>`	Change Employee Name
`ChgEmp <EmpID> Address <address>`	Change Employee Address
`ChgEmp <EmpID> Hourly <hourlyRate>`	Change to Hourly
`ChgEmp <EmpID> Salaried <salary>`	Change to Salaried
`ChgEmp <EmpID> Commissioned <salary> <rate>`	Change to Commissioned
`ChgEmp <EmpID> Hold`	Hold Paycheck
`ChgEmp <EmpID> Direct <bank> <account>`	Direct Deposit
`ChgEmp <EmpID> Mail <address>`	Mail Paycheck
`ChgEmp <EmpID> Member <memberID> Dues <rate>`	Make Employee a Union Member
`ChgEmp <EmpID> NoMember`	Make Employee Non-Union Member

Alternatives
Transaction Errors

If the structure of the transaction is improper, or **<EmpID>** does not refer to a real employee, or **<memberID>** already refers to a member, then print a suitable error, and take no further action.

This use-case is very revealing. It has told us all the aspects of an employee that must be changeable. The fact that we can change an employee from hourly to salaried means that the diagram in Figure 3-5 is certainly invalid. Instead, it would probably be more appropriate for **Employee** objects to contain some kind of **PaymentClassification** object, as in Figure 3-10. This is an advantage because we can change the **PaymentClassification** object without changing any other part of the **Employee** object. When an hourly employee is changed to a salaried employee, the **HourlyClassification** of the corresponding **Employee** object is replaced with a **SalariedClassification** object.

PaymentClassification objects come in three varieties. **HourlyClassification** objects maintain the hourly rate and a list of **TimeCard** objects. **SalariedClassification** objects maintain the monthly salary figure. **CommissionedClassification** objects maintain a monthly salary, a commission rate and a list of **SalesReceipt** objects. I have used contains-by-value relationships in these cases, because I believe that **TimeCards** and **SalesReceipts** should be destroyed when the employee is destroyed.

The method of payment must also be changeable. This strengthens the model from Figure 3-3, which depicts an **Employee** object containing some kind of **PaymentMethod** object. Figure 3-10 expands upon this idea by deriving three different kinds of **PaymentMethod** classes. If an **Employee** object contains a **MailMethod** object, the corresponding employee will have his paychecks mailed to him. The address to which the checks are mailed is recorded in the **MailMethod** object. If the **Employee** object contains a **DirectMethod** object, then his pay will be directly deposited into the bank

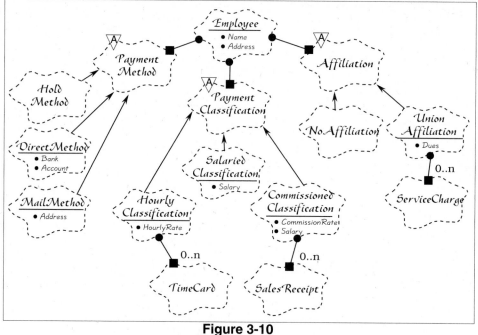

Figure 3-10
Revised Class Diagram for `Payroll`

account that is recorded in the **DirectMethod** object. If the **Employee** contains a **HoldMethod** object, his paychecks will be sent to the paymaster to be held for pickup.

Finally, Figure 3-10 shows how we can model union membership. Each **Employee** object contains an **Affiliation** object, which has two forms. If the **Employee** contains a **NoAffiliation** object, then his pay is not adjusted by any organization other than the employer. However, if the **Employee** object contains a **UnionAffiliation** object, that employee must pay the dues and service charges that are recorded in that **UnionAffiliation** object.

Payday

Use-Case 7
Run the Payroll for Today

Upon receipt of the Payday transaction, the system finds all those employees that should be paid upon the specified date. The system then determines how much they are owed, and pays them according to their selected payment method. An audit-trail report is printed showing the action taken for each employee.

`Payday <date>`

Although it is easy to understand the intent of this use-case, it is not so simple to determine what impact it has upon the static structure of Figure 3-10. We need to answer several questions.

First, how does the **Employee** object know how to calculate its pay. Certainly if the employee is hourly, the system must tally up his time cards and multiply by the hourly rate. If the employee is commissioned, the system must tally up his sales receipts, multiply by the commission rate, and add the base salary. But where does this get done? The ideal place seems to be in the **PaymentClassification** derivatives. These objects maintain the records needed to calculate pay, so they should probably have the methods for determining pay. Figure 3-11a shows an object diagram that describes how this might work.

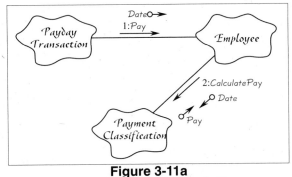

Figure 3-11a
Calculating an Employee's Pay

When the **Employee** object is asked to calculate pay, it refers this request to its **PaymentClassification** object. The actual algorithm employed depends upon the type of **PaymentClassification** that the **Employee** object contains. Figures 3-11b through 3-11d show the three possible scenarios. These diagrams show that the **TimeCard** and **SalesReceipt** objects are contained within **Set** classes, and that **Iterator** objects are used to iterate over them. Thus, we can refine our static model as shown in Figure 3-12.

Reflection: What Have We Learned?

We have learned that a use-case analysis provides a wealth of information and insights into object modeling. Compare Figure 3-3 with Figures 3-10 through 3-12. Most of the structural and conceptual difference between these diagrams comes from thinking about the use-cases, that is, thinking about behavior. Also, we have learned that compiling a list of nouns does not provide much insight. This is not to say that noun lists are a bad idea, but you should not expect too much from them. Noun lists can only provide the crudest of initial approximations for the model.

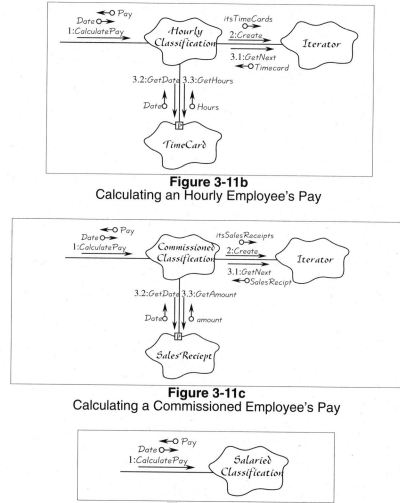

Figure 3-11b
Calculating an Hourly Employee's Pay

Figure 3-11c
Calculating a Commissioned Employee's Pay

Figure 3-11d
Calculating a Salaried Employee's Pay

Another interesting thing about the use-case analysis is the creation of abstractions that are not part of the essential problem domain. For example, the **PaymentClassification** class is a contrivance that has been created so that we can change the status of an employee. The same is true of the **Affiliation** class, which has been added so that we can change the union membership status of an employee. Other classes that are not obviously part of the problem domain are the transaction classes in Figure 3-4. Why do these classes exist if they are not part of the problem domain?

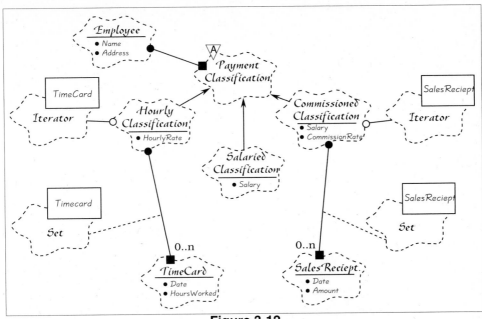

Figure 3-12
Refined Static Structure for `PaymentClassification`

The Viability of Real-World Models

OOA is often touted as being superior to other methodologies because the analyst can model his application in terms of real-world objects from the problem domain. If this is true, then why are we creating objects that are contrivances? If we were modeling employees as real-world objects, we might consider Figure 3-5 to be a more accurate model. After all, according to the requirements, employees are either hourly, salaried, or commissioned. Why have we abandoned the real-world nature of our objects and built our model from objects that could not have been predicted directly from the requirements?

The answer is that we are writing a software application, we are not modeling the real world. A software application is a contrivance in and of itself; thus, it must be composed of components that are contrivances. These components connect the real-world entities within the model to the pragmatics of the job at hand.

For example, the transaction classes from Figure 3-4 connect the real-world **Employee** class to the pragmatic issue of adding new employees. The contrived **PaymentClassification** objects connect the real-world **Employee** class to the pragmatic issue of how employees get paid. Thus, we should not feel bad if our model contains contrivances. Indeed, we should be comforted that it does! It means that our model is addressing the pragmatic issues of the application requirements. To quote Jacobson, "We do not believe that the best (most stable) systems are built by *only* using objects that correspond to real-life entities."[3]

Finding the Underlying Abstractions

We have explored some useful tools. We have created noun lists and analyzed use-cases, and this has moved the analysis of the payroll application along quite well. But analysis is not deterministic! No set of tools and procedures can guarantee a proper analysis and design. Tools and procedures are a help, but they cannot do the whole job. Eventually the real effectiveness of design and analysis arises from the experience and talent of the analysts and designers.

The most important word in the object-oriented paradigm is *abstraction*. Abstraction cannot be automated. The ability to find abstractions is based upon the insight and experience of the analysts and designers. Abstraction is key to any successful application because it is at the root of the open-closed principle. We can create objects that are closed for modification but open to extension because those objects are used through an abstract interface that is divorced from, and thus independent of, implementation.

To use the open/closed principle effectively, we must hunt for abstractions and find those that underlie the application. Often these abstractions are not stated or even alluded to by the requirements of the application, or even the use-cases. Requirements and use-cases are too steeped in details to express the generalities of the underlying abstractions.

What are the underlying abstractions of the Payroll application? Let's look again at the requirements. We see statements like this: "Some employees work by the hour," and "Some employees are paid a flat salary," and again "Some [...] employees are paid a commission." This hints at the following generalization: "All employees are paid, but they are paid by different schemes." The abstraction here is that "All employees are paid." Our model of the **PaymentClassification** in Figures 3-11 and 3-12 expresses this abstraction nicely. Thus, this abstraction has already been found by the use-case analysis.

The Schedule Abstraction

Looking for other abstractions we find "They are paid every Friday," "They are paid on the last working day of the month," and "They are paid every other Friday." This leads us to another generality: "All employees are paid according to some schedule." The abstraction here is the notion of the *Schedule*. It should be possible to ask an **Employee** object whether a certain date is its payday. The use-cases barely mention this. The requirements associate an employee's schedule with his payment classification. Specifically, hourly

---

3. Ivar Jacobson, *Object-Oriented Software Engineering: A Use-Case-Driven Approach* (Addison-Wesley, 1992), p. 133.

employees are paid weekly, salaried employees are paid monthly, and employees receiving commissions are paid biweekly; however, is this association essential? Might not the policy change one day, so that employees could select a particular schedule, or so that employees belonging to different departments or different divisions could have different schedules? Might not schedule policy change independent of payment policy? Certainly, this must be so.

If, as the requirements imply, we delegated the issue of schedule to the **Payment-Classification** class, then our class could not be closed against issues of change in schedule. When we changed payment policy, we would also have to test schedule; when we changed schedules, we would also have to test payment policy.

An association between schedule and payment policy could lead to bugs in which a change to a particular payment policy caused incorrect scheduling of certain employees. Bugs like this may make sense to programmers, but they strike fear in the hearts of managers and users. They fear, and rightly so, that if schedules can be broken by a change to payment policy, then *any* change made *anywhere* might cause problems in *any* other unrelated part of the system. This means that we cannot predict the effects of a change. When effects cannot be predicted, confidence is lost and the program assumes the status of "dangerous and unstable" in the minds of its managers and users.

Despite the essential nature of the schedule abstraction, neither our noun list nor our use-case analysis gave us any clues about its existence. To spot it required careful consideration of the requirements and an insight into the wiles of the user community. Over-reliance upon tools and procedures, and under-reliance upon intelligence and experience are recipes for disaster.

Figures 3-13a and 3-13b show the static and dynamic models for the schedule abstraction. The **Employee** class contains the abstract **Schedule** class. There are three varieties of **Schedule** that correspond to the three known schedules by which employees are paid.

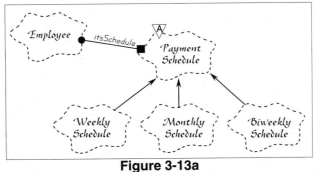

Figure 3-13a
Static Model of a **Schedule** Abstraction

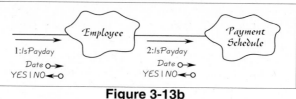

Figure 3-13b
Dynamic Model of Schedule Abstraction

Payment Methods

Another generalization that we can make from the requirements is "All employees receive their pay by some method." The abstraction is the **PaymentMethod** class. Interestingly enough, this abstraction was mentioned in our noun list, and is already expressed in Figure 3-10.

Affiliations

The requirements imply that employees may have affiliations with a union; however, the union may not be the only organization that has a claim to some of an employee's pay. Employees might want to make automatic contributions to certain charities, or have their dues to professional associations paid automatically. The generalization therefore becomes "The employee may be affiliated with many organizations that should be automatically paid from the employee's paycheck."

The corresponding abstraction is the **Affiliation** class that is shown in Figure 3-10. That figure, however, does not show the **Employee** containing more than one **Affiliation**, and it shows the presence of a **NoAffiliation** class. This model does not quite fit the abstraction we need. Figures 3-14a and 3-14b show the static and dynamic models that represent the **Affiliation** abstraction.

Transactions

Looking again at the use-cases, we see that each transaction is like an object in that it contains data and has a behavior. Figures 3-4 and 3-11 have already begun to explore the notion that we can represent transactions by classes. But what is the underlying abstraction? The generality that applies to transactions is relatively simple: Transactions are built by some agency, and then they are executed. Figure 3-15 shows that we can represent this generality as an abstract base class named **Transaction**, which has an instance method named **Execute()**.

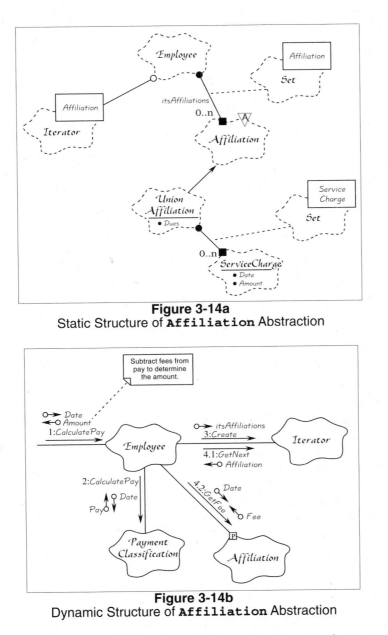

Figure 3-14a
Static Structure of **Affiliation** Abstraction

Figure 3-14b
Dynamic Structure of **Affiliation** Abstraction

This model allows several different processing modes. For example, transactions can be executed as they are parsed, or they can be parsed and then stored in an ordered set of **Transaction** objects to be executed later. Also, transactions become a convenient unit of work. If this system were ported to a GUI, then the GUI could build **Transaction** objects and execute them. Also, since transactions can remember everything that they

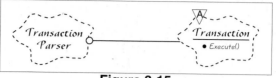

Figure 3-15
Abstract Base Transaction Class

have done, they can be given the power to undo their actions. Thus, if we ever needed an "undo" capability, we could provide a pure virtual **Undo** function in class **Transaction** and then implement this function in the derivatives.

Adding Employees

Figure 3-16 shows a potential structure for the transactions that add employees. Note that it is within these transactions that the employees' payment schedule is associated with their payment classification. This is appropriate, since the transactions are contrivances instead of part of the real-world model. Thus, the real-world model is unaware of the association; the association is merely part of one of the contrivances and can be changed at any time. For example, we could easily extend the application to allow us to change schedules.

Note, too, that the default payment method is to hold the paycheck with the Paymaster. If an employee wants a different payment method, it must be changed with the appropriate **ChgEmp** transaction.

The **AddEmployeeTransaction** class uses a class called **PayrollDatabase**. This class maintains all the existing **Employee** objects in a **Dictionary** that is keyed by **EmpID**. It also maintains a **Dictionary** that maps union **MemberIDs** to **EmpID**s. The structure for this class appears in Figure 3-17.

Figure 3-18 shows the dynamic model for adding an employee. Note that the **AddEmployeeTransaction** object sends messages to *itself* in order to get the appropriate **PaymentClassification** and **PaymentSchedule** objects. These messages are implemented in the derivatives of the **AddEmployeeTransaction** class.

Deleting Employees

Figures 3-19 and 3-20 present the static and dynamic models for the transactions that delete employees.

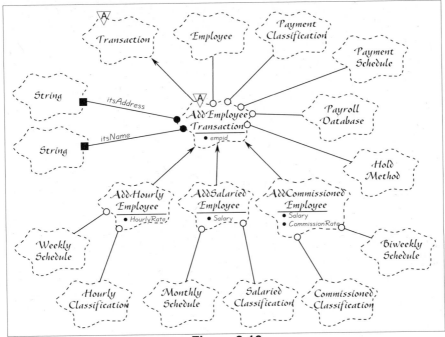

Figure 3-16
Static Model of `AddEmployeeTransaction`

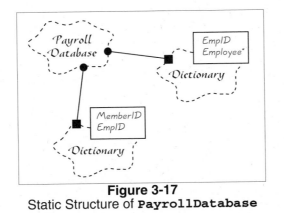

Figure 3-17
Static Structure of `PayrollDatabase`

Time Cards, Sales Receipts, and Service Charges

Figure 3-21 shows the static structure for the transaction that posts time cards to employees. Figure 3-22 shows the dynamic model. The basic idea is that the transaction gets the **Employee** object from the **PayrollDatabase**, asks the **Employee** for its **Pay-**

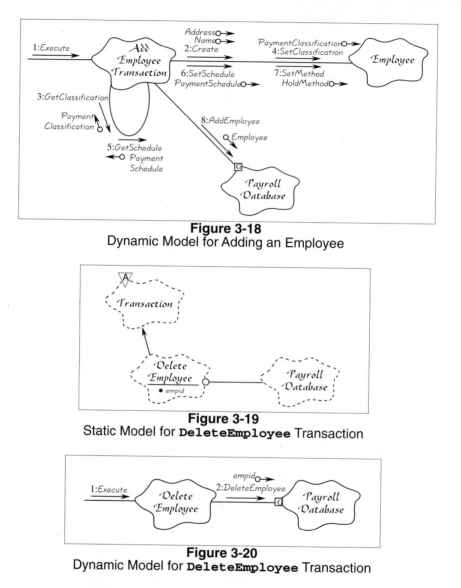

Figure 3-18
Dynamic Model for Adding an Employee

Figure 3-19
Static Model for `DeleteEmployee` Transaction

Figure 3-20
Dynamic Model for `DeleteEmployee` Transaction

mentClassification object, and then creates and adds a **TimeCard** object to that **PaymentClassification**.

Notice that we cannot add **TimeCard** objects to general **PaymentClassifica-tion** objects; we can only add them to **HourlyClassification** objects. This implies that we must downcast the **PaymentClassification** object received from the **Employee** object to an **HourlyClassification** object. This is a good use for the **dynamic_cast** operator in C++, as shown in the following code:

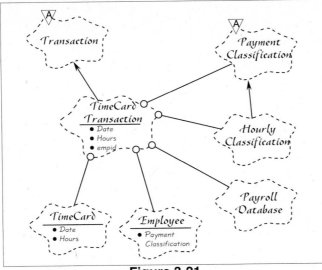

Figure 3-21
Static Structure of `TimeCardTransaction`

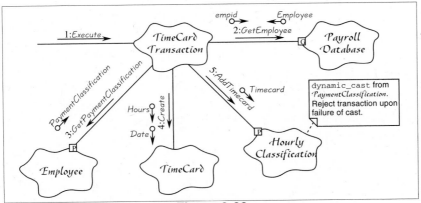

Figure 3-22
Dynamic Model for Posting a `TimeCard`

```
Employee* e = thePayrollDatabase.GetEmployee(empID);
if (e)
{
    HourlyClassification *hc;
    hc = dynamic_cast<HourlyClassification*>
                    (e->GetPaymentClassification());
    if (hc)
    {
        hc->AddTimeCard(new TimeCard(date, hours));
    }
}
```

Figures 3-23 and 3-24 show a similar design for the transaction that posts sales receipts to a commissioned employee. Figures 3-25 and 3-26 show the design for the transaction that posts service charges to union members.

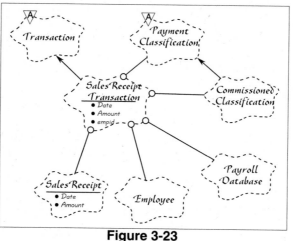

Figure 3-23
Static Model for `SalesReceiptTransaction`

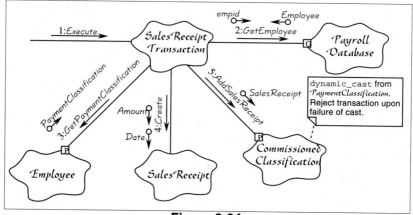

Figure 3-24
Dynamic Model for `SalesReceiptTransaction`

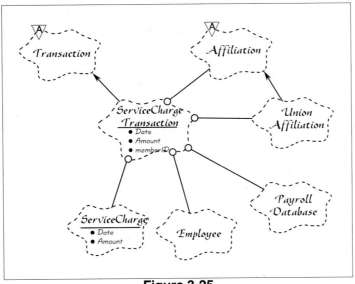

Figure 3-25
Static Model for `ServiceChargeTransaction`

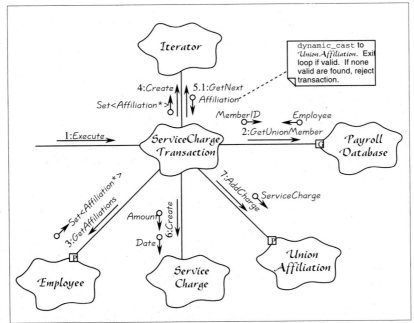

Figure 3-26
Dynamic Model for `ServiceChargeTransaction`

These models point up a mismatch between the transaction model and the real-world model that we have created. Our real-world **Employee** object can be affiliated with many different organizations, but the transaction model assumes that any affiliation must be a union affiliation. Thus, the transaction model provides no way to identify a particular kind of affiliation. Instead, it simply assumes that if we are posting a service charge, then the employee has a union affiliation.

The dynamic model addresses this dilemma by searching the set of **Affiliation** objects contained by the **Employee** object for a **UnionAffiliation** object. It then adds the **ServiceCharge** object to that **UnionAffiliation**. This is another use for the **dynamic_cast** feature of C++, as shown in Listing 3-1.

Listing 3-1

Example of **dynamic_cast**

```
Set<Affiliation*>& s = theEmployee.GetAffiliations();
Iterator<Affiliation*>i(s);
UnionAffiliation* ua = 0;
for (; i && !ua; i++)
    ua = dynamic_cast<UnionAffiliation*>(*i);
if (ua)
    ua->AddCharge(new ServiceCharge(date, amount));
else
    //error.
```

Changing Employees

Figures 3-27 and 3-28 show the static structure for the transactions that change the attributes of an employee. This structure is easily derived from Use-Case 6. All the transactions take an **EmpID** argument, so we can create a top-level base class called **Change-EmployeeTransaction**. Below this base class are the classes that change single attributes, such as **ChangeNameTransaction** and **ChangeAddress-Transaction**. The transactions that change classifications have a commonality of purpose, in that they all modify the same field of the **Employee** object. Thus, they can be grouped together under an abstract base, **ChangeClassificationTransaction**. The same is true of the transactions that change the payment and the affiliations. This can be seen by the structure of **ChangeMethodTransaction** and **Change-AffiliationTransaction**.

Figure 3-29 shows the dynamic model for all the change transactions. In every case, the **Employee** object corresponding to the **EmpID** must be retrieved from the **Pay-rollDatabase**. Thus the **Execute** function of **ChangeEmployeeTransaction** implements this behavior, and then sends the **Change** message to itself. This message will be declared as a pure virtual function and implemented in the derivatives, as shown in Figures 3-30 and 3-31.

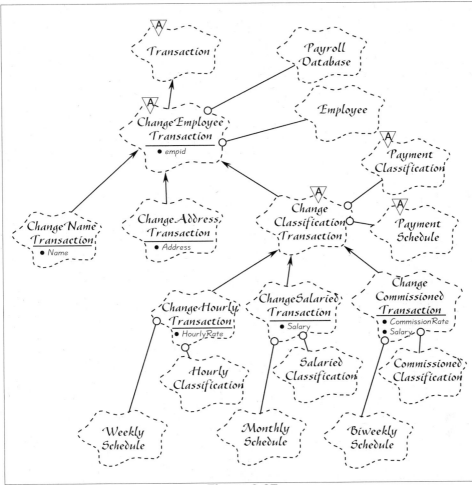

Figure 3-27
Static Model for `ChangeEmployeeTransaction`

Figure 3-32 shows how the hierarchy beneath `ChangeClassificationTransaction` is implemented. All of these transactions must create a new `PaymentClassification` object and then hand it to the `Employee` object. This is accomplished by sending the `GetClassification` message to itself. This pure virtual function is implemented in each of the classes derived from `ChangeClassificationTransaction`, as shown in Figures 3-33 through 3-35.

A similar mechanism is employed for the implementation of `ChangeMethodTransaction`. The pure virtual `GetMethod` function is used to select the proper derivative of `PaymentMethod`, which is then handed to the `Employee` object (see Figures 3-36 through 3-39).

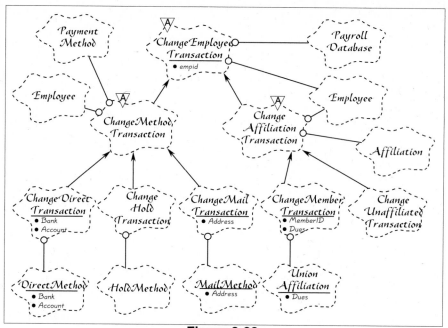

Figure 3-28
Static Model for `ChangeEmployeeTransaction` (cont.)

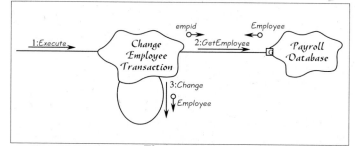

Figure 3-29
Dynamic Model for `ChangeEmployeeTransaction`

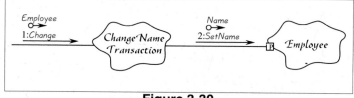

Figure 3-30
Dynamic Model for `ChangeNameTransaction`

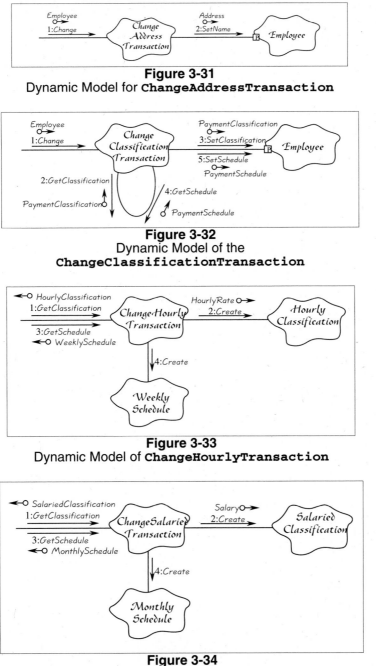

Figure 3-31
Dynamic Model for **ChangeAddressTransaction**

Figure 3-32
Dynamic Model of the
ChangeClassificationTransaction

Figure 3-33
Dynamic Model of **ChangeHourlyTransaction**

Figure 3-34
Dynamic Model of **ChangeSalariedTransaction**

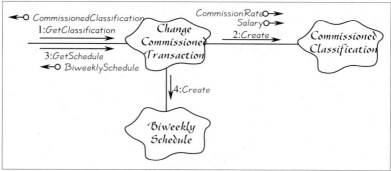

Figure 3-35
Dynamic Model of **ChangeCommissionedTransaction**

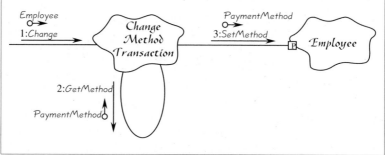

Figure 3-36
Dynamic Model of **ChangeMethodTransaction**

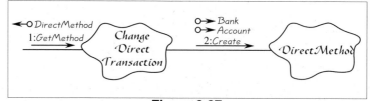

Figure 3-37
Dynamic Model of **ChangeDirectTransaction**

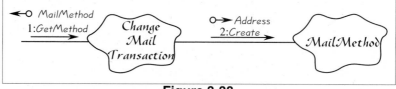

Figure 3-38
Dynamic Model of **ChangeMailTransaction**

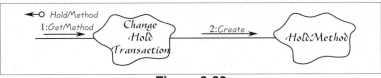

Figure 3-39
Dynamic Model of `ChangeHoldTransaction`

Figure 3-40 shows the implementation of the **ChangeAffiliationTransaction**. Once again we use a pure virtual function to select the **Affiliation** derivative that should be handed to the **Employee** object. Notice that when this transaction executes, the set of **Affiliations** in the **Employee** object is cleared before the new **Affiliation** is added. Also notice that the **GetAffiliation** function can return a zero pointer. Thus, with this implementation, an **Employee** object can have either a single **UnionAffiliation** or no **Affiliation** at all (see Figures 3-40 through 3-42).

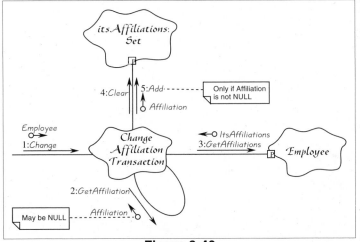

Figure 3-40
Dynamic Model of `ChangeAffiliationTransaction`

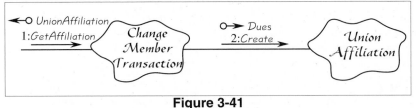

Figure 3-41
Dynamic Model of `ChangeMemberTransaction`

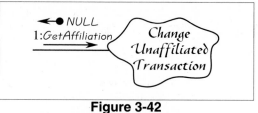

Figure 3-42
Dynamic Model of
ChangeUnaffiliatedTransaction

Paying Employees

Finally, we will consider the transaction that is at the root of this application: the transaction that instructs the system to pay the appropriate employees. Figure 3-43 shows the static structure of the **PaydayTransaction** class. Figures 3-44 through 3-47 describe the dynamic behavior.

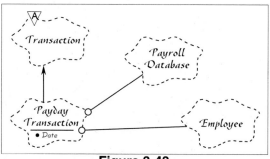

Figure 3-43
Static Model of **PaydayTransaction**

These few dynamic models express a great deal of polymorphic behavior. The algorithm employed by the **CalculatePay** message depends upon the kind of **Payment-Classification** that the **Employee** object contains. The algorithm used to determine if a date is a payday depends upon the kind of **PaymentSchedule** that the **Employee** contains. The algorithm used to send the payment to the **Employee** depends upon the type of the **PaymentMethod** object. This high degree of abstraction allows the algorithm employed in Figures 3-44 through 3-47 to be closed against the addition of new kinds of payment classifications, schedules, affiliations, or payment methods.

The algorithm modeled in Figures 3-46 and 3-47 introduces the concept of *posting*. After the correct pay amount has been calculated and sent to the **Employee**, the payment is posted; that is, the records involved in the payment are updated. Thus, we can define the **CalculatePay** method as calculating the pay from the last posting until the specified date.

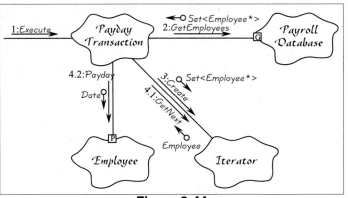

Figure 3-44
Dynamic Model for `PaydayTransaction`

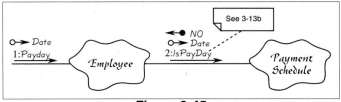

Figure 3-45
Dynamic Model Scenario: "Payday is not today."

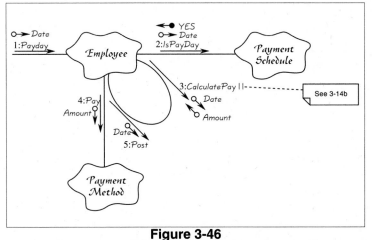

Figure 3-46
Dynamic Model Scenario: "Payday is today."

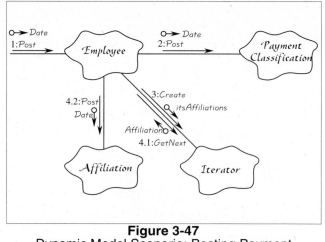

Figure 3-47
Dynamic Model Scenario: Posting Payment

Main Program

The main payroll program can now be expressed as a loop that parses transactions from an input source and then executes them. Figures 3-48 and 3-49 model the statics and dynamics of the main program. The concept is simple: the **PayrollApplication** sits in a loop, alternately requesting transactions from the **TransactionSource** and then telling those **Transaction** objects to **Execute**. Note that this is different from the diagram in Figure 3-15 and represents a shift in our thinking to a more abstract mechanism.

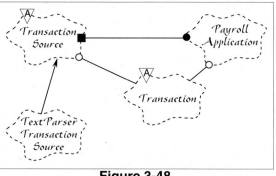

Figure 3-48
Static Model for the Main Program

TransactionSource is an abstract class that we can implement in several ways. The static diagram shows the derivative named **TextParserTransactionSource**, which reads an incoming text stream and parses out the transactions as described in the

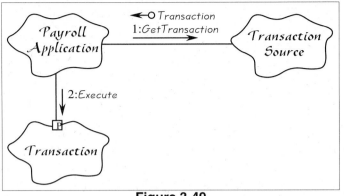

Figure 3-49
Dynamic Model for the Main Program

use-cases. This object then creates the appropriate **Transaction** objects and sends them along to the **PayrollApplication**.

The separation of interface from implementation in the **TransactionSource** allows the source of the transactions to be abstract; for example, we could easily interface the **PayrollApplication** to a **GUITransactionSource** or a **RemoteTransactionSource**.

Application Framework

Figures 3-50 and 3-51 show a further refinement of the application structure. We can model the application itself as a class that has an **Initialize** function, an **Idle** function that is called each time around the main loop, and a **Cleanup** function that is called just prior to program exit. We can then derive **PayrollApplication** from **Application**, and the **Idle** function will invoke the dynamic scenario shown in Figure 3-49.

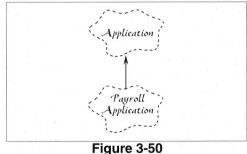

Figure 3-50
Static Model of **Application** Class

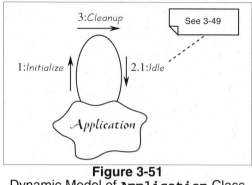

Figure 3-51
Dynamic Model of **Application** Class

The Database

Now that most of the application has been analyzed and designed, we can consider the role of the database. The class **PayrollDatabase** clearly encapsulates something involving persistence. The objects contained within the **PayrollDatabase** must live longer than any particular run of the application. How should this be implemented? We have several options.

We could implement **PayrollDatabase** using an object-oriented database management system (OODBMS). This would allow the actual objects to reside within the permanent storage of the database. As designers, we would have no more work to do, since the OODBMS would not add anything new to our model. One of the great benefits of OODBMS products is that they have little or no impact on the object model of the applications. As far as the design is concerned, the database barely exists.[4]

Another option would be to use simple flat text files to record the data. Upon initialization, the **PayrollDatabase** object could read that file and build the necessary objects in memory. At the end of the program, the **PayrollDatabase** object could write a new version of the text file. Certainly this option would not suffice for a company with hundreds of thousands of employees, or one that wanted real-time concurrent access to its payroll database. However, it might suffice for a smaller company, and it could certainly be used as a mechanism for testing the rest of the application classes without investing in a big database system.

Still another option would be to incorporate a relational database management system (RDBMS) into the **PayrollDatabase** object. The implementation of the **Payroll-Database** object would then make the appropriate queries to the RDMBS to temporarily

---

4. This is optimistic. In a simple application like Payroll the use of an OODBMS would have very little impact upon the design of the program. As applications become more and more complicated, the amount of impact that the OODBMS has upon the application increases. Still, the impact is far less than an RDBMS would have.

create the necessary objects in memory. We will discuss this option in more detail in the next chapter.

The point is that, as far as the application is concerned, databases are simply mechanisms for managing storage. They should usually not be considered as a major factor of the design. As we have shown here, they can be left for last and handled as a detail.[5] By doing so, we leave open a number of interesting options for implementing the needed persistence, and creating mechanisms to test the rest of the application. We also do not tie ourselves to any particular database technology or product. We have the freedom to choose the database we need, based upon the rest of the design, and we maintain the freedom to change or replace that database product in the future as needed.

Summary of Payroll Design

In roughly 50 diagrams, we have documented a reasonably complete design for the payroll application. The design employs a large amount of abstraction and polymorphism. The result is that large portions of the design are closed against changes of payroll policy. For example, the application could be changed to deal with employees who were paid quarterly based upon a normal salary and a bonus schedule, and who were paid in shares of preferred stock. This change would require *addition* to the design, but none of the existing design would change. Moreover, if the design has been coded, these changes would require almost no changes to existing working code.

The design consists of three different types of objects. There are real-world objects, such as **Employee** and **TimeCard**, which represent something intrinsic to the problem domain. These objects could be used in other applications associated with this problem domain. Then there are the objects that are contrived as part of this particular application; among these are the hierarchy of **Transaction** objects, the **PaymentSchedule** and **PaymentMethod** hierarchies and, to some extent, the **PaymentClassification** hierarchy. These objects are more related to this particular application, than they are to the whole problem domain. Finally, there are objects that relate to the physical details of the application. Among these are **Set**, **Iterator**, **Application**, **PayrollApplication**, **TransactionSource**, and **TextParserTransactionSource**. These classes have almost nothing to do with paying employees; we need them as components of the superstructure that supports the entire application.

During this design process we rarely considered whether we were performing analysis or design. Instead we concentrated upon issues of clarity and closure. We tried to find the underlying abstractions wherever possible. The result is that we have a good design for

---

5. Sometimes the nature of the database is one of the requirements of the application. RDBMSs provide powerful query and reporting systems that may be listed as application requirements. However, even when such requirements are explicit, the designers should still decouple the application design from the database design. The application design should not have to depend on any particular kind of database.

a payroll application, and we have a core of objects that are germane to the problem domain as a whole. These real-world entity objects (such as **Employee**, **TimeCard**, **SalesReceipt**, etc.) may not be completely ready for integration into other applications, but they are not far from it. Moreover, we *know* that these objects *are* appropriate to at least one application.

If we were concerned with providing a general structure for more than just the **Payroll** application, we would have a good start. At this point, following the successful design of one application, we are ready to consider how the other applications impact our core model.

High-Level Closure Using Categories

The logical analysis and design of the payroll application is complete; however, we still have many design decisions to make. The design of the payroll application documents at least 50 different classes. If all are written into their own implementation and interface modules (**.cc** and **.h** files), we will have over 100 source files in this application. Although this is not a huge number, it does represent an organizational burden. How should we manage these source files?

Along similar lines, how should we divide the work of implementation so that the development can proceed smoothly without the programmers getting into each other's way. We would like to divide the classes into groups that we can assign to individuals or teams for implementation and support. We would like all the developers to know what part of the project they are responsible for, who is responsible for the parts they depend upon, and who is responsible for the parts that depend upon them.

Is this part of design, or is this project management? It is both. Some issues of project management impinge directly upon the design. If we do not consider the management of the project during the design, we may create a design that cannot be managed. Of course such a design would be useless. The following sections show how to manage the issues of closure and reuse by coordinating the design of the application with the design of the development and support environment.

Class Categories

Booch defines class categories as "clusters of classes that are themselves cohesive, but are loosely coupled relative to other clusters."[6]

---

6. Grady Booch, *Object-Oriented Analysis and Design with Applications,"* 2d ed., (Copyright © 1994 by The Benjamin/Cummings Publishing Company), p. 181.

Categories are packages of related classes. Typically one developer, or one team of developers, is responsible for all the classes within a particular category. Such a team may be responsible for many categories, but categories are not usually worked upon by more than one team.

Categories are often used as releasable units. That is, once the team has compiled and tested the classes within a category, they will release that category for use by other teams working on the project. Typically they will assign release numbers to the categories and make copies of the released source and object code that the other development teams will use.

Once a category is released and copied, the development team can continue to develop and modify the classes within the category. The other development teams are unaffected by this because they continue to use the previous release of that category. Thus the team responsible for the category is free to modify the classes within the category without concern for the effect it will have on other teams.

Categories "use" other categories, which means that some categories depend upon others. A dependency may arise because a class in one category inherits from a class in another. Dependencies also arise because using, containing, or instantiation relationships exist between classes in different categories. The most useful definition of a dependency is simply this: Category A depends upon Category B if any of the classes within A cannot be completely compiled and tested without access to at least one of the classes in Category B.

Thus, if Category A depends upon Category B, then Category A cannot be released until it can be compiled and tested with a working release of Category B. Once Category A is released, that release is tied to the release of Category B that it was tested with. Thus, the release of categories must proceed in an orderly, bottom-up fashion. The categories at the bottom do not depend upon others; those at the top depend heavily upon other categories, but are not themselves depended upon.

This bottom-up dependency structure can give project leaders a tool for planning the release of the project as a whole. By examining the category dependency structure, they can determine which categories must be released, and the order in which they must be released, so that the whole system can come together for integration testing and then release.

Note that the concept of categories that I present in this book is slightly different from Booch's concept. Booch's categories are purely logical entities that are not released and do not represent anything physical about the development environment. Booch has a similar but separate entity that he calls a *subsystem*. A subsystem is a physical structure that can be released and for which engineers can assume responsibility.

I have merged these two concepts within this book, so that a category is both a logical entity for grouping classes together and a physical entity that can be released. I have done so, because I find that there is often a 1:1 correspondence between the physical and logical partitions at this level.

Category Structure and Notation

The diagram in Figure 3-52 shows a possible category structure for the payroll application. We will address the appropriateness of this structure in a subsequent section. For now we will confine ourselves to how such a structure is documented and used.

Class categories are drawn as rectangles in the Booch notation. They are annotated with the name of the category and the names of the important classes within the category. Dependencies between the categories are drawn as **uses** relationships with the user being dependent upon the used. By convention, category diagrams are drawn with the using relationships pointing downwards. Thus the dependence is highest at the top and lowest at the bottom.

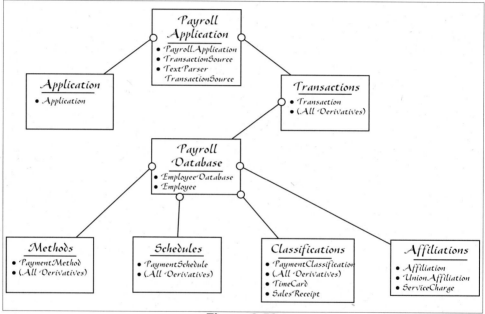

Figure 3-52
Possible Payroll Category Diagram

Figure 3-52 has divided the payroll application into eight categories. The **Payroll-Application** category contains the **PayrollApplication** class and the **TransactionSource** and **TextParserTransactionSource** classes. The **Transactions** category contains the complete **Transaction**-class hierarchy. The constituents of the other categories should be clear by carefully examining the diagram.

The **uses** relationships should also be clear. The **PayrollApplication** category depends upon the **Transactions** category because the **PayrollApplication** class calls the **Transaction::Execute** method. The **Transactions** category depends upon the **PayrollDatabase** category because each of the many derivatives of **Transaction** communicate directly with the **PayrollDatabase** class. The other **uses** relationships are likewise justifiable.

The structure of this diagram is a directed acyclic graph (DAG). It is a graph because it is composed of vertices (the categories) and edges (the **uses** relationships). It is directed because the **uses** relationships are directional; that A uses B does *not* imply that B uses A. Finally, it is acyclic because it is not possible to begin at any arbitrary category and follow the **uses** relationships to wind up back at that starting category.

A quick glance at this diagram is enough to inform the developers who their clients are and who their servers are. The team responsible for the **PayrollDatabase** category, for example, can easily tell that they depend upon four categories below them: **Methods**, **Schedules**, **Classifications** and **Affiliations**. They can also tell that their sole client is **Transactions**.

When the **PayrollDatabase** team wants to make a new release, they know that they need new releases from the teams that they depend upon, and they know that they must notify the developers of **Transactions** that a new release of **Payroll-Database** is imminent.

Circularity in the Category Structure

The acyclic nature of category diagrams is essential. Cycles, when they appear, must be eliminated if the structure is to remain useful. For example, consider Figure 3-53, in which we have added a new category named **Report**. The function of this category is to gather the classes having to do with generating a report of the current day's transaction run. Certainly this category will depend upon the **PayrollDatabase** category for much of its information. Another new category, **ReportViewer** encapsulates a general purpose GUI system that allows us to browse reports on a workstation screen.

The team that is responsible for the **Methods** category needs to display some information in a field of the report, so they make use of the appropriate functions in the **Report** category. Unfortunately, this creates a dependency cycle between **Methods**, **Report**, and **Database**.

The effect of this cycle is that we cannot release **Methods** without **Report**, which we cannot release without **Database**, which we cannot release without **Methods**. In other words, all three categories must be released together, as though they were one big category. This is unfortunate, because it means that the teams that develop and support these three categories will be effectively merged into one team. They will be able to do nothing independently.

Worse, however, is the cycle's effect upon the team that develops and supports the **Transactions** category, which now finds itself dependent upon **ReportViewer**! As far as that team is concerned, such a dependency is absurd. Why should the developers of transactions need to worry about a GUI interface? This team will be very displeased when they discover that they can neither test nor compile until the bugs are worked out of the

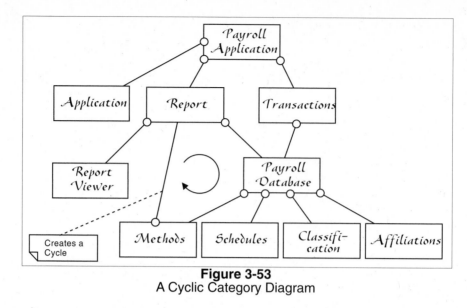

Figure 3-53
A Cyclic Category Diagram

GUI. Moreover, they will arm themselves with spears and daggers when they discover that, just to run their unit tests, they must link in the GUI library, which is 100 times larger than their own object code, and therefore takes 100 times longer to link in, and for which they have absolutely no use.

A development environment can be kept orderly and sane when the teams that use it can work with a degree of independence. When we allow dependencies in a computer application to propagate uncontrolled, the result is chaos.

Resolving Issues of Circularity

How can we eliminate the circularity in Figure 3-53? Figure 3-54 shows a possible solution. The **Report** category is split into two categories, one named **Report** and the other named **ReportFields**. **Report** depends upon **ReportFields**, and so does **Methods**. Thus, the circularity is broken, and rational behavior is restored to the development environment.

It is always possible to break a cycle in a category diagram by splitting one of the categories in the cycle. Moreover, this is beneficial. As the application grows, more and more classes get added to the existing categories. Sometimes new categories are added by design, but sometimes they are added to resolve circularities. Although this increases the number of categories, it also helps to keep the size of each category manageable.

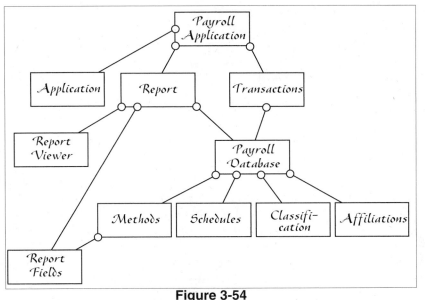

Figure 3-54
Breaking a Cycle in a Category Diagram

The Category Structure Is Always Flexible

Development environments must be able to adapt as the size and complexity of the application grows. As an integral part of the development environment, the category structure of an application is constantly adapting to the changes in the volume and intricacy of the software. The categories and relationships between them should be allowed to change and grow as the application matures.

Such growth, however, should not be unconstrained or arbitrary. The category structure should be *designed* to help manage the development and release of the software. This design must be ongoing as long as the application is undergoing major evolution.

Cohesion, Closure, and Reusability

In the past, the terms *coupling* and *cohesion* have helped us to decide how to group software entities together. These concepts were popularized by structured analysis and design in the early 1980s. Among the structured techniques, cohesion, the tendency of two or more software entities to "belong together," should be maximized in any grouping, while coupling between groupings should be minimized.

The difficulty with applying this criterion in the past has been that the terms *coupling* and *cohesion* had no quantitative definition. There are many kinds of cohesion, many different ways that a group of classes can be said to *cohere*. For example, they may have similar functions, or work together to achieve a common purpose. Perhaps they share similar hierarchical structures, or manage a set of client classes in the same manner. So which kind of cohesion is "right"?

For example, consider Figure 3-52 again—a somewhat arbitrary grouping of classes into categories. Consider the **Transaction** category. We have grouped these classes together because they appear to have a common purpose: they are all transactions. Is this a good grouping?

Consider what happens if we make a change to the **Classifications** category. This change will force a recompilation and retest of the **EmployeeDatabase** category, and well it should. But it will also force a recompilation and retest of the **Transactions** category. Certainly the **ChangeClassificationTransaction** and its three derivatives from Figure 3-27 *should* be recompiled and retested, but why should the others be recompiled and retested?

Technically, those other transactions don't need recompilation and retest. However, if they are part of the **Transactions** category, and if the category is going to be rereleased to deal with the changes to the **Classifications** category, then it could be viewed as irresponsible not to recompile and retest the category as a whole. Even if all the transactions aren't recompiled and retested, the category itself must be rereleased, and then all of its clients will require revalidation at very least, and probably recompilation.

The Cohesion of Common Closure

One of the reasons for grouping the classes into categories is to control the development of the software as it changes. It stands to reason then, that the criteria for grouping should be based upon the propagation of change. Specifically, we would like to organize the categories in such a way that the majority of expected changes will not propagate through the category hierarchy. Thus, we want to base our category groupings upon *closure*.

Closure becomes a criterion for cohesion: classes are cohesive if they are closed against the same modifications. The classes that are grouped into a category should therefore have common closure characteristics: they should all be closed to the same kinds of changes.

Certainly closure is not the only criterion for cohesion; we must consider other criteria, but closure is perhaps the most important. If the classes within a category are closed together, then the category has the enviable attribute that it will resist most kinds of change, and when change is needed, all the classes will change together.

Now let's look again at the **Transactions** category. The classes in this category do not share the same closure. Each one is sensitive to its own particular changes. The **ServiceChargeTransaction** is open to changes to the **ServiceCharge** class, whereas the **TimeCardTransaction** is open to changes to the **TimeCard** class. In fact, as the diagram in 3-52 implies, some portion of the **Transactions** category is dependent upon nearly every other part of the software. Thus, this category suffers a very high rate of release. Every time something is changed anywhere below, the **Transactions** category will have to be revalidated and rereleased.

The **PayrollApplication** category is even more sensitive: any change to any part of the system will affect this category, so its release rate must be enormous. You might think that this is inevitable—that as one climbs higher up the category-dependency hierarchy, the release rate must increase. Fortunately, however, this is not true, and avoiding this syndrome is one of the major advantages of using the OOA/D paradigm.

Creating a Hierarchy of Closed Categories

Consider Figure 3-55. This diagram groups the classes of the payroll application together according to their closure. For example, the **PayrollApplication** category contains the **PayrollApplication** and **TransactionSource** classes. These two classes both depend upon the abstract **Transaction** class, which is in the **PayrollDomain** category. Note that the **TextParserTransactionSource** class is in another category that depends upon the abstract **PayrollApplication** class. This creates an upside-down structure in which the details depend upon the generalities, and the generalities are independent.

The most striking case of generality and independence is the **PayrollDomain** category. This category contains the *essence* of the whole system, yet it depends upon nothing! Examine this category carefully. It contains **Employee**, **PaymentClassification**, **PaymentMethod**, **PaymentSchedule**, **Affiliation**, and **Transaction**. This category contains all of the major abstractions in our model, yet it has no dependencies. Why? Because all of the classes it contains are abstract.

Consider the **Classifications** category, which contains the three derivatives of **PaymentClassification**. It also contains the **ChangeClassificationTransaction** class and its three derivatives, along with **TimeCard** and **SalesReceipt**. Notice that any change made to these nine classes is isolated; other than **TextParser**, no other category is affected! Such isolation also holds for the **Methods** category, the **Schedules** category and the **Affiliations** category. This is quite a bit of isolation.

Notice that the bulk of the detailed code that will eventually be written is in categories that have few or no dependents. Since almost nothing depends upon them, we call them *irresponsible*. The code within those categories is tremendously flexible; it can be changed without affecting many other parts of the project. Notice also that the most general categories of the system contain the least amount of code. These categories are heavily depended upon, but depend upon nothing. Since many categories depend upon them, we call them *responsible*, and since they don't depend upon anything, we call them *independent*. Thus, the amount of responsible code (i.e., code in which changes would affect lots of other

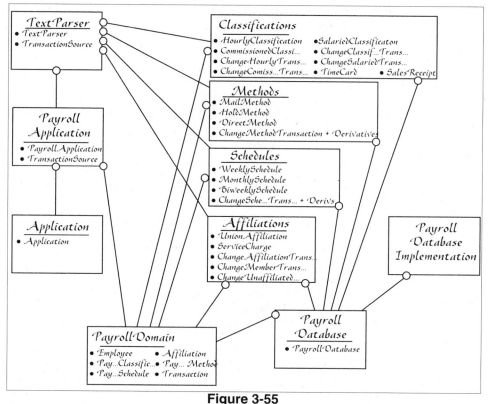

Figure 3-55
A Closed Category Hierarchy for the Payroll Application

code) is very small. Moreover, that small amount of responsible code is also independent, which means that no other modules will induce it to change. This upside-down structure, with highly independent and responsible generalities at the bottom, and highly irresponsible and dependent details at the top, is the hallmark of a well-closed hierarchy.

Contrast Figure 3-52 with Figure 3-55. Notice that the details at the bottom of Figure 3-55 are independent and highly responsible. This is the wrong place for details! Details should depend upon the major architectural decisions of the system and should not be depended upon. Notice also that the generalities, the categories that define the architecture of the system, are irresponsible and highly dependent. Thus, the categories that define the architectural decisions depend upon, and are thus constrained by, the categories that contain the implementation details. It would be better if the architecture constrained the details!

The Main Sequence: Plotting Stability vs. Generality

Consider the graph in Figure 3-56. The vertical axis measures the number of dependents, and the horizontal axis measures the number of dependencies. We can plot class categories upon this graph. Categories that are irresponsible will be close to the bottom, while highly responsible categories will be high up the vertical axis. Independent categories will be far to the left, while highly dependent categories will be to the right. The band that extends from the upper left to the lower right is where most class categories will fall. Categories tend to fall somewhere near the line that connects independent-responsibility with dependent-irresponsibility. This is natural, because categories near the top of a diagram have no dependents but many dependencies, while at the bottom they have many dependents but no dependencies. The higher the category is in a category diagram (such as Figure 3-52), the closer to the upper left corner it will be in Figure 3-56.

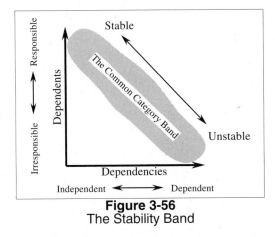

Figure 3-56
The Stability Band

Categories that are both independent and responsible are stable; that is, they are not likely to change. Their responsibility makes them difficult to change, and their independence gives them no outside reason to change. Responsibility means that many other categories depend upon them. To change a responsible category is to induce changes into all the dependent categories as well. Thus, responsible categories are difficult to change. Moreover, since they are independent, no other categories can induce changes in them; so they have no outside cause to change. Thus, we say that the farther to the upper left a category falls, the more stable it is.

Likewise, the categories in the lower right are very unstable. They are irresponsible, so there is nothing to anchor them. We can change them at will, because the changes will not affect other categories. Moreover, they are highly dependent, so they are affected by changes to the categories on which they depend.

Figure 3-57 shows another graph. The horizontal axis measures a class category's instability (i.e., its position in the band in Figure 3-56). To the left is stability (independent-responsibility) and to the right is instability (dependent-irresponsibility). The vertical axis is "generality" or "abstractness." The more general or abstract the category is, the higher it is placed on the graph. The categories that contain the implementation details go at the bottom. Notice the band that stretches from the upper left to the lower right. I call this band the *main sequence* for closed hierarchies. A category that is plotted near this band is called a *main-sequence category*. A main-sequence category is instable only if it contains implementation details. The more general a main-sequence category is, the more stable it is.

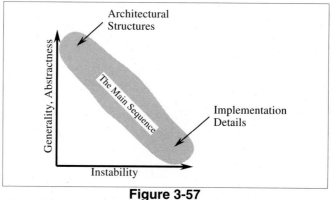

Figure 3-57
The Main Sequence for Closed Category Hierarchies

We would like categories to fall on or near the main sequence. Main-sequence categories exhibit the upside-down dependencies that we found desirable in Figure 3-55. The categories that are the most general and that form the architectural foundation of the software are the most stable. They don't depend upon other categories, but are highly depended upon, whereas the categories that contain the implementation details are the least stable. Other categories do not depend upon them, and they depend heavily upon the general categories that define the architecture of the system.

The Abstraction vs. Stability Characteristics of Traditional Software Methods

Traditional software methods do not conform to the main sequence. Consider a structure chart or a data flow diagram. The more detailed the module in the structure chart, or the more detailed the bubble in the data flow diagram, the more other modules or bubbles depend upon it. Changes at the lowest layers of a structure chart propagate upward to the highest levels, forcing changes in all the intervening modules. Changes in the lower bubbles of a data flow diagram propagate upward through the containing bubbles, forcing changes to the higher-level diagrams. Indeed, when changes are made to the code produced with these techniques, the changes can ripple up from the lowest levels to the highest levels. Figure 3-58 shows how the software entities generated from traditional software design methods would lie on a abstraction vs. instability graph.

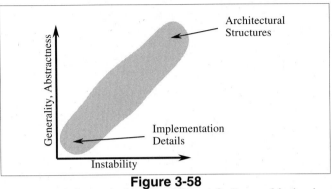

Figure 3-58
The Band Occupied by Traditional Software Methods

That traditional software methods produce software entities that do not follow the main sequence is easy to show. Their most general entities, those that specify the major design decisions and the architecture of the application, depend upon the entities that contain the implementation details. Consider a simple traditional application. It has a main loop that calls several other functions. The main loop is an abstract entity that defines the architecture of the system, yet it depends upon the functions that contain the implementation details. This pattern is repeated in each of the functions called by the main loop. Those functions specify the major design decisions of their part of the application, yet they depend upon the detailed functions that they call.

Thus, traditional methods produce generalities that are highly dependent upon implementation details. The generalities are also irresponsible, because no other entities depend upon them. This combination makes the generalities highly instable. On the other hand, since the details are heavily depended upon by the generalities, they are difficult to change. Every time a detail is changed, the implications of that change ripple up through the application. This is difficult and error-prone. Thus the details are more stable than the generalities and are *resistant* to change.

This leads to an incredible absurdity. In traditional software methods, *the design decisions are easier to change than the implementation details*; or stated perhaps more accurately, it is easier to make a change by *subverting* the design than by conforming to it. Perhaps this is why the designs of traditional software applications so seldom survive the life cycle of the application.

The instability of the general, or abstract, software entities interferes with their reusability. They are tied to their details and constrained by them, so they are, at best, difficult to reuse in a different environment.

When software entities follow the main sequence, however, the generalities are stable, and the details are instable. This makes changing the details easy, but makes changing the design difficult. Since the generalities do not depend upon the details, we can change the details without affecting the design; that is, the design is stable in the presence of change. This means that we can reuse the generalities in many other applications without fear of pollution by the details. Since the generalities are not tied to or influenced by the details, we can reuse the generalities with ease.

One might think that the stability of the generalities leads to inflexibility of the design. However, a design that is hard to change is not necessarily hard to *extend*. After all, this is what the open-closed principle is all about. The generalities can be *extended* without modifying them by ensuring that they have well–designed abstract interfaces.

The Impact of Abstract Classes on the Main Sequence

It should be clear that conformance to the main sequence depends upon the use of abstract classes. Look at Figure 3-55 again. The ability to create the upside-down main sequence structure came about because the **PayrollDomain** category contained nothing but abstract classes. If these classes had not been abstract, then it would not have been possible to create the main-sequence structure. Other abstract classes that have significant effects upon the structure are **TransactionSource**, **Application**, and **Payroll-Database**. Each of these classes specifies generalities upon which other detailed entities depend.

PayrollDatabase was converted to an abstract class at the last minute, as I drew Figure 3-55. I could see by examining the category diagram that the four detail categories (**Classifications**, **Methods**, **Schedules,** and **Affiliations**) depended upon the details of the database. Thus, I split the **PayrollDatabase** into an abstract general category and an implementation-detail category.

The prodigious use of abstract classes thus allows for an increase of closure and the ability to build main-sequence category structures. In turn, main-sequence closure yields the benefits of maintainability and reuse that OO promises.

Categories That Deviate from the Main Sequence

A category that does not fall upon the main sequence is a weakness in the dependency structure of the development environment. Certainly we should minimize such exceptions, because they complicate the development effort; however, we must sometimes compromise the stability of the development environment to support a more important goal.

For example, consider a category of geometrical classes, such as **Point**, **Line**, **Square**, and so on. In order to put such a category on the main sequence, we would like it to consist of abstract classes with no implementation. We would then create another category that depends upon it and provides a particular implementation. Both these categories would be on the main sequence, since one would be abstract and stable, and the other would be concrete and instable. However, these classes are very simple. Once these classes are working, they will probably not be subject to very much change. Thus, making abstract interfaces for them smacks of overkill, and slightly affects their performance. It might be better to make these classes concrete.

It is a matter of judgment as to which of these options to accept. If the stability of the development environment is critical, then we should force the categories onto the main sequence. On the other hand, if performance is vital, or if we are certain of the high stability of a particular concrete category, then we may accept the complexity of depending upon a concrete category.

The Category Is the Granule of Reuse

What portions of the payroll application can we reuse? If another division of our company wanted to reuse our payroll system, but they had a completely different set of policies, they could not reuse **Classifications**, **Methods**, **Schedules**, or **Affiliations**; however, they could reuse **PayrollDomain**, **PayrollApplication**, **Application**, **PayrollDatabase**, and possibly **PDImplementation**. On the other hand, if another department wanted to write software that analyzed the current employee database, they could reuse **PayrollDomain**, **Classifications**, **Methods**, **Schedules**, **Affiliations**, **PayrollDatabase**, and **PDImplementation**. In each case, the granule of reuse is a class category.

Seldom, if ever, would only a single class from a category be reused. The reason is simple: the classes within a category should be cohesive. That means that they depend upon one another and cannot be easily, or sensibly separated. It would make no sense, for example, to use the **Employee** class without using the **PaymentMethod** class. In fact, in order to do so, you would have to modify the **Employee** class so that it did not contain a **PaymentMethod** class. Certainly we don't want to support the kind of reuse that forces us to modify the reused components. Therefore, the granule of reuse is the category. This gives us another cohesion criterion to employ when trying to group classes into categories: not only should the classes be closed together, they should also be reusable together.

Consider again our original category diagram in Figure 3-52. Since this hierarchy does not place the categories on the main sequence, the ones that we might like to reuse, like **Transactions** or **PayrollDatabase**, are not independently reusable. The value of "independence" at the upper left of the main sequence is that we can reuse the independent category without dragging along a lot of extra baggage.

In Figure 3-52 the **PayrollApplication** category is horribly dependent (it depends upon everything). If we wanted to create a new payroll application that used a different set of schedule, method, affiliation, and classification policies, we would not be able to use this category as a whole. Instead, we would have to take individual classes from **PayrollApplication**, **Transactions**, **Methods**, **Schedules**, **Classifi-**

cations, and **Affiliations**. By disassembling the categories in this way, we destroy their release structure. We cannot say that Release 3.2 of **PayrollApplication** is reusable.

Moreover, the reuser, having accepted the reusable fragments of our various class categories, will be faced with a difficult management problem: he will not be able to depend upon our release structure. A new release of **Methods** affects him because he is reusing the **PaymentMethod** class. Most of the time, the changes will be to classes that he is not reusing, yet he must still track our new release number and probably recompile and retest his code.

This will be so difficult to manage that his most likely strategy will be to make a copy of the reusable components and evolve that copy separately from ours. This is not reuse. The two pieces of code will become different, and will require independent support, effectively doubling the support burden.

Categories that lie on the upper left of the main sequence are independently reusable. They do not have to be copied or independently evolved in order to be reused; they are reused as a unit. Since all the classes within such a category are reused together, they can be tracked as a single releasable element with a single evolutionary path. Thus, there is only a single support burden, regardless of the number of reusers. The changes we make in such a cohesive category will almost always be pertinent to all of its reusers, because the category is cohesive for closure. Thus, reusers will not often have to deal with releases that are tangential to their needs.

Cohesion of Policy and Function

The final aspect of cohesion that we will discuss is related to policy and function. Certain classes belong together because they participate in the fulfillment of a particular application policy or function. For example, in Figure 3-55 the reason that **Methods**, **Classifications**, **Schedules**, and **Affiliations** are separate from each other is that they implement different policies. This separation isolates the policies from one another. New schedule policies will not cause a rerelease of the payment-method policies, for example.

In traditional software methodologies, the cohesion of policy and function was supreme. The reason for grouping modules together into larger blocks was that they cooperated in implementing the same function or policy. In OOA/D this form of cohesion is important, but it is subordinate to closure and reuse. That is, a group of classes that are functionally cohesive should be placed in separate categories if they do not share similar closure or reuse characteristics. This is why we separated **PayrollDatabase** from **PayrollDomain**. Even though they are functionally cohesive, their closure characteristics are very different.

Reflections on Cohesion

That the classes within a class category should be cohesive is clear. The preceding paragraphs have defined what cohesion means. To be cohesive, the classes in a category

1. Must be closed together
2. Must be reused together
3. Should share a common function or policy

The order of this list is significant; the first rule is more important than the second, and the second is more important than the last.

Having common closure means that the classes are all subject to the same kinds of changes, and are all immune to other kinds. Thus, most changes to the application will leave the category untouched. The changes that do touch the category will be concentrated within it. This eliminates (or at least mitigates) the syndrome where certain changes cause small modifications in many categories.

Having common reusability means that the classes are inseparable. Any attempt to reuse any class within the category will cause all of them to be reused.

Finally, we should arrange categories so that their dependencies put them on the main sequence. The most general categories should have the fewest dependencies, and the most dependents. The categories that contain the implementation details should have the fewest dependents, and the most dependencies.

When we organize classes into categories that obey these rules, the resulting software will consist of units that are releasable, maintainable, and reusable.

Reflections Upon the Payroll Application

The astute reader will notice that the category diagram in Figure 3-55 does not completely conform to the guidelines quoted above. Specifically, the classes within **PayrollDomain** do not form the smallest reusable unit. The **Transaction** class does not need to be reused with the rest of the category. We could design many applications that access the **Employee** and its fields, but never use a **Transaction**.

This suggests a change to the category diagram, as shown in Figure 3-59. This separates the transactions from the elements that they manipulate. For example, the classes in the **MethodTransactions** category manipulate the classes in the **Methods** category. We have moved the **Transaction** class into a new category named **TransactionApplication**, which also contains **TransactionSource** and a class named **TransactionApplication**. These three form a reusable unit. The **PayrollApplication** class has now become the grand unifier. It contains the main program and also a derivative of **TransactionApplication** called **PayrollApplication**, which ties the `TextParserTransactionSource` to the `Transaction-Application`.

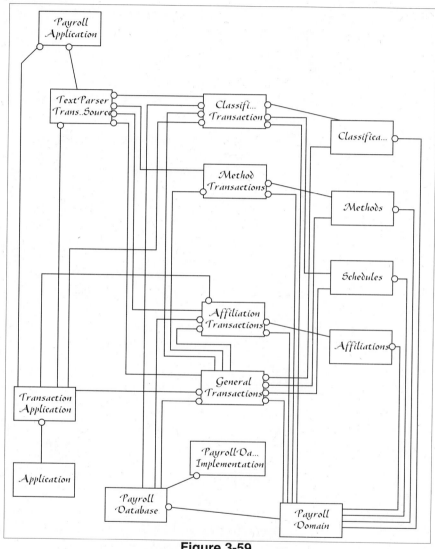

Figure 3-59
Updated Payroll Category Diagram

These manipulations have added yet another layer of abstraction to the design. The **TransactionApplication** category can now be reused by any application that obtains **Transactions** from a **TransactionSource** and then **Executes** them. The **PayrollApplication** category is no longer reusable, since it is extremely dependent. It has slid all the way down to the lower right of the main sequence. However, the **TransactionApplication** category has taken its place, and is more general. Now we can reuse the **PayrollDomain** category without any **Transactions**.

This certainly improves the reusability and maintainability of the project, but at the cost of five extra categories and a more complex dependency architecture. The value of the trade-off depends upon the type of reuse that we might expect, and the rate at which we expect the application to evolve. If the application remains very stable, and few clients reuse it, then perhaps this change is overkill. On the other hand, if many applications will reuse this structure, or we expect the application to experience many changes, then perhaps the new structure would be superior—it's a judgment call.

Coupling and Encapsulation

In traditional approaches to software, such as SA/SD, coupling was considered a necessary evil. The more coupled a software entity was, the harder it was to maintain, because a coupling was viewed as a complication to both entities. However, in OOA/D the coupling issue is not so clear-cut. We want categories to be reusable; the more reusable—the better. Yet each reuse represents a coupling. Thus, we consider some types of couplings to be beneficial! On the other hand, we don't want general categories to depend upon more detailed categories. Each such dependency represents a coupling that is not beneficial. In general, beneficial dependencies flow in the direction of stability. It is good to depend upon a stable category.

Afferent and Efferent Coupling

From the point of view of a particular category, there are two types of couplings. *Afferent* couplings are the dependencies of other categories upon that category, while *efferent* couplings are the dependencies of that category upon others (see Figure 3-60).

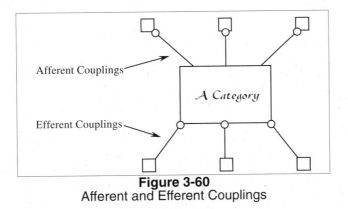

Figure 3-60
Afferent and Efferent Couplings

Whether a particular kind of coupling is beneficial or detrimental depends upon the kind of category that we are dealing with. Afferent couplings are beneficial to abstract, main-sequence class categories, since they represent reuse and flow in the direction of stability. The more afferent couplings a category has, the more responsible that category is. In order to stay on the main sequence, abstract categories should be very responsible; however, abstract main-sequence categories should also be independent, which means that they should have few, if any, efferent couplings.

The opposite is true for main-sequence categories that contain implementation details. Such categories should be irresponsible and dependent, meaning that they should have few afferent couplings but many efferent couplings.

Thus, it is not couplings that we want to restrict, but the *kind* of couplings compared to the generality of the category. The more abstract the category, the more we want to diminish efferent couplings and enhance afferent couplings. The more detailed the category is, the more we want to diminish afferent couplings and encourage efferent couplings.

Controlling Coupling with Encapsulation

Just as the coupling among classes is managed by encapsulation boundaries in C++, so the couplings among categories can be managed by the export adornments of the Booch notation. We will see later how to enforce export decisions by using the **namespace** feature of C++.

If a class within one category is to be used by another category, that class must be exported. In Booch notation, classes are exported by default, but we may adorn a class category to denote that certain classes should not be exported. Figure 3-61, a blowup of the **Classifications** category, shows that the three derivatives of **PaymentClassification** are exported, but that **TimeCard** and **SalesReceipt** are not. This means that other categories will not be able to use **TimeCard** and **SalesReceipt**; they are private to the **Classifications** category.

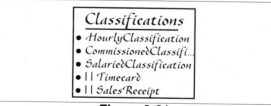

Figure 3-61
Private Classes in Classifications Category

We may want to hide certain classes within a category to prevent afferent couplings. **Classifications** is a very detailed category that contains the implementations of several payment policies. In order to keep this category on the main sequence, we want to limit its afferent couplings, so we hide the classes that other categories don't need to know about.

TimeCard and **SalesReceipt** are good choices for private classes. They are implementation details of the mechanisms for calculating an employee's pay. We want to remain free to alter these details, so we need to prevent anyone else from depending upon their structure.

A quick glance at Figures 3-21 through 3-24 shows that the **TimeCardTransaction** and **SalesReceiptTransaction** classes already depend upon **TimeCard** and **SalesReceipt**. We can easily resolve this problem, however, as shown in Figures 3-62 and 3-63.

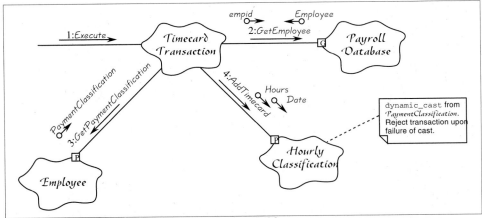

Figure 3-62
Revision to **TimeCardTransaction** to Protect **TimeCard** Privacy

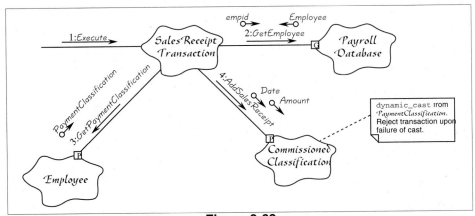

Figure 3-63
Revision to **SalesReceiptTransaction** to Protect **SalesReceipt** Privacy

Metrics

We can quantify the attributes of cohesion, coupling, stability, generality, and conformance to the main sequence with a few simple heuristics. But why should we want to? To paraphrase Tom DeMarco: You can't manage what you can't control, and you can't control what you don't measure.[7] To be effective software engineers or software managers, we must be able to control software development practice. If we don't measure it, however, we will never have that control.

By applying the heuristics described below, and calculating some fundamental metrics about our object-oriented designs, we can begin to correlate those metrics with measured performance of the software and of the teams that develop it. The more metrics we gather, the more information we will have, and the more control we will eventually be able to exert.

I present these metrics as experimental. I have used them myself with a reasonable amount of success, but I cannot say that they have been subjected to a sufficient and comprehensive test. I can say this: The metrics are simple enough to calculate by hand, and they are unambiguous enough to be calculated automatically from a program that parses C++ programs or Booch diagrams.

- (*H*) **Relational Cohesion**. One aspect of the cohesion of a class category can be represented as the average number of internal relationships per class. Let R be the number of class relationships that are internal to the category (i.e., that do not connect to classes outside the category). Let N be the number of classes within the category. Then $H = (R + 1)/N$. The extra 1 in the formula prevents $H = 0$ when $N = 1$. It represents the relationship that the category has to all its classes.
- (C_a) **Afferent coupling** can be calculated as the number of classes from other categories that depend upon the classes within the subject category. These dependencies are class relationships, such as `inheritance`, `contains`, and `uses`.
- (C_e) **Efferent coupling** can be calculated as the number of classes in other categories that the classes in the subject category depend upon. As before, these dependencies are class relationships.
- (*A*) **Abstractness** or **Generality** can be calculated as the ratio of the number of abstract classes in the category to the total number of classes in the category.[8] This metric ranges from 0 to 1.
- (*I*) **Instability** can be calculated as the ratio of efferent coupling to total coupling. ($C_e \div (C_e + C_a)$). This metric also ranges from 0 to 1.
- (*D*) **Distance from the Main Sequence** $= |(A + I - 1) \div \sqrt{2}|$. The main sequence is idealized by the line $A + I = 1$. The formula above calculates the distance of any particular category from the main sequence. It ranges from ~.7 to 0;[9] the closer to

---

7. Tom DeMarco, *Controlling Software Projects* (Yourdon Press, 1982), p. 3.
8. One might think that a better formula for *A* is the ratio of pure virtual functions to total member functions within the category. However, I have found that this formula weakens the abstraction metric too much. Even one pure virtual function will make a class abstract, and the power of that abstraction is more significant than the fact that the class may have dozens of concrete functions.

0, the better.

- **(D') Normalized Distance from the Main Sequence** = $|(A + I - 1)|$. This metric represents the D metric normalized to the range [0,1]. It is perhaps a little more convenient to calculate, and to interpret. The value 0 represents a category that is coincident with the main sequence. The value 1 represents a category that is as far from the main sequence as is possible.

Applying the Metrics to the Payroll Application

Table 3-1 shows how the classes in the payroll model have been allocated to class categories. Figure 3-64 shows the class category diagram for the payroll application with all the metrics calculated. And Table 3-2 shows all of the metrics calculated for each category.

Each category **uses** relationship in Figure 3-64 is adorned with two numbers. The number closest to the 'using' category (i.e. the number closest to the open circle) represents the number of classes in that category that depend upon the 'used' category. The number closest to the 'used' category represents the number of classes in that category that the 'using' category depends upon.

Table 3-1: Allocation of Classes to Class Categories

Category	Classes in Category		
Affiliations	ServiceCharge	UnionAffiliation	
AffiliationTrans-actions	ChangeAffillia-tionTransaction	ChangeUnaffiliat-edTransaction	ChangeMember-Transaction
	ServiceCharge-Transaction		
Application	Application		
Classifications	Commissioned-Classification	Hourly-Classification	Salaried-Classification
	SalesReceipt	Timecard	
Classification-Transaction	ChangeClassifica-tionTransaction	ChangeCommisioned Transaction	ChangeHourly-Transaction
	ChangeSalaried-Transaction	SalesReceipt-Transaction	Timecard-Transaction
GeneralTransac-tions	AddCommissioned-Employee	AddEmployee-Transaction	AddHourlyEmployee
	AddSalaried-Employee	ChangeAddress-Transaction	ChangeEmployee-Transaction

---

9. It is impossible to plot any category outside the unit square on the A vs. I graph. This is because neither A nor I can exceed 1. The main sequence bisects this square from (0,1) to (1,0). The points within the square that are farthest from the main sequence are the two corners (0,0) and (1,1). Their distance from the main sequence is $\sqrt{2}/2 = 0.7071067812...$

Table 3-1: Allocation of Classes to Class Categories (Continued)

Category	Classes in Category		
	ChangeName-Transaction	DeleteEmployee-Transaction	PaydayTransaction
Methods	DirectMethod	HoldMethod	MailMethod
MethodTransac-tions	ChangeDirect-Transaction	ChangeHold-Transaction	ChangeMail-Transaction
	ChangeMethod-Transaction		
PayrollApplica-tion	Payroll-Application		
PayrollDatabase	PayrollDatabase		
PayrollDatabase-Implementation	PayrollDatabase-Implementation		
PayrollDomain	Affiliation	Employee	Payment-Classification
	PaymentMethod	PaymentSchedule	
Schedules	BiweeklySchedule	MonthlySchedule	WeeklySchedule
TextParserTrans-actionSource	TextParser-TransactionSource		
TransactionAppli-cation	Transaction-Application	Transaction	TransactionSource

Table 3-2: Category Metrics Spreadsheet

Category Name	N	A	Ca	Ce	R	H	I	A	D	D'
Affiliations	2	0	2	1	1	1	.33	0	.47	.67
AffilliationTransactions	4	1	1	7	2	.75	.88	.25	.09	.12
Application	1	1	1	0	0	1	0	1	0	0
Classifications	5	0	8	3	2	.06	.27	0	.51	.73
ClassificationTransaction	6	1	1	15	5	1	.94	.17	.07	.10
GeneralTransactions	9	2	4	12	5	.67	.75	.22	.02	.03
Methods	3	0	4	1	0	.33	.20	0	.57	.80
MethodTransactions	4	1	1	6	3	1	.86	.25	.08	.11
PayrollApplication	1	0	0	2	0	1	1	0	0	0
PayrollDatabase	1	1	11	1	0	1	.08	1	.06	.08
PayrollDatabaseImpl...	1	0	0	1	0	1	1	0	0	0
PayrollDomain	5	4	26	0	4	1	0	.80	.14	.20
Schedules	3	0	6	1	0	.33	.14	0	.61	.86
TextParserTransactionSource	1	0	1	20	0	1	.95	0	.03	.05
TransactionApplication	3	3	9	1	2	1	.1	1	.07	.10

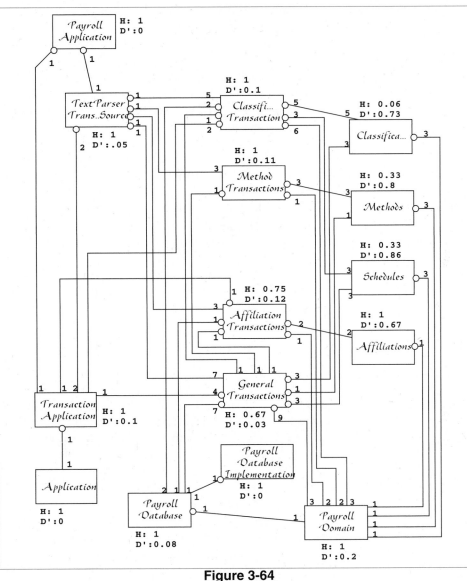

Figure 3-64
Category Diagram with Metrics

Each category in FIgure 3-64 is adorned with the metrics that apply to it. Many of these metrics are encouraging. **PayrollApplication**, **PayrollDomain**, and **PayrollDatabase**, for example, have high relational cohesion and are either on or close to the main sequence. However, the **Classifications**, **Methods**, and **Schedules** categories show generally poor relational cohesion and are almost as far from the main sequence as is possible!

These numbers tell us that the partitioning of the classes into categories is weak. If we don't find a way to improve the numbers, then the development environment will be sensitive to change, which may cause unnecessary rerelease and retesting. Specifically, we have low-abstraction categories like **ClassificationTransactions** depending heavily upon other low-abstraction categories like **Classifications**. Classes with low abstraction contain most of the detailed code and are therefore likely to change, which will force rerelease of the categories that depend upon them. Thus the **Classification-Transactions** category will have a very high release rate since it is subject to both its own high change rate, and that of **Classifications**. As much as possible, we would like to limit the sensitivity of our development environment to change.

Clearly, if we have only two or three developers, they will be able to manage the development environment "in their heads," and the need to maintain categories on the main sequence, for this purpose, will not be great. The more developers there are, however, the more difficult it is to keep the development environment sane. Moreover, the work required to obtain these metrics is minimal compared to the work required to do even a single retest and rerelease.[10] Therefore, it is a judgment call as to whether the work of computing these metrics will be a short-term loss or gain.

Object Factories

Classifications and **ClassificationTransactions** are so heavily depended upon because the classes within them must be instantiated. For example, the **TextParserTransactionSource** class must be able to create **AddHourly-EmployeeTransaction** objects; thus there is an afferent coupling from the **Text-ParserTransactionSource** category to the **ClassificationTransactions** category. Also, the **ChangeHourlyTransaction** class must be able to create **HourlyClassification** objects, so there is an afferent coupling from the **ClassificationTransactions** category to the **Classification** category.

Almost every other use of the objects within these categories is through their abstract interface. Were it not for the need to create each concrete object, the afferent couplings upon these categories would not exist. For example, if **TextParserTransaction-Source** did not need to create the different transactions, it would not depend upon the four categories containing the transaction implementations.

This problem cannot be entirely solved, but it can be significantly mitigated. The technique employs classes known as *object factories*. Each category provides an object factory that is responsible for creating all the public objects within that category. The object factory provides virtual functions that act as the representatives of the constructors

---

10. I spent about two hours compiling the statistics and computing the metrics for the payroll example.

of the objects that it creates, and returns pointers to those objects. The factory inherits its interface from an abstract class that specifies the interface for all of the constructor representatives as pure virtual functions. This abstract version of the factory is kept as the sole class in a companion category, the "factory" category. Users who want to create objects within a category depend upon the factory category instead of the concrete category (see Figure 3-65).

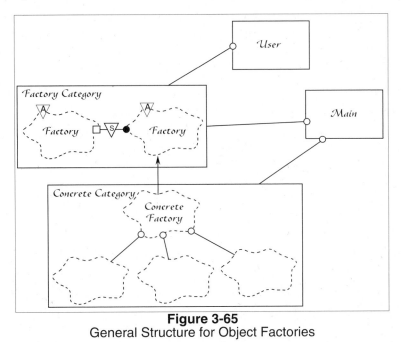

Figure 3-65
General Structure for Object Factories

The abstract factory class contains a static member that is a pointer to its own type. The main program creates the appropriate concrete factory object and then loads the static pointer in the abstract class. Thus, all other categories that want to create objects from the concrete category can use the abstract interface within the factory category to do so. This places all of the afferent creation dependencies upon an abstract category, and leaves the concrete category much closer to the main sequence.

We will examine how to structure an object factory in the next section, but first we need to consider some other deficiencies from the category diagram in Figure 3-64.

Rethinking the Cohesion Boundaries

We initially separated **Classifications**, **Methods**, **Schedules**, and **Affiliations** in Figure 3-52. At the time it seemed like a reasonable partitioning. After all, other users may want to reuse our schedule classes without reusing our affiliation classes. This partitioning was maintained after we split out the transactions into their own categories, creating a dual hierarchy. Perhaps this was too much. The diagram in Figure 3-64 is very tangled.

A tangled category diagram makes the management of releases difficult if it is done by hand. Although category diagrams would work well with an automated project-planning tool, most of us don't have that luxury. Thus, we need to keep our category diagrams as simple as is practical.

In my view, the transaction partitioning is more important than the functional partitioning. Thus, in Figure 3-69 (the final category structure) we will merge the transactions into a single **TransactionImplementation** category. We will also merge the **Classifications**, **Schedules**, **Methods**, and **Affiliations** categories into a single **PayrollImplementation** category.

The Object Factory for **TransactionImplementation**

Figure 3-66 shows how to build an object factory for the **TransactionImplementation** category. The **TransactionFactory** category contains the abstract base class, which defines the pure virtual functions that represent the constructors for the concrete transaction objects. The **TransactionImplementation** category contains the concrete derivative of the **TransactionFactory** class, and uses all the concrete transactions in order to create them.

The **TransactionFactory** class has a static member declared as a **TransactionFactory** pointer. This member must be initialized by the main program to point to an instance of the concrete **TransactionFactoryImplementation** object.

Initializing the Factories

If other categories are to create objects using the object factories, the static members of the abstract object factories must be initialized to point to the appropriate concrete factory. This must be done before any user attempts to use the factory. The best place to do this is usually the main program, which means that the main program depends upon all the factories, *and* upon all the concrete categories. Thus, each concrete category will have at least one afferent coupling from the main program. This will force the concrete category off the main sequence a bit, but it cannot be helped.[11] It means that we must rerelease the main program every time we change any of the concrete categories. Of course we should probably rerelease the main program for each change anyway, since it will need to be tested regardless.

Figures 3-67 and 3-68 show the static and dynamic structure of the main program in relation to the object factories.

---

11. As a practical solution, I usually ignore couplings from the main program.

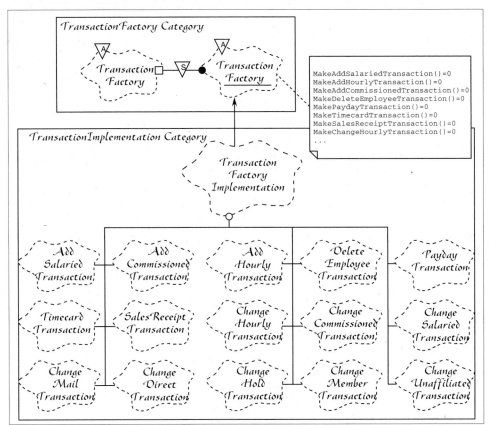

Figure 3-66
Object Factory for Transactions

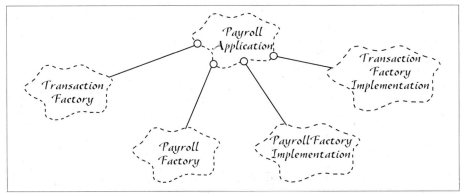

Figure 3-67
Static Structure of Main Program and Object Factories

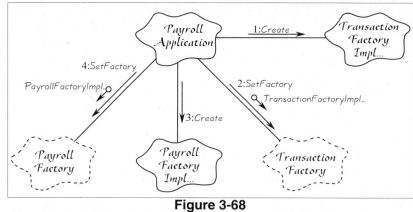

Figure 3-68
Dynamic Structure of Main Program and Object Factories

The Final Category Structure

Table 3-3 shows the final allocation of classes to class categories. Table 3-4 contains the metrics spreadsheet. Figure 3-69 shows the final category structure, which employs object factories to bring the concrete categories near the main sequence

Table 3-3: Allocation of classes to class categories

Category	Classes in Category		
Abstract-Transactions	AddEmployee-Transaction	ChangeAffilia-tionTransaction	ChangeEmployee-Transaction
	ChangeClassifica-tionTransaction	ChangeMethod-Transaction	
Application	Application		
Payroll-Application	Payroll-Application		
PayrollDatabase	PayrollDatabase		
PayrollDatabase-Implementation	PayrollDatabase-Implementation		
PayrollDomain	Affiliation	Employee	Payment-Classification
	PaymentMethod	PaymentSchedule	
PayrollFactory	PayrollFactory		
Payroll-Implementation	BiweeklySchedule	Commissioned-Classification	DirectMethod
	HoldMethod	Hourly-Classification	MailMethod

Table 3-3: Allocation of classes to class categories (Continued)

Category	Classes in Category		
	MonthlySchedule	PayrollFactory-Implementation	Salaried-Classification
	SalesReceipt	ServiceCharge	Timecard
	UnionAffiliation	WeeklySchedule	
TextParser-TransactionSource	TextParser-TransactionSource		
Transaction-Application	Transaction	Transaction-Application	TransactionSource
Transaction-Factory	Transaction-Factory		
Transaction-Implementation	AddCommissioned-Employee	AddHourlyEmployee	AddSalaried-Employee
	ChangeAddress-Transaction	ChangeCommis-sionedTransaction	ChangeDirect-Transaction
	ChangeHold-Transaction	ChangeHourly-Transaction	ChangeMail-Transaction
	ChangeMember-Transaction	ChangeName-Transaction	ChangeSalaried-Transaction
	ChangeUnaffiliat-edTransaction	DeleteEmployee	PaydayTransaction
	SalesReceipt-Transaction	ServiceCharge-Transaction	Timecard-Transaction
	TransactionFacto-ryImplementation		

Table 3-4: Category Metrics Spreadsheet

Category Name	N	A	Ca	Ce	R	H	I	A	D	D'
AbstractTransactions	5	5	13	1	0	.20	.07	1	.05	.07
Application	1	1	1	0	0	1	0	1	0	0
PayrollApplication	1	0	0	5	0	1	.21	1	.15	.21
PayrollDatabase	1	1	19	5	0	1	.21	1	.15	.21
PayrollDatabaseImpl...	1	0	0	1	0	1	1	0	0	0
PayrollDomain	5	4	30	0	4	1	0	.80	.14	.20
PayrollFactory	1	1	12	4	0	1	.25	1	.18	.25
PayrollImplementation	14	0	1	5	3	.29	.83	0	.12	.17
TextParserTransactionSource	1	0	1	3	0	1	.75	0	.18	.25
TransactionApplication	3	3	14	1	3	1.33	.07	1	.05	.07
TransactionFactory	1	1	3	1	0	1	.25	1	.18	.25
TransactionImplementation	19	0	1	14	0	.05	.93	0	.05	.07

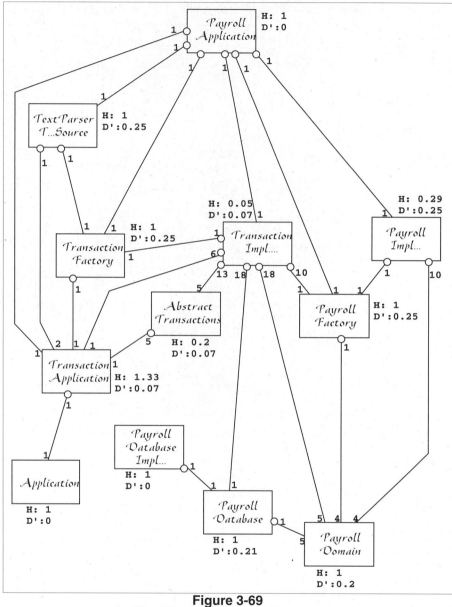

Figure 3-69
Final Payroll Category Structure

The metrics on this diagram are heartening. The relational cohesions are all very high (thanks in part to the relationships of the concrete factories to the objects that they create), and there are no significant deviations from the main sequence. Thus, the couplings between our categories are appropriate to a sane development environment. Our abstract categories are closed, reusable, and heavily depended upon, while having few dependencies of their own. Our concrete categories are segregated on the basis of reuse, are heavily dependent upon the abstract categories, and are not heavily depended upon themselves.

Reflections upon Object Factories

Object factories strongly mitigate the need for the unhealthy dependencies required for creating concrete objects. Instead of creating them directly, users create them through an abstract interface. The concrete factory object gets created once at program initialization time, and usually only in one place, thus rationalizing the remaining dependencies. But how far should one go? Should every object be created through a factory? How about objects like **Strings** or **Complex** numbers? Probably not.

Factories should be employed only when necessary. If you can survive with a less-than-optimal dependency structure among your categories, then factories are probably overkill, but if at some places in your category structure you believe you should minimize the sensitivity to change, then factories can be a big help.

The astute reader may suspect that the dependency of the main program on the concrete object factory could be broken. If this were possible, then categories with factories would need no afferent couplings at all, and would sit square on the main sequence.

In C++ it is possible to create static objects. What if a module within a concrete category created a static instance of the concrete factory? Moreover, what if the constructor for that concrete factory loaded the address of the created object into the static pointer within the abstract factory? Then the main program would not have to create the concrete factory, and the dependency would be broken!

However, this depends upon a facility that the language does not give us; it does not guarantee that static objects are constructed before main is called. It only guarantees that static objects are constructed before the first use of any function or object within the module that contains the static object. Thus, there is no solid guarantee that the constructors will be called before someone actually tries to employ the abstract interface of the factory.

Exercises

1. Why is it inadvisable to finish the analysis of a project before you begin its design?

2. Write a specification for a system that plays Tic-Tac-Toe. Perform a noun list analysis in an attempt to identify the objects in the system. Now perform a use-case analysis.

3. What are the underlying abstractions in the Tic-Tac-Toe program? Can these abstractions be reused in a program that plays Othello?

4. Modify the Payroll Design to add Employees who are paid a flat salary on a quarterly basis, but are also given a yearly bonus. The bonus is decided by management and fed into the payroll system as bonus slips.

5. Modify the Payroll Program to include tax deductions. Update the category hierarchy and recompute the metrics.

6. Add the **Undo** method to the **Transaction** class and implement it throughout all the Payroll transactions.

7. Create a category structure for the container classes from Chapter 2. Compute the metrics. Do you think that an Object Factory would be beneficial?

8. Compute the metrics for the CoffeeMaker example in chapter 1.

9. What is the significance of a class that sits on the main sequence at coordinates (.5,.5)?

10. If we performed top-down design, we would try to come up with the category structure before we came up with the class and object diagrams. Yet in the payroll example, the category structure was the *last* thing that was designed. Do you think this is appropriate? Why?

A Partial C++ Implementation of Payroll

At last we are ready to discuss the implementation.[12] We have created a logical design for the payroll application, and we have fit it into a physical category structure that will help keep our development environment sane.

Categories and Namespaces

Class categories can be physically represented as the directories in which the source files are kept. They can also be logically represented as C++ namespaces. Each category is given two namespaces. One contains the names of the classes that the category exports for public use; the other is reserved for names that are private to the category.

---

12. In an actual project, we would have written much of the code prior to creating the category structure.

The Header Files

The header files from three of the categories of the payroll application are presented below. Each category has a file named **namespaces.h** that contains the definition of the namespaces for that category. Notice that every header file within a category includes the **namespaces.h** file.

The **PayrollDomain** Category

PayrollDomain/namespaces.h

```
//-------------------------------------------------
// The namespaces for the PayrollDomain Category
//
namespace PublicPayrollDomain
{
    class Employee;
    class PaymentSchedule;
    class PaymentMethod;
    class PaymentClassification;
    class Affiliation;
};

//---------------------------------------------
// The published alias that clients should use
//
namespace PayrollDomain = PublicPayrollDomain;
```

Note that the name of the public namespace is **PublicPayrollDomain**, although users are expected to use the alias **PayrollDomain**. The purpose of the alias is to make it difficult for users to add more names to the public namespace. Under the rules for C++ namespaces, users may add names to a namespace if they use the actual namespace name, but not if they use an alias.

Certainly the use of the alias does not prevent a user from specifically using the namespace name instead of the alias. However, if we establish the convention that only the alias may be referenced within user code and never the true name of the namespace, then it is easy to develop tools that can check that convention by searching for uses of the proscribed names.

PayrollDomain/employee.h

```
#include "PayrollDomain/namespaces.h"
#include "Components/namespaces.h"
using namespace Components;

#include "Components/string.h"
#include "Components/u_set.h"
//---------------------------------------------
```

```
// Name
//   Employee
class PayrollDomain::Employee
{
  public:
    void PayDay(const Date&);
    void SetClassification(PaymentClassification*);
    void SetMethod(PaymentMethod*);
    void SetSchedule(PaymentSchedule*);

  private:
    double CalculatePay(const Date&) const;

    String                   itsName;
    String                   itsAddress;
    UnboundedSet<Affiliation*> itsAffiliation;
    PaymentSchedule*         itsSchedule;
    PaymentClassification*   itsClassification;
    PaymentMethod*           itsMethod;
};
```

PayrollDomain/pmtClass.h

```
#include "PayrollDomain/namespaces.h"
#include "Components/namespaces.h"
using namespace Components;

//------------------------------------
// Name
//   PaymentClassification
//
// Description
//   This class represents the policy for determination of the payment
//   due an employee.

class PayrollDomain::PaymentClassification
{
  public:
    virtual double CalculatePay(const Date&) = 0;
    virtual void   Post(const Date&) = 0;
  private:
};
```

PayrollDomain/pmtMethod.h

```
#include "PayrollDomain/namespaces.h"

//------------------------------------
// Name
//   PaymentMethod
//
// Description
//   This class represents the policy by which an employee
//   recieves his pay.
//

class PayrollDomain::PaymentMethod
{
  public:
    virtual void Pay(double theAmount) const = 0;
};
```

PayrollDomain/pmtSched.h

```
#include "PayrollDomain/namespaces.h"
#include "Components/date.h"
using Components::Date;

//------------------------------------
// Name
//   PaymentSchedule
//
// Description
//   This class represents the policy which determines when an
//   employee is to be paid.
//

class PayrollDomain::PaymentSchedule
{
  public:
    virtual int IsPayDay(const Date&) const = 0;
};
```

PayrollDomain/affiliation.h

```
#include "PayrollDomain/namespaces.h"
#include "Components/namespaces.h"
using namespace Components;

//-------------------------
// Name
//   Affiliation
//
// Description
//   This class represents an affiliation for an employee.  An
//   affiliation is a membership in a group which is paid its dues and
//   fees through payroll deductions.
//

class PayrollDomain::Affiliation
{
  public:
    virtual double GetFee(const Date&) const = 0;
    virtual void   Post(const Date&) = 0;
};
```

The `PayrollFactory` Category

PayrollFactory/namespaces.h

```
//-----------------------------------------------
// The namespaces for the PayrollFactory category
//
namespace PayrollFactoryPublic
{
    class PayrollFactory;
};

namespace PayrollFactory = PayrollFactoryPublic;
```

PayrollFactory/payrollFac.h

```
#include "PayrollFactory/namespaces.h"
#include "PayrollDomain/namespaces.h"
#include "Component/namespaces.h"
using namespace PayrollDomain;
using namespace Component;

//----------------------------------------
// Name
//   PayrollFactory
//
// Description
//   This class specifies the interface for creating all the
//   payroll objects.
//

class PayrollFactory::PayrollFactory
{
  public:
    static void SetFactory(PayrollFactory* theFactory)
    {theirFactory = theFactory;}

    static PayrollFactory* GetFactory() const
    {return theirFactory;}

    virtual PaymentClassification*
    MakeSalaried(double theSalary) = 0;

    virtual PaymentClassification*
    MakeHourly(double theRate) = 0;

    virtual PaymentClassification*
    MakeCommissioned(double theSalary, double theRate) = 0;

    virtual PaymentMethod* MakeHoldMethod() = 0;

    virtual PaymentMethod*
    MakeDirectMethod(const String& theBank,
                     const String& theAccount) = 0;

    virtual PaymentMethod*
    MakeMailMethod(const String& theAddress) = 0;

    virtual PaymentSchedule* MakeWeeklySchedule() = 0;
    virtual PaymentSchedule* MakeMonthlySchedule() = 0;
```

```
    virtual PaymentSchedule* MakeBiweeklySchedule() = 0;

    virtual Affiliation* MakeUnionAffiliation() = 0;

  private:
    static PayrollFactory* theirFactory;
};
```

This class is the abstract interface for the object factory of the **PayrollImple-mentation** category. One pure virtual function is provided for each concrete class that can be created through this interface. Notice, however, that the functions return the abstract base class of the objects being created.

The **PayrollImplementation** Category

PayrollImplementation/namespaces.h

```
//-----------------------------------------
// The namespaces for the PayrollImplementation category.
//

namespace PayrollImplementationPublic
{
    class PayrollFactoryImplementation;
};

namespace PayrollImplementationPrivate
{
    class HoldMethod;
    class MailMethod;
    class DirectMethod;
    class WeeklySchedule;
    class MonthlySchedule;
    class BiweeklySchedule;
    class HourlyClassification;
    class SalariedClassification;
    class CommissionedClassification;
    class UnionAffiliation;
    class ServiceCharge;
    class TimeCard;
    class SalesReceipt;
};

namespace PayrollImplementation = PayrollImplementationPublic;
```

The namespaces for the **PayrollImplementation** category are revealing. All of the classes are private except for the factory, which severely limits the number of afferent couplings that can depend upon this category. All the other classes in the category must be used though the abstract interfaces of the **PayrollDomain** category!

PayrollImplementation/factory.h

```
#include "PayrollImplementation/namespaces.h"

#include "PayrollFactory/payrollFac.h"
using namespace PayrollFactory;

//----------------------------------------
// Name
//   PayrollFactoryImplementation
//
// Description
//   This class specifies the interface for creating all the
//   payroll objects.
//

class PayrollImplementation::PayrollFactoryImplementation
: public PayrollFactory
{
  public:
    virtual PaymentClassification*
    MakeSalaried(double theSalary);

    virtual PaymentClassification*
    MakeHourly(double theRate);

    virtual PaymentClassification*
    MakeCommissioned(double theSalary, double theRate);

    virtual PaymentMethod* MakeHoldMethod();

    virtual PaymentMethod*
    MakeDirectMethod(const String& theBank,
                     const String& theAccount);

    virtual PaymentMethod*
    MakeMailMethod(const String& theAddress);

    virtual PaymentSchedule* MakeWeeklySchedule();
    virtual PaymentSchedule* MakeMonthlySchedule();
    virtual PaymentSchedule* MakeBiweeklySchedule();

    virtual Affiliation* MakeUnionAffiliation();
};
```

PayrollImplementation/timecard.h

```
#include "PayrollImplementation/namespaces.h"
#include "Components/date.h"
using Components::Date;

//----------------------------------------
// Name
//   TimeCard
//
// Description
//   These objects represent the timecards that are filled
//   out by hourly employees.  They are contained by
//   HourlyClassification objects.
//

class PayrollImplementationPrivate::TimeCard
```

```
{
  public:
    TimeCard(const Date&, double theHours);
    Date   GetDate() const;
    double GetHours() const;

  private:
    Date    itsDate;
    double itsHours;
};
```

PayrollImplementation/salesReceipt.h

```
#include "PayrollImplementation/namespaces.h"
#include "Components/date.h"
using Components::Date;

//-------------------------------------
// Name
//   SalesReceipt
//
// Description
//   These objects represent the sales receipts that are given to
//   commissioned employees when they make a sale.  They are contained
//   by the CommissionedClassification objects.

class PayrollImplementationPrivate::SalesReceipt
{
  public:
    SalesReceipt(const Date&, double theAmount);
    Date   GetDate() const;
    double GetAmount() const;

  private:
    Date    itsDate;
    double itsAmount;
};
```

PayrollImplementation/svcCharge.h

```
#include "PayrollImplementation/namespaces.h"
#include "Components/date.h"
using Components::Date;

//-------------------------------------
// Name
//   ServiceCharge
//
// Description
//   These objects represent the service charges that are levied
//   against union members.  They are contained by the
//   UnionAffiliation object.
//

class PayrollImplementationPrivate::ServiceCharge
{
  public:
    ServiceCharge(const Date& theDate, double theAmount);
    double GetAmount() const;
    Date   GetDate() const;

  private:
```

```
    Date    itsDate;
    double itsAmount;
};
```

PayrollImplementation/hourlyClass.h

```
#include "PayrollImplementation/namespaces.h"
#include "PayrollDomain/pmtClass.h"
using namespace PayrollDomain;

#include "Components/namespaces.h"
using namespace Components;

#include "Components/u_set.h"

//-------------------------------------
// Name
//   HourlyClassification
//
// Description
//   Employees containing the HourlyClassification
//   are paid according to the number of hours logged
//   in their most current time cards.
//

class PayrollImplementationPrivate::HourlyClassification
: public PaymentClassification
{
  public:
    virtual double CalculatePay(const Date&);

  private:
    UnboundedSet<TimeCard*> itsTimeCards;
    double                  itsHourlyRate;
};
```

PayrollImplementation/slryClass.h

```
#include "PayrollImplementation/namespaces.h"
#include "PayrollDomain/pmtClass.h"
using namespace PayrollDomain;

//-------------------------------------
// Name
//   SalariedClassification
//
// Description
//   Employees containing the SalariedClassification
//   are paid according to their salary.
//

class PayrollImplementationPrivate::SalariedClassification
: public PaymentClassification
{
  public:
    SalariedClassification(double theSalary);
    virtual double CalculatePay(const Date&);

  private:
    double itsSalary;
};
```

PayrollImplementation/commClass.h

```
#include "PayrollImplementation/namespaces.h"
#include "PayrollDomain/pmtClass.h"
using namespace PayrollDomain;

#include "Components/namespaces.h"
using namespace Components;
#include "Components/u_set.h"

//-------------------------------------
// Name
//   CommissionedClassification
//
// Description
//   Employees containing the CommissionedClassification
//   are paid according to a base salary and their total sales
//   as recorded in their sales receipts
//

class PayrollImplementationPrivate::HourlyClassification
: public PaymentClassification
{
  public:
    virtual double CalculatePay(const Date&);

  private:
    UnboundedSet<SalesReceipt*> itsSalesReceipts;
    double                      itsBaseSalary;
    double                      itsCommissionRate;
};
```

PayrollImplementation/weeklySched.h

```
#include "PayrollImplementation/namespaces.h"
#include "PayrollDomain/pmtSched.h"
using namespace PayrollDomain;

//-------------------------------------
// Name
//   WeeklySchedule
//
// Description
//   Employees containing the WeeklySchedule will be paid
//   every Friday
//

class PayrollImplementationPrivate::WeeklySchedule
: public PaymentSchedule
{
  public:
    WeeklySchedule();
    virtual int IsPayDay(const Date&) const;
};
```

PayrollImplementation/biweekSched.h

```
#include "PayrollImplementation/namespaces.h"
#include "PayrollDomain/pmtSched.h"

using namespace PayrollDomain;

//-------------------------------------
// Name
//   BiweeklySchedule
//
// Description
//   Employees containing the BiweeklySchedule will be paid
//   every other Friday
//

class PayrollImplementationPrivate::BiweeklySchedule
: public PaymentSchedule
{
  public:
    virtual int IsPayday(const Date&) const;
};
```

PayrollImplementation/monthlySched.h

```
#include "PayrollImplementation/namespaces.h"
#include "PayrollDomain/pmtSched.h"
using namespace PayrollDomain;

#include "Components/namespaces.h"
using namespace Components;

//-------------------------------------
// Name
//   MonthlySchedule
//
// Description
//   Employees containing the MonthlySchedule will be paid
//   on the last working day of the month.
//

class PayrollImplementationPrivate::MonthlySchedule
: public PaymentSchedule
{
  public:
    MonthlySchedule();
    virtual int IsPayDay(const Date&) const;
};
```

PayrollImplementation/mailMethod.h

```
#include "PayrollImplementation/namespaces.h"
#include "PayrollDomain/pmtMethod.h"
using namespace PayrollDomain;

#include "Components/namespaces.h"
using namespace Components;

#include "Components/string.h"
```

```
//-------------------------------------
// Name
//   MailMethod
//
// Description
//   Employees containing the MailMethod will have their
//   paychecks mailed to the specified address
//

class PayrollImplementationPrivate::MailMethod : public
PaymentMethod
{
  public:
    MailMethod(const String& thePaymentAddress);
    virtual void Pay(double theAmount) const;
  private:
    String itsPaymentAddress;
};
```

PayrollImplementation/holdMethod.h

```
#include "PayrollImplementation/namespaces.h"
#include "PayrollDomain/pmtMethod.h"
using namespace PayrollDomain;

//-------------------------------------
// Name
//   HoldMethod
//
// Description
//   Employees containing the HoldMethod will have their
//   paychecks held for pickup by the paymaster.
//

class PayrollImplementationPrivate::HoldMethod : public
PaymentMethod
{
  public:
    virtual void Pay(double theAmount) const;
};
```

PayrollImplementation/directMethod.h

```
#include "PayrollImplementation/namespaces.h"
#include "PayrollDomain/pmtMethod.h"
using namespace PayrollDomain;

#include "Components/namespaces.h"
using namespace Components;

#include "Components/string.h"

//-------------------------------------
// Name
//   DirectMethod
//
// Description
//   Employees containing the DirectMethod will have their
//   pay directly deposited into the bank account of their
//   choice
//
```

```
class PayrollImplementationPrivate::DirectMethod : public
PaymentMethod
{
  public:
    DirectMethod(const String& theBank, const String& theAccount);
    virtual void Pay(double) const;
  private:
    String itsBank;
    String itsAccount;
};
```

PayrollImplementation/unionAff.h

```
#include "PayrollImplementation/namespaces.h"
#include "PayrollDomain/affiliation.h"
using namespace PayrollDomain;

#include "Components/date.h"
#include "Components/u_set.h"
using namespace Components;

//-------------------------------------
// Name
//   UnionAffiliation
//
// Description
//   Employees containing the UnionAffiliation are members
//   of the union, and must pay dues and service charges
//

class PayrollImplementationPrivate::UnionAffiliation : public
Affiliation
{
  public:
    UnionAffiliation(double theDuesRate);
    virtual double GetFee(const Date&) const;
    virtual void   Post(const Date&);

  private:
    double                          itsDuesRate;
    UnboundedSet<ServiceCharge*> itsServiceCharges;
};
```

4

Paradigm Crossings

Hay don't you remember, you called me Al . . .

—Song from the depression era.

*Meanwhile, the poor Babel fish, by effectively removing
all barriers to communications between different races and cultures,
has caused more and bloodier wars than anything else in the history of creation.*

—Douglas Adams, from The Hitchhiker's Guide to the Galaxy

According to *Webster's Third New International Dictionary* (unabridged version) a paradigm is an example or a pattern. Object-oriented programs follow a particular kind of pattern or paradigm in the way they are designed. But OO is not the only programming paradigm; there are many others, such as procedural programming, relational database programming, multiprocessing, and so on. These other paradigms must often coexist in a single object-oriented application, which can cause problems that are difficult to resolve. This chapter discusses these problems and some methods for resolving them.

Introduction

Consider the problem faced by an American traveling in Europe. He has brought his hair dryer from home, but he finds (with his hair dripping) that the wall socket won't take American-style plugs. Hair still dripping, he walks to the local hardware store and buys the proper sort of plug. Back at his hotel room, he cuts the American plug off the end of the hair dryer cord and replaces it with the new plug.

Now it fits! He wets his head, picks up his hair brush, aims his hair dryer, and BAM! In a flurry of screaming motors, blue sparks, and ozone, the hair dryer self-destructs. Our plucky lad was unaware that the voltage in Europe is twice as high as in the States. The poor little hair dryer, designed for 110V, was not prepared for 220V.

Realizing his error, he runs back to the hardware store to buy a 2:1 transformer. He happens to have another hair dryer, and he is determined to make this work. He attaches the transformer to the plug and the dryer, so that the voltage entering the dryer will be half of what is entering the plug, and voila! The hair dryer works!

Well, not quite. The fan does not seem to blow as hard as it ought to, and the thermostat keeps popping every minute or so, forcing him to wait for it to reset. This is because European power is supplied at a lower frequency than American power is.

The moral of this story is that crossing a paradigm boundary is seldom simple and often leads to subtle problems. This chapter is about crossing from the OO paradigm to other paradigms. Sometimes this is easy and straightforward, and sometimes it is frustrating and fraught with obstacles. We will discuss some of these obstacles, and some ways of maneuvering around them.

Do not expect any magical solutions, however; I shall not provide any. Even if you use the techniques I outline, you will still have problems. Crossing paradigms is *hard*. There are no quick fixes.

The Object-Oriented Paradigm

We will first discuss the OO paradigm and the specific restrictions placed upon that paradigm by C++. From there we will go on to discuss other paradigms and how they can be bridged to applications with an OO design.

The OO paradigm is a method of writing programs in which data structures are exclusively operated upon by a single set of functions, which are accessed through an interface. The combination of data structures, functions, and their interfaces is called a *class*. The interface of a class is all that is accessible to functions that are not part of the class. These client functions communicate with the class by invoking its interface. A particular interface is not unique to a particular class; many classes can share the same interface. Clients that invoke this interface are not required to know which class they are invoking. New classes may be written in terms of other classes. The data structures, functions, and interfaces of the old class may be inherited by the new class and then specifically overridden.

A class describes an object. An object actually takes up physical space in the computer memory. Client functions invoke class interfaces by "sending messages" to objects. The client function is not required to know what class an object belongs to in order to send a message. When a client sends a message to an object, the class that the object belongs to is determined at run time, and the appropriate function of that class is called.

This decoupling of interface from data structure and function allows clients to depend upon interface and nothing but interface. Clients can use objects of any class that conforms to the interface that they depend upon. No compiler or linker dependencies need to exist between the client class and the classes of the server objects it uses. Clients don't have to depend upon servers. This allows designers to reuse clients for many different kinds of servers and to reuse servers with many different kinds of clients.

The C++ Interpretation of the OO Paradigm

C++ interprets the OO paradigm within the framework of *static typing*. Static typing places restrictions upon the recognition of an interface. In C++ a client function cannot arbitrarily invoke any interface upon an object. The client must first ensure that the object has that interface. The compiler enforces this surety by insisting that all objects have a type, and that the interface being invoked is declared within that type. The compiler allows interfaces to be inherited; thus, a client may invoke an interface declared within any of the base classes of a class. Moreover, the compiler allows objects of a derived class to be manipulated as though they were objects of a base class.

The decoupling of interface from data structure and function still exists in the statically typed form of OO as supported by C++, but that decoupling is achieved only through the mechanism of inheritance. Thus, in C++ clients can be reused for different servers only if the client uses a service interface presented in an abstract base class that the servers can inherit from. Adherence to this form avoids the need for compiler or linker dependencies between clients and servers; both the clients and the servers, however, will have compiler and linker dependencies upon the abstract base class that presents the service interface.

This dependency of the client and server upon an abstract base class affects the way C++ programs evolve. When new clients are created that need extended services, the service interface must change. Those changes then propagate down from the abstract base class to its derivatives—the servers; thus, all the servers need to be changed.

An OO language that is *dynamically typed* (e.g., Objective-C or Smalltalk) does not enforce the declaration of interfaces within types. With such languages there is no need for an abstract base class, and so the servers need not be derivatives and need not be changed. This makes programs in such languages easier to change; however, they are more prone to run-time errors, since the invocation of unsupported interfaces cannot be detected at compile time.

Crossing the Procedural-Paradigm Boundary

The procedural paradigm (PP) is typified by the "structured" methodology. Structured analysis (SA), structured design (SD) and structured programming (SP) are techniques that operate within the procedural paradigm.

In the procedural paradigm, data structures and functions are separate entities. A particular function may operate on many different data structures, and each data structure may have many different functions operating upon it. Functions have compile and link-time dependencies upon the data structures that they manipulate and upon the other functions that they call.

Since there is no separation between an interface and the function it invokes, clients have compile-time and link-time dependencies upon their servers. This precludes the possibility of reusing clients with different servers.[1] Thus, changes that are made to servers affect clients. Moreover, in order to reuse a client in another context, its code must be copied and disentangled from the servers that it employs. This is seldom a straightforward process.

Wrapping Procedural Programs in OO Classes

For several reasons, it is often necessary to mix procedural and OO programs. There are several motivations for this. First, there is a huge investment in procedural function libraries; these libraries must be usable from OO applications. Second, many development teams want to start using an OO paradigm on projects that are currently procedural. They want to add new features using the OO paradigm while maintaining their investment in the procedural base.

The OO-PP boundary is at once the simplest and most difficult boundary to cross. The use of procedural functions within class methods is straightforward, as is the use of pre-existing objects within procedural modules. As we will see, however, "objectifying" a procedural client to the extent that it is reusable with other servers is tantamount to rewriting the client altogether.

Wrapping Procedural Servers within Classes

A procedural server is nothing more than a function or an associated set of functions. Such functions are usually placed in a library. A typical example might be the string-manipulation functions from the standard C library.

Although these functions can be used directly from a C++ program, wrapping them behind an OO class can hide them behind an abstract interface. This decouples the clients of that interface from the implementations of the string functions. The clients are then free to make use of other implementations that conform to the same interface.

---

1. Of course we can use several tricks to approximate the effect of abstract interfaces in order to decouple clients from servers, but these tricks leave the procedural paradigm and encroach upon the OO paradigm. Moreover, in a procedural language, such tricks are often relatively complex, difficult to maintain, and prone to errors that the compiler cannot detect.

Listing 4-1 and Listing 4-2 present a class that wraps the standard string library into a **String** class. Notice that this class provides a consistent set of policies for dealing with strings. These policies may not be the best for every kind of application, but wrapping them behind a class interface allows us to change them without interfering with the clients who use that interface.

Listing 4-1

Wrapping a string function behind an abstract class interface

```
#ifndef STRING_CLASS_H
#define STRING_CLASS_H

//----------------------------------------------------------
// Name
//   String
//
// Description
//   This class encapsulates the functions in <strings.h> into a
//   coherent set of policies for managing strings of characters.
//
class ostream;

class String
{
  public:
    String(char* theChars=0);
    virtual ~String();
    String(const String&);
    String& operator=(const String&);

    // Comparators
    int operator==(const String&)    const;
    int operator!=(const String& s) const {return !operator==(s);}
    int operator< (const String&)    const;
    int operator<=(const String&)    const;
    int operator> (const String&)    const;
    int operator>=(const String&)    const;

    // Queries
    int GetLength() const;

    // Catenation
    String& operator+=(const String&);
    String  operator+ (const String&);

    // Character indexing
    char    operator[](int)          const;
    int     operator()(char)         const;
    int     operator()(const String&) const;

    // Substring manipulation
    String operator()(int pos, int len) const;
    String operator()(int pos, int len, const String& insert);
```

Listing 4-1 (Continued)

Wrapping a string function behind an abstract class interface

```
    // Output.
    friend ostream& operator<<(ostream&, const String&);

  private:
    char* itsChars;
    int   itsLength;
};
#endif
```

Listing 4-2

strclass.cpp—implementation of String class

```
#include "strclass.h"
#include <string.h>
#include <iostream.h>

String::String(char* theChars)
{
    if (theChars == 0)
        theChars = "";
    itsLength = strlen(theChars);
    itsChars = new char[itsLength+1];
    strcpy(itsChars, theChars);
}

String::~String()
{
    delete [] itsChars;
}

String::String(const String& theString)
{
    itsChars = 0;
    *this = theString;
}

String& String::operator=(const String& theString)
{
    if (&theString != this) // not the same
    {
        delete [] itsChars;
        itsLength = strlen(theString.itsChars);
        itsChars = new char[itsLength+1];
        strcpy(itsChars, theString.itsChars);
    }
    return *this;
}

int String::operator==(const String& theString) const
{
    if (itsLength== 0 && theString.itsLength == 0)
```

Listing 4-2 (Continued)

---

strclass.cpp—implementation of String class

```cpp
        return 1;
    else
        return strcmp(itsChars, theString.itsChars) == 0;
}

int String::operator<(const String& s) const
{
    return strcmp(itsChars, s.itsChars) < 0;
}

int String::operator<=(const String& s) const
{
    return strcmp(itsChars, s.itsChars) <= 0;
}

int String::operator>(const String& s) const
{
    return strcmp(itsChars, s.itsChars) > 0;
}

int String::operator>=(const String& s) const
{
    return strcmp(itsChars, s.itsChars) >= 0;
}

int String::GetLength() const
{
    return itsLength;
}

String& String::operator+=(const String& s)
{
    int newLength = strlen(itsChars)+strlen(s.itsChars);
    char* x = new char[newLength+1];
    strcpy(x, itsChars);
    strcat(x,s.itsChars);
    delete [] itsChars;
    itsChars = x;
    itsLength = newLength;
    return *this;
}

String String::operator+(const String& s)
{
    String x(itsChars);
    return (x += s);
}

char String::operator[](int i) const
{
    if (i<0 || i>itsLength)
        return 0;
    else
```

Listing 4-2 (Continued)

strclass.cpp—implementation of String class

```cpp
            return itsChars[i];
}

int String::operator()(char c) const
{
    char* cp = strchr(itsChars, c);
    int offset = cp ? cp - itsChars  : -1;
    if (offset >= itsLength)
        offset = -1;
    return offset;
}

int String::operator()(const String& s) const
{
    char* cp = strstr(itsChars, s.itsChars);
    int offset = cp ? cp - itsChars  : -1;
    if (offset >= itsLength)
        offset = -1;
    return offset;
}

String String::operator()(int pos, int len) const
{
    String retval;
    if (pos >= 0 && pos < itsLength)
    {
        len = (pos+len > itsLength) ? (itsLength-pos) : len;
        char* cp = new char[len+1];
        strncpy(cp, itsChars+pos, len);
        cp[len] = 0;
        retval = String(cp);
        delete [] cp;
    }
    return retval;
}

String String::operator()(int pos, int len, const String& s)
{
    String retval = operator()(0,pos);
    retval += s;
    int postLen = itsLength - (pos+len);
    retval += operator()(pos+len, postLen);
    return retval;
}

ostream& operator<< (ostream& o, const String& s)
{
    o << s.itsChars;
    return o;
}
```

"Objectifying" Procedural Clients

Procedural clients have strong physical dependencies upon their servers. Breaking these dependencies is the goal of "objectifying" such clients. The motivation for achieving this goal is the ability to reuse the clients in other applications.

For example, the high-level control mechanisms for an ATM machine involve user recognition and transaction processing. A procedural client that embodies these high-level policies might be written as shown in Listing 4-3. The goal of objectifying this client would be to reuse it in the context of a credit card advance machine, or a ticket-purchase machine, or even a door-security system. In fact, the same policies apply to any application that must identify users before allowing them to request transactions.

Listing 4-3

High-level procedural client for an ATM machine

```
void ProcessUser(User);
void ATMClient
{
    for(;;)
    {
        User u = GetUserID();
        if (IndentifyAndValidateUser(u) == VALID_USER)
        {
            ProcessUser(u);
        }
    }
}

void ProcessUser(User u)
{
    for(Transaction t = GetTransaction(); t.type != END;
        t = GetTransaction())
    {
        ProcessTransaction(t,u);
    }
}
```

In order to achieve this objectification, we must build abstract interfaces between the high-level procedural clients and their servers. We would like to wind up with code that looks something like Listing 4-4. This design allows us to separate and reuse the clients with servers adapted for applications other than ATMs.

A procedural client that is well designed according to the tenets of structured design can be *relatively* simple to objectify, since one of those tenets advocates the separation of concerns. It is not a huge intuitive leap from Listing 4-3 to Listing 4-4. The procedural designer of Listing 4-3 has already begun the process of abstraction. The OO designer simply extends the process by adding abstract polymorphic interfaces, so that the client code is separable and reusable.

Listing 4-4

High-level "objectified" client for an ATM machine

```
class UserProcessor
{
  public:
    virtual void ProcessUser(User&) = 0;
};

class UserIdentifier
{
  public:
    virtual User* GetValidUser() = 0;
};

class UserApplication
{
  public:
    UserApplication(UserIdentifier& ui, UserProcessor& up)
    : itsIdentifier(ui), itsProcessor(up) {}
    void Run();
  private:
    UserIdentifier& itsIdentifier;
    UserProcessor&  itsProcessor;
};

void UserApplication::Run()
{
    for(;;)
    {
        User* u = itsIdentifier.GetValidUser();
        if (u) itsProcessor.ProcessUser(*u);
    }
}

Class Transaction
{
  public:
    virtual void Process(User&) = 0;
};

class TransactionSelector
{
  public:
    virtual Transaction* GetTransaction() = 0;
};

class UserTransactionProcessor : public UserProcessor
{
  public:
    UserTransactionProcessor(TransactionSelector& ts)
    : itsSelector(ts) {}
    virtual void ProcessUser(User&);
  private:
    TransactionSelector& itsSelector
};
```

Listing 4-4 (Continued)

High-level "objectified" client for an ATM machine

```
void UserTransactionProcessor::ProcessUser(User& u)
{
    for(Transaction* t = itsSelector.GetTransaction();
        t->IsEnd() != true; t = itsSelector.GetTransaction())
    {
        t->Process(u);
    }
}

class ATMTransactionSelector : public TransactionSelector
{
    //...Stuff specific to selecting ATM transactions
};

class ATMUserIdentifier : public UserIdentifier
{
    //...Stuff specific to identifying ATM users
};

void main()
{
    ATMTransactionSelector s;
    UserTransactionProcessor up(s);
    ATMUserIdentifier ui;
    UserApplication atmApp(ui, up);
    atmApp.Run();
}
```

Unfortunately the impetus for building procedural designs that employ the separation of concerns is weak. The benefit is tenuous at best, and the cost of abstraction is high in comparison. Therefore most procedural designs don't follow that rule strictly and look more like Listing 4-5, in which the abstractions are much harder to see. If they ever existed in the first place, they were buried under the implementation. The gap between the procedural code in Listing 4-5 and the object-oriented code in Listing 4-4 is so wide that it is unlikely to be crossed within the context of an objectification effort. Crossing it entails the complete redesign and reimplementation of the client code as well as the objectification of the server code.

Managing the PP-to-OO Transition

The fact that servers are easy to wrap behind OO interfaces, but clients are difficult to wrap, makes the concept of a "flash-cut" to OO technology unrealistic. The clients will dominate the application and make the transition to OO difficult at best. The most likely

---

Listing 4-5

A more typical design for the high-level procedural client of an ATM

```
void ATMClient
{
    for(;;)
    {
        User u = GetUserID();
        if (IndentifyAndValidateUser(u) == VALID_USER)
        {
            for(Transaction t = GetTransaction();
                t.type != END; t = GetTransaction())
            {
                switch(t.type)
                {
                case deposit:
                    ProcessDeposit(t,u);
                break;

                cast withdrawal:
                    ProcessWithdrawal(t,u);
                break;

                case transfer:
                    ProcessTransfer(t,u);
                break;

                default:
                    LogInvalidTransaction(t,u);
                break;
                }
            }
        }
    }
}
```

result is a procedural application with a few OO servers scattered throughout. The benefits of OOD will not be adequately realized.

Thus, the manager of a procedural application who hopes to move that application into the OO paradigm must employ a long-term strategy. It is not sufficient simply to train the designers and programmers in C++ and OOD and then expect that the product will suddenly be OO. In fact, the procedural nature of the application will so dominate the designers and programmers that they will probably forget the training and continue as procedural designers and programmers.

So, how can we convert a procedural application to OO? The following paragraphs describe a strategy that has met with some success. It is a phased approach which guarantees that, with each phase, parts of the product will be converted to OO, and parts of the staff will become OO fluent.

First, train a small core of developers and programmers in C++ and OOD—the product architects or the lead engineers. These people should then convert a small but important server or subsystem within the application to OO. This subsystem could either be an existing procedural subsystem, or part of a new feature that must be added. It would be wise to recruit the help of an OO *expert* in the design of this subsystem, since it will be the keystone upon which the conversion strategy rests.

The presence of the OO subsystem splits the project staff into three teams. Team A is the OO core responsible for the new subsystem. Team B consists of the engineers who are responsible for the clients that use Team A's OO subsystem. Team C includes those engineers whose responsibilities are not affected by Team A's activities. Team A's project should be chosen so that Team B is relatively small—perhaps 2–3 times larger than Team A.

Team B must be trained in C++, since they must use it in order to interface with Team A's server. However, Team B does not need to be trained in OOD, since they will continue to program procedurally while they use Team A's new subsystem. Team C is unaffected by these activities. They do not need to convert to C++, nor do they need to understand anything about OO at this time.

The net result of this phase is that a small core of the staff becomes OO-fluent, and a larger circle of engineers becomes aware of C++ and OO. The next phase begins by completing the training of Team B. They should be trained in OOD and the OO uses of C++, so that they may join the ranks of the OO-fluent. The process can then be repeated. Team A is now much larger and can work on the conversion of more than one subsystem. These subsystems will be used by new Team Bs, which must be trained in C++. The ranks of Team C shrink.

The Representational Paradigm

The representational paradigm employs data structures to represent the structure and relationships of elements within the application domain. For example, consider an application that plays Blackjack. We could represent a **Card** as an instance of a class that defined instance variables for suit and rank. We could represent a **Deck** of cards as an **Ordered-Set** of cards. We could represent a **Hand** as a smaller **Set** of cards (see Figure 4-1).

Clearly this simple scheme is adequate to represent the cards in a game of Blackjack. In fact, we could reuse the same scheme to represent the cards in a game of Poker, Bridge, Hearts, Fish, or even War. The representation is reusable in many different contexts.

Representations are, by their nature, reusable, but for the opposite reason that objects are reusable. Objects present an *abstract behavioral* interface that hides the underlying representation. This allows us to reuse high-level policy functions with many different sets of details. On the other hand, representations present *concrete static* interfaces that are devoid of significant behavior. Thus, we can reuse them in many different behavioral contexts.

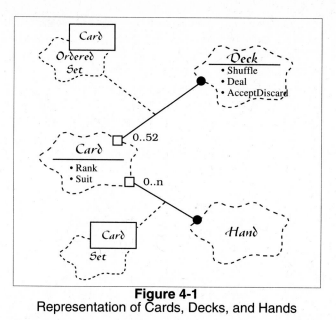

Figure 4-1
Representation of Cards, Decks, and Hands

Consider the **Card** object. What behavior does it have? Taken by itself, a **Card** has no behavior whatsoever. To be sure, there is behavior associated with a **Card** within the context of a game. For example, in Poker there is an ordinal relationship between the cards: given any two, one will always be of greater value than the other. However, this relationship does not hold for other games; some games lack the concept of comparing one card with another. Thus, the behaviors that we can associate with a **Card** depend upon the game being played; the **Card** has no intrinsic behaviors. A **Card** is a pure representational entity.

Representational concepts arise in a surprising number of applications. Large systems often require large amounts of configuration information, which is typically arranged into data structures that the rest of the application reads and interprets. These data structures are representations of the configuration information. Compilers and translators often convert their input into an internal representation prior to generating code. CASE tools, likewise, often create an internal representation of the diagrams being drawn. CAD/CAM systems create representations of mechanical and electrical designs.

Representational Modeling Is Not Object-Oriented Modeling

Unfortunately, representational modeling is often taken for object-oriented modeling. Many current so-called OOA methodologies are really just representational methodologies that have little to do with objects. It is easy to see why people make this mistake. Representational models are extremely similar to the static models of object-oriented designs. They use many of the same relationships, including **Contains** and **Inheritance**, and they can be drawn with the same diagrams, but the difference is deep and significant. Representational models are an abstraction of static entities and relationships, devoid of behavior; object-oriented models are abstractions of dynamic behavior devoid of representation.

The OO / Representational Difference

Employing methodologies that confuse OOA and representational modeling leads to some unfortunate consequences. Consider again the game of Blackjack. If we believed that our representations of **Cards**, **Decks**, and **Hands** were the objects in the system, we would search for behaviors that implement the rules of Blackjack within these objects. For example, we might add a **Score** method to the **Hand** object that calculates how many points the **Hand** contains. We could also add a **Value** method to the **Card** object that indicated the number of points per card.

Doing these things, however, would mean that the once-elegant representational scheme that could represent any game of cards could now represent only a game of Blackjack. True, we can derive **BlackjackHand** and **PokerHand** from an abstract base **Hand**, but then Poker games must explicitly use **PokerHand** objects and Blackjack games must explicitly use **BlackjackHand** objects. We have lost the reusability of the representation.

In OOA we try to find behavioral abstractions as opposed to representational abstractions. In an OO analysis of Blackjack, cards and decks could be abstracted away to some generalized scoring tokens. The primary abstractions might be the dealers and players. We can state generalities such as the following: Dealers randomize the pool of scoring tokens and then distribute them to the Players; Players negotiate with the Dealer for more scoring tokens; Players compute their scores; Players place bets; and so on. From this kind of behavioral analysis, we can establish high-level behavioral policies that are reusable for many different games.

The Need for Pure Representations

Consider a more significant and important example: a CAD tool for designing electronic circuits. A designer inputs designs for circuit boards though a rich and complex GUI. The tool records the designs in an internal representation consisting of circuit components and connections.

Now consider the range of applications for which the CAD tool will use that internal representation. It may model the electronic behavior of the designed circuitry. It may design a circuit-board layout, including copper etching masks, drilling instructions, solder-resist instructions, and so on. It may produce a bill of materials for the board, a nicely printed schematic diagram, or a test procedure. The number of applications that could make use of the representation of an electronic design is probably beyond counting.

Moreover, the rich GUI is not the only source for an electronic design. The input to the CAD tool may be textual, or perhaps based upon a hand-drawn diagram that is scanned in. Regardless of the source, the information boils down to a single representational model, and then applications are run against that model to yield interesting output.

Thus, the representation needs to be pure. It can't depend upon its source, because it can have many sources; and it can't specify its behavior, since many behaviors may be applied to it. We dare not make objects out of the representational entities and thereby load them up with dozens of methods supporting each different application. If we did so, we could never close those objects; new applications would require us to open them again and add more methods. Worse, the objects would become so *fat* with all the different methods for all the different applications that they would be very difficult to maintain. Thus, we need pure representations—representations that are devoid of behavior and whose static implementation is visible, so that separate applications can interpret it.

Representational Models and Run-Time Type Identification

Run-time type identification (RTTI), the ability to ask an object what class it belongs to, is usually considered a poor practice in an object-oriented environment. The reason is simple: If a function tests the type of an object and then selects a behavior based upon that type, that function cannot be closed against new classes being derived. This practice is known as *type-casing*. Every time a new derivative class is created, we must open that function and add a new type-case. Thus, using RTTI to implement type-cases violates the open/closed principle.

When accessing a representational model, which is devoid of behavior, you have no choice: you must query the various entities for their types, and you must choose behaviors based upon those types. Your programs will therefore have type-cases, and cannot be closed against changes to the representation. This should not be surprising. Programs that interpret a representational model must depend upon that model, because the model has no intrinsic behavior. The programs that interpret the model must supply the appropriate behaviors. Since the dependency already exists, no detriment is added by the use of RTTI and type-casing.

When Is a Representational Model More Appropriate Than an OO Model?

For any particular application, an object-oriented model will have a stronger dependency structure than the corresponding representational model. In a representational model, the detailed declarations of the representation are highly depended upon. When we can hide representation behind abstract behavior, we can invert dependency structures, so that details can depend upon abstractions.

Sometimes, in order to satisfy many applications, we load objects with many behaviors. Each behavior is needed by at least one application, but none is needed by all. These objects become fat and difficult to maintain, and in such cases, we may prefer a representational model.

Object-oriented models and representational models are not mutually exclusive. They can, and should, coexist in the same application. Entities that can be described by abstract behaviors should conform to the OO model. Entities that we can describe only by data structures that are interpreted differently for many different applications should be pure representations.

The Representational Model of a State Machine Compiler

A state machine compiler (SMC) reads a textual description of a finite state machine (FSM) and generates the C++ code that implements it. This compiler parses a text file and builds a representational model of the state machine. It then generates the C++ code by interpreting the representational model. Figure 4-2 shows the category design for this compiler.

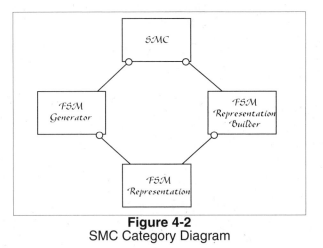

Figure 4-2
SMC Category Diagram

The **FSMRepresentation** category allows the **FSMGenerator** category to be completely isolated from the **FSMRepresentationBuilder** category. The **FSM-Generator** can generate the C++ code for a finite state machine, regardless of the mechanism that builds the representation. Thus, we can reuse the **FSMGenerator** in any application that can build the state machine representation. For example, instead of a text parser, we could have a GUI-based CASE tool build the representation. Also, we can replace the **FSMGenerator** with a different category that generates C code or Pascal code from representations built with the same front-end parser or CASE tool.

The representational model, in this program, is modeled as a set of classes. Behaviors that aid the formation and interpretation of the representation, such as constructors, destructors, assignment operators, and query methods, are all present in these classes. Figure 4-3 shows the static structure of the representation.

The fundamentals of a state machine should be evident. A state map contains a collection of state entities. Each state has a name, some actions to be performed upon entry, some actions to be performed upon exit, and a set of transitions. All transitions contain the name of the event that triggers them and the list of actions to perform when that event occurs. There are two types of transition. Internal transitions do not cause the state to change. External transitions do cause the state to change, so they contain a reference to the appropriate next state.

This compiler supports substates and superstates. Superstates are abstract states that cannot be named in an external transition. Substates inherit transitions from super states. Superstates can also be substates. Such super-substates are also abstract, cannot be named in an external transition, and inherit all the transitions of their superstate. Concrete states are states that are not superstates. They can be named in external transitions, meaning that they are legitimate target states for those transitions. A concrete state may be a substate, inheriting some of its transitions from its superstate.

The representational model enforces the appropriate relationships by declaring the types of the objects in those relationships. Substates contain references to their superstate. Any state may be the source of a transition, but the target state of a transition and the initial state of the FSM must be concrete.

At the time of this writing, most compilers did not support RTTI. In order to allow the **FSMGenerator** category to query the type of the states and transitions, a quasi-RTTI has been added to the model, as shown in Figure 4-4.

The **State** class has a method that takes a **StateHandler** as an argument. The **StateHandler** class declares a method corresponding to each concrete derivative of **State**. The derivatives of **State** respond to the **Handle** message by calling the appropriate method within the **StateHandler**. Thus, users can derive from **StateHandler** and write methods that act upon each state separately.

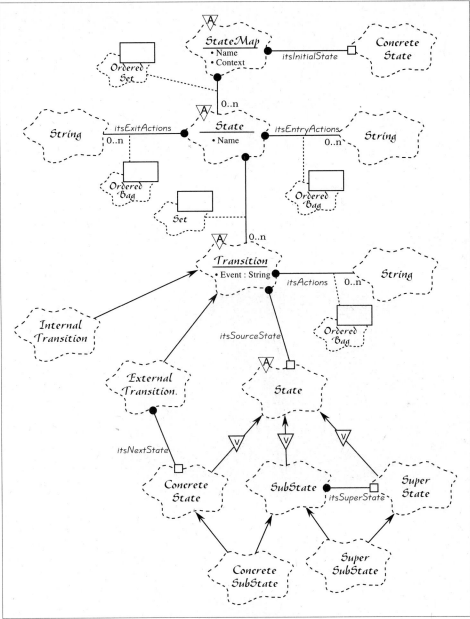

Figure 4-3
State Map Representation

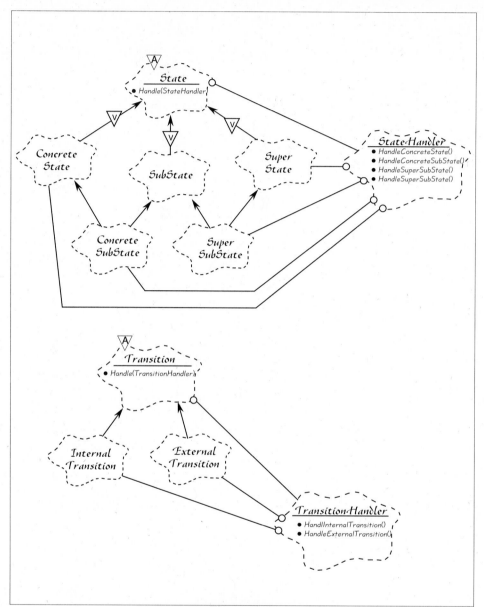

Figure 4-4
Quasi-RTTI for States and Transitions

The SMC Representational Model in C++

Listing 4-6 shows the C++ code for the state class and its derivatives.

Listing 4-6

The **State** class hierarchy

```
class State
{
 public:
    State(const String& theName)
    : itsName(theName)
    {}

    virtual void Handle(StateHandler&) = 0;

    void AddTransition(Transition* t) {itsTransitions.Add(t);}

    const Set<Transition*>& GetTransitions() const
    {return itsTransitions;}

    String GetName() const {return itsName;}

    const OrderedBag<String>& GetEntryActions() const
    {return itsEntryActions;}

    const OrderedBag<String>& GetExitActions() const
    {return itsExitActions;}

    void SetEntryActions(const OrderedBag<String>& theActions)
    {itsEntryActions = theActions;}

    void SetExitActions(const OrderedBag<String>& theActions)
    {itsExitActions = theActions;}

  private:
    UnboundedSet<Transition*> itsTransitions;
    UnboundedOrderedBag<String> itsEntryActions;
    UnboundedOrderedBag<String> itsExitActions;
    String itsName;
};

class StateHandler
{
  public:
    virtual void HandleConcreteState(ConcreteState&) = 0;
    virtual void HandleConcreteSubState(ConcreteSubState&) = 0;
    virtual void HandleSuperSubState(SuperSubState&) = 0;
    virtual void HandleSuperState(SuperState&) = 0;
};

class ConcreteState : public virtual State
{
  public:
    ConcreteState(const String& theName) : State(theName) {}
```

Listing 4-6 (Continued)

The **State** class hierarchy

```
    virtual void Handle(StateHandler& h)
    {h.HandleConcreteState(*this);}
};

class SuperState : public virtual State
{
  public:
    SuperState(const String& theName) : State(theName) {}
    virtual void Handle(StateHandler& h)
    {h.HandleSuperState(*this);}
  private:
};

class SubState : public virtual State
{
  public:
    SubState(const String& theName, SuperState* ss)
    : State(theName), itsSuperState(ss) {}
    SuperState* GetSuperState() const {return itsSuperState;}

  private:
    SuperState* itsSuperState;
}

class SuperSubState : public SubState, public SuperState
{
  public:
    SuperSubState(const String& theName, SuperState* ss)
    : State(theName), SubState(theName, ss), SuperState(theName) {}
    virtual void Handle(StateHandler& h)
    {h.HandleSuperSubState(*this);}
};

class ConcreteSubState : public ConcreteState, public SubState
{
  public:
    ConcreteSubState(const String& theName, SuperState* ss)
    : State(theName), SubState(theName, ss), ConcreteState(theName)
    {}

    virtual void Handle(StateHandler& h)
    {h.HandleConcreteSubState(*this);}
};
```

In the absence of a compiler that implements RTTI, the state hierarchy employs the **StateHandler** mechanism to simulate **dynamic_cast**, as shown in Listing 4-7. A similar mechanism is employed to create **dynamic_cast** operations for the transition hierarchy.

In a compiler that correctly implements RTTI and the **dynamic_cast** operator, these machinations are not necessary. In fact, they are detrimental since the source code of

---

Listing 4-7

State hierarchy `dynamic_cast`

```
class StateCastHandler : public StateHandler
{
  public:
    StateCastHandler()
    : itsConcreteState(0)
    , itsConcreteSubState(0)
    , itsSuperSubState(0)
    , itsSuperState(0)
    , itsSubState(0)
    {}
    virtual void HandleConcreteState(ConcreteState& s)
    {itsConcreteState = (ConcreteState*) &s;}

    virtual void HandleConcreteSubState(ConcreteSubState& s)
    {
        itsConcreteState = (ConcreteState*) &s;
        itsSubState = (SubState*) &s;
    }

    virtual void HandleSuperSubState(SuperSubState& s)
    {
        itsSuperState = (SuperState*) &s;
        itsSubState = (SubState*) &s;
    }

    virtual void HandleSuperState(SuperState& s)
    {itsSuperState = (SuperState*) &s;}

    ConcreteState*    GetConcreteState()
    {return itsConcreteState;}

    ConcreteSubState* GetConcreteSubState()
    {return itsConcreteSubState;}

    SuperSubState*    GetSuperSubState()
    {return itsSuperSubState;}

    SuperState*       GetSuperState()       {return itsSuperState;}
    SubState*         GetSubState()         {return itsSubState;}

  private:
    ConcreteState* itsConcreteState;
    ConcreteSubState* itsConcreteSubState;
    SuperSubState* itsSuperSubState;
    SuperState* itsSuperState;
    SubState* itsSubState;
};

ConcreteState* dynamic_cast_ConcreteState(State* s)
{
    StateCastHandler h;
    s->Handle(h);
    return h.GetConcreteState();
```

Listing 4-7 (Continued)

State hierarchy `dynamic_cast`

```
}

ConcreteSubState* dynamic_cast_ConcreteSubState(State* s)
{
    StateCastHandler h;
    s->Handle(h);
    return h.GetConcreteSubState();
}

SubState* dynamic_cast_SubState(State* s)
{
    StateCastHandler h;
    s->Handle(h);
    return h.GetSubState();
}

SuperSubState* dynamic_cast_SuperSubState(State* s)
{
    StateCastHandler h;
    s->Handle(h);
    return h.GetSuperSubState();
}

SuperState* dynamic_cast_SuperState(State* s)
{
    StateCastHandler h;
    s->Handle(h);
    return h.GetSuperState();
}
```

---

the base class depends upon the source code of the derived classes. If we could remove the **Handler** classes, we would break this dependency.

Listing 4-8 shows the implementation of the transition hierarchy.

Listing 4-8

Transition class hierarchy

```
class Transition
{
 public:
    Transition(const String& theEvent, State* theSourceState)
    : itsEvent(theEvent)
    , itsSourceState(theSourceState)
    {}

    String GetEvent() const {return itsEvent;}
    State* GetSourceState() {return itsSourceState;}
    const OrderedBag<String>& GetActions() const
    {return itsActions;}
```

Listing 4-8 (Continued)

`Transition` class hierarchy

```
    void AddAction(String a) {itsActions.Add(a);}

    virtual void Handle(TransitionHandler&) const = 0;

  private:
    State*   itsSourceState;
    String   itsEvent;
    UnboundedOrderedBag<String> itsActions;
};

class InternalTransition : public Transition
{
  public:
    InternalTransition(const String& theEvent,
                        State* theSourceState)
    : Transition(theEvent, theSourceState)
    {}

    virtual void    Handle(TransitionHandler& h) const
    { h.HandleInternalTransition(*this);}
};

class ExternalTransition : public Transition
{
  public:
    ExternalTransition(const String& theEvent,
                        State* theSourceState,
                        ConcreteState* theNextState)
    : Transition(theEvent, theSourceState)
    , itsNextState(theNextState)
    {}

    ConcreteState* GetNextState() const {return itsNextState;}
    void           SetNextState(ConcreteState* s) {itsNextState = s;}
    virtual void   Handle(TransitionHandler& h) const
    {h.HandleExternalTransition(*this);}

  private:
    ConcreteState* itsNextState;
};
```

Finally, Listing 4-9 shows the abstract interface of the **StateMap** class. A derived implementation of this class is the responsibility of the agent that builds the representation.

Listing 4-9

StateMap abstract class

```
class StateMap
{
 public:
    virtual       ConcreteState*       GetInitialState()          = 0;
    virtual const OrderedSet<State*>& GetOrderedStates() const = 0;
    virtual const Set<String>&        GetEvents()        const = 0;
    virtual const Set<String>&        GetActions()       const = 0;
    virtual const String&             GetName()          const = 0;
    virtual const String&             GetContextName()   const = 0;
    virtual const OrderedBag<String>& GetHeaders()       const = 0;
    virtual const String&             GetVersion()       const = 0;
};
```

Crossing the OO/Representational Boundary (Interpreting the Model)

Listing 4-10 shows a portion of the **FSMGenerator** class. This class contains the functions that traverse the state map internal representation and generate C++ code. The functions shown are responsible for generating a class declaration for each concrete state and providing member-function declarations for each transition that can occur from that state. This involves walking up the superstate hierarchy and adding those inherited transitions that are not overridden in the substates.

Listing 4-10

FSMGenerator::GenerateStateClassDeclarations

```
void FSMGenerator::GenerateStateClassDeclarations()
{
    OrderedSet<State*>& states = itsStateMap.GetOrderedStates();
    for (Iterator<State*> si(states); si; si++)
    {
        State* s = *si;
        ConcreteState* cs = dynamic_cast_ConcreteState(s);

        if (cs != 0) // if the state is concrete
        {
            itsHeaderFile << endl;
            itsHeaderFile << "//-----------------------------------"
                          << endl;
            itsHeaderFile << "// State: " << s.GetName() << endl;
            itsHeaderFile << "//" << endl;
            itsHeaderFile << "class " << MakeStateName(s.GetName())
                          << " : public " << itsBaseStateName
                          << endl;
            itsHeaderFile << '{' << endl;
```

Listing 4-10 (Continued)

FSMGenerator::GenerateStateClassDeclarations

```
                itsHeaderFile << "  public:" << endl;
                itsHeaderFile << "    virtual const char* StateName() "
                                 "const"
                         << endl;
                itsHeaderFile << "      {return \"" << cs->GetName()
                         << "\";}" << endl;
                itsOverriddenEvents.Clear(); // clear the overrides
                GenerateTransitionDeclarations(*cs);
                itsHeaderFile << "};" << endl;
            } // State is concrete
        } // for each state
    }


    void FSMGenerator::GenerateTransitionDeclarations(State& s)
    {
        for (Iterator<Transition*> ti(s.GetTransitions()); ti; ti++)
        {
            Transition* t = *ti;
            if (!itsOverriddenEvents.IsMember(t->GetEvent()))
            {
                itsOverriddenEvents.Add(t->GetEvent());
                // remember override.
                itsHeaderFile << "    virtual void " << t->GetEvent()
                         << "(" << itsFSMName << "&);" << endl;
            }
        }

        SubState* ss = dynamic_cast_SubState(&s);
        if (ss)
        {
            GenerateTransitionDeclarations(*(ss->GetSuperState()));
        }
    }
```

The important thing to notice about these functions is their use of the special **dynamic_cast** functions. These functions could easily be replaced by C++ **dynamic_cast** operators in an RTTI compliant compiler. Note that the functions use the **dynamic_cast** functions to determine the kind of entity they are dealing with, so that they can deal with it appropriately.

In the **FSMGenerator::GenerateStateClassDeclarations()** function from Listing 4-10, declarations are generated only if the state is concrete; thus, only **ConcreteState** entities and **ConcreteSubState** entities will have declarations generated. The function **FSMGenerator::GenerateTransitionDeclarations()** in Listing 4-10 is recursive. It generates declarations for each transition in the current state, as long as that transition has not appeared in that state before. This allows substate transitions to override superstate transitions. If the current state is a substate, then the function determines the superstate and calls itself recursively. Thus, the function walks up the superstate hierarchy for **ConcreteSubState** and **SuperSubState** entities.

Categories and Representational Models

Some of the classes in the SMC representational model are truly abstract classes. **State** and **Transition** each have a pure virtual function named **Handle**. However, this is an artifact of the mechanism used to implement the quasi-**dynamic_cast** functions. With a compiler that supports RTTI and the **dynamic_cast** operator, the **Handle** function would not exist. In fact, representational models often consist entirely of concrete classes as opposed to abstract classes.

Representational classes are not abstract with respect to the application. Even if such classes contain pure virtual functions, those functions do not represent an abstraction of the application's behavior. Instead, representational classes *always* contain concrete data structures, although they are sometimes incomplete. For example, the **State** class and the **Transition** class do not completely specify any of the concrete representations, but the fact that they are partial representations does not make them behaviorally abstract.

Thus, for the purposes of calculating the A metric from Chapter 3, a representational class should be considered a concrete class. A category that contains nothing but representational categories is a concrete category. It holds a position near the origin on the abstraction/instability (A/I) graph, far to the lower left of the main sequence (see Figure 4-5).

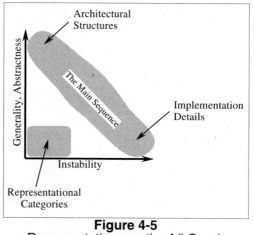

Figure 4-5
Representations on the A/I Graph

This position on the *A/I* graph indicates graphically what we already know to be true about representations: they are extremely detailed, and the rest of the application depends heavily upon them. It graphically depicts that the open/closed principle has been violated for that application; that is, we cannot close the application against changes to the representation.

Representational Reflections

Representational models are an essential element of software engineering. They appear in a surprising number of applications and are used to communicate within and between them. Databases are huge representational models; they contain data needed by many applications but usually lack any application-related behavior. Configuration specifications are representational models of the resources and requirements used by the applications being configured. Internal representations are used by compilers, CASE tools, CAD/ CAM tools, drawing tools, word processors, spreadsheets, and so on.

However, the analysis and design of representational models is not object-oriented analysis and design. Representational modeling deals with data structures and the relationships between them. Object-oriented models deal with abstract behaviors and their partitioning into classes and categories. Behaviors are irrelevant to representations, and representations are irrelevant to abstract behaviors.

Despite the need for representational models, they violate the open/closed principle and weaken the dependency structure of the application. Representational models do not conform to the main sequence. Thus, in the majority of cases where representational models *can* be used, OO models are superior. In such cases we should abstract the representations from the problem description and replace them with behavioral abstractions. Where possible, we should prefer OO modeling to representational modeling.

In those cases where representational modeling cannot or should not be eliminated, the use of RTTI is an appropriate mechanism for interpreting the elements of the representation. While RTTI is often inappropriate within an OO design, it provides strong support for crossing the OO/representational paradigm boundary.

The Relational Paradigm

The relational paradigm is a special, highly restrictive case of the representational paradigm that is employed in relational data base management systems (RDBMS). The restrictive nature of the representational format allows the design of very general query languages. Using these languages, we can compose powerful queries that print reports, update records, manage transactions, and so on. This is the foundation for the so-called fourth-generation languages (4GLs) that surround the current menagerie of relational database products.

Because of the extreme flexibility and power of RDMBS query languages, relational database technology is an extremely important aspect of software technology. Whole classes of applications can be written entirely in 4GLs. Writing programs in a 4GL is far simpler than writing programs in C or C++, so this ability offers a large advantage.

On the opposite side of the spectrum, there is a class of programs for which 4GLs are completely impractical. These programs typically do not store their data in relational databases.

Between these two extremes is a large class of hybrid applications that can make use of 4GLs for some of their functions, but have features for which 4GLs are inappropriate. Such programs are the focus of this section.

Tuples and Tables

A relational representation is a set of *relations*, or tables. Each table comprises many *tuples*, or *rows*. The tuples of a table are identical in form, but different in content. Each tuple is comprised of a set of *fields*, or attributes, which are also called *columns*, since they stack up "vertically" in the table.

Consider a table that represents people. Each row, or tuple, represents a different person. Each tuple has attributes for Name, Address, and Date of Birth. Looking at this table we can easily see how the row/column nomenclature came about. Each horizontal row corresponds to a tuple. When the rows are stacked up vertically, the attributes of the tuples line up into vertical columns.

Name	Address	Date of Birth
Julie Kirk	1428 Willow Creek Rd.	12/5/52
Jessie Rottweiler	666 Destructor Blvd.	6/6/66
Morry Cardwether	11423 Susquehana St.	11/5/32
Willy Wilburn	7789 N. 421st Ave.	1/17/43
James T. Kirk	1701 Enterprise Dr.	6/4/84
Methuseleh Adams	42 Deep Thought Pkwy.	9/10/48

Within a table, each row must be identified by a *key*. A key is simply the attributes of a tuple that identify that tuple. For example, the key in the above table is Name. Attributes that are part of the key are called *key attributes*; the others are called *non-key attributes*.

Tables relate to each other by using keys. For example, we can create a new table that represents the offspring of the people in the first table:

Parent	Child
Morry Cardwether	Jessie Rottweiler
Morry Cardwether	Julie Kirk
Julie Kirk	James T. Kirk

Notice that this new table uses the key of the Person table to identify people. Notice also that each child is recorded separately in its own tuple. If a person had five children, there would be five tuples in the Parent/Child table. This conforms to the first rule of relational representation: no tuple should have repeating fields.

The *Normal Forms* of a Relation

The six rules that govern relational representation are called *normal forms*. The process of applying the normal forms is called *normalization*. The query languages and 4GLs of RDBMS products depend upon normalized representations. Each abnormality within the representation causes problems for the 4GL programmer and weakens the structure of the representation. Thus, database designers spend a great deal of their time normalizing the structure of their representations.

The first three normal forms are at the core of normalization theory. We will discuss each of them in turn. The other three are beyond the scope of what I want to accomplish in this chapter. The interested reader should consult a text on relational database design.

- First Normal Form

  Tuples must be "flat" structures with no repeating groups. Each attribute is an atomic value, having no subattributes nor any other hierarchical components. This means that there can be no arrays within a tuple, nor even any repeating groups of fields. For example, the tuple representing a person cannot record the dates for the last three dentist appointments since that would be a repeating group of three dentist-appointment dates.

- Second Normal Form

  Tuples must be in first normal form, and all non-key attributes must depend upon the *whole* key. This means that, in cases where the key is made up of more than one attribute, all the other attributes in the tuple must depend upon *all* the key attributes. For example, assume we create a table that records birthday parties. The key for this table could be composed of a person's name and celebrated age. The non-key attributes might be the time of the party and the name of the place where it was held. However, it would violate the second normal form to make the person's birthdate one of the non-key attributes, since the birthdate does not depend upon the celebrated age.

- Third Normal Form

  Tuples must be in second normal form, and the non-key attributes must depend upon no other attributes besides the key attributes. For example, our table of birthday parties already contains the name of the place where the party was held; therefore, it should not contain the address of that place. The address of the party location depends upon more than just the key; it also depends upon one of the non-key attributes.

The Relational Representation of the Payroll Application

To understand the problems inherent in crossing the OO/relational boundary, we need to study an example of a relational representation. We will examine the payroll application from Chapter 3 because we understand that problem domain well from an object-oriented viewpoint.

Figure 4-6 shows an entity-relationship diagram that describes the representation of the payroll data. The rectangles represent entities, and the diamonds represent the relationships among those entities. All rectangles will become tables in the relational representation. All diamonds *could* become tables, but there are often ways to simplify the table structure so that most diamonds simply become key fields in the tables associated with an entity.

Compare this diagram with the diagram in Figure 3-10. Although there is a great deal of similarity, there are also quite a few differences. Specifically, information about behavioral abstraction has been lost. In Figure 3-10 it was clear that all three payment classifications had a common behavioral interface, but this is not indicated in Figure 4-6. Also, several relationships have been changed. The **TimeCard** and **SalesReceipt** entities have been directly related to the **Employee** entity as opposed to a particular **Payment-Classification** as in Figure 3-10. This was done because the **Employee** entity and all the payment classifications share the same key; they are all keyed off of **empid**.

The tables derived from the diagram in Figure 4-6 are shown in Listing 4-11. Notice how the placement of keys within the tables implements the relationships shown in Figure 4-6. By issuing queries based upon these keys, we can access all the relevant data associated with an **Employee** and his payroll.

Using a Relational Database

The interface between C/C++ programs and a relational database product is highly dependent upon the specific product. Each RDMBS has its own ways of implementing the details of the interface. In concept, however, the interface can be reduced to the notion that the C/C++ program sends a query to the database, and the database responds with an array of C structures. It is simplest if we suppose that those C structures correspond exactly to the schema for a table, although this is not strictly true.

We can read table rows from the database by issuing a query with the key of the row in question. If several rows have that key, then the array of C structure that is returned will have that many elements. The data in the C structure can then be changed, and the structure written back to the database by issuing the appropriate update call.

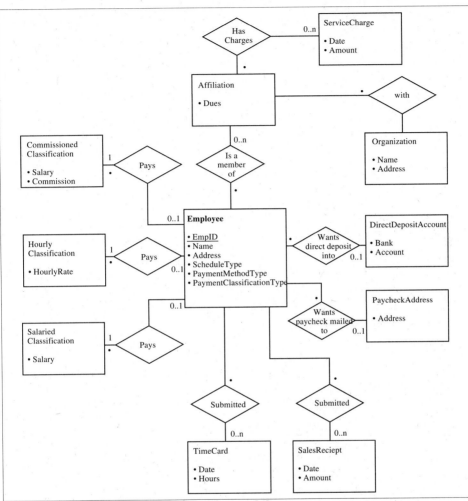

Figure 4-6
Entity-Relationship Diagram for Payroll Database Representation

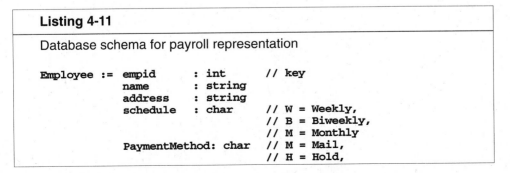

Listing 4-11

Database schema for payroll representation

```
Employee := empid      : int      // key
            name       : string
            address    : string
            schedule   : char     // W = Weekly,
                                  // B = Biweekly,
                                  // M = Monthly
            PaymentMethod: char   // M = Mail,
                                  // H = Hold,
```

Listing 4-11 (Continued)

Database schema for payroll representation

```
                                   // D = Deposit
                  PaymentClass: char   // S = Salaried,
                                   // H = Hourly,
                                   // C = Commissioned

CommissionedClassification :=
          empid      : int      // key
          salary     : float
          commission : float

HourlyClassification :=
          empid      : int      // key
          rate       : float

SalariedClassification :=
          empid      : int      // key
          salary     : float

TimeCard := empid      : int      // key
          date       : date
          hours      : float

Salesreceipt :=
          empid      : int      // key
          date       : date
          amount     : float

PaycheckAddress :=
          empid      : int      // key
          address    : string

DirectDepositAccount :=
          empid      : int      // key
          bank       : string
          account    : string

Organization :=
          orgid      : int      // key
          name       : string
          address    : string

Affiliation :=
          empid      : int      // key
          orgid      : int      // key
          dues       : float

ServiceCharge :=
          empid      : int      // key
          orgid      : int      // key
          date       : date
          amount     : float
```

A Wide Chasm

It should be clear that the relational entities shown in Listing 4-11 do not correspond well to the classes depicted in Figure 3-10. There are certainly similarities, but there are significant differences too. Primary among those differences are the flags, in the **Employee** table, that must be used to identify the appropriate **Schedule**, **PaymentMethod**, and **PaymentClassification** tables. In the OO model, the **Employee** object neither knew nor cared what kind of **PaymentMethod** object it contained. It simply invoked the abstract interface of its contained **PaymentClassification** object and expected the right thing to happen. Unfortunately, the relational **Employee** entity specifically identifies the type of the **PaymentMethod** that it uses. This violates the open/closed principle in the code that uses the **Employee** table and forces its dependency structure to revert to top-down (i.e., abstractions depending upon details).

If we must use a relational database, we have little choice about these issues. We must accept that the portions of our code that interface with the relational database will violate the open/closed principle and will be very far away from the main sequence. These portions of the code will therefore experience very high levels of change as the application evolves. Thus, it is to our benefit to make this code as small as possible.

Unfortunately, the size of the relational interface code is proportional to the size of the relational schema. The more tables and queries there are, the more interface code is necessary to cross the boundary. Worse still, this code is highly dependent upon both the relational representation of the database and the object representation of the application. Whenever there are changes in either side, the interface code must change too. So this code is going to be involved in almost every change made to the system—it will breed nightmares.

Crossing the Chasm

Our primary concern in crossing the relational/OO boundary is to keep the original object model as pure as possible. Since the dependency structure of the code that deals with the relational model cannot be properly inverted, we want to prevent any notion of the relational model from infiltrating the object model. Not only does this protect our dependency structure and keep the previously designed categories on the main sequence, it also protects us from the RDBMS itself. If the code that deals with the RDBMS is appropriately isolated from the rest of the application, then we can change RDMBS systems with a minimum of disruption.

Changing the RDBMS might not seem like an important issue at the beginning of a project, but the evolutionary pressures exerted upon a project often push it in directions that its chosen database cannot support. The best choice of RDBMS may therefore change as the project evolves and as new RDBMS products become available. We would like to remain as independent as possible from the RDBMS vendor, so that our options remain open during the lifetime of the project.

To achieve these ends, we need a layer of code between the object model and the relational model. This layer must be transparent to the object model; that is, the objects in the object model should not know that they are using the interface layer. Ideally, none of the currently existing code in the payroll application would need to change in order to use a relational database. This is a true test of the open/closed principle.

Surrogation

Surrogation is the strategy of replacing existing objects with surrogate objects. The surrogates have interfaces identical to those of the objects that they are replacing. Figure 4-7 shows how a surrogate might be used in the payroll application. Compare this diagram with the diagram for adding a **TimeCard** to an **Employee** in Figure 3-21. The important features of this diagram involve the **Employee** class and its two new derivatives. The **Employee** class has become abstract, and this abstract interface is used by the **Time-CardTransaction** class. The **RealEmployee** class contains the implementation of a concrete employee object. This class contains the instances of **PaymentMethod**, **PaymentClassification**, **PaymentSchedule**, and **Affiliation**. The **EmployeeHandle** class is the surrogate for **RealEmployee**. **RealEmployee** objects must be constructed from data that is contained in the relational model. **EmployeeHandle** objects know how to access the relational model and build the **RealEmployee** object that they represent. Once the **RealEmployee** is built, it is remembered by the **EmployeeHandle**. The **EmployeeHandle** then delegates the messages it receives via the **Employee** interface to the remembered **RealEmployee**.

The **EmployeeHandle** class also derives from **DBHandle**, which is an abstract base class that represents the need to administer the relational model and the RDBMS. **DBHandle** is used by a class called **DBController**, which is responsible for the management of RDBMS transactions and for resource acquisition and release within the RDBMS. When a **DBHandle** object is created, it registers itself with the **DBController**, so that the **DBController** can manage the RDBMS transactions and resources that pertain to it.

The **RDBMSPayrollApplication** class derives from the **PayrollApplication** class. Its purpose is to inform the **DBController** that a transaction is beginning or ending.

The **PayrollRelationalDatabase** class is derived from the abstract **PayrollDatabase** class. This class now returns **EmployeeHandle** objects instead of **RealEmployee** objects, and it collaborates with the **DBController** object to access these handles.

Figure 4-8 shows one of the dynamic scenarios behind this model. Compare this diagram with the dynamic model for adding a **TimeCard** in Figure 3-22

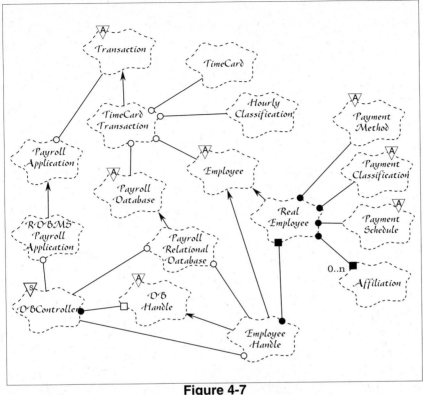

Figure 4-7
An Example of a Surrogate

While the complexity of this scenario has increased substantially, it is completely contained within the new classes that we have created. None of the classes that were part of the original object model have been touched. They still send the same messages to the same interfaces, but now those interfaces perform more complex tasks. The RDMBS has remained entirely behind the scenes, and the object model remains ignorant of its existence.

Relational Reflections

If you carefully consider the above example, you will realize that it takes quite a bit of work to implement. We must write surrogates for many objects, and those surrogates are horribly dependent. They depend upon both the object model *and* the relational model. Thus, the surrogate classes will be involved in nearly every change made to the system.

Efficiency is also difficult to control. Surrogates cannot easily optimize the efficiency of database access, since they know nothing about the current state of the application. One

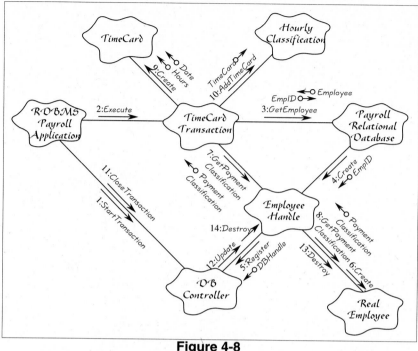

Figure 4-8
Dynamic Model for Adding a `TimeCard` Using a Surrogate

could try to establish communication between the application and the **DBController** so that the various surrogates could query the controller to determine the most efficient tack, but this could lead to significant ugliness.

These disadvantages arise from the mismatch in paradigms, and there is no perfect solution. The need for isolation is real, but isolation breeds the volatile interface layer and disconnects the application from some of its options for efficiency.

Still, the advantages of isolation in general, and surrogation in particular, are quite real. In the example above, we were able to insert an RDBMS without changing the underlying object model. We did not quite achieve our goal of entirely closing the source code; we had to split **Employee** into abstract and concrete classes. These changes are almost insignificant, however; not a single line of executable code is involved.

Moreover, if we had been a little more prescient in our original design—if we had known, or even suspected, that an RDBMS was going to be used—then we would have created the abstract **Employee** class in the first place. We might even have created the abstract class on the general principle that abstract interfaces open our options. If we had, then the only source code changes required would have been to the main program. The rest of the RDBMS could have been added to the system with new source code. We would have achieved nearly 100% closure!

It should be clear that changing the RDBMS product does not affect the structure of the design in the slightest. Certainly the change would be costly in terms of time required to create the new **DBController** and all the **DBHandle** derivatives. Still, the job is straightforward and bounded. We know what needs to be changed, and we know that those changes will not affect any of the application-related code.

The Multiprocessing Paradigm

The multiprocessing paradigm is different from the previous paradigms, which interfered with the source-code dependency structure of the software. They each forced us to violate the open/closed principle. This is not true of the multiprocessing paradigm. There is nothing inherent in the multiprocessing paradigm that forces our class categories off the main sequence.

The multiprocessing (MP) paradigm is completely orthogonal to the OO paradigm; the two deal with very different aspects of software. Whereas OO deals with abstractions of state and behavior, MP deals with abstractions of schedule and sequence. These abstractions have very little overlap, so the two paradigms work quite well together.

The concepts, vocabulary, and notation of the multiprocessing paradigm are thoroughly discussed in Appendix B. If you have not had much experience in MP, you should read Appendix B before you proceed. If you are reasonably familiar with MP, then a quick perusal of Appendix B would probably be helpful.

Lightweight Processes in an OO Environment

Lightweight processes are those that share a single address space and have direct access to each other's data. Objects that run in this kind of an environment are sometimes called active objects. In a lightweight environment it is not necessary, or even desirable, for all of the methods of a particular object to run within the same process. In fact, many of the methods of such objects can be written to be responsible for communicating across the process boundaries. For example, consider Figures 4-9 and 4-10.

Figure 4-9 shows a common division of objects. The application is a system in which users can demand that a test be performed. We want to capture this policy decision in abstract classes, so that we can reuse it in different contexts. Thus, we form two abstract base classes: one representing the user, and another representing the test controller.

The diagram shows the intended derivatives of these abstract bases. The user interface will be supported by a GUI of some kind, and there will be many associated objects. The test controller will support remote tests, probably over a modem or some other wide-area network scheme.

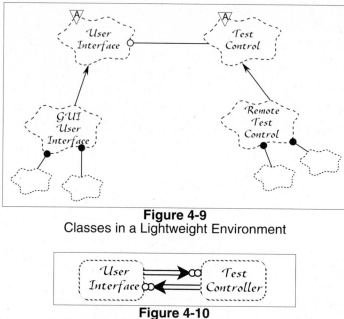

Figure 4-9
Classes in a Lightweight Environment

Figure 4-10
Process Diagram for the Test System

Figure 4-10 shows the scheduling abstractions that are part of the design. The user interface and the test controller must run according to different schedules (i.e., concurrently) and are therefore placed in different processes. We made this decision because tests can be lengthy affairs, and the user may want to perform other activities while the test is running.

The double circles at the tips of the arrows between the two processes depict queues into which communications messages are stored. Thus, the user interface can request several tests that will queue up behind each other. The test controller will execute each in sequence and then return the results to the user. The user interface queues up the results until it is ready to display them to the user.

Figure 4-11 shows the object diagram that implements the high-level policy shared by the two abstract classes. The **UserInterface** class instructs the **TestController** class to perform a test. Some time later the **TestController** class responds with the **TestComplete** message, which carries the results of the test.

Notice the half-arrow notation used for the messages. This is Booch notation for *asynchronous* messages. In an asynchronous message, the invocation and the execution occur according to different schedules (i.e., in different processes). Thus, these messages represent communication across a process boundary. Figures 4–12 through 4-15 show one strategy for implementing such messages.

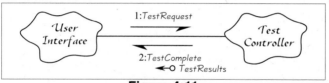

Figure 4-11
Test System High-Level Object Diagram

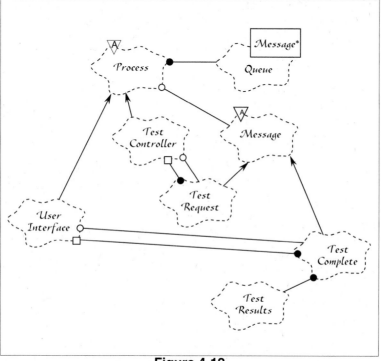

Figure 4-12
Process Hierarchy

Figure 4-12 shows that **UserInterface** and **TestController** both derive from an abstract base class, **Process**, which contains a **Queue<Message*>** object that holds any pending messages.

When the **TestRequest** message is received by the **TestController**, it creates a **TestRequestMessage** object and places it on the queue (see Figure 4-13). This function operates within the thread of execution of the user interface process.

After the context of execution switches and the test controller process gains control, a method within the **Process** class pulls the next message out of its queue and tells it to execute (Figure 4-14).

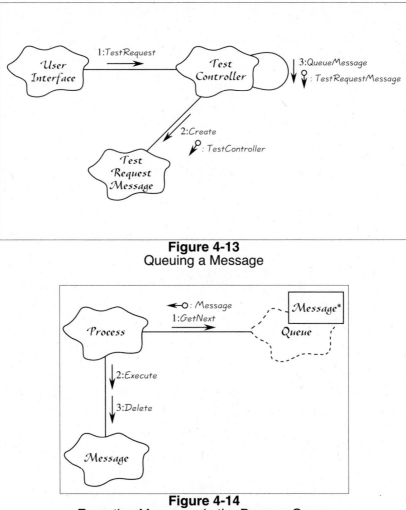

Figure 4-13
Queuing a Message

Figure 4-14
Executing Messages in the Process Queue

When the **TestRequest** message is told to execute, it tells its corresponding **TestController** to perform the requested test.

This mechanism is simple to implement and provides an effective way for classes to communicate across process boundaries. It should be clear that this mechanism will work as well in a multiprocessing model with multiple threads as it will in a run-to-completion (RTC) model (see Appendix B). In the RTC model, there is only one queue, instead of one queue per process.

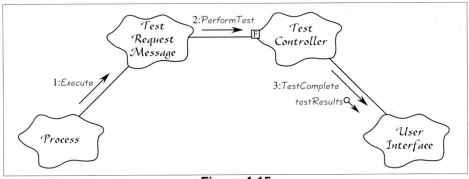

Figure 4-15
Executing the Test-Request Message

Multiprocessing Pollution

The preceding model has a problem. Figures 4-9 and 4-11 depicted a simple statement of policy between two base classes. If we ignore the half-arrows in Figure 4-11, this policy could easily have been implemented in a single process. By making **Process** a base class of **UserInterface** and **TestController**, however, we have polluted the simple policy with multiprocessing concerns. Thus, we could not reuse the policy in an environment that did not demand multiprocessing. Figure 4-16 shows how to rid the base classes of the multiprocessing pollution.

By isolating the **UserInterface** and **TestController** classes from the **Process** class, we have preserved the purity of the simple policy that exists between them. Derived from these base classes are two classes that also derive from **Process**. They perform the message deferral needed to manage the execution of the two classes in separate processes. They are also responsible for any concurrency management, semaphores, monitors, guards, and queues necessary for managing the multiprocessing environment. Thus, the base classes remain reusable in any kind of execution environment.

Heavyweight Processes

Heavyweight processes do not execute in the same address space. Their address spaces are typically isolated from each other by the memory management hardware in the computer. In most operating systems it is physically impossible for a program running in one process to arbitrarily access the data space of another process.

In such an environment, the simple communications mechanism used in the previous section is not practical. **Message** objects can be passed between lightweight processes in order to communicate method invocations. In a heavyweight environment objects cannot be passed across the process boundary because any pointers within the objects (including

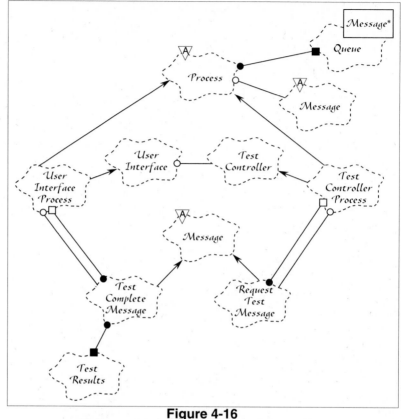

Figure 4-16
Ridding the Base Classes of MP Pollution

hidden **vtbl** pointers or virtual base class pointers) will not be valid within the address space of the receiving process. Moreover, all the methods within an object must execute within the heavyweight process that contains the object. An object cannot execute across heavyweight process boundaries.

Thus, we need a different strategy for communicating between objects in heavyweight environments. The goals, however, remain the same: we want to protect our high-level policies from being polluted by the multiprocessing environment, and we want the multiprocessing environment to be transparent to those high-level policies. Thus, we must hide the concurrency and message-passing mechanism as much as possible.

Surrogation between Heavyweight Processes.

We can achieve the above goals by using surrogation, as we did in the relational paradigm. Figures 4-17 through 4-23 show one possible mechanism for using surrogation between processes.

Figure 4-17 shows a simple alarm management system. A **Sensor** object uses an **AlarmManagement** object. The **AlarmManagement** object is apparently responsible for presenting alarms to a user and for remembering them until a user instructs it to clear the alarm. This could be as simple as a household burglar alarm, or as complex as a system monitoring an automated factory.

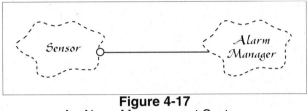

Figure 4-17
An Alarm Management System

Figure 4-18 shows the scenario when an alarm is detected. An **AlarmEvent** message is sent to the **AlarmManager** object along with a copy of the alarm details. This is a simple statement of high-level policy. In some of the contexts where this high-level policy is reused, however, the two objects must live in separate heavyweight processes. We do not want to pollute the high-level policy with multiprocessing concerns, so we use surrogation to hide the multiprocessing complications from the high-level classes.

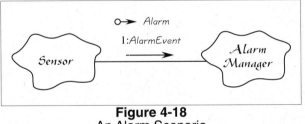

Figure 4-18
An Alarm Scenario

Figure 4-19 shows how surrogation is employed within the **Sensor** process. The **AlarmManager** object has become abstract. The **Sensor** object uses the abstract interface of the **AlarmManager** class, so its assumptions have not changed. Derived from the **AlarmManager** abstract class is a concrete class called **AlarmManagerSurrogate**, which is responsible for transmitting method invocations across the process boundary.

When a method is invoked within the **AlarmManagerSurrogate**, it creates an appropriate derivative of the **Packet** class. In this case, when an **AlarmEvent** method is invoked by a **Sensor** object, the **AlarmManagerSurrogate** creates an **AlarmEventPacket**. The **Packet** object is then transmitted across the process boundary.

In an earlier section, we asserted that objects cannot be sent across process boundaries. However, the data within an object *can* be sent as long as it is sent with enough

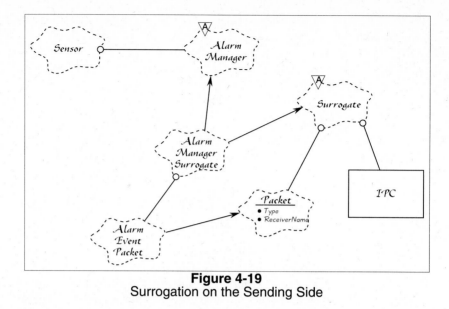

Figure 4-19
Surrogation on the Sending Side

information to rebuild the object that contained it. Thus, we must encode the type of the packet object into the data that gets sent across the process boundary.

The **AlarmManagerSurrogate** class also derives from the abstract base class **Surrogate**. The **Surrogate** class knows how to use the interprocess communications (IPC) mechanisms of the operating system to transmit the data and type encoded within a packet to the appropriate receiving process.

Figure 4-20 shows the structure of a process that receives packets. The **Process** class uses the IPC mechanisms to receive a packet. The **PacketDecoder** class maintains a list of **Receiver** objects and their names. The sending process must load the name of the appropriate **Receiver** object into the packet before it is sent, so that the proper **Receiver** object will be given charge of the incoming packet. Derivatives of the **Receiver** class know how to decode the type information of the packet and extract the data from the packet so that it can be turned into a method invocation (member function call) for the appropriate object. We will see a typical scenario in Figure 4-23, but first let's look at some housekeeping issues.

Figure 4-21 shows how objects in the receiving process are created. The **Alarm-ManagerProcess** object creates the **RealAlarmManager** object and the **Alarm-ManagerReceiver** object. The **AlarmManagerReceiver** object then registers itself with the **PacketDecoder** object. This ensures that the **PacketDecoder** knows both the name and address of the **Receiver** for packets that contain alarm events.

Although this diagram shows a one-to-one correspondence between **Receivers** and the objects that they serve, this is not strictly required. If there were many **Alarm-Manager** objects, they could all be handled by a single **AlarmManagerReceiver**.

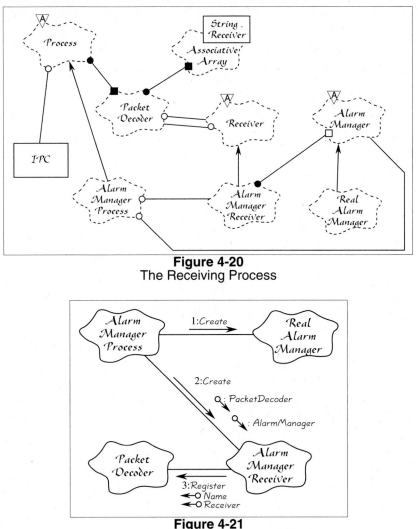

Figure 4-20
The Receiving Process

Figure 4-21
Creation and Registration of a Receiver

The sender could place some kind of selector in the packet, so that the correct **Alarm-Manager** object would be selected.

Figure 4-22 shows that when a packet is received by the **Process** object, the name of the appropriate **Receiver** object is extracted, and the packet is sent to the **Packet-Decoder** along with the name of the **Receiver**. The packet is then sent to the appropriate **Receiver** object.

Figure 4-23 shows how the **AlarmManagerReceiver** object queries the packet for the type of object it represents. The **AlarmEventPacket** is then recreated from this

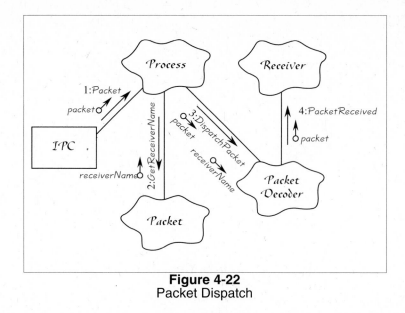

Figure 4-22
Packet Dispatch

information and the other data contained within the packet. The **AlarmEventPacket** is then queried for the alarm code. Finally, the alarm code is sent to the **RealAlarmManager** via the **AlarmEvent** method invocation.

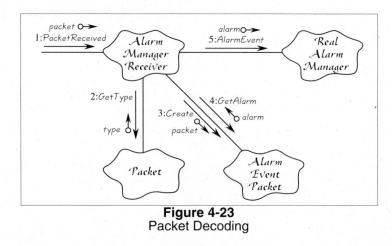

Figure 4-23
Packet Decoding

Thus, we have transparently sent a method invocation across the process boundary. The high-level policy represented by the **Sensor** and **AlarmManager** classes has not been polluted by any multiprocessing concerns. Instead, we have invoked the open/closed principle in order to manage the complexity of multiprocessing by adding new code to the system, rather than modifying the working model.

Summary

In this chapter we have discussed five different software paradigms: object-oriented, procedural, representational, relational, and multiprocessing. Each of these paradigms has advantages and disadvantages. None is intrinsically inferior to any of the others; they simply serve different needs.

Paradigm chauvinism is a poor substitute for design skills. There is no reason to force the use of the object-oriented paradigm in all aspects of software; many aspects of a software application may be better served by one of the other paradigms. It is important to remember that the prime advantage of the object-oriented paradigm is the ability to manage source code dependencies so that details depend upon abstractions. While this is a noble goal that supports the reusability of high-level policies and greatly enhances the maintainability of an application, it is not appropriate in every case.

Where a flexible query language is needed, the relational paradigm is almost essential. Where a single representation must be shared by many different programs, a representational paradigm is probably most appropriate. For quick programs that are not candidates for reuse, the procedural paradigm is very effective. The multiprocessing paradigm is necessary for any projects that must operate according to many schedules.

All of these paradigms can be mixed with the object-oriented paradigm. The techniques presented in this chapter can be effective in achieving such paradigm crossings.

Exercises

1. What is the frequency the main electrical current in Europe?

2. What kind of type system does C++ have?
   a. Static
   b. Strong
   c. Dynamic
   d. Regional

3. If your operating system has function calls for manipulating the current time and date, wrap them beneath a **Time** class.

4. Using procedural design techniques (e.g., Structured Analysis and Design), design and write a program that plays blackjack. Then convert the program to OO.

5. Create the representational model for a PERT chart. Write a program that draws the chart. Write another that finds the critical path. Write another that calculates the probability that any particular task might lie on the critical path.

6. Convert the PERT representation to a relational model. Develop an object ori-
    ented design for interactively drawing a PERT diagram. Use surrogation to tie the
    object model to the relational database.

7. Design and write an object-oriented program that simulates a ball bouncing
    across the screen. Using RTC, modify the model so that the screen can be split
    into many virtual screens, each with its own bouncing ball

5

High-Level OOAD:
A Case Study

. . . because how one lives is so far distant from how one ought to live,
that he who neglects what is done for what ought to be done,
sooner effects his ruin than his preservation . . .

—Machiavelli, circa 1514

. . . one of the most, if not <u>the</u> most, essential properties of a system
is that it must have a stable structure during its lifetime.

—Ivar Jacobson

The two quotes above, one from an ancient political pragmatist and the other from a contemporary design master, reflect the naturally opposing forces—the yin and yang—within software engineering. On the one hand, we need to do what is necessary to reduce our time-to-market and respond quickly to market demands. On the other hand, we must spend the time needed to ensure that our designs will enjoy reasonable maintenance costs for a decent lifetime. The balancing act that strives to satisfy these two extremes adequately is known as engineering.

This chapter begins the case study of a building security system. Unlike our previous examples, this project is sufficiently complicated to expose the struggle between pragmatics and propriety, practicality, and precision. In this chapter we will examine the requirements and high-level design and analysis of this case study. In the chapters that follow, we will study lower-level design and implementation issues.

Introduction

This chapter and those that follow present an investigation of the object-oriented analysis and design of a building security system. The complexity of this project is significant. Its implementation would probably take several hundred thousand lines of C++ code.

Why should we be interested in examining a problem of such complexity? In my opinion, the real issues of software engineering cannot be faithfully represented by anything less than a significant project; we cannot learn the techniques for building a house by gluing popsicle sticks together.

Software engineering is a balancing act between two diametrically opposed forces. If a project is to be worthwhile, it must provide usable benefit early in its life cycle. Time-to-market is a critical issue. A product that is late to market may not be able to compete against those that were there before it. If a software project cannot be developed quickly, then regardless of how wonderfully designed it is, it may be worthless. On the other hand, the maintainability of the software is also a critical issue. A software project must be able to evolve over its intended life cycle without requiring huge maintenance budgets. If the project cannot support a reasonable budget for evolution and maintenance, then—regardless of how quickly it was developed—it is worthless. The true beauty of a software design is in the creativity that the designers employ to balance these two issues.

It is not easy to design software that is easy to maintain over a long life cycle. It is also not easy to design software that can be implemented quickly.[1] Balancing these two difficulties into a workable design that is robust enough to survive and practical enough to be implemented quickly is nothing short of miraculous—yet we must work this miracle on a regular basis.

Object-oriented design gives us some tools that help us with both aspects of the problem. The inversion of source-code dependencies allows us to decouple the high-level abstractions from the details that they manipulate. Thus, we can evolve and maintain the details with minimal effects upon each other and the abstractions. The inversion of dependencies also allows us to reuse abstractions in different detailed contexts. By building a library of abstract reusable components, we can shorten the time required to build new systems. Finally, the strong reliance upon well-defined abstract interfaces between the separate components of the application makes the process of integration far more efficient and less error-prone.

The case study that follows reveals many examples of the struggle between the opposing forces in design. Often we must trade robustness off against pragmatics and vice versa. This is normal and healthy. It is engineering.

---

1. There is a difference between software that is designed for speedy implementation and software that is implemented quickly. The first usually gets done faster than the second. The second usually doesn't work anyway.

A word of warning: This is a long chapter. It covers a lot of ground and requires a fair amount of effort and diligence to read. Yet, when it is complete, we will have little more than an outline of the design. Chapters 6 and 7 continue the process and flesh out the design.

Case Study: The Requirements Document

Building Security Manager

This document describes the software requirements for a new product that provides security-management functions for a medium- to large-sized building. The purpose of this system is to prevent/report unauthorized entry into a building or a secure area of a building. It monitors the patrols of security guards and reports any anomalies in their patrol schedules. It is also responsible for monitoring fire and smoke detectors, and raising the appropriate alarms.

The detailed functions of the system are as follows:

1. Monitor and control the normal entry and exit of building occupants through the use of personal security cards. This includes entry and exit from the building proper, and entry and exit from particular security zones within the building. The system controls the locks on the doors, and will not unlock a door unless the appropriate security card is swiped through the security-card reader by the door.

2. Detect a forced break-in of doors or windows. Break-ins are monitored both for outside entrances or windows, and entrances or windows leading to particular security zones within the building.

3. Fire and smoke detectors are strategically placed throughout the building. These detectors must be monitored. If fire or smoke is detected, the appropriate alarms must be raised.

4. The tracking of security-guard patrols is accomplished by having the security guards swipe their ID cards at checkpoint locations along their patrol routes. The system knows the normal schedule for such patrols, and reports any anomalies in the monitored patrols.

5. The system allows multiple levels of security for restricting access to certain security zones, possibly based on the time of day.

6. In the case of certain major violations of security, the system must have the ability to lock down the violated security zone or an enclosing zone in order to prevent exit of the perpetrators from the building or a zone.

7. In the case of fire or other emergency, the system will allow "emergency evacuation" from the affected zones. This will allow unrestricted exit from those zones, but will not allow entry. Sirens in the affected zones are activated to alert the occupants that they must evacuate.

8. There is at least one security control center that contains a computer screen and a printer. Such a control center may cover the entire building, or be for a set of

security zones. Every security zone must report to one and only one control center. Alarms, security violations, and security events are logged on the printer. The screen shows a list of unresolved violations and alarms. An audible alarm will sound as long as this list is not empty. The control center operators can resolve a violation or alarm by interacting with the computer keyboard.

9. Security Events: An authorized entrance or exit; a security guard swiping his card at a control checkpoint at the appropriate time.

Security Violations: An unauthorized attempt to enter or exit a security zone; a security guard being 5 minutes late to a checkpoint. A security door being held open for more than 1 minute.

Security Alarm: A break-in; a security guard being more than 10 minutes late to swipe his card at a checkpoint. A door being held open for more than 5 minutes. A fire or smoke detector signal.

Analyzing the Requirements

This rather uninspiring document is typical of an early requirements document. It contains a list of features that are considered to be essential for the success of the product. It does not attempt to describe too much of the structure of the system, or very much about the way in which the system operates.

We will now walk through each requirement in turn, considering how each impacts the design of the product. Each requirement is unique, and I will employ different techniques accordingly. I may use noun lists, use-cases, STDs, or simply ad hoc analysis, depending upon which seems most appropriate.

Requirement 1: Doors, Locks, and Security Card Readers

1. *Monitor and control the normal entry and exit of building occupants through the use of personal security cards. This includes entry and exit from the building proper, and entry and exit from particular security zones within the building. The system controls the locks on the doors, and will not unlock a door unless the appropriate security card is swiped through the security-card reader by the door.*

Let's begin by translating this requirement into its corresponding use-cases. In this case, there is only one.

Use-Case 1-A

Request entry through door

When a user swipes his security card through a card reader, the system checks to see if that user is authorized to pass through the corresponding door. If so, a security event is logged, and the door is unlocked. If not, a security violation is logged, and the door will remain locked.

Now let's create some simple static models. If we examine use-case 1-A, we find that we will have to model the concept of doors, security-card readers, security cards, and locks.

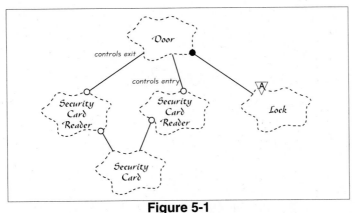

Figure 5-1
Static Model for Door, Lock, and Card Readers

Figure 5-1 is no more than an initial guess. We have two **SecurityCardReader** objects for each door; one to control entry, and one to control exit. Each door also has a lock. Security cards are used by the **SecurityCardReader**.

Whenever there are two of something, it makes me nervous. Why two? Why not three? What is the difference between the two, really? Will a **Door** ever require more than two **SecurityCardReader** objects? I can't think of a reason right now, but the assumption of two specific readers is very limiting. If the assumption turns out to be wrong, we could have a lot of difficulty later.

There is another issue about doors that bothers me. How does a **Door** or a **SecurityCardReader** know whether a person is entering or exiting the door? Can a door be entered? Can it be exited? If you think about this a minute, you will see that it is nonsense. A door can only be passed through.

Imagine a door that connects Security Zone 2 with Security Zone 3. If I pass through the door one way, I exit Zone 2 and enter Zone 3. If I pass through the door in the opposite direction, I will exit Zone 3 and enter Zone 2. Whenever you pass through a door, then, you are both entering and exiting a zone. This is good thing to know. It also gives us an interesting generalization: The outside of the building is a valid security zone.

Another interesting thing to note is that the **SecurityCardReader** "knows" where the person is. It knows which way the person is trying to pass through the door, so it knows which zones are being entered and exited. This means that the **SecurityCardReader** should be the central abstraction in this static model, and that **Zones** and **Doors** should be related to it.

Thus, we can restate the association between a **Door**, a **Zone**, and a **SecurityCardReader** as follows: A **SecurityCardReader** controls access into one **Zone** and out of another **Zone** by opening a **Door**. This is shown in Figure 5-2.

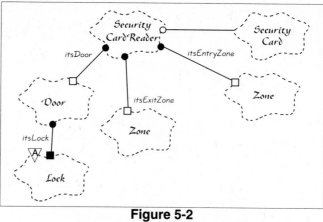

Figure 5-2
SecurityCardReader Model

Note that this solves the other problem we had about how many **Security-CardReaders** a **Door** can have—they don't seem to have any at all. Instead, **Doors**, **Zones**, and **SecurityCardReaders** exist in a four-way association. There appears to be no limit to the number of such associations that may exist; thus, we can associate many **SecurityCardReaders** with a particular **Door**. That result was not a goal of the model; it just happened to work out that way.

This is typical of the way that problems go away when you look at the bigger picture in the right way. Whenever you are faced by what appears to be an unsolvable problem, it is often wise to rethink your initial assumptions.

Let's run some behavioral scenarios on this model, and see if it works. Suppose that a person is trying to open a door with her security card. Figure 5-3 shows what happens.

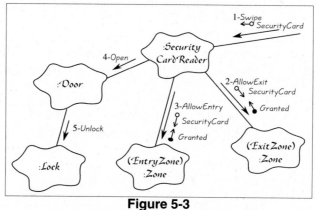

Figure 5-3
Card Swipe Opens Door

Some object we haven't identified yet detects the swipe of a security card through the reader, which causes the swipe message to be sent to the **SecurityCardReader** along with some representation of the security card that was swiped. The **Security-CardReader** then checks to see if that security card has permission to exit and enter the respective zones. In this case permission is granted, so the **SecurityCardReader** tells the **Door** to open, and the **Door** tells the **Lock** to unlock.

This scenario leaves out a great deal: How long will the door remain unlocked? How does the system know if the door is left open? What object sends the initial message to **SecurityCardReader**? We will have to investigate these questions later. Still, we have learned a great deal already about how to model the security-card mechanisms, and how they work.

We should look at two more scenarios before we leave this part of the model. What happens if either of the two **Zones** denies permission to pass through the **Door**? What should the system do? According to the use-case and Requirement 9, such an event must be logged at the security control center. We will deal with that part of the model later. What should the **Door**, **Zone**, and **SecurityCardReader** do? Probably nothing at all. In any breach of security, the best course of action is to give the violator as little feedback as possible. Figures 5-4 and 5-5 show the scenarios.

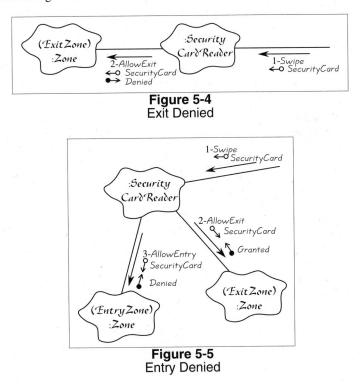

Figure 5-4
Exit Denied

Figure 5-5
Entry Denied

The central object in all these scenarios is certainly the **SecurityCardReader**. It is easy to identify because the primary incoming message (i.e., **swipe**) terminates there, and all the primary outgoing messages originate there. This is a problem. We have bound **SecurityCardReader** objects to the job of controlling access between doors, but they ought to be reusable in other contexts such as Teller Machines, Elevators, and so on. Figure 5-6 shows how we can isolate the **SecurityCardReader** class from the job of controlling access between security zones.

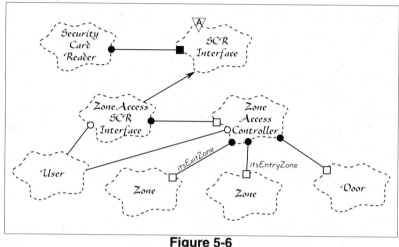

Figure 5-6
ZoneAccessController Static Model

Two important concepts are employed here. First, we have disassociated the zone-access function from the **SecurityCardReader**. This function is now the domain of the **ZoneAccessController**. This is probably wise, since zone access is an abstract concept, and the card reader is a physical entity. We would like to separate physical entities from the jobs that we assign to them, so that we can use them for many different kinds of jobs.

The second thing of interest is the **SCRInterface** class, an abstract base class that is contained by the **SecurityCardReader**. This class provides an interface that the **SecurityCardReader** uses, and from this class we derive the **ZoneAccess-SCRInterface** class. This class can receive messages from the **Security-CardReader** and translate them into commands that the **ZoneAccessController** can understand. Thus, the **SecurityCardReader** and the **ZoneAccess-Controller** are utterly isolated from each other; neither class knows about the other.

This makes use of a very important design pattern called a *BRIDGE*.[2] A BRIDGE exists whenever a client class (such as **SecurityCardReader**) contains an abstract server

---

2.   Erich Gamma, Richard Helm, Ralph Johnson, and John Vlissides, *Design Patterns: Elements of Reusable Object-Oriented Software* (Addison Wesley, 1995).

class (such as **SCRInterface**). The client can invoke the server without depending upon the implementation of the server; thus, we can use the *client* in many different contexts. We will see this pattern several more times in the pages that follow.

Figure 5-7 shows the dynamic model for the **ZoneAccessController**. Notice that the **swipe** message is now generated by the **SecurityCardReader** object and is translated to an **AccessRequest** message by the **ZoneAccessSCRInterface** object. Notice also that the concept of the security card has been altered to the more abstract concept of a **user**. The other dynamic models should be changed accordingly.

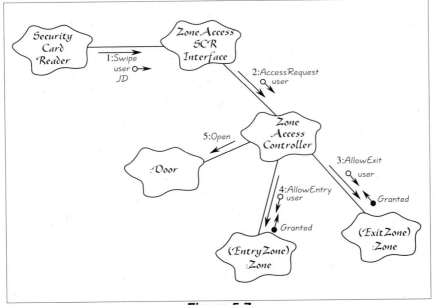

Figure 5-7
ZoneAccessController Dynamic Model

This model allows us to use other devices to gain access to a zone. For example, it would be simple to modify the model so that we can use retinal scanners, thumbprint scanners, or voice-print identifiers. Also, requests for access could come from other sources, such as the security control room or even external management systems. Finally, the model allows for the reuse of the **SecurityCardReader** class in many different contexts.

Since **ZoneAccessControl** is the central abstraction in this model, it would probably help us to understand it if we modeled it as a finite state machine. Figure 5-8 shows the appropriate state transition diagram.

This is pretty simple. You can see most of the three scenarios modeled in this STD. You can also see that we have found a place for logging the security violations and events, as dictated by Requirement 9. However, the STD has forced us to consider a few other

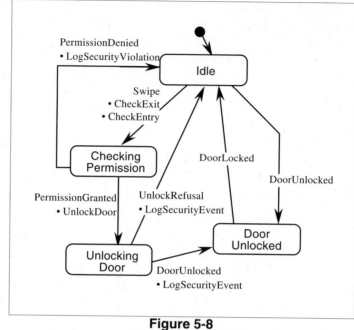

Figure 5-8
`ZoneAccessController` Finite State Machine

problems. What happens, for example, if the door is opened due to interaction with a different `ZoneAccessController` (i.e., the one attached to the card reader on the other side of the door)? I don't think we want the `ZoneAccessController` to attempt to unlock a door that is already open. Thus the `ZoneAccessController` must be kept abreast of the status of the lock on its door. If a user swipes a card while the door is unlocked, nothing happens.

Note that unlocking the door takes place in two stages. Since the **Door** must tell us that it has been unlocked, I separated the unlocking mechanism into two states: **UnlockingDoor** is the state in which the **Unlock** message has been sent, but the **Door** has not yet responded. If the **Door** responds by telling us that it is unlocked, then we move to the **DoorUnlocked** state. However, the fact that the **Door** has to tell us that the door has been unlocked invites the possibility that the door may not be able to be unlocked. Perhaps doors can be manually locked to prevent access. Thus, I have modeled the situation in which the **Door** refuses to accept the **Unlock** message. Although the requirements don't specify this as a possibility, it seems so likely to me, that I am including it in the functional model of the system.

Now we should go back and update our scenarios, and deal with the new ones that we have uncovered. The results are shown in Figures 5-9 through 5-12.

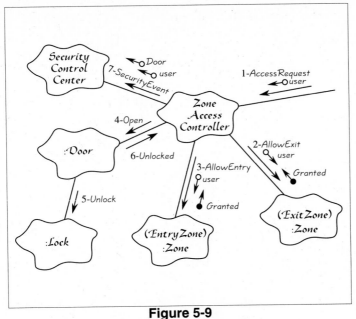

Figure 5-9
`AccessRequest` Opens Door

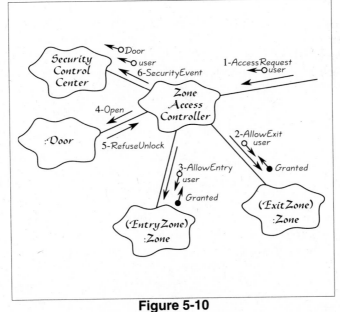

Figure 5-10
`Door` Refuses to Unlock

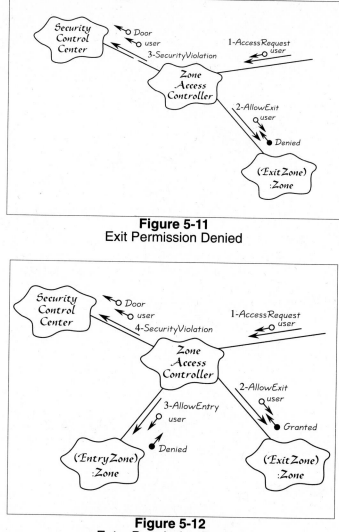

Figure 5-11
Exit Permission Denied

Figure 5-12
Entry Permission Denied

     Since we have added the **SecurityControlCenter** object to these scenarios, we ought to figure out how it fits into the static structure. Requirement 8 states that we can have more than one security control center, and that such a center is responsible for a set of zones. Figure 5-13 shows an unrefined relationship that exists between **Zone** and **SecurityControlCenter**. I don't yet know what form that relationship takes, whether **Zone** should contain **SecurityControlCenter** or vice versa, so I have merely diagrammed the association.

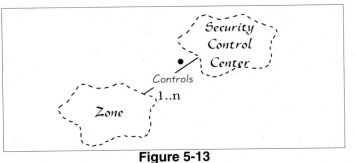

Figure 5-13
Static Model of Zone and **SecurityControlCenter**

This diagram isn't consistent with the behavioral scenarios in Figures 5-9 through 5-12, which show the **ZoneAccessController** communicating directly with the **SecurityControlCenter**, rather than through a **Zone**. This is a bug. If a security card is used to attempt an unauthorized exit from some zone, the security violation must be sent to the security control center for *that particular zone*. Thus, we need to change the behavioral scenarios once again. The updated models are shown in Figures 5-14 through 5-18.

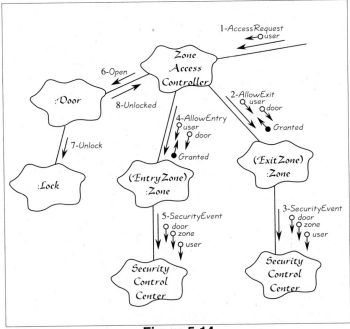

Figure 5-14
Zone Access Request Accepted

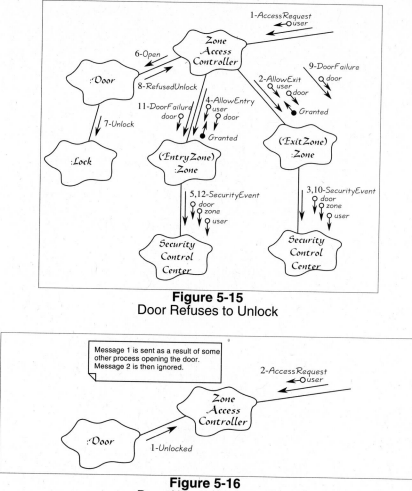

Figure 5-15
Door Refuses to Unlock

Figure 5-16
Door Already Unlocked

Notice in Figure 5-14 that two security events are now reported for every card use. This is correct: the **SecurityControlCenter** for both affected **Zones** must report the appropriate event. The **ExitZone** must report the authorized exit, and the **EntryZone** must log the authorized entry.

In Figure 5-15, both zones are notified if the door that separates them refuses to unlock. If it turns out that both the exit and entry zones use the same **SecurityControlCenter**, the messages will be somewhat redundant. If this becomes a problem, we could install a filter in **SecurityControlCenter** to prevent redundant messages.

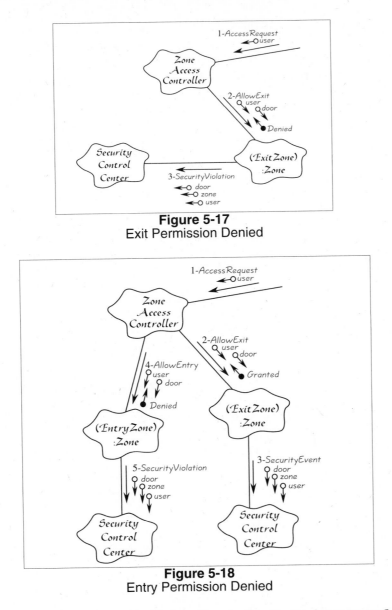

Figure 5-17
Exit Permission Denied

Figure 5-18
Entry Permission Denied

I am not entirely happy with this last scenario. The **SecurityControlCenter** for the **ExitZone** is told that the exit request was granted, but no exit actually took place, since entry permission was not granted. This seems to be a contradiction, but it does represent an accurate description of the decisions that were made. Perhaps, to add more detail, we should declare a **SecurityEvent** whenever a door is opened, and send the event to the **SecurityControlCenter**s for both the **ExitZone** and the

EntryZone. Let's keep this in mind.

Figure 5-19 reexamines the finite state machine for the **ZoneAccessController** class. The only changes involve the removal of the security events that are no longer the responsibility of **ZoneAccessController**.

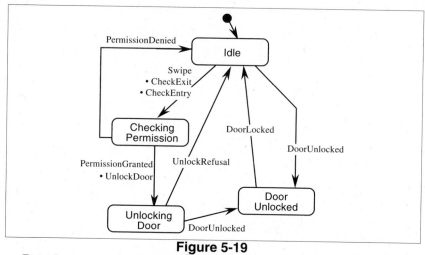

Figure 5-19
ZoneAccessController State Transaction Diagram (updated)

It is clear from the dynamic scenarios that each **Zone** must be able to send messages to its corresponding **SecurityControlCenter**. Thus, we can eliminate some of the ambiguity from Figure 5-13 by showing, in Figure 5-20, that **Zone** must contain the **SecurityControlCenter** that it reports to.

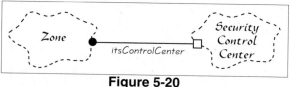

Figure 5-20
Zone Contains **SecurityControlCenter**

Reflections

This concludes our preliminary analysis of Requirement 1. The gyrations we went through to get to this point are typical. We oscillated back and forth between the static model and the dynamic model, as each improvement in one revealed deficiencies in the other. Each change increased both the accuracy and complexity of the model. The process only stopped when both models appeared reasonably consistent.

Notice also that we kept the scope of the analysis quite narrow, considering only Requirement 1. This was intentional. Had we widened the scope too early, we might have created a huge static model attempting to describe the whole application—a formidable amount of work. By the time we had begun the behavioral analysis, our investment in the static model would have tempted us to force the dynamic model to work rather than fix the flaws in the static model. By limiting the scope, we became vested in neither model, and could easily repair flaws.

This is *stepwise refinement*. It is a powerful tool both for creating accurate models, and for preventing premature vesting in any particular scheme.

Although the use-case I wrote for this requirement provided some insights, it was little more than a restatement of the requirement. The object diagrams and STDs were, in my opinion, far more fertile ground for the discovery of abstractions.

Requirement 2: Break-in Detection

> 2. *Detect a forced break-in of doors or windows. Break-ins are monitored both for outside entrances or windows, and entrances or windows leading to particular security zones within the building.*

The second requirement says that the system must be able to detect break-ins of a door or a window. To detect a break-in, we must have a break-in detector. Figure 5-21 shows how such an object might fit into a static model.

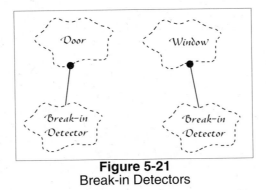

Figure 5-21
Break-in Detectors

This seems simple enough. Every door and window has a detector; however, are we sure that we can support this relationship? If a single detector could cover more than one window or door, we would need to change the relationships around, as shown in Figure 5-22.

I like this better. It gives us the flexibility of having one detector per door or window, but it also allows the user to protect more than one door or window with a single detector. This give us some options.

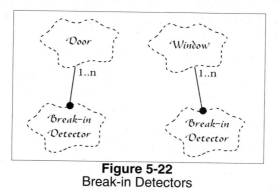

Figure 5-22
Break-in Detectors

Notice the symmetry of this model. Both **Door** and **Window** share identical relationships with **Break-inDetector**. This suggests that **Door** and **Window** *may* be related by inheritance to some parent class. Figure 5-23 shows a possible inheritance hierarchy.

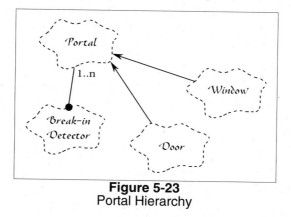

Figure 5-23
Portal Hierarchy

This inheritance relationship is tentative, since we have not yet established a common interface for **Door** and **Window**. In the object paradigm, inheritance should not be used without the justification of common behavioral interfaces. If there are no methods that **Window** and **Door** share in common, there should be no base class **Portal**. The containment of **Portal** by **Break-inDetector** implies that **Break-inDetector** can send messages to **Portal**. Whatever those messages are, they must be part of the abstract interface for both **Window** and **Door**. Thus, the inheritance relationship is indirectly justified. The dynamic scenarios should bear it out.

We need to make one more addition to this model. When a break-in is detected, a security alarm must be raised. We already know from our analysis of Requirement 1 that security events, violations, and alarms must be sent to the **Zone** so that they can be forwarded to the appropriate **SecurityControlCenter**. Thus, the detector must have access to a **Zone**. But which one? **Doors** and **Window**s represent separations between two **Zone**s, so each detector must know about the two security zones that its doors and windows divide.

Figure 5-24 shows that each **Break-inDetector** knows about two **Zones**. This allows the **Break-inDetector** objects to send **SecurityAlarm** messages to its **Zone** objects. But how can we be sure that these two **Zones** are the same ones that are divided by the doors and windows that the detector protects? This is an important constraint. If for some reason the detector protected a portal that provided access to a zone that the detector knew nothing about, then security alarms generated by that detector would not be sent to the appropriate control centers.

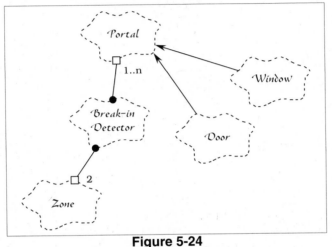

Figure 5-24
Zones and **Break-inDetectors**

Perhaps our model is incorrect. Figure 5-25 shows an alternative.

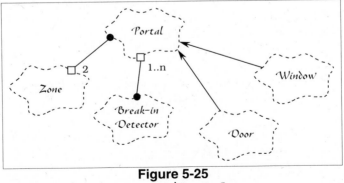

Figure 5-25
Zones and **Portals**

This model is interesting because it allows a detector to protect any set of **Portal**s, regardless of which **Zone**s they protect. Thus, the user has the most flexibility. Now when a break-in is detected, the security alarm is raised in every **Zone** that is divided by a **Portal** protected by that detector. Figure 5-26 shows the behavioral scenario.

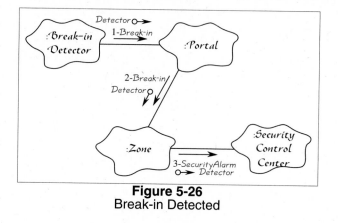

Figure 5-26
Break-in Detected

Nothing is particularly complex about this. The detector alerts all its **Portal**s, which in turn alert both their **Zone**s. Notice that the **Break-in** message sent from the **BreakinDetector** to the **Portal** provides the abstract interface that we needed to justify making **Portal** the base class for **Door** and **Window**.

Reflections

During the analysis of this requirement, we looked at many different ways to represent the static model. The behavioral model seemed trivial in comparison; however, consideration of the behavioral model motivated many of the changes to the static model. We didn't create a behavioral model until the end, because we couldn't even get one started until the static model could support it.

You might argue that, so far, we have created a representational model, not an object-oriented model. Certainly the classes have a strong representational flavor, but the static structure that has evolved has been strongly influenced by behavioral requirements. As a result, the classes have a strong contingent of application-related behaviors. So, although many of the classes represent real-world objects, the focus is on behavior, and the paradigm is object-oriented.

For this requirement I used *ad hoc* analysis. The requirement was so simple that I did not feel the need for anything more elaborate.

Requirement 3: Fire and Smoke Detectors

> *3. Fire and smoke detectors are strategically placed throughout the building. These detectors must be monitored. If fire or smoke is detected, the appropriate alarms must be raised.*

Since the only way to raise an alarm is through a **Zone**, fire and smoke detectors must apparently know what zone they are in. We model this as shown in Figure 5-27.

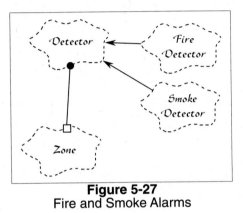

Figure 5-27
Fire and Smoke Alarms

There is only one behavioral scenario, and it is just as simple as the static model. It is shown in Figure 5-28.

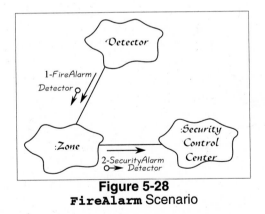

Figure 5-28
FireAlarm Scenario

What justification do we have for deriving **FireDetector** and **SmokeDetector** from the base class **Detector**? We have not documented any abstract interfaces that could reside in **Detector**. It is important to remember the Liskov Substitution Principle. The primary justification for inheritance is that it provides dissimilar classes with an abstract interface, so that derived classes can be used by any function that expects a base. Figures 5-29 through 5-31 make a case for making **Detector** a base class of **Fire-Detector** and **SmokeDetector**.

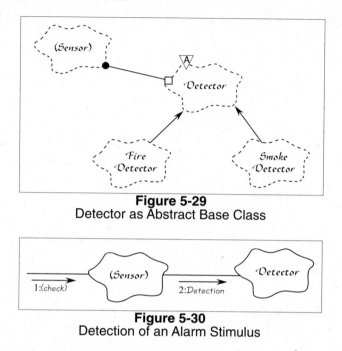

Figure 5-29
Detector as Abstract Base Class

Figure 5-30
Detection of an Alarm Stimulus

In Figures 5-29 and 5-30 we have again invoked the BRIDGE pattern. **Detector** is meant to be used as an abstract interface that can accept the **Detection** method from some kind of sensor object. We don't know what the sensor is, but we do know that somehow the mechanisms related to the sensor manage to send a **Detection** method to an object that has the **Detector** interface.

This alone is justification for making **Detector** an abstract base class. We don't want the mechanisms that send the **Detection** method to have source-code dependencies on the mechanisms that process that detection. However, this is not justification for **FireDetector** and/or **SmokeDetector**. We could simply have a **FireSmokeDetector** derived from **Detector**. Figure 5-31 provides a possible justification for keeping **FireDetector** and **SmokeDetector** as individual classes.

Figure 5-31
Detection-Message Scenario

It seems likely that some client, perhaps within the **SecurityControlCenter**, will want to ask the **Detector** for a message string describing what it detected. Such a string could be generated by the derivative of **Detector**. A **FireDetector** might generate **FireDetected**, and a **SmokeDetector** might generate **SmokeDetected**.

These justifications are admittedly weak. I would want to see dynamic scenarios that were less ambiguous before I accepted them. However, there are other reasons, having to do with representational integrity, that we might want to keep **FireDetector** and **SmokeDetector** separate. We will probably want to maintain segregated lists of the **Detector** objects. Some lists will have only **FireDetector** objects, and others will have only **SmokeDetector** objects. By describing these **Detector** objects as separate classes in C++ we provide static type checking for the consistency of these lists, making it impossible to put a **SmokeDetector** into a **FireDetector** list.

This points out one of the difficulties with statically typed OO languages. Inheritance is overloaded as both the mechanism for providing abstract behavioral interfaces and as a means for providing static representational integrity. This sometimes makes it difficult to choose when inheritance is appropriate and when it is not.

In light of Figures 5-29 and 5-30, Figure 5-27 has a flaw: it shows **Detector** containing **Zone**. However, we just said that we didn't want the clients of **Detector** to know anything about the mechanisms for processing **Detection** messages. That is, we don't want the bridge between the **sensor** client and the **Detector** server to be polluted by **Zone**. Thus, we need another level of abstraction to shore up the dependency structure, as shown in Figure 5-32.

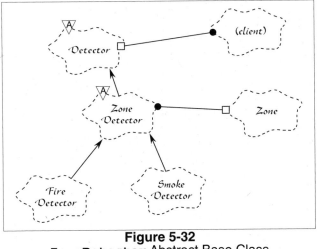

Figure 5-32
ZoneDetector Abstract Base Class

This nicely breaks any dependency between the clients of **Detector** and **Zone**. Now **Detector** provides the abstract interface, **ZoneDetector** provides the connection that the **Detectors** in this application need to their **Zone**, and the two derived classes provide the appropriate strings in response to the **GetMessage** method.

Reflections

It appears, at this point, that **Break-inDetector** could benefit from the same kind of abstraction as **ZoneDetector**. In fact, we can probably make it a derivative of **Detector**, as shown in Figure 5-33.

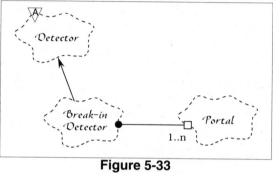

Figure 5-33
Break-inDetector Revisited

It is amusing to me that in my first draft of this chapter, this design had only Figures 5-27 and 5-28. None of the justifications for inheritance or levels of abstraction were present. This shows, I think, one of the fundamental truths of design: "No design is ever finished."

Again, this requirement was so simple that I fell back on *ad hoc* analysis. In retrospect, this may have been a poor decision. Had I written use-cases for Requirements 2 and 3, I would probably have discovered that they were extremely similar. For example, consider the following:

> **Use-Case:**
> Break-in
>
> When a break-in is detected, log a **SecurityAlarm** with the appropriate **SecurityControlCenter**.

> **Use-Case:**
> Fire and smoke detection
>
> When fire or smoke is detected, log a **SecurityAlarm** with the appropriate **SecurityControlCenter**.

This might have led me to the **Detector** abstraction a bit earlier.

It would be foolish, however, to adopt a policy of unconditionally writing use-cases, or noun lists, or using any other technique. The fact that use-cases might have been better in this particular instance does not mean that they are *always* better. Regardless of which technique we choose at the outset, we will often look back when we are done and notice that we could have gotten there faster using a different technique.

Requirement 4: Security-Guard Patrol Tracking

> 4. *Security-guard patrol tracking is accomplished by having the security guards swipe their ID cards at checkpoint locations along their patrol routes. The system knows the normal schedule for such patrols, and reports any anomalies in the monitored patrols.*

The nouns in this paragraph give us a good idea of what kinds of objects ought to be in the model: **SecurityGuard**, **Patrol**, **IDCard**, **Checkpoint**, **PatrolRoute**, and **Schedule**. The **PatrolRoute** is probably not something we want to model independently of the **Schedule**. Thus we can eliminate it as a separate object. So, too, we can eliminate the **IDCard**. The other objects are probably appropriate. Let's provide some initial definitions:

SecurityGuard	Encapsulates the identity and important attributes of a particular security guard.
Patrol	One circuit through a **PatrolSchedule**. Patrols are probably transient objects that represent patrols currently in progress.
Checkpoint	A device through which a security guard swipes his ID card to inform the system that he has arrived at a particular point in his patrol.
PatrolSchedule	This object represents the choreography of a single patrol. It specifies the times when the guard running the route should appear at each checkpoint along the route.

We can arrange these objects into an apparently rational model, as shown in Figure 5-34. Again, this is little more than an educated guess.

PatrolSchedule objects contain many **Checkpoints**, each of which is within a **Zone** to which events, violations, and alarms are sent. **Patrol** objects use a particular **PatrolSchedule**, and are manned by specific **SecurityGuard**s that know the **Patrol** they are currently supposed to be running. Each **Patrol** knows the **Patrol-Schedule** it is supposed to maintain. Each **PatrolSchedule** knows the list of **Checkpoints** that must be passed during the schedule. Finally, each **Checkpoint** knows the **Zone** that it belongs to.

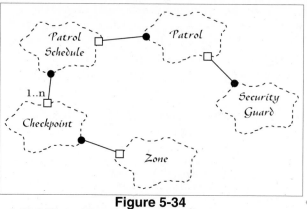

Figure 5-34
Initial Class Diagram for Security Patrol Feature

We can run a dynamic scenario through this static model by asking the question "What happens when the security guard swipes his ID card at the appropriate checkpoint?" Figure 5-35 shows the object diagram.

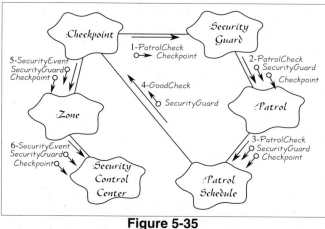

Figure 5-35
Security Guard Checkpoint Accepted

This seems to work all right, although it implies some using relationships that are not shown in the static model. The **Checkpoint** gets the **SecurityGuard** object from the data imprinted on the card that was swiped (or whatever other identification technique is involved). It tells the **SecurityGuard** object that it has been involved in a checkpoint. The **SecurityGuard** then tells its **Patrol** about the checkpoint, and the **Patrol** consults its **PatrolSchedule**. The **PatrolSchedule** tells the **Checkpoint** that the **SecurityGuard** got there on time, and the **Checkpoint** logs the appropriate security event with its **Zone**. Figure 5-36 shows what happens when the guard swipes his card at the wrong checkpoint. Almost identical! I think we are on a roll.

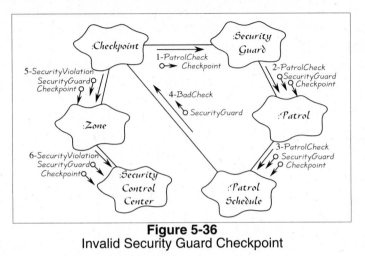

Figure 5-36
Invalid Security Guard Checkpoint

Some of the anomalies that can occur during a patrol are listed in Requirement 9. They have to do with the guard being late to the scheduled checkpoint. If our system is to autonomously determine that a guard was late, it must have a clock that can spontaneously initiate some action. We can add this to our static model, and then examine some of the associated behaviors. Figure 5-37 shows the updated static model. Once again, we are employing the BRIDGE pattern to isolate the **Timer** from the objects to which it must send messages.

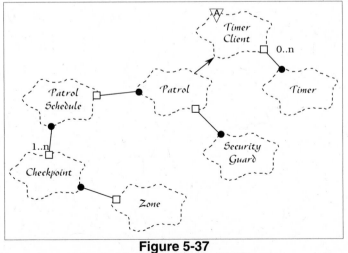

Figure 5-37
Static Model of Patrol with Timer

The **Timer** contains a number of objects derived from **TimerClient**. **Patrol** derives from **TimerClient**, which gives it the ability to accept the **Trigger** message from the **Timer**. This scheme prevents **Timer** from depending upon **Patrol**; thus, we can reuse **Timer** in other contexts.

The **Timer** "triggers" the **Patrol** object. How it does this is not important at the moment; we can presume that it fires off a **trigger** message once per minute or something like that. Note that the **Timer** may talk to more then one **Patrol** object, because more than one patrol can be in progress at any given time.

Figure 5-38 shows that the **Timer** sends a **Trigger** message to **Patrol**. The **Patrol** object gets the time of the last successful checkpoint and sends it to the **PatrolSchedule** to see if the guard is late for his next checkpoint. In this case, he is not late, so nothing more happens.

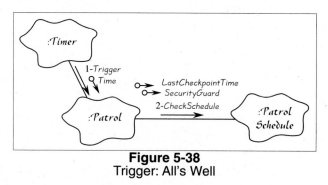

Figure 5-38
Trigger: All's Well

In Figure 5-39, the guard is tardy. According to Requirement 9, a security violation is declared if the guard is more than 5 minutes late to a checkpoint.

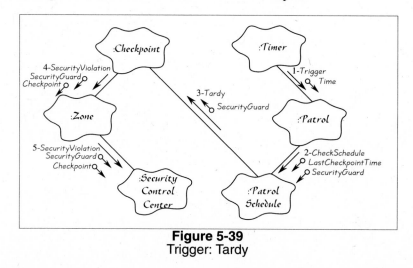

Figure 5-39
Trigger: Tardy

Figure 5-40 shows that if the guard is more than 10 minutes late, a security alarm will be raised.

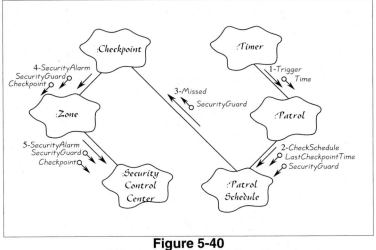

Figure 5-40
Trigger: Checkpoint Missed

How does a patrol get started? How does the system know when a patrol begins, and who is manning it? We probably don't want to bind particular security guards to a schedule, since we would then have to update the schedules whenever there was a personnel change. What if we made the concept of **SecurityGuard** more abstract? What if, instead of referring to a specific person, it referred to a role that any appropriate person could play.

For example, say the patrol schedule called for security guard 7 to check in at checkpoint 17 at 23:15 every night. Who is Security Guard 7? It is whoever is in possession of ID Card 7. If Security Guard 7 is a role that any of the security personnel can play, then the system does not have to deal with the fact that Ted Cahall got food poisoning today, or Bill Vogel was late because his motorcycle was stolen. The shift supervisor can hand out the appropriate ID cards and direct the available staff to perform any particular patrol.

Thus, the system can start patrols autonomously . No operator intervention is necessary to get a patrol running. All we need is for some object to scan the schedules to see what time they should start, and then create **Patrol** objects for the ones that are ready to be started.

Figure 5-41 shows the updated static model. Each **PatrolSchedule** object has a **SecurityGuard** object that is responsible for all the checkpoints. This **Security-Guard** object gets passed to the **Patrol** object when it is created. No change to the behavioral scenarios is implied by this addition to the static model.

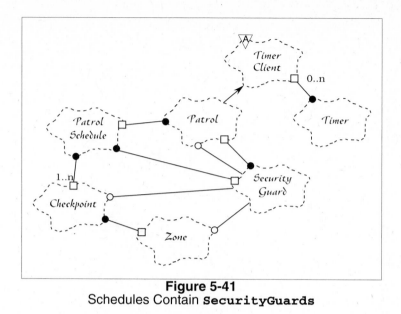

Figure 5-41
Schedules Contain `SecurityGuards`

The new static model also shows the **uses** relationships that we can infer from the dynamic models. The **SecurityGuard** class is known to the **Patrol**, **Checkpoint**, and **Zone** classes, even though it is not contained by them.

Some object must be responsible for creating **Patrol** objects when it is time for them to start. We can call this object the **PatrolManager**. Figure 5-42 shows how it fits into the static model.

Now, finally, we see how all the **PatrolSchedules** and **Patrol**s are managed. The **PatrolManager** knows about all the schedules and starts them up based on triggers from the **Timer**. This boils down to the two scenarios in Figures 5-43 and 5-44: one where a trigger does not correspond to a start time, and another where a trigger does.

The first scenario checks all the **PatrolSchedule** objects to see if it is time for any of them to start. Since it isn't, nothing more happens. In the second scenario, it *is* time for a **Patrol** to start, so the **Patrol** object is constructed and passed the **Patrol-Schedule** it will use and to the **SecurityGuard** that will be manning the patrol. The **SecurityGuard** is then told which **Patrol** it is manning.

Patrol objects are destroyed when the **PatrolSchedule** for that **Patrol** is complete. Who has this information? The **PatrolSchedule** does. However, Figure 5-45 depicts a problem.

By the time the **PatrolSchedule** finds out that the final **Checkpoint** has been hit, it has no way to tell the **PatrolManager** which **Patrol** is complete! The **Patrol** is not passed to the **PatrolSchedule**. Something has to change. We could pass the **Patrol** to the **PatrolSchedule**, but that adds more data to the collaboration, which is busy enough as it is!

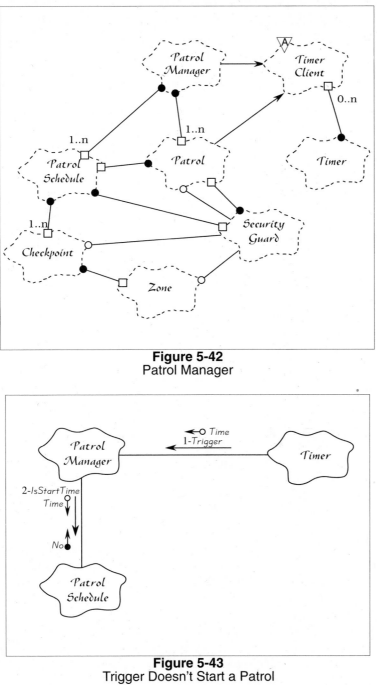

Figure 5-42
Patrol Manager

Figure 5-43
Trigger Doesn't Start a Patrol

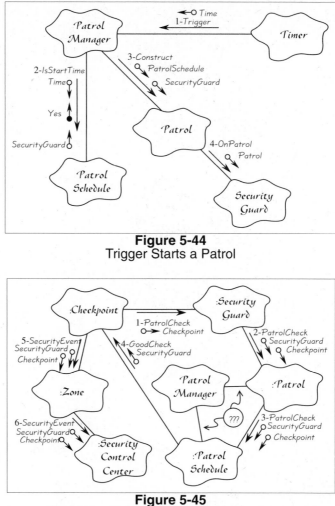

Figure 5-44
Trigger Starts a Patrol

Figure 5-45
Final Accepted Security-Guard Checkpoint

Perhaps we should rearrange things a bit. We currently show the **PatrolSchedule** informing the **Checkpoint** that it was good or bad. Why not make this information wend its way back as the return from the **PatrolCheck** message that the **Checkpoint** originally sent to the **SecurityGuard**. Figure 5-46 shows the scenario.

Now the **Patrol** object can tell the **PatrolManager** that the patrol is complete by sending it the **FinalCheck** message. This signal indicates that the checkpoint was good, and that it was the last one scheduled. Presumably the **PatrolManager** will dispose of the **Patrol** at its earliest convenience. Why not now? Because the **Patrol** object is still actively involved in the current collaboration; killing it now could be danger-

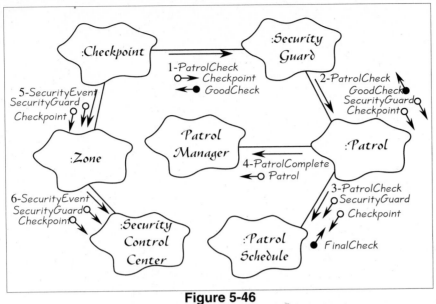

Figure 5-46
Fix: Final Accepted Security-Guard Checkpoint

ous. Figures 5-47 and 5-48 show what this change in strategy does to the other related scenarios.

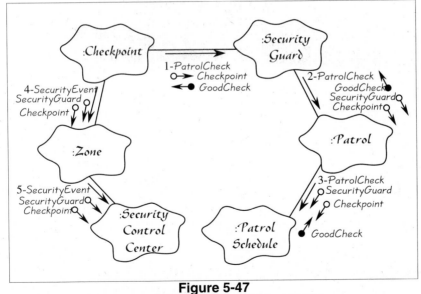

Figure 5-47
Accepted Security-Guard Checkpoint

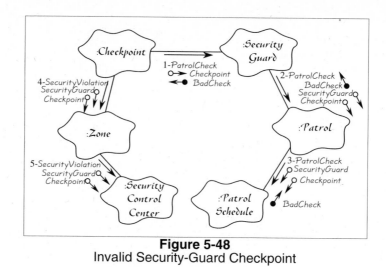

Figure 5-48
Invalid Security-Guard Checkpoint

There is one other scenario that I thought of while doing this last batch. What happens if the ID card swiped at a checkpoint currently has no **Patrol** assigned to it? Figure 5-49 shows the scenario. Returning either **BadCheck** or **GoodCheck** from the **Patrol-Check** message has made this whole set of scenarios simpler.

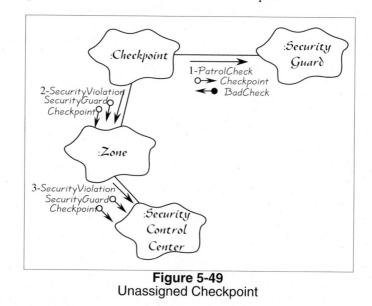

Figure 5-49
Unassigned Checkpoint

The final scenario involves the destruction of **Patrol** objects. I am making the completely arbitrary assumption that the **PatrolManager** will do this at the next trigger event. Figure 5-50 shows the scenario.

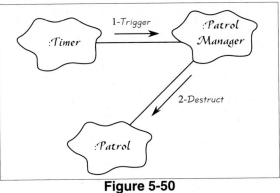

Figure 5-50
Destruction of `Patrol` Objects

This concludes our analysis of Requirement 4.

Reflections

Overall, we were pretty lucky with this requirement. Our first tries at the static model went unchallenged by the behavioral model. Perhaps this means that we are getting a "feel" for this application.

The decisions we made for this requirement covered the spectrum from analysis to design. Some decisions were very high-level; others, such as when to destroy `Patrol` objects, were extremely low-level. This typifies the notion of a combined, continuous analysis and design phase.

Although I could have identified several use-cases for this requirement, I found it to be unnecessary; I got up a pretty good head of steam by simply using a noun list.

Requirement 5: Multiple Levels of Security

> 5. *The system allows multiple levels of security for restricting access to certain security zones, possibly based on the time of day.*

What does this requirement mean? What behaviors does it imply? Perhaps it means that there are security classifications that apply to security zones. For example, Classification A might be more restrictive than Classification B, and B more restrictive than C, and so on. If this is so, then we must define the restrictions. To what do the restrictions apply? Probably they apply to the carriers of security ID cards. Perhaps each security card is marked with a clearance code. There may be many clearance codes, each with different restrictions for entering and leaving zones of a particular classification, as suggested in Figure 5-51. Let's call this the classification/clearance scheme.

		Zone Classification		
		A	B	C
Clearance	1	Allowed	Allowed	Allowed
	2	Denied	8P.M.-5P.M.	Allowed
	3	Denied	Denied	8P.M.-5P.M.

Figure 5-51
Classification/Clearance Scheme

Another possibility, shown in Figure 5-52, is to forget about the idea of classification and simply treat each zone independently. This has the advantage that zones do not have to be classified, but it has the disadvantage of having to deal with each zone independently.

		Zone ID		
		Zone 1	Zone 2	Zone3
Clearance	1	Allowed	Allowed	Allowed
	2	Denied	8P.M.-5P.M.	Allowed
	3	Denied	Denied	8P.M.-5P.M.

Figure 5-52
Zone/Clearance Scheme

We can take this one step further if we remove the concept of a clearance code, and simply treat each user independently, as shown in Figure 5-53. This has the advantage that users do not have to be associated with a clearance code, but it has the disadvantage that we have to deal with all the users independently.

		Zone ID		
		Zone 1	Zone 2	Zone3
User ID	User #1	Allowed	Allowed	Allowed
	User #2	Denied	8P.M.-5P.M.	Allowed
	User #3	Denied	Denied	8P.M.-5P.M.

Figure 5-53
Zone/User Scheme

This last scheme is certainly the easiest to model and implement, since it has fewer abstractions than the others; however, the others provide facilities that users might need. It seems most likely that users will *want* to create classifications and clearances, so that they can generalize the security behavior of groups of zones and users. Thus, for this model, I choose the classification/clearance scheme. Figure 5-54 shows the initial static model for this requirement.

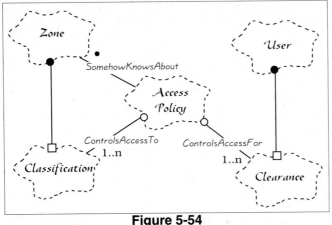

Figure 5-54
Initial Static Model for Zone Security

This model is a good start. **Zone** objects have **Classifications**, and **User** objects have **Clearances**. The **AccessPolicy** class encapsulates the access-control table (like the one in Figure 5-51). It contains the policies that specify which **Clearances** are granted access to which **Classifications**.

The only sticky part in this model is the unrefined relationship between the **Zone** and the **AccessPolicy** classes. Does every **Zone** know about the **AccessPolicy**? Can some **Zones** know about a different **AccessPolicy** than others? The model seems to imply this, but it is probably not desirable. We can fix this, however, if we cause all **Zones** to be contained by a higher-level object that maintains the **AccessPolicy** (see Figure 5-55).

I chose the name **SecuritySystem** because of the nagging feeling that the entire system will need a root object.[3] I expect that **SecuritySystem** will be used for much more than just associating **Zone** objects with the **AccessPolicy**. The **uses** relationship between **Zone** and **SecuritySystem** is adorned to indicate that **Zone** uses a static instance of **SecuritySystem**.

By coupling **Zone** to **SecuritySystem**, **Classification**, and **AccessPolicy**, we have violated the open/closed principle. Now all the users of **Zone**, such as the **ZoneAccessController** in Figure 5-6, will be affected whenever we change the **AccessPolicy** or **Classification**. Clearly, this is undesirable, and some abstraction is in order. Figure 5-56 shows how we can abstract **Zone**, **User**, and **AccessPolicy** to afford the isolation we require.

This new model employs the BRIDGE pattern three more times. **Zone** and **User** have been isolated from the concept of access policies, clearances, or classifications, which

---

3. A root object is not a main program; it does not necessarily contain very much intelligence. Its function is to act as the starting place for traversing a representation. Usually the root object is one of the few global objects in the system, from which all the others can be found.

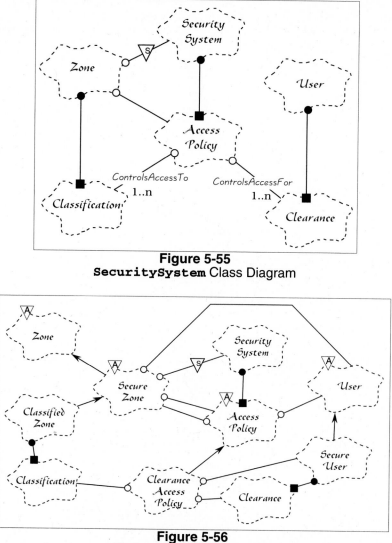

Figure 5-55
SecuritySystem Class Diagram

Figure 5-56
Abstraction to Protect **Zone**

means that changes to the access polices will not affect the other users of **Zone** and **User**. We have also abstracted the **AccessPolicy** class, so that we can implement any of the schemes from Figures 5-51 through 5-53 without affecting **SecuritySystem** or **SecureZone**. The **SecureZone** class is a further abstraction of **Zone**; it knows about **AccessPolicy** objects but does not know the details about **Classifications** or **Clearances**. The **ClassifiedZone** is the concrete class that understands about **Classifications**.

This splitting of concerns within the static model insulates the design that describes the security requirements from the design that describes the other requirements. Thus, our design conforms to the open/closed principle, in that we can make changes to one requirement without affecting the design of the others.

Now let's look at the behaviors of this model. Figure 5-57 shows what happens when a **Zone** receives an **AllowEntry** message from the scenarios of Requirement 1.

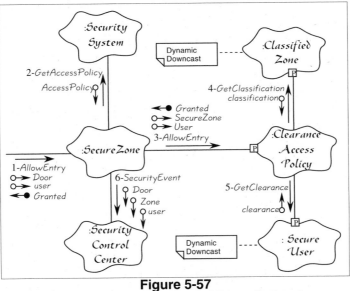

Figure 5-57
Zone Receives Request for Entry: Granted

When a **SecureZone** object receives an **AllowEntry** message, the first thing it does is get the **AccessPolicy** object from the **SecuritySystem**. Just how the **SecuritySystem** decides what kind of **AccessPolicy** object to return is unknown at this time. Perhaps there is only one **AccessPolicy** for the entire system, or perhaps there are many that are selected according to various criteria. The **SecureZone** then passes the **user** and itself as parameters of the **AllowEntry** message that is sent to the **AccessPolicy** object, which in this scenario happens to be an instance of **ClearanceAccessPolicy**.

The **ClearanceAccessPolicy** knows about **Clearance** and **Classification** objects. It knows that **SecureUser** objects can be asked for their **Clearance** objects; and that **ClassifiedZone** objects can be asked for their **Classification** objects. However, the **AllowEntry** message is an interface of the **AccessPolicy** class, which knows nothing of **Clearances**, **Classifications**, or any of the derivatives of **User** and **SecureZone**. Thus, the **User** and **SecureZone** objects that are passed through that interface must be dynamically downcast to their appropriate types. The code should look something like this:

```
AccessPolicy::AccessStatus ClearanceAccessPolicy::
AllowEntry(SecureZone& z, User& u)
{
    AccessStatus retval = denied;
    ClassifiedZone* cz = dynamic_cast<ClassifiedZone*>(&z);
    SecureUser* su = dynamic_cast<SecureUser*>(&u);
    if (cz && su)
    {
        Classification& classification = cz->GetClassification();
        Clearance &clearance = su->GetClearance();
        retval = FigureOutStatus(classification, clearance);
    }
    return retval;
}
```

The **dynamic_cast** operators in this bit of code do not violate the open/closed principle because **ClearanceAccessPolicy** *must* depend upon the downcast classes anyway. Therefore, there is no harm in using the downcast; in fact, there is a great benefit. Without the downcast, the interface between **SecureZone** and **AccessPolicy** could not be abstract.

Figure 5-58 shows what happens when a request for entry is denied. It is very similar to Figure 5-57. The scenarios that show exit requests are not shown, since they are just the same as those for entry requests.

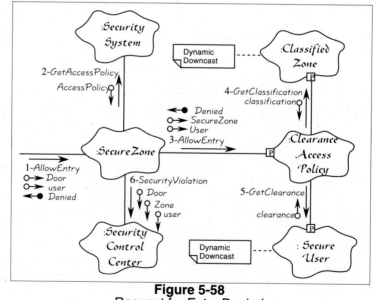

Figure 5-58
Request for Entry Denied

Reflections

We appear to be making pretty good progress through these requirements. This was the first set of scenarios that interfaces with work that we have already done (Requirement 1). Interestingly enough, it was the analysis of this requirement that caused us to add the abstractions to the **Zone** and **User** classes of the other requirement. This is typical. Abstraction is often added as a way of building fire walls between different functional requirements. In so doing we prevent changes that take place in one requirement from breaking code in another.

This is an important issue. The liberal use of abstraction allows us to separate one part of the code and make it independent of other parts. Thus, it is usually good practice to anticipate the need for such separation by using plenty of abstract classes, even where the justification is not immediately apparent.

Requirement 6: Lockdown

6. *In the case of certain major violations of security, the system must have the ability to lock down the violated security zone or an enclosing zone in order to prevent exit of the perpetrators from the building or a zone.*

What is an "enclosing zone," and how do we model it? Do some zones contain other zones? Is that something that the system should know? Well, frankly, I don't like it. When I think of a building divided into zones, I think of a jigsaw puzzle. The zones lie adjacent to one another and fill the building with their irregular shapes. *Sometimes* one zone may entirely contain another, as when high-security areas are buried within lower security areas. Still, in my mind, this is the exception rather than the rule, so most zones will neither be enclosed nor enclose others.

To model the concept of one zone enclosing another is not difficult, but it complicates the job of configuring and using the system. There will have to be user gestures that allow the user to specify that "zone A contains zone B." It also implies that there should be some integrity checking, so that in the above case the user could not later specify that "zone B contains zone A." There will also have to be user gestures for lockdown that involve enclosing zones. Perhaps the lockdown command would specify how many enclosing zones should be locked. All this seems like too much complexity for very little benefit.

Should an analyst put herself above the requirements in this fashion? Has he the right to ignore portions of the requirements, if he doesn't think they are correct? Indeed! In fact, it is his job to question the requirements and correct them where necessary, but he had better not do it in a vacuum as I did in the previous paragraph! He had better consult with the users of the system to make sure that his conclusions are correct.

In this hypothetical example, I consult with my hypothetical users. It turns out that the writer of the requirements thought of the idea of locking enclosing zones one day, and thought it was interesting enough to include. After listening to the complexity arguments, however, he and the rest of the users agreed that the feature should not be included in the model of the system.

This makes lockdown much simpler to model. We already have an object that is in a position to know about all the **zones** in the system: the **SecuritySystem** object that we created for Requirement 5. Lockdown should be simply a matter of sending the **SecuritySystem** a message specifying which **Zone** to lock.

One part of this model that we don't have yet is an object that allows operators to enter commands. Let's call this object an **OperatorTerminal**. If we put all these pieces together, we get the model shown in Figure 5-59.

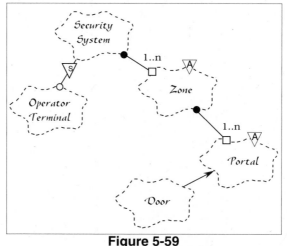

Figure 5-59
Initial Lockdown Static Model

This captures the proper intent. The **SecuritySystem** object can have one or more **OperatorTerminal** instances that represent terminals from which security commands can be entered. The **SecuritySystem** has many **Zones**, and these have many **Portals**, some of which are **Doors**.

There is something I don't like about that last statement: "some of which" is imprecise and implies a hidden decision. Let's see if we have any trouble putting a scenario together. Figure 5-60 shows an initial attempt at the lockdown scenario.

There is indeed a problem here. What should the **Zone** send to the **Portal**? A **Portal** is an abstract concept that represents the different objects that separate **Zones**, but not all the objects derived from **Portal** need to know what **Lockdown** is all about. In fact, only **Doors** need to know. Windows are never opened, locked, or unlocked in this model, so they have no need to participate in **Lockdown**.

We could allow **Portal** to deal with a **LockDown** message, and then have the derivatives of **Portal** ignore the message if it doesn't apply to them, but this is a hidden

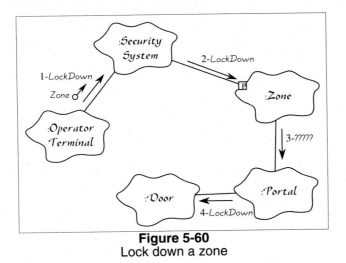

Figure 5-60
Lock down a zone

constraint upon derivatives of **Portal**. It also causes information that should remain specific to **Door** to spread into **Portal** and all its derivatives. It is also just plain sloppy. It would be better to have **Zones** know about **Doors** and dynamically test each **Portal** to see if it is a **Door** (e.g., by using **dynamic-cast**). This keeps the model clean and does not involve any hidden constraints. Figure 5-61 shows the updated model.

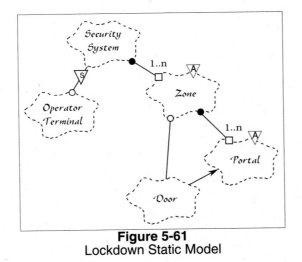

Figure 5-61
Lockdown Static Model

Although this model involves a new relationship between **Zone** and **Door**, it is cleaner than the previous model. I am not completely happy with the idea of using a **dynamic_cast** in this instance, but I think it is better than having **Zone** contain a separate list of **Door** objects or modifying **Portal** to maintain an interface that is specific to **Door**. Figure 5-62 shows the updated dynamic model.

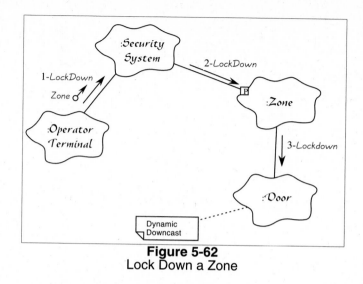

Figure 5-62
Lock Down a Zone

This model implies that **Doors** have a state that they must remember. The finite state machine, as shown in Figure 5-63, is pretty trivial.

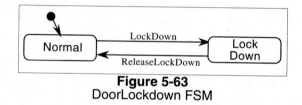

Figure 5-63
DoorLockdown FSM

In the **normal** state, **Doors** behave as usual. However, in the **LockDown** state, they refuse to open. This means we must go back to the other behavioral scenarios from previous requirements and model how **Doors** behave when in the **LockDown** state.

This is ugly. If **Door** objects change behavior based upon their state, then every client of **Door** depends upon the state machine. It seems very unfortunate that many other features will be dependent upon one aspect of the lockdown feature. Perhaps there is another solution . . .

What about **Zones**? Does their state change too? This seems likely, since it is the **Zone**, working with an **AccessPolicy** object, that grants or denies access to a **Door**; the **Door** object does not participate in the decision at all. But if this is true, then the state of the **Door** does not need to change! **Doors** don't need to know about lockdown.

Aha! We have been chasing the wrong model! Lockdown does not really *lock* any doors, it simply changes the access rights of a **Zone** that is in the **LockDown** state. It doesn't have any thing to do with **Doors** at all!

Let's look at the problem in a different way by writing an informal use-case: *When an operator requests that a certain zone be locked down, he expects that most users will be unable to make their security cards grant them access in or out of the zone.* But shouldn't some security cards still work? Shouldn't the chief of security still be allowed to open those doors with his security card? If this is the case, then lockdown represents a new **AccessPolicy** used by the **Zone**. This implies a change to the static model for **Zone** and **AccessPolicy** classes in Figure 5-56. The appropriate changes are shown in Figure 5-64.

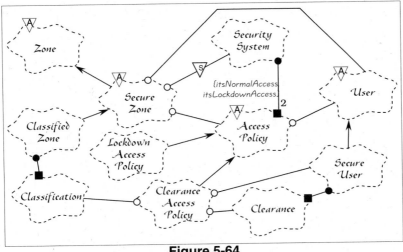

Figure 5-64
Multiple **AccessPolices** used by **Zone**

This model shows that the **SecuritySystem** object maintains *two* **AccessPolicies**: one for normal **Zones**, and one for **Zones** in the **LockDown** state. This makes the finite state machine for **Zone**, shown in Figure 5-65, a bit more complex, since it must now choose which **AccessPolicy** it needs to use.

I think this will work, but something else is bothering me. Look at Requirement 7. It specifies that a **Zone** can be placed in "Emergency Evacuation" state, in which all exits are allowed, and no entries are allowed. This implies yet another **AccessPolicy** and yet another state for the **Zone** finite state machine. We now have three **Zone** states that we know of: **Normal**, **LockDown**, and **Evacuate**. Are there more? Not according to the requirements. However, three is an uncomfortable number. It makes me think that there are more such states—perhaps many more.

Currently, **AccessPolicy** contains a two-dimensional table. It uses **Clearance** and **Classification** as keys to determine access rights. Let's add the dimension of **ZoneState** to this table. This gives us the ability to model an unlimited number of zone states, without undue complication of the static model, and without complicating the finite state machine for the **Zone** class. Figure 5-66 shows the resultant static model.

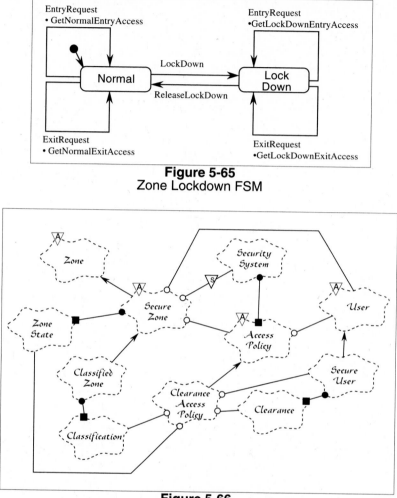

Figure 5-65
Zone Lockdown FSM

Figure 5-66
Lockdown Static Model with `ZoneState`

Notice that we are back to just one **AccessPolicy**, but now it uses **ZoneState** as one of its inputs. Note also that **Zone** now contains a **ZoneState**. I think this is a better way to model things. Now we can define any number of access states that a zone can be in, and can tailor the access policies of each zone.

The behavioral scenarios must change just a bit in order to pass the **ZoneState** to the **AccessPolicy**. Figure 5-67 shows the entry request scenario. The others change in a similar fashion.

The original model that allowed **Zone** objects to be put into the **LockDown** state can be simplified as shown in Figures 5-68 and 5-69.

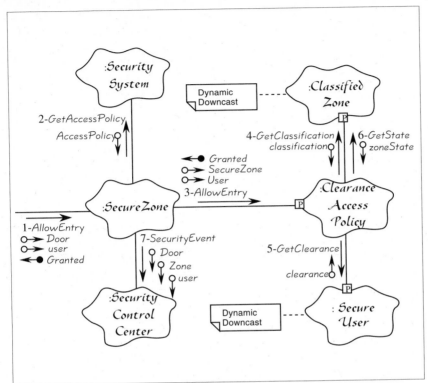

Figure 5-67
Zone Receives Request for Entry: Granted

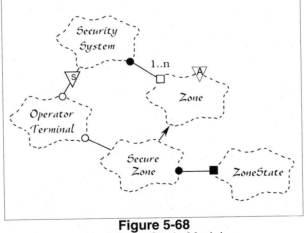

Figure 5-68
Lockdown Static Model

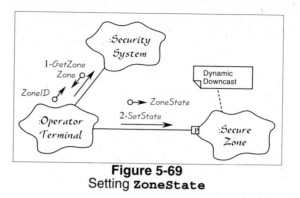

Figure 5-69
Setting `ZoneState`

Once again we are using a **dynamic_cast** to hide a dependency. The abstract **Zone** class knows nothing of the **SecureZone** class nor its associated **ZoneState** class. This is a pleasant fire wall, and we would like to keep it. However, the **Operator-Terminal** class needs to query the **SecuritySystem** for a **Zone** and then set the state of that **Zone**. Rather than force **SecuritySystem** to depend upon **SecureZone** and **ZoneState**, I prefer to dynamically downcast the **Zone** to a **SecureZone** within the **OperatorTerminal** class.

Reflections

We went pretty far afield while analyzing this requirement. We started out with some bad assumptions, and wound up significantly modifying the model for Requirement 5. This is not atypical. On the surface, Requirements 5 and 6 do not seem to have much to do with each other, but at a deeper level they are intimately related. It is the function of analysis to expose these deep connections between requirements.

Requirement 7: Emergency Evacuation

> 7. *In the case of fire or other emergency, the system will allow "emergency evacuation" from the affected zones. This will allow unrestricted exit from those zones, but will not allow entry. Sirens in the affected zones are activated to alert the occupants that they must evacuate.*

This requirement raises two issues that our current model does not address. First, we have not modeled any way to sound sirens within a zone. This is simple to remedy, and we will do so presently. The second issue is more subtle. In the case where one zone completely contains another, how do the people in the inner zone get out if the outer zone is placed in the **Evacuate** state? The enclosing zone will let its own people out, but will not allow the people from the inner zone to enter it in order to pass through! This would be a problem for those people trapped within the inner zone.

This is not a trivial problem; we cannot solve it simply by allowing entry into a condemned zone from an enclosed zone. The problem in the condemned zone may be poison gas or lethal gamma rays—something that the people in the enclosed zone would be better off staying out of. Moreover, a zone does not have to be enclosed by another in order to be cut off. Any zone or set of zones can be cut off if it is completely surrounded by a ring of condemned zones, as Figure 5-70 shows.

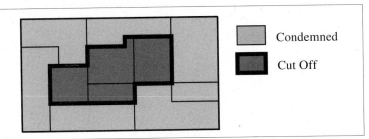

Figure 5-70
Zones Cut Off by a Ring of Condemned Zones

Solving this problem is complex. It will require us to model the topology of the zones within a building. If the system knows the topology, it can determine if a zone is cut off or not, and can decide whether or not to grant "exceptional" access to condemned zones from within zones that are cut off. Such a model is very complex. Is the benefit worth the cost? Is there an external solution?

The problem could be solved by documentation, for example. The user documentation could describe the situation and recommend against dangerous topologies. Perhaps zone configuration could remain the responsibility of the system supplier rather than the customer. The system supplier would receive special training that would prevent him from creating the potential for cutting off zones.

Pitfalls like this are often discovered during the analysis of the requirements. The analyst should find as many as possible, as early as possible. Finding them early allows strategic decisions to be made about the product and its requirements.

Fortunately for me, this is an example, and I am free to manipulate its context to suit my goals. My goals in this case are instructional, and have been met. Therefore, I am going to make a unilateral decision that the "cut-off problem" will be handled externally, and that zone topology does not have to be modeled.

As to the first issue that we raised, we need to change the model to show that **Zones** are equipped with sirens, and that the operators have certain gestures that sound those sirens. Figure 5-71 shows the static model.

It should be clear that we don't want **SecureZone** or any of its clients to have any source-code dependencies upon a siren entity. The nature of the siren is a detail, and we want to be able to change it without affecting the rest of the system, so we created the **ZoneAnnunciator** abstraction. The **ZoneAnnunciator** is an abstract class that

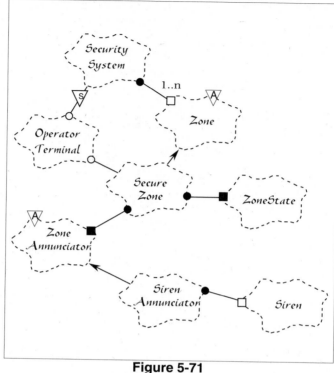

Figure 5-71
Sirens for Zones

supplies an interface that can be used by **SecureZone**. A derivative of **ZoneAnnunciator** (say **SirenAnnunciator**) connects the abstraction to a physical siren object. This is another example of the BRIDGE pattern. Figure 5-72 shows the dynamic scenario.

Figure 5-73 shows the finite state machine for the **SecureZone** class. Note that the transitions control the sounding and silencing of the **ZoneAnnunciator**.

The dynamic scenario of Figure 5-67 still applies. The **AccessPolicy** object must now consider a new **ZoneState**, but to **AccessPolicy** the design remains the same. Thus, there is nothing left to model in this requirement.

Reflections

Most of the design for this requirement was anticipated by the other requirements. The only thing that we had to consider was the siren, yet even that simple job yielded an interesting abstraction. The use of **ZoneAnnunciator** to separate the **SecureZone** from the **Siren** exemplifies the classic mechanism for inverting source-code dependencies.

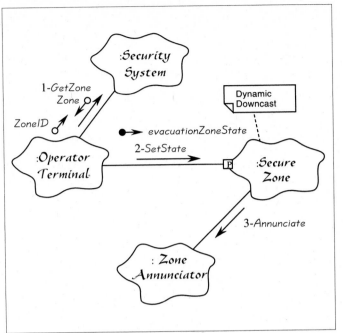

Figure 5-72
Setting a Zone to Evacuation state

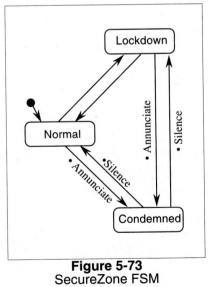

Figure 5-73
SecureZone FSM

Requirement 8: Security Control Centers

> 8. *There is at least one security control center that contains a computer screen and a printer. Such a control center may cover the entire building, or be for a set of security zones. Every security zone must report to one and only one control center. Alarms, security violations, and security events are logged on the printer. The screen shows a list of unresolved violations and alarms. An audible alarm will sound as long as this list is not empty. The control center operators can resolve a violation or alarm by interacting with the computer keyboard.*

The words of this requirement give us a first approximation of its static model, which is shown in Figure 5-74.

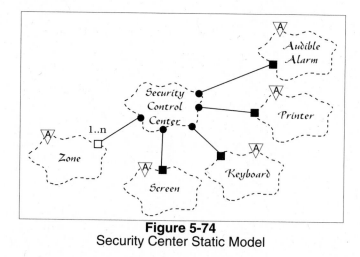

Figure 5-74
Security Center Static Model

This diagram displays a traditional characteristic of an OO design: a central client class representing high level policy, using abstract server classes representing lower level details. We provide these abstract classes so that we can hide the details of the actual keyboard, printer, screen, and alarm software from the **SecurityControlCenter** class. Each of these classes represents another invocation of the BRIDGE pattern.

Our previous behavioral models have already sent three different types of messages to the **SecurityControlCenter**: **SecurityEvent**, **SecurityViolation**, and **SecurityAlarm**. Let's look at how our static model responds to these messages.

SecurityEvent, in Figure 5-75, is the simplest. All it has to do is log the event on the printer. Notice that something called **Data** gets passed along with the **SecurityEvent**. This represents all the different parameters of the **SecurityEvent** message. If you look through all the previous behavioral scenarios, you will see that several different sets of parameters are associated with the message that gets sent to the **SecurityControlCenter** class. The only reason that all these parameters are passed into the

SecurityControlCenter is so they can be printed on the printer and displayed on the screen. I do not wish to model the differences in the way these parameters are displayed. Thus, at least for the moment, I am considering them as details that can be generalized.

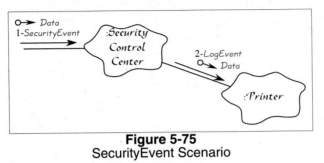

Figure 5-75
SecurityEvent Scenario

The next two messages, **SecurityViolation** and **SecurityAlarm** in Figures 5-76 and 5-77, are handled identically. Both get logged to the printer, and both get added to the list on the screen.

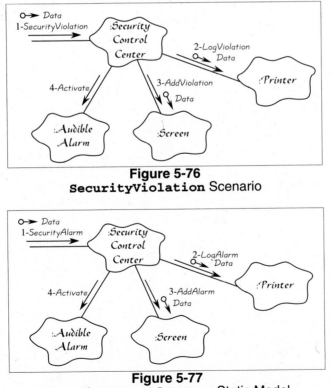

Figure 5-76
SecurityViolation Scenario

Figure 5-77
SecurityControlCenter Static Model

Notice that the reception of a **SecurityViolation** or **SecurityAlarm** activates the **AudibleAlarm**. This begs the question, "How does the alarm get turned off?" Probably, it gets turned off when the last item on the screen is resolved. This seems to imply that the **Screen** should turn the alarm off, since the **Screen** knows if the list of items is empty. But if the **Screen** turns the alarm off, then it should probably turn it on. If we make these changes, the **Screen** will be the only class collaborating with the **AudibleAlarm**, so **AudibleAlarm** should probably be related to the **Screen** and to nothing else. This is shown in Figure 5-78.

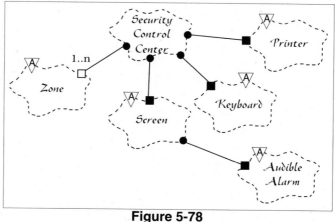

Figure 5-78
SecurityControlCenter Static Model

What is wrong with this structure? Certainly the reasoning above is quite sound, yet something about this structure nags at me. The problem is that the alarm policy will now be controlled by the **Screen**. This is not at odds with the requirements; they tightly relate the alarm and the list of elements on the screen. Yet, could the alarm be used for other purposes in the future? Shouldn't it remain directly available to the **SecurityControl-Center** object, so that the **SecurityControlCenter** can control the policy for audible alarms? I believe that it should, so I am going to revert to the previous static model shown in Figure 5-74.

However, I don't think that the **SecurityControlCenter** object should be responsible for determining if the violation list on the screen is empty or not. Quite the contrary, I think it should know nothing about the list at all. Yet it does need to know when to sound the alarm. Thus, the **Screen** must somehow describe its state to the **SecurityControlCenter**, so that the **SecurityControlCenter** can sound the alarm when necessary.

We might accomplish this by having the **Screen** send the **SecurityControl-Center** a message named **SoundAlarm** when the list becomes nonempty, and another message named **SilenceAlarm** when the list becomes empty again. However, this makes the **SecurityControlCenter** the slave of the **Screen**, rather than the

administrator of alarm policy. In my view, it would be better if **Screen** sent status messages to **SecurityControlCenter** rather than commands that directly control the
alarm. The **SecurityControlCenter** could then interpret these status messages to
decide when to sound the alarm. Consider the following list of status messages: **List-
Empty**, **ListHasViolations**, **ListHasAlarms**. These messages allow the
Screen to tell the **SecurityControlCenter** something about the state of the list.
The **SecurityControlCenter** can then decide when to sound the alarm. Moreover,
it can sound the alarm in different ways for different statuses. For example, it might ring a
soft bell when there are violations on the list, but blast a ferocious air-horn when alarms
are present.

The finite state machine in Figure 5-79 shows the states that the **Screen** object can
have, the events that cause its state to change, and the actions it takes when those state
changes occur. We can couple this state machine with the behavioral scenarios in Figures
5-80 through 5-85 to describe how events, violations, and alarms are controlled by the
SecurityControlCenter objects.

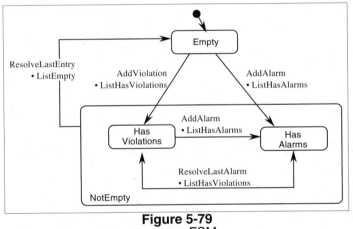

Figure 5-79
Screen FSM

Figures 5-80 through 5-83 show us how the alarm is turned on, but how is it turned
off? We know from the requirement that the alarm can only be turned off when the list of
alarms and violations on the screen is empty. Items are removed from this list when the
operator resolves them, using the keyboard. This means that the operator must type some
code that uniquely identifies the violation. This code should be set by the **Screen** object
and displayed in the list of alarms and violations. When the user types it, it is sent to the
Screen, so that the correct item is deleted from the list. A typical scenario is shown in
Figure 5-84.

If the item removed from the list is the last violation, or the last alarm, then one of the
transitions in the **Screen's** finite state machine will occur, causing the alarm to be
altered or turned off. Figure 5-85 shows this scenario.

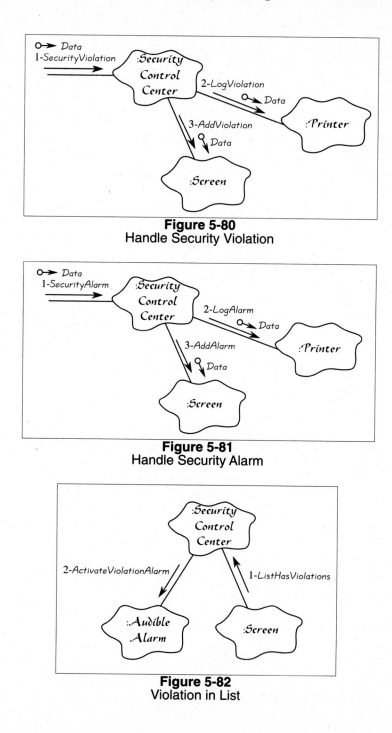

Figure 5-80
Handle Security Violation

Figure 5-81
Handle Security Alarm

Figure 5-82
Violation in List

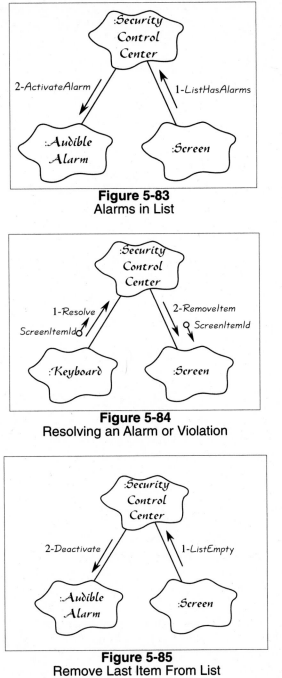

Figure 5-83
Alarms in List

Figure 5-84
Resolving an Alarm or Violation

Figure 5-85
Remove Last Item From List

Figure 5-74 shows the **SecurityControlCenter** using several different abstract classes. How are these abstract classes implemented? Figures 5-86 through 5-89 show possible schemes.

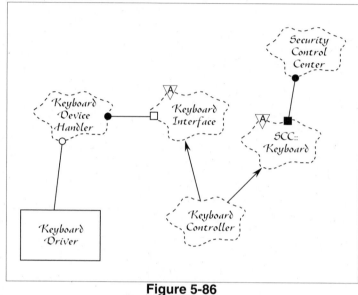

Figure 5-86
Keyboard Controller

Figure 5-86 shows how to hook up the **Keyboard** class to the operating system's keyboard driver. In this diagram the **Keyboard** class is prefixed with **SCC::** to show that it is the same class that is associated with the **SecurityControlCenter**.

The keyboard driver of the operating system is manipulated by a class called the **KeyboardDeviceHandler**. Since a keyboard is an input device, this class must be able to call some external function when it has received input data. It provides an interface for that external function in the abstract **KeyboardInterface** class. The **Keyboard-Controller** multiply inherits from both the **KeyboardInterface** and from the **SCC::Keyboard**. Thus, both the **KeyboardDeviceHandler** and the **Security-ControlCenter** can communicate with the **KeyboardController**. This allows the **KeyboardDeviceHandler** to tell the **KeyboardController** when new input has been received. It also allows the **SecurityControlSystem** to query the **Key-boardController** about command input.

This doubly abstract system allows us to reuse the **KeyboardDeviceHandler** in many other different contexts, and it allows us to reuse the **SecurityControlCenter** with many different keyboard-management schemes.

Figures 5-87 through 5-89 show that the abstract classes that represent the output devices of the **SecurityControlSystem** can be implemented by deriving classes that use the output mechanisms of the current operating system. This simple form of abstraction allows us to reuse the **SecurityControlCenter** in many different operating systems, or with many different kinds of output mechanisms.

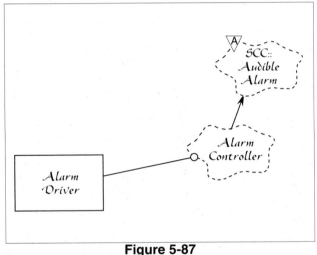

Figure 5-87
AlarmController Static Model

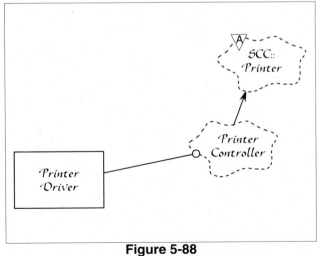

Figure 5-88
PrinterController Static Model

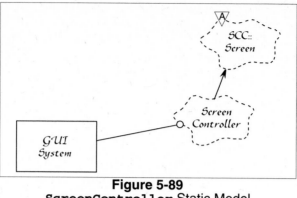

Figure 5-89
ScreenController Static Model

This completes the analysis of Requirement 8.

Reflections

The design of this requirement was somewhat involved. It required a fair amount of back-tracking and some conceptual juggling. Some extra complexity was added to the model for managing the policy for sounding alarms. I felt this extra complexity was worth the cost, since the policy for sounding the alarm is likely to change often over the lifetime of the product.

Requirement 9: Events, Violations, and Alarms

> 9. *Security Events: An authorized entrance or exit; a security guard swiping his card at a control checkpoint at the appropriate time.*
>
> *Security Violations: An unauthorized attempt to enter or exit a security zone; a security guard being 5 minutes late to a checkpoint. A security door being held open for more than 1 minute.*
>
> *Security Alarm: A break-in; a security guard being more than 10 minutes late to swipe his card at a checkpoint. A door being held open for more than 5 minutes. A fire or smoke detector signal.*

Most of the items mentioned in this list have already been covered by the analysis of previous requirements, except for the raising of violations and alarms when a door is held open too long. We have already studied a similar timing-dependent situation in Requirement 4, which had to do with tracking security patrols. We have also studied the mechanisms by which **Doors** can send violations and alarms to the **Zones** they divide in Requirement 2 when we discussed break-in detection.

In light of these facts, Figure 5-90 depicts an update of the static model surrounding the **Door** class. Since the **Door** class must now receive timer events, it becomes a derivative of the **TimerClient** class. Furthermore, I have made **Door** abstract and have derived **SensedDoor** from it, which prevents clients of **Door** from depending upon **Sensor**. A **SensedDoor** must be able to receive messages from its **Sensor**, so it must also be derived from **SensorClient**.

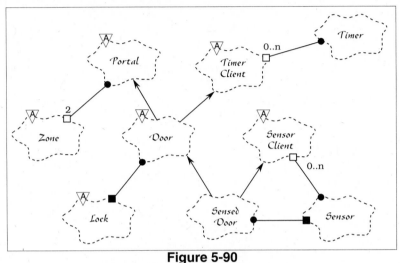

Figure 5-90
Static Model Surrounding **Door**

The level of abstraction in this model is quite high. Much of the intelligence of the system is embedded within the abstract classes in this diagram, which allows us to reuse that intelligence in different detailed contexts. Thus, the high-level policies represented by the abstract classes are reusable.

The behavior of this system is quite simple. The **Sensor** sends a **StateChange** message to its **SensorClient**s. The **SensedDoor** reinterprets that message into a **DoorOpen** or **DoorClosed** message, which it sends to itself so that its base class, **Door**, can keep track of its state. The **Timer** sends **Trigger** messages to the **Timer-Client** base of **Door** on a regular basis. This allows the **Door** to determine when to lock itself after it has been unlocked. It also allows the **Door** to measure the time that it has been left open, so that it can send violations and alarms to the **Zone**s that it divides. Figures 5-91 through 5-94 depict the scenarios.

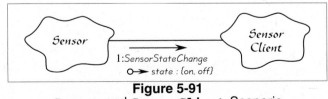

Figure 5-91
Sensor and **SensorClient** Scenario

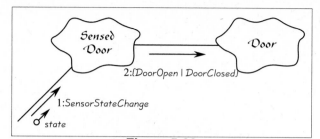

Figure 5-92
Reinterpretation of **StateChange** Message

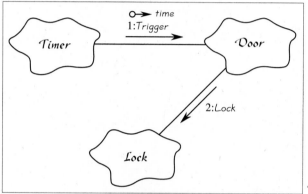

Figure 5-93
Automatic Locking of Door Based upon Timer

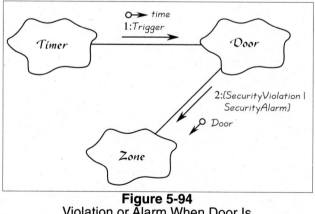

Figure 5-94
Violation or Alarm When Door Is
Held Open Too Long

Summary

This completes the high-level analysis and design of the building security system. It has been an instructive exercise. We certainly did not use a top-down approach. In fact, the approach was more sideways, since we analyzed one requirement at a time. Certainly we demonstrated the malleability and fluidity of the concepts of high-level analysis and design. We often went back and changed parts of the model because of insights gained while analyzing an apparently separate part of the problem. This is both common and essential to the process of analysis and design.

We also employed a wide variety of techniques in the analysis and design of the requirements. Sometimes we wrote use-cases. At other times, we employed noun lists or STDs. Sometimes we simply "winged" it. This points out that there is no "one true technique." The techniques you employ to help you analyze a requirement should remain a matter of judgment.

This design is far from complete. The preceding diagrams and text are little more than elaborations of the requirements. They describe the behavior of the system with more rigor and accuracy than the requirements do. They also *begin* to add a static structure to that behavior. Still, we must do much more to elucidate that structure. To stop now, thinking that we have a workable design would be extremely unfortunate. We have not yet created the structures that will make this design reusable and maintainable. Those structures will be designed in the next chapter, when we break the model down into categories. Also, we have not yet considered the platform or the multiprocessing needs of the model. We deal with those considerations in Chapter 7. So far, all we really have are a few good ideas and a very rough structure.

Exercises

1. Which is the more important issue: Time to market or maintainability? Should software be created as quickly as possible, irrespective of its structure, and then fixed later? Or should it be carefully designed so that it can be maintained over a long lifetime, irrespective of the time such design might take?

2. In Figure 5-2, why is **Lock** an abstract class?

3. In Figure 5-38 the **Timer** class sends **Trigger** messages to a **Patrol** object. This message is sent periodically. Would it be better to have the **Patrol** object tell the **Timer** when to send the **Trigger**?

4. Justify the use of *downcasts* in Figure 5-58. When are downcasts acceptable in general?

5. Name the analysis mechanisms employed in this chapter. Describe the benefits and drawbacks of each. Are any superior to the others? Which should be used most often?

6. Do you think the couple named **Data** in Figure 5-75 should be described in more detail? Supply such a description.

7. Justify the use of abstraction in Figure 5-90. Describe each abstract class, explain why it is abstract, and what effect its abstractness has upon the other classes in the figure.

8. Write a specification for, and then provide an analysis of a system which manages elevators in a skyscraper.

6

Physical Architecture

There was a most ingenious architect, who had contrived a new method for building houses, by beginning at the roof, and working downwards to the foundation; which he justified to me, by the like practice of those two prudent insects, the bee and the spider.

— Jonathan Swift, from Gulliver's Travels,

In this chapter we will continue the case study of the building security system by breaking the design into releasable categories. In one sense, this will be the most important activity of the whole design. The reusability and maintainability of the entire design rest upon the category architecture developed in this chapter. Not that the category structure designed here will be static and unchanging; rather, it will be a flexible foundation upon which the development, maintenance, and reusability will evolve.

Introduction

In this chapter we will be applying the principles that we learned in Chapter 3 to the case study begun in Chapter 5. What we currently have is a high-level logical model of the building security system. What we want to produce is a main-sequence category structure. We will do this by mapping out the dependencies within the logical design. Wherever details depend upon abstractions, we will draw category boundaries. Wherever abstractions depend upon details, we will attempt to create further abstractions in order to invert the dependency.

We will employ the three rules of category cohesion that we learned in Chapter 3:

1. Classes within a category should be closed together against common changes.
2. Classes within a category should be reused together.

3. Classes within a category should share a common function.

These principles are in order of their priority. The first is the most important and is worth violating the other two for. The second is more important than the third. The third is only important if it can be satisfied without violating the first two.

When we have completed this exercise, we will have a set of categories bound together by **uses** relationships in a Directed Acyclic Graph (DAG). Each category will be a granule of release and a granule of reuse. We will assign version numbers to the categories in order to implement configuration management and version control. Thus, we will have the beginnings of our development environment and the structure with which to manage it. We will also have the beginnings of a catalog of reusable components and the facilities with which to manage their evolution.

Reviewing the Logical Design

One strategy for reviewing the logical design is to condense it into as few diagrams as possible. In our case, two (cluttered) diagrams, Figures 6-1a and 6-1b, suffice. In larger, more complex projects, we would use more diagrams.

The purpose of condensing these diagrams is not to help review logical content; that is better accomplished by using the smaller separate diagrams in Chapter 5. Instead, we want to examine the diagrams for physical dependencies as a prelude to separating them into categories.

Breaking Dependency Cycles

Figure 6-1a shows several dependency cycles. A cycle exists between **Security-ControlCenter** and **Zone**. Another exists between **Portal** and **Zone**. Still another between **SecurityGuard** and **Patrol**. There is a long cycle that begins at **Zone** and proceeds through **SecurityGuard**, **Patrol**, **PatrolSchedule**, **Checkpoint**, and back to **Zone**. Another between **Door**, **Portal** and **Zone**.

There is nothing intrinsically wrong with dependency cycles in the logical design; however, they have a significant effect on the breakdown of the design into categories. Because category dependencies must never be cyclic, and because classes in a dependency cycle must be reused together, all the classes within a dependency cycle must belong to the same category.

Some of the cycles mentioned above seem appropriate for inclusion into a category. For example, **Portal** and **Zone** probably belong in the same category. However, **Zone** and **PatrolSchedule** probably do not.

Consider the first rule of category cohesion: All the classes in a category must be closed together. This means that when one class changes, all the other classes in the cate-

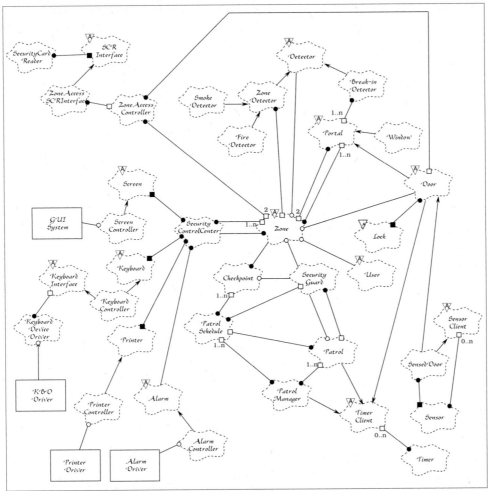

Figure 6-1a
Composite Logical Design for the Building Security System

gory ought to require changes too. This seems probable for **Zone** and **Portal**; if either changes, the other is likely to need changing. However, there ought to be many changes that we could make to **PatrolSchedule** that would not affect **Zone**. Thus by Rule 1, they should not be in the same category.

Consider the second rule: All the classes in a category should be reused together. It seems very unlikely that we would want to reuse the **Zone** class without reusing the **Portal** class with it. However, it seems very likely that we would want to reuse **Zone** without involving **PatrolSchedule**. So by Rule 2, **Zone** and **PatrolSchedule** are not cohesive.

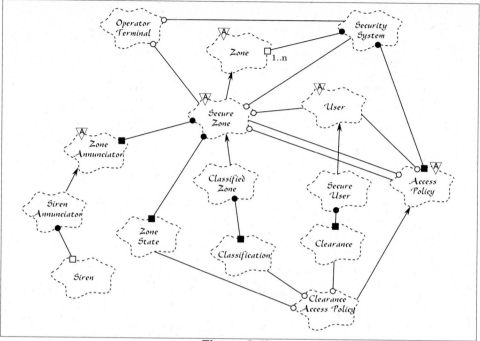

Figure 6-1b
Composite Logical Design for the Building Security System

Rule 3, that the classes in a category should share a common function, is met by **Portal** and **Zone**, since they are both related to security access. However, **Zone** and **PatrolSchedule** have very little functionally in common.

I have done this detailed analysis to make the point that reasonable logical dependencies may create poor category dependencies. The logical dependencies of the current model dictate that **Zone** and **PatrolSchedule** must be in the same category, yet that inclusion violates all three rules of category cohesion. There is nothing wrong with the *logic* of any of the relationships between the classes, but the physical relationships that result are badly flawed.

How should we solve this problem? We could accept the three rules of category cohesion and put **Zone** and **PatrolSchedule** in separate categories, but that would result in a dependency cycle between the two categories. As we found in Chapter 3, when cycles exist between categories, they cannot be released independently. They become, for all intents and purposes, a single category. This solution is therefore invalid.

We could ignore the three rules of category cohesion and put **Zone** and **PatrolSchedule** together in the same category. However, this would make it impossible to reuse **Zone** without **PatrolSchedule**.

The real solution is to change the logical design so that it fits a better physical model. Specifically, we want to break the cycle that involves **Zone** and **PatrolSchedule**. We can do that by converting **SecurityGuard** into an abstract class and deriving a **PatrolingSecurityGuard** from it as shown in Figure 6-2.

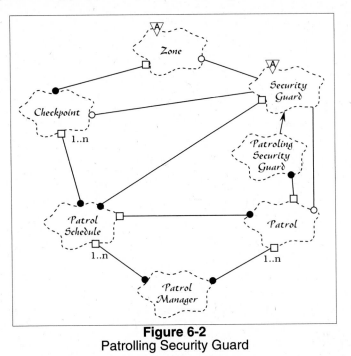

Figure 6-2
Patrolling Security Guard

This breaks the cycles, and allows us to place **Zone** and **PatrolSchedule** in separate categories. However, there is still something odd about it. Where should we draw the category boundary? We could put **Zone** in one category and all the other classes in another, but then a cycle would exist between those two categories. The only way to separate them so that there are no cycles is to place **Zone** and **SecurityGuard** into one category, and all the other classes into another, but then we force **Zone** to be reused with **SecurityGuard**. This seems silly. There must be many possible uses for the **Zone** class that do not include security guards. It seems likely, for example, that we will need to create security systems that do not have the concept of security patrols. In such a system, the **SecurityGuard** class would be excess baggage that we would have to sidestep with the kind of ugly code that is every software maintainer's worst nightmare.

Breaking Unwanted Dependencies

We must step back and look at the problem again. Why does **Zone** depend upon **SecurityGuard**? We must examine the object diagrams from Chapter 5 to see why. Figure 5-35 shows us the answer. **SecurityGuard** is passed to **Zone** as an argument of the **SecurityEvent** message. **Zone** doesn't do anything interesting with the **SecurityGuard** object; it simply passes it along to the **SecurityControlCenter**.

It is silly to have **Zone** depend upon something that it does not use. Thus, we should eliminate this dependency altogether. We can do that by creating a **SecurityMessage** abstract class that encapsulates all the possible security messages that the **SecurityControlCenter** needs to deal with. We can then create individual derivatives of this base class for each kind of security message. Figures 6-3a and 6-3b show how this is done.

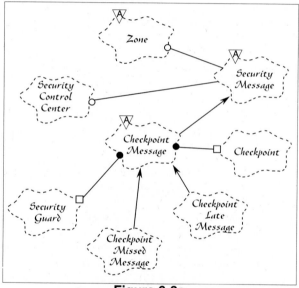

Figure 6-3a
Static Model for **SecurityMessage**

Figure 6-3a shows that the dependency from **Zone** to **SecurityGuard** has been broken. Now we are free to reuse **Zone** without dragging **SecurityGuard** along.

Accidental Duplication

Figure 6-1a shows a case of accidental duplication. Notice that **Zone** seems to be contained with a cardinality of 2 by both **ZoneAccessController** and by **Portal**. This

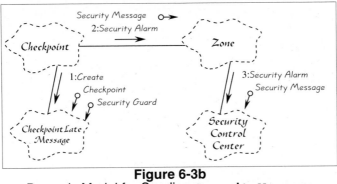

Figure 6-3b
Dynamic Model for Sending `SecurityMessage`

is suspicious. In fact, **ZoneAccessController** contains a reference to a **Door**, which is a kind of **Portal**. Thus, the containment of **Zone** by **ZoneAccessController** is redundant. We can get from the **ZoneAccessController** to the two contained **Zone** objects by traversing through the **Door**. The redundant relationship has been removed in Figure 6-4.

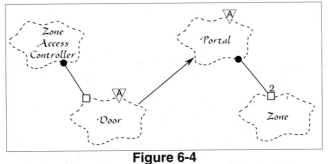

Figure 6-4
Duplicate Containment of **Zone** Eliminated

This begs a question. Why does **ZoneAccessController** contains a **Door**? Shouldn't it contain a **Portal** instead? Probably not. **Door** has the **Lock** and **Unlock** methods; **Portal** does not.

Cycles Revisited

We should eliminate some of the other dependency cycles that we spotted earlier. The cycle between **Zone** and **SecurityControlCenter** is particularly bad, since the **SecurityControlCenter** depends upon so many other classes. We don't want to have to drag along all these other classes every time we reuse **Zone**. We can break this dependency by creating an abstract class, as shown in Figure 6-5.

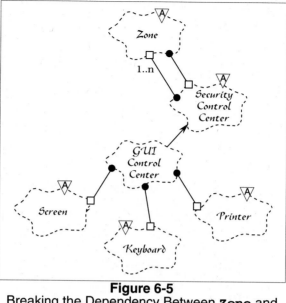

Figure 6-5
Breaking the Dependency Between **Zone** and
SecurityControlCenter

The cycle remains, but it is now in a form that we can place wholly within the category that contains **Zone**. This does not affect the reusability of **Zone**, since it is reasonable to expect that all **Zone** objects must report events, violations and alarms to some instance of the **SecurityControlCenter** class.

But why does the cycle still exist? More specifically, why does **SecurityControlCenter** contain a list of **Zone** objects? This relationship was presented in Figure 5-74 and maintained throughout the rest of the chapter. It seems to originate from Requirement 8, which states "a control center may . . . be for a set of security zones." However, I can find no justification in any of the dynamic scenarios. There appears to be no occasion when a **SecurityControlCenter** actually sends a message to a **Zone**. Thus, I think we can delete the relationship, as shown in Figure 6-6. This does not mean that we don't need the abstract **SecurityControlCenter** class anymore. That class is still necessary to buffer the **Zone** from the **Keyboard**, **Printer**, and **Screen** classes.

Finally, there is the cycle that includes **Door**, **Portal**, and **Zone**. This is a strange case. **Zone** needs to send **Lockdown** messages to **Door**. **Door** derives from **Portal**, and **Portal** needs to send **Break-in** messages to **Zone**. There seems to be no reasonable escape from this cycle; it was created in Figure 5-61 for good reasons, and those reasons still apply. Thus, the three classes must be kept together within the same category.

Do **Zone**, **Portal**, and **Door** conform to the three rules of category cohesion? The conformance isn't perfect, but it seems reasonable. Certainly the bulk of changes that either of the three classes could experience would be felt by the other two. Also, the

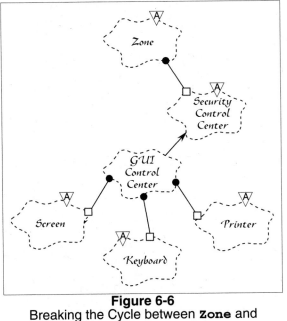

Figure 6-6
Breaking the Cycle between `Zone` and
`SecurityControlCenter`

classes will certainly be reused together for most purposes, although it seems a shame to drag break-in detection and lockdown into every possible reuse of **Zone**. Finally, the three classes certainly work together to fulfill a common purpose. About the only complaint one could make about their cohesion is that there could be some changes to **Door** that would not affect **Zone**, or some uses of **Zone** that would not require **Portal** or **Door**. This small deviation is probably not worth bothering about, but we will keep it in mind as we consider other physical design issues.

Reflection

This has been interesting. By putting the whole logical model together in this way, we have found, and fixed, some significant problems. Prior to this exercise, even though the model was *logically* consistent, it was put together in a way that would have prevented successful reuse of its most fundamental components. It would also have been difficult to maintain, since changes to **SecurityGuard**, for example, would have forced recompilation and retest of just about everything.

This is an example of the importance of *physical* design. A design may be logically consistent, and yet fail horribly due to poor physical characteristics. A good physical design is at the core of producing reusable and maintainable software.

This case study has also shown that physical and logical design are not independent. In every case where we found a physical problem, the solution was to alter the logical design. Thus, the primary activity of physical design is to find alternate logical designs that have good physical properties.

`SecurityZone` Category

The first category we will attempt to assemble is the `SecurityZone` category, which contains **Zone** and all its cohesive partners. Figure 6-7 shows the class diagram that describes this category. The first thing to notice is that every class in this category is abstract. The second thing is that the classes within this category do not depend upon any other categories. Therefore, this category fits perfectly upon the main sequence. If we were to work out the metrics described in Chapter 3 for this category, we would find: Abstraction (A) = 1. Afferent Coupling (C_a) is certainly greater than 0, since other categories must depend upon this one. Efferent Coupling (C_e) is 0. Instability (I) = $C_e \div (C_e + C_a) = 0$. Thus, the distance from the main sequence (D) = $|A + I - 1| \div \sqrt{2} = 0$.

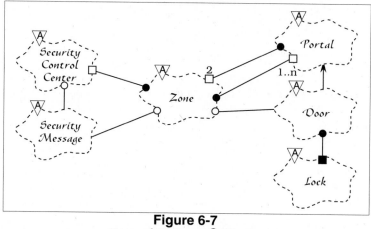

Figure 6-7
`SecurityZone` Category

Quantitative analysis is comforting, *but it does not guarantee a good design.* Let's examine the diagram qualitatively. **Zones** know where their `SecurityControl-Center` objects are and collaborate with them via `SecurityMessage` objects. A quick perusal of the dynamic scenarios in Chapter 5 shows that a **Zone** object appears very often in the context of sending `SecurityMessage` instances to its `Security-ControlCenter` object. Thus, this triad seems to support a major function of the system.

Portals divide Zones from one another. This is nicely encoded by the fact that Portal contains two Zone objects. This allows Portal objects to inform their Zones of various events such as break-in detections.

Zones contain many Portals, some of which are Doors. Zone uses dynamic downcasting to send Lockdown messages to Door objects, as was shown in Figure 5-62.

Something about this bothers me. Why does Zone contain a list of all its Portals? In Chapter 5 we assumed that Zone needed this relationship; however, in searching through the dynamic scenarios of Chapter 5, I cannot find any justification for it. It seems to me that Zone should simply contain a list of its Doors. This will obviate the need for the downcasting and simplify the relationships between Zone, Portal, and Door somewhat. Figure 6-8 shows the resultant static diagram.

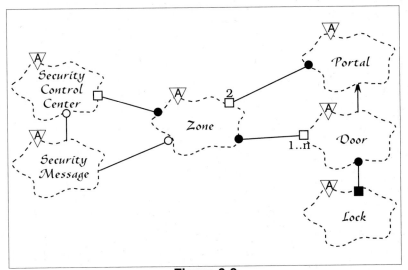

Figure 6-8
SecurityZone Category (simplified)

This change weakens the cycle between Zone, Portal, and Door significantly. It now might be possible for a class derived from Zone (e.g., SecureZone) to contain the list of Doors, and break the cycle completely. The purpose for containing that list is to send the Lockdown message to the Doors. Thus, we could remove the concept of lockdown from the highest level categories. This is tempting because it means we could separate Zone from Portal and Door, so that we could reuse Zone purely for event reporting, without dragging Portal and Door along.

Many of the diagrams that follow in this chapter will depict the classes within a category, and these classes will often have relationships with classes from other categories. I will show these imported classes with a two-letter abbreviation prepended to their names, separated from the names by two colons. This abbreviation represents the category to which the imported class belongs. Thus, **SZ::Zone** means the **Zone** class from the **SecurityZone** category.

The category structure implied by breaking the **Zone, Portal, Door** cycle is shown in Figure 6-9. The **SecurityZone** category consists of nothing but **Zone, SecurityControlCenter**, and **SecurityMessage**. It represents the event-handling and dispatch facilities of **Zone**, as shown in Figure 6-10. The **Portals** category contains **Portal** and its detectors and **SecurityMessage** derivatives. It encapsulates the notion that **Portals** can trap events and broadcast them to their **Zones**, as Figure 6-11 shows. The **ZoneAccess** category depicted in Figure 6-12 contains **Door, ZoneAccessController, SecureZone**, and their collaborators. This category represents the facilities that allow **Zones** to be accessed by users, evacuated, and locked down.

Note that **SecuritySystem** no longer contains **Zone** objects; it now contains **SecureZone** objects. This is justified by the fact that all uses of **SecuritySystem** pertain to facilities of **SecureZone**.

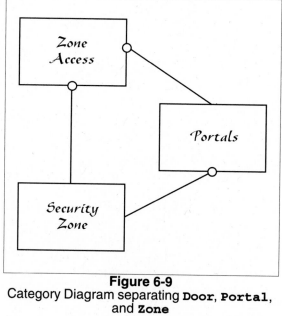

Figure 6-9
Category Diagram separating **Door, Portal,** and **Zone**

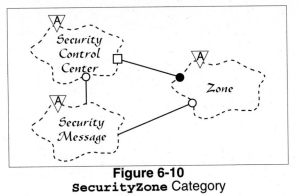

Figure 6-10
SecurityZone Category

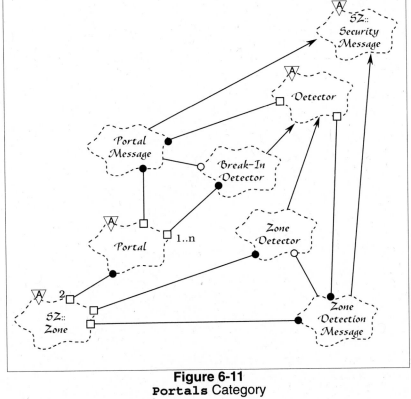

Figure 6-11
Portals Category

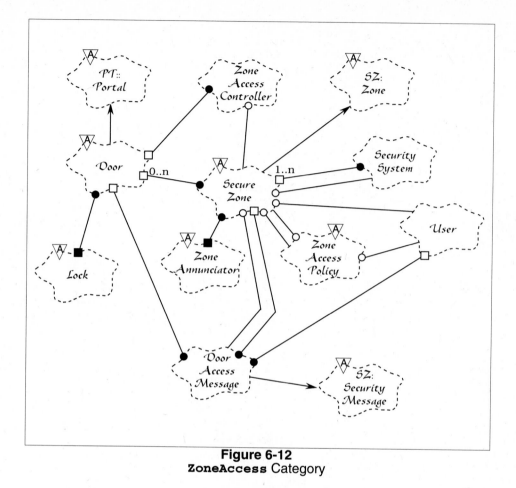

Figure 6-12
ZoneAccess Category

Keeping the Dynamic Scenarios Current

These changes to the static model should be reflected in the dynamic model. For example, Figure 6-13 shows how the dynamic design of Figure 5-14 has changed. This dynamic model describes how a user gains access to cross the boundary between two zones. Notice that several details of this dynamic scenario have changed. The security events are now communicated to the **SecurityControlCenter** in the form of **SecurityMessage** derivatives. **Zones** are being retrieved from the **Door** and downcast into **SecureZones**. Clearly these changes will affect other dynamic scenarios. Each should be examined in a similar manner.

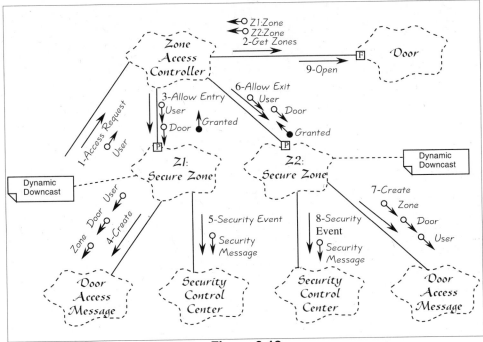

Figure 6-13
Zone **AccessRequest** Accepted

Breaking Unwanted Dependencies

Looking over Figure 6-9, we can see that there is a dependency from the **ZoneAccess** category to the **Portals** category. This is unfortunate, since we probably don't want the ability to control access to zones to depend upon the ability to detect break-ins and fires. The only dependency between these two categories is the inheritance of **Portal** by **Door**. We could easily move **Portal** into the **SecurityZone** category, which would break the dependency between **ZoneAccess** and **Portals**. It also changes the nature of the **Portals** category sufficiently to cause me to rename it **Detectors**.

The worst effect of this change is upon the **SecurityZone** category, since it adds a class which is not involved in passing **SecurityMessage** objects from **Zone** objects to **SecurityControlCenter** objects. This violates the third rule of category coupling. We can fix this by putting the **Portal** class all by itself in the **Portal** category. Figure 6-14 shows the resultant category diagram. Figures 6-15 and 6-16 show the two affected categories.

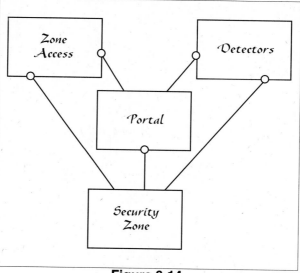

Figure 6-14
Category Structure with **Portal** and **Detector**

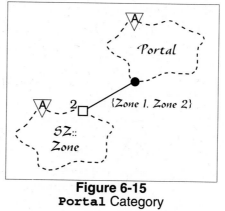

Figure 6-15
Portal Category

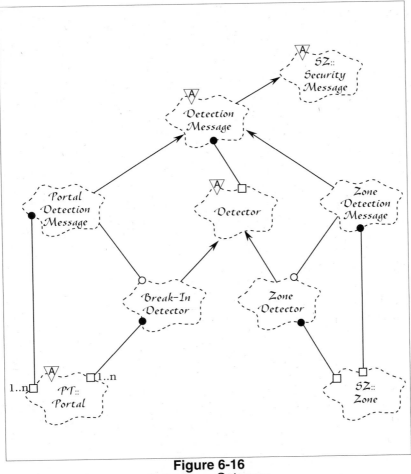

Figure 6-16
Detector Category

Metric Analysis

Table 6-1 and Figure 6-17 show the metrics for the current category design. Certainly the **SecurityZone** category is well placed with D = 0. The **ZoneAccess** and **Detectors** categories also appear to be in good shape since they both have A ≈ 0.5, and C_e is relatively small. These categories will remain close to the main sequence as long as $C_e \approx C_a$.

Table 6-1: Category Metrics Spreadsheet

Category Name	N	AC	Ca	Ce	R	H	I	A	D	D'
ZoneAccess	9	5	?	3	15	1.78	?	0.56	?	?
Detector	6	2	?	3	6	1.17	?	0.33	?	?
Portal	1	1	3	1	0	1	0.25	1	0.17	0.25
SecurityZone	3	3	6	0	3	1.33	0	1	0	0

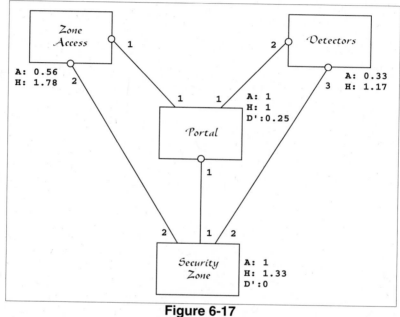

Figure 6-17
Metric Analysis

The **Portal** category is interesting. It is completely abstract, and yet it has a dependency upon the **SecurityZone** category. This forces it away from the main sequence by about 25%. We will see such categories quite often. They result from the tension between the main-sequence dependency structure and the rules of category cohesion. **Portal** was separated into its own category by applying the category-cohesion rules. We felt that **Zone** could be reused independently of **Portal** and that the two would have different closure characteristics. Yet this separation created an abstract category with a dependency, which means that it cannot be reused independently of the **Zone** category. Moreover, whenever the **Zone** category is released, a new release or at least a revalidation of the **Portal** category will be necessary.

We cannot avoid this tension. If we were to follow only the rules of category cohesion, we would try to put every class in its own category. The closure and reuse characteristics of two classes will rarely be *identical*. Thus, the ultraconservative approach would be to isolate as many classes as possible. On the other hand, if we followed only the main-sequence dependency structure, we would try to put all the abstract classes into one category and all the concrete classes into another. This would give us a wonderfully conformant dependency structure that would have terrible closure characteristics and negligible reusability.

Reflection on Metrics

We have begun a metric analysis that will continue through the remainder of this chapter. I will be diligent in considering these metrics, and will try hard to create a structure that conforms to the main sequence. My diligence might give you the impression that I believe in following the metrics at all costs. In fact, I do not.

Metrics are not ends in themselves. Good metrics do not necessarily accompany good designs, and bad metrics do not necessarily accompany bad designs. Metrics are nothing more and nothing less than *measurements*. A good designer *measures* his designs in order to understand them. He then adjusts his design until the measurements reflect the kind of design he wants. A designer may not want or need main-sequence dependency for some of his categories. That is his decision and part of his design. Whether it is a good or bad decision depends entirely on the kind of design he is trying to create.

Splitting `Detectors`

The symmetry of Figure 6-16 is revealing. There appear to be two identical halves to the diagram, which may indicate that some design component is being duplicated, and that the duplicates should be in separate categories. Indeed, the design is split between `ZoneDetector` and `Break-inDetector`. It seems likely that a client might want to use one kind of detector without using the other. By the second rule of category cohesion, therefore, we should probably split this category. Table 6-2 and Figure 6-18 show one possibility.

Table 6-2: Category Metrics Spreadsheet

Category Name	N	AC	Ca	Ce	R	H	I	A	D	D'
`ZoneAccess`	9	5	?	3	15	1.78	?	0.56	?	?
`Detector`	2	2	4	1	1	1	0.2	1	0.14	0.2
`Portal`	1	1	3	1	0	1	0.25	1	0.18	0.25
`SecurityZone`	3	3	5	0	3	1.33	0	1	0	0
`Break-inDetector`	2	0	?	3	1	1	?	0	?	?
`ZoneDetector`	2	0	?	3	1	1	?	0	?	?

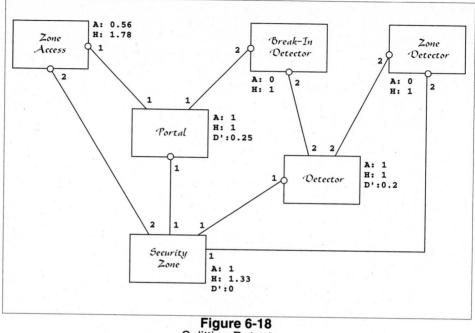

Figure 6-18
Splitting Detectors

The category structure shows no surprises. The three new categories show reasonable conformance to the main sequence and provide independent reusability for the two types of detectors. We might be concerned that our categories are very small, but they will probably fill out as the design progresses.

Figures 6-19 through 6-21 show the contents of the three new categories.

Timers and Patrols

Figure 6-22 depicts the **Timer** category, which is completely abstract. It contains the **Timer** and **TimerClient** classes. **Timer** is an abstract base class that knows it must send **Trigger** messages to all the **TimerClients** in its list. Users of the **Timer** class must derive a new class from it to provide it with an implementation that uses the operating-system facilities.

TimerClient is meant to be a base class of those classes that need to be alerted by the **Timer**. Figures 6-23 and 6-24 show three such classes. Figure 6-23 depicts the **ZoneAccess** category. This diagram is no different than Figure 6-12, except that it

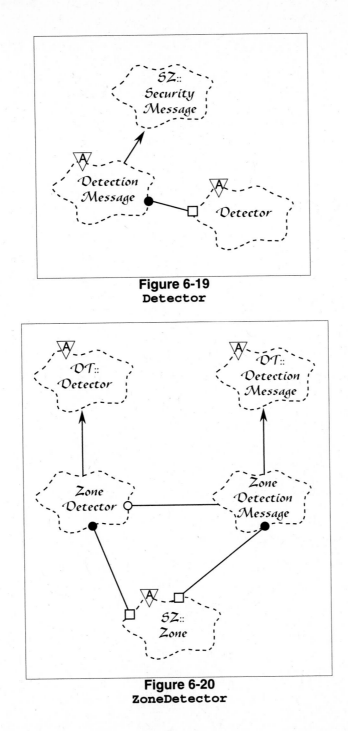

Figure 6-19
`Detector`

Figure 6-20
`ZoneDetector`

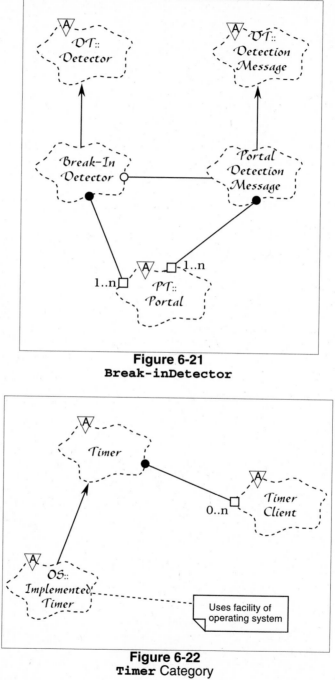

Figure 6-21
Break-inDetector

Figure 6-22
Timer Category

shows that **Door** inherits from both **TimerClient** and **Portal**. Such uses of multiple inheritance are both common and very useful for allowing a class to act as a client to many different facilities.

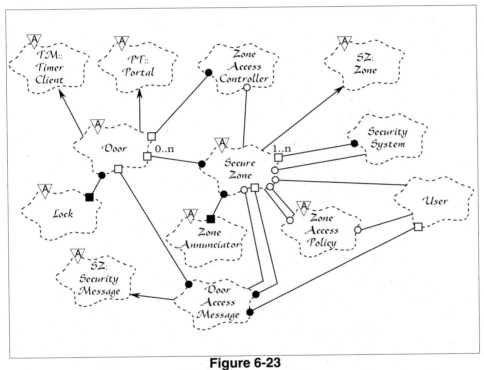

Figure 6-23
ZoneAccess Category

Figure 6-24 shows the **Patrol** category, which contains the classes that manage the scheduling and monitoring of the security guard patrols. Two classes in this category make use of the **Timer** facilities by deriving from **TimerClient**.

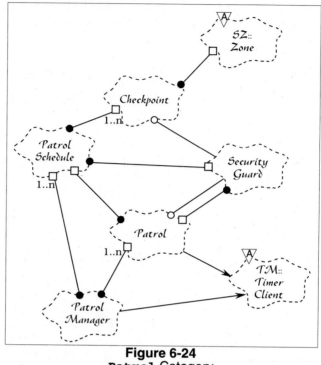

Figure 6-24
Patrol Category

Figure 6-25 and Table 6-3 show how these new categories fit into our growing category structure. Notice that I have included a category named **O/S-Specifics**, which represents the concrete derivatives of classes that require operating-system facilities. So far, we have only the derivative of the **Timer** class, but others will certainly appear.

Table 6-3: Category Metrics Spreadsheet

Category Name	N	AC	Ca	Ce	R	H	I	A	D	D'
ZoneAccess	9	5	?	4	15	1.78	?	0.56	?	?
Detector	2	2	4	1	1	1	0.2	1	0.14	0.2
Portal	1	1	3	1	0	1	0.25	1	0.18	0.25
SecurityZone	3	3	6	0	3	1.33	0	1	0	0
Break-inDetector	2	0	?	3	1	1	?	0	?	?
ZoneDetector	2	0	?	3	1	1	?	0	?	?
Patrol	5	0	0	2	8	1.8	1	0	0	0
Timer	2	2	4	0	1	1	0	1	0	0
O/S Specific	1	0	0	1	0	1	1	0	0	0

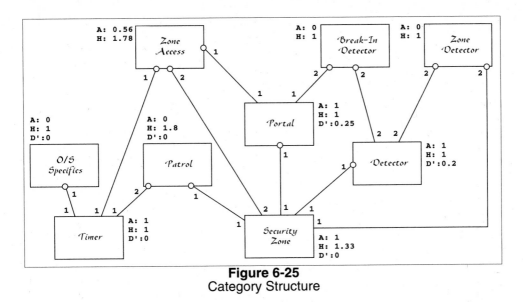

Figure 6-25
Category Structure

The category structure remains very close to the main sequence and provides ample opportunity for interesting combinations of reuse. For example, we could easily implement a system that did nothing but monitor security guards by reusing only the **SecurityZone**, **Timer**, and **Patrol** categories, or one that did nothing but detect fire alarms by reusing only the **SecurityZone**, **Detector**, and **ZoneDetector** categories. We could also provide a system that did nothing but grant or deny access requests to users by reusing only the **SecurityZone**, **Portal**, **ZoneAccess**, and **Timer** categories. In short, we can mix and match these categories into a variety of very interesting combinations, without having to worry about what code is being dragged along because of strange dependencies.

Sensors

Figure 6-26 shows the category divisions for the sensors used to detect if doors are open or closed. Again we see how operations that are specific to the operating system are abstracted, so that we can reuse their abstract interfaces without regard to the actual operating-system facilities.

The category **SensedDoor** has a single class of the same name. It represents the interface between **Doors** and **SensorClients**, and was separated from the **Zone-Access** category because it seemed likely that **Doors** could be reused without **Sensors**. This points out an error in the design. Our previous diagrams have shown **Door** as an abstract class. Close inspection of Figure 5-90 and the associated text, however, have convinced me that **Door** does not need to be, and should not be, abstract.

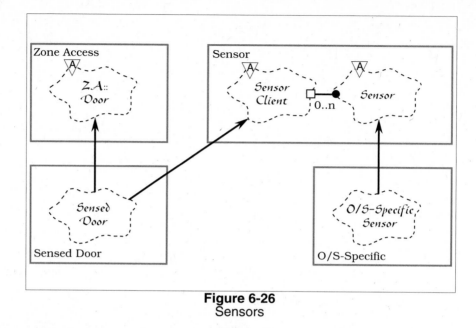

Figure 6-26
Sensors

I had made **Door** an abstract class almost out of reflex, because it was the base class for **SensedDoor**; however, **Door** contains no pure virtual functions that **SensedDoor** overrides. This should be clear from Figure 5-92. The **SensedDoor** simply sends a message to itself that is specified in the **Door** class. Thus, the **Door** class can be reused in the absence of any kind of **Sensor**, which means that **SensedDoor** should not be in the same category with **Door**. Therefore, I have placed it by itself in its own category.

The **Sensor** category encapsulates the concept of a **Sensor** and its **Sensor-Clients**. Any class desiring to be notified by a **Sensor** must derive from **Sensor-Client** in order to be sent the **SensorChangedState** message.

Finally, an operating-system-specific derivative of the **Sensor** is placed in the **O/S-Specific** category.

Security Card Reader

Figure 6-27 shows how the **SecurityCardReader** and its ancillary classes are split up into categories. The pattern should be familiar by now.[1] We have an abstract class that contains a set of abstract clients. Any class wishing to be alerted to an incoming swipe of a

---

1. Patterns are important to all good designers. When we find a particular pattern that works well, we try to use it over and over again in subsequent designs. Perhaps one day, we can compile a reference book of such patterns so that old patterns don't have to be constantly reinvented.

security card must derive from **SCRInterface**. The actual implementation of **SecurityCardReader** must be deferred to an operating-system-specific class.

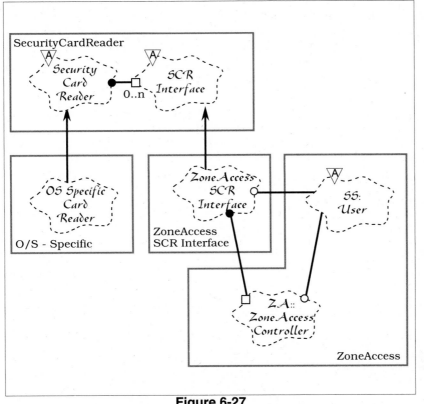

Figure 6-27
SecurityCardReader Category

The **ZoneAccessSCRInterface** also represents a familiar pattern. It is a class in a category by itself, supplying the client interface to **ZoneAccessController**, which has no knowledge of security-card readers.

GUI Control Center

The **GUIControlCenter** category in Figure 6-28 provides an abstract implementation for the **SecurityControlCenter**. Notice that its abstract components are all implemented by the operating system.

I have no illusions about the apparent simplicity of this category. Most of the GUI interface has simply not yet been designed, and I will not attempt such a design in the con-

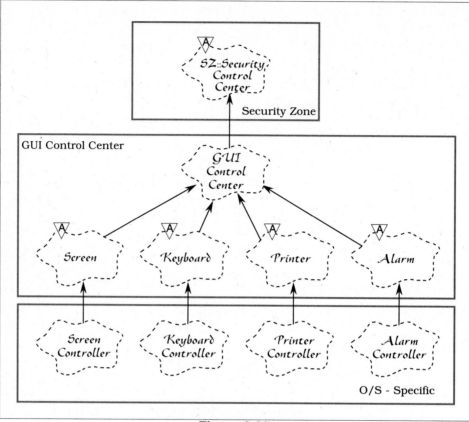

Figure 6-28
GUIControlCenter Category

text of this book. Suffice it to say that any GUI interface is a design challenge in its own right, and that such designs yield to the same strategies that we are employing here.

Security System and Clearance-Access Policy

Finally we come to the last two categories that we will discuss in this chapter: the **SecuritySystem** and the **ClearanceAccessPolicy**. Both are highly detailed categories. Figure 6-29 shows the class diagrams depicting them.

SecuritySystem is a class that associates **Zones** and **AccessPolicy** objects, knows where all the **Zone** instances are, and can act as a liaison for the **Operator-Terminal**. **ClearanceAccessPolicy** provides a particular kind of zone-access policy.

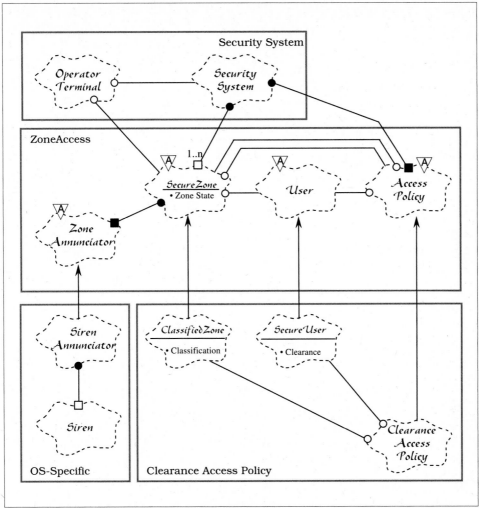

Figure 6-29
SecuritySystem and **ClearanceAccessPolicy**

Notice that we can completely replace the **ClearanceAccessPolicy** category with a category that supplies a very different kind of policy for accessing zones, without affecting the rest of the system.

The Final Category Diagram

Figure 6-30 and Table 6-4 shows all the categories together. Notice that abstractions are on the bottom, and details are on the top, and that product identity is at the bottom, and implementation specifics are at the top. These are characteristics of a robust category structure.

Table 6-4: Category Metrics Spreadsheet

Category Name	N	AC	Ca	Ce	R	H	I	A	D	D'
ZoneAccess	9	4	8	4	15	1.78	0.33	0.44	0.16	0.22
Detector	2	2	4	1	1	1	0.2	1	0.14	0.2
Portal	1	1	3	1	0	1	0.25	1	0.18	0.25
SecurityZone	3	3	8	0	3	1.33	0	1	0	0
Break-inDetector	2	1	1	3	1	1	0.75	0.5	0.18	0.25
ZoneDetector	2	1	1	3	1	1	0.75	0.5	0.18	0.25
Patrol	5	0	0	2	8	1.8	1	0	0	0
Timer	2	2	4	0	1	1	0	1	0	0
O/S Specific	7	0	0	7	0	0.14	1	0	0	0
ZoneAccessSCRInterface	1	0	0	3	0	1	1	0	0	0
SecurityCardReader	2	2	2	0	1	1	0	1	0	0
SecuritySystem	2	0	0	2	1	1	1	0	0	0
ClearanceAccessPolicy	3	0	0	3	2	1	1	0	0	0
Sensor	2	2	2	0	1	1	0	1	0	0
GUIControlCenter	5	4	4	1	4	1	0.2	0.8	0	0
SensedDoor	1	0	0	2	0	1	1	0	0	0

Physical Representation

The category diagram presents us with a viable strategy for containing and managing the source code for this system. We can create a set of directories within a file system that correspond to the categories on the diagram. Each directory bears the name of the category it represents. Within each directory we can place the source code of the classes contained by the corresponding category.

Not only does this scheme provide a convenient place for all the source code, but it also lends itself well to release management. Since categories are the granule of release, we must give them release numbers, and maintain old releases. This is easy to do by copying the contents of the corresponding directory into a "release" directory whose name combines the category and release number (e.g., **ZoneAccess_1_3**).

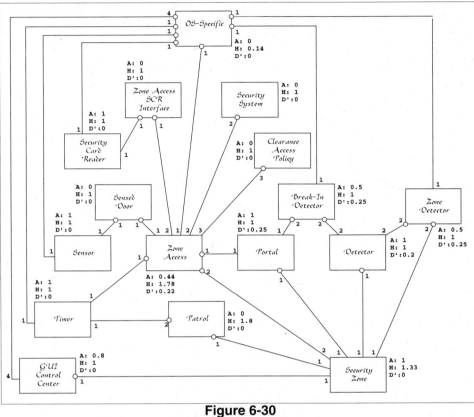

Figure 6-30
Integrated Category Diagram

The ability to maintain previous releases of a category is essential for a successful reuse strategy. Reusers will want to choose the particular release of the category that they need. It is also important for developers working on other categories to be able to choose the version of the other categories that they depend upon. The directory structure shown in Figure 6-30 satisfies these needs quite simply.

How Reusable Is This

We can test the reusability of the category structure in Figure 6-30 by conducting a few "thought experiments." Let's assume that the Lunar Zoo is building a huge dome that will simulate the various habitats of the former South American rain forests. Some of the habitats are exposed to each other, while others are isolated. The visitors to the zoo can walk along paths that remain in sight of, but apart from, the animal habitats.

The directors of the zoo want to be able to track the position of every animal and visitor under the dome. They want to know if animals get out of their intended habitats, or if a visitor violates the posted pathways. To accomplish this, a bioneurological (BN) net has been woven into the fabric of the dome. This net is capable of registering, locating, and identifying any kind of biologically active creature. No two individuals will ever have the exact same BN fingerprint, so the system will be able to track every individual, from the lowliest worm to the most rebellious teenager.

What portions of our system can we reuse to implement this system? Starting with the abstractions, it seems clear that we can reuse the **SecurityZone** category verbatim. **Portal**, **Detector**, **Break-inDetector**, and **ZoneDetector** may also be useful for alerting the zoo keepers to fires or malicious mischief. **ZoneAccess** becomes the core of the "tracking" software. It knows when an animal or human moves from one **Zone** (habitat) to another, and it will report such movement to the appropriate **Zones**, which will in turn report to the **SecurityControlCenter**.

The **SecurityControlCenter** will probably need a completely different implementation. The Lunar officials would be deeply upset if antique GUI systems were used in place of standard virtual-reality, voice-recognition, and holographic-projection systems.

The **ClearanceAccessPolicy** would be completely replaced by a subsystem that recorded the changing positions of each visitor and animal and checked them against zoo policy. This new system that would complain if an animal or visitor got out of place.

Sensor, **Timer**, and **SensedDoor** would all probably be brought into the system, but of course new O/S-specific implementations would need to be supplied. **Security-CardReader** and **ZoneAccessSCRInterface** will be completely replaced by the subsystem that encapsulates the BN net.

We have stripped away the implementation details and access policy details, and replaced them with completely different details. The rest of the system can remain as it is, maintained by the same project team that currently supports the security system.

Splitting up the **O/S-Specific** Category

The **O/S-Specific** category is something of an anomaly. It has grouped together all the implementations of the physical I/O and timing devices. We should probably add some structure beneath this category. Figure 6-31 shows that the category could be split into a set of subcategories that support each component.

The benefit of this hierarchical structure is that the entire **O/S-Specific** category will be exchanged for another whenever the product is ported to a new platform. When new products are made, however, not all of the subcategories need be used.

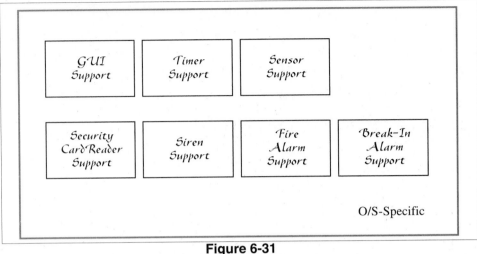

Figure 6-31
`O/S-Specific` subcategories

The `Main` Category

The `Main` category has been omitted from Figure 6-30. It is the most detailed and application-specific category of all. It always applies only to a single application and always adds dependencies upon other detailed categories. In this sense it is pathological, since it is a detailed category depending upon details. In most designs, it should not be included in the metric analysis. This is especially true if the design represents a framework for many different kinds of applications.

Metric Analysis

A close examination of Figure 6-30 and Table 6-4 will show some discrepancies with the previous diagrams. For one thing, I have made the **Break-InDetector** and **ZoneDetector** classes abstract, with implementations supplied by the **O/S-Specific** category. The exact representation of these changes is left as one of the exercises at the end of the chapter.

Figure 6-32 shows a simple analysis of the category metrics. A simple mean and standard deviation of all the $\mathbf{D}^2$ scores were taken and plotted on the $\mathbf{A/I}$ graph along with all the categories. Note how tightly the 1σ and 2σ lines cling to the main sequence. Note also that only a few categories are outside the 2σ line, and not by much. This is heartening.

---

2. The D metric was used because it measures absolute distance from the Main Sequence, and is therefore easy to plot on the graph.

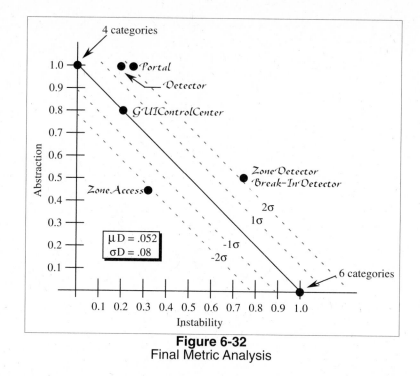

Figure 6-32
Final Metric Analysis

Should we try to fix the categories that are outside the 2σ line? Why? I don't see anything particularly wrong with them. I think that metrics can be valuable in helping you to judge the quality of a design, but they lose their value when they become a law unto themselves. I prefer to leave these categories alone. Besides, a **D'** score of 0.25 is hardly a major violation.

Summary

We have created the first physical design for our building security system. As expected, the physical concerns forced us to alter some of the logical model. Yet the result is quite positive. The structure appears flexible and well isolated. The metric analysis shows a very strong correlation to the main sequence. All in all, we are well positioned for dealing with the detailed design issues of the next chapter.

Exercises

1. Draw the new class diagrams for **Break-inDetector** and **ZoneDetector**. Which classes have become abstract? Why? Draw object diagrams that support your decisions.

2. A close inspection of Figure 5-66 and 6-1b shows a **uses** relationship from **SecureZone** to **SecuritySystem**, that was "accidentally" omitted from Figure 6-29. This **uses** relationship creates a cycle among the categories in Figure 6-29 that is not shown in Figure 6-30. Find it and fix it. Supply class and object diagrams to support your design changes. Reevaluate the metrics for the categories. Do those metrics still make sense?

3. Create a design for the Lunar Zoo. Reuse as many of the existing categories as possible.

4. The value of H for the O/S–Specific category is 0.14. This means that the category has a very low relational cohesion. Why? Is this bad? Explain?

5. Verify that the metrics in Figure 6-30 and Table 6-4 are correct. Are they? How long did this calculation take you?

6. The dependency of the Detector category upon the SecurityZone category is odd. Break it. Recalculate the metrics. Is the result superior? Explain?

7. New feature: Certain doors should be automatically locked and unlocked at certain times. For example, the main entrance should be open from 8AM to 5PM on weekdays. Otherwise it should be locked. Add this to the design. Recalculate the metrics.

7

Detailed Design:
The Case Study Continues

If we have learned anything in three decades of building software systems,
it is that this design on the fly leads to disaster.
There is no substitute for thinking first and acting later,
acting only when all the essential thinking is completed.
Design is the thinking process that has to precede the action of implementation.

—Tom DeMarco, 1982

Design and programming are human activities; forget that and all is lost.

—Bjarne Stroustrup, 1991

This chapter concludes the case study that we started in Chapter 5. It extends the analysis and design of the building security system into a detailed design, using the tools and concepts we have learned in previous chapters. Along with adding a considerable amount of detail, we will investigate such issues as the appropriate multiprocessing structures and real-time response. The end product will be a general blueprint for a low-level design and implementation.

This chapter uses the multiprocessing conventions and nomenclature described in Appendix B. I strongly recommend a review of that appendix prior to an in-depth study of this chapter.

Introduction

Our first chore in this chapter is to decide upon an execution model for the system that will describe the process structure and the manner in which the processes communicate. Then we will examine the details of the communications between the processes and the structure of the communicated messages. Finally we will show the structure of each process at the class-diagram level.

At the same time, we will explore the mechanisms by which the behavioral model interfaces to the real world. This will involve the invention of more classes that act as interfaces for physical devices and physical control mechanisms.

Finally, we will examine how the structure of the system is built from configuration data. That is, how does the system know how many zones, doors, detectors, patrol schedules, and so on, it has? This configuration data must be easy to create and maintain, and mechanisms must exist that allow the system to read that data and build the necessary internal structures.

The Execution Model

A process is an abstraction of a schedule. Several separate schedules operate concurrently within the security system. Access requests and alarms can take place at any time, and must be answered very quickly. Patrols must be monitored according to their timetables. The control-center terminals must display alarms and, like the operator terminals, they must accept commands. The existence of these separate schedules implies that a multi-processing architecture might be appropriate.

The Single-Process Option

First let's explore the possibility of combining all these autonomous functions into a single process. Such an execution model would require one function, somewhere in the system, to send *poll* messages down the containment hierarchy. These poll messages would eventually reach every card reader, sensor, detector, and patrol object in the system. The poll message acts as a very simple thread controller. As each object receives the poll message, it is given its chance to take control and emit one of the autonomous messages described in the object diagrams of the behavioral model. For example, a **Break-inDetector** could not send the **Break-in** message to its **Zone**, as described in Figure 5-26, until that detector had received a poll message.

One of the big advantages of this approach is that it is simple. We don't need to invent an interprocess communication scheme, since all the objects communicate with each other through member function calls. Also, we don't need to design a process architecture.

One disadvantage to the polling approach is that it is difficult to prioritize the polls. For example, it would be very embarrassing if a fire alarm were delayed because the system was too busy polling the patrol schedules. Ideally, we would like to give certain functions a higher priority than others. This is often better accomplished by a multiprocess model.

This argument is fairly weak, however, since any reasonable polling model would probably run through all the objects in a very short time. Moreover, although high-priority alarms sound nice in theory, they are very difficult to implement in practice. This is because the objects must be designed to be interruptable; that is, an object that is busy handling a low-priority event must be interrupted to handle the high-priority event. This is not impossible, but it can be complicated. The polling delay is probably not sufficient reason to justify the extra complexity.

However, polling has other, more crucial, disadvantages. The constant polling will consume many CPU cycles. Each object must be checked as quickly as possible, so the computer cannot afford to share the processor with other applications. This is very unfriendly behavior, and does not satisfy a market in which customers expect to run many applications on a single computer.

Polling ties the application to a single computer. A reasonable process architecture, however, can be divided among several computers on a network, perhaps separated by long distances.

Polling is difficult, if not impossible, to integrate with third party packages such as databases and GUI frameworks.

But, worst of all, every subsystem in the product will be mercilessly constrained by the polling scheme. Each subsystem will have to guarantee not to hold the processor for longer than some minimum interval. As more and more features are added to the system, these constraints will be more and more difficult to live with. Moreover, violating them does not produce instant failures. Instead the system fails only occasionally. The more violations, the more frequently failures occur; but because they are failures in timing instead of logic, they are extremely difficult to find.

The Multiple-Process Option

How would we split the application into multiple processes? We must inspect the application for major subsections that are cohesive enough to withstand the relative autonomy of life in a separate process and that have a low-enough communication load to be economic through interprocess communications links. There are several obvious candidates.

The first major candidate is the set of classes that comprise the security control center (see Figure 6-28). The object diagrams relating to these classes show that the only external communications of these classes are **SecurityEvents**, **SecurityAlarms**, and **SecurityViolations**. To calculate the communications load, we must know the frequency of these events.

Developing an Estimate of Message Rate

Consider a building with a capacity of 5,000 people. How many times will the average occupant swipe his security card in an 8-hour day? This depends upon many factors: the number of security zones between the entrance he uses and his office; the number of zones between his office and the bathroom, break room, and cafeteria; and how often he leaves his office to go to one of these places. Let's say, for the sake of argument, the average occupant must cross two security zones each time he changes his position in the building. Let's also say that he takes two breaks, one lunch hour, and four bathroom breaks during a normal 8-hour shift. If we include his entry at the beginning of the shift and his exit at the end, we get a total of 32 swipes in an 8-hour period.[1] If we multiply that times the population, we get 160,000 (!) swipes every 8 hours, or just over 5.5 swipes per second.

To make matters worse, a quick look at the object diagrams will reveal that most card swipes will generate two messages to the **SecurityControlCenter**: one to report exit from the current zone, and one to report entry to the next zone. Thus, the message rate into **SecurityControlCenter** is approximately 11 messages per second.

A message rate of 11 messages per second is quite low for most interprocess communications channels, so the selection of **SecurityControlCenter** as a process is not likely to cause an IPC bottleneck.

But we are forgetting something. The flux of card swipes is not distributed evenly throughout the 8-hour day. Entry, exit, breaks, and lunch probably occur at fixed times during the day. The bathroom breaks will probably be more uniformly distributed. Thus, nearly half the card swipes will fall into eight major clumps: entry, exit, and the beginning and end of lunch and the two breaks.

Now, let's assume that the peaks are 5 minutes wide; that is, it takes 5 minutes for people to stop what they are doing and go to lunch, or to break. Moreover, let's say that the distribution in this time is fairly random. Then we have 5,000 occupants passing through an average of two security zones in a 5-minute period. This gives us a rate of just over 33 swipes per second, or 66 messages per second.

For most IPC systems, 66 messages per second is clipping along at a pretty good rate. Also, during some seconds, the peak could be substantially higher. Our IPC mechanism will have to be pretty robust to manage it all. Certainly if the frequency of messages is too

---

1. Remember that each break, lunch, or bathroom break is two position changes: one out and one back.

high, the messages will be queued. Queue space is limited, however, and eventually the queues could fill up.

The message-rate problem gives me the jitters. But let's continue exploring the execution model for awhile. Perhaps a solution will present itself.

Beginning the Process Structure

How do we decide how to partition the application into processes? At first we might consider categories to be good places to look for process boundaries. However, classes and categories are abstractions of state and behavior, while processes are abstractions of schedule.[2] Thus, categories actually do not fit well into processes. Some categories may be present in more than one process, while others may be divided between processes.

To find the processes, we must hunt for the schedule abstractions: the features of the system that operate on independent schedules. For the security system, we have the following schedule abstractions:

- Monitoring patrols
- Processing access requests
- Handling security events and commands at the security control centers
- Handling commands at the operator terminals
- Detecting and processing alarms

These five features must operate independently. Patrols must not be delayed by access requests, nor may alarm detection be delayed by operator terminal interactions.

The schedule abstraction for processing access requests is an excellent candidate for a process. It is very self-contained. Its major function is to validate access requests that come into a **Zone**, and to send security messages to the appropriate security control center. These security control centers are also good candidates for processes, since they are also schedule abstractions.

However, the IPC message rate that was nagging me before is now really bothering me. Every IPC message that travels between the **ZoneAccess** process and the **SecurityControlCenter** process is the result of an **AccessRequest** message that comes into the **ZoneAccess** process. Moreover, for nearly every access request that is received by the **ZoneAccess** process an **OpenDoor** message will be sent back as a response. Thus, the IPC rate is roughly 198 messages per second. Figure 7-1 shows the situation.

Something has to give. Either we must downgrade the population rating of the system, or come up with a different process architecture to support the message flux.

We could combine the **ZoneAccess** process and the **SecuritySystem** process into a single process named **ZoneAccessControl** process (see Figure 7-2). This

---

2.   This notion was communicated to me by Jim Coplien in personal correspondence.

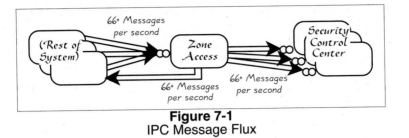

Figure 7-1
IPC Message Flux

would significantly decrease the message flux. However, since there can be many security control centers, we would be forced to create our own thread controller to manage them.

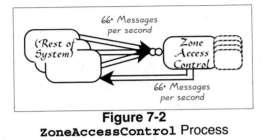

Figure 7-2
ZoneAccessControl Process

Another disadvantage to this scheme is that each of the **SecurityControl-Center** threads manages a keyboard that must be polled. Although the polling rate doesn't have to be very fast, it still may use a significant number of CPU cycles.

We could resolve this problem by creating independent processes that use the operating system to wait for keyboard events, and then send them to the **ZoneAccess-Control** process, as depicted in Figure 7-3.

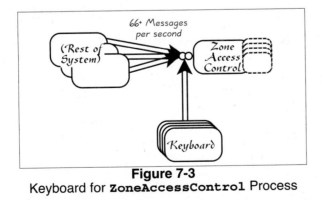

Figure 7-3
Keyboard for **ZoneAccessControl** Process

However, I dislike this entire line of reasoning. The **ZoneAccess** process and the **SecurityControlCenter** processes do not belong together. They are separate schedule abstractions and deserve to be treated as first-class processes. Also, I don't trust a thread controller to do justice to the tasks required of the `SecurityControlCenter` process—tasks such as dealing with a GUI and handling user commands coming in from the keyboard while simultaneously handling access requests. I think such a thread controller would have to be very complex to ensure smooth and timely behavior. Finally, it is very likely that the `SecurityControlCenter` processes will run on separate computers that communicate with the system via network services.

Controlling Message Flux by Buffering

There is another method for managing the message flux. Each sending process could buffer up the messages that it needed to send for 1 second, and then send them all in one big message. This would add some noticeable delays in the response of the system, but they would average out to about 1 additional second per transaction.

Consider, for example, a card swipe. When the swipe is detected, an `Access-Request` message must be sent to the `ZoneAccess` process, but the message will be buffered for up to 1 second before being sent. Thus, the average delay will be about 0.5 seconds. The `ZoneAccess` process will then send the `Open` message back. This too will be buffered and delayed for an average of 0.5 seconds. Thus, the total delay will be 0–2 seconds, with an average delay of 1 second.[3]

We can gain great efficiencies by using this technique, but only if the particular IPC mechanism has a high overhead for individual messages. IPC overhead is typically high, and the overhead is usually *not* closely related to the number of bytes in the message.[4]

Message buffering only provides a benefit if most of the messages are sent by just a few processes. The fewer sending processes there are, the more buffering is possible, and the more efficiency we can gain. If each message is sent by a different process, then no buffering can occur, and we gain no efficiency at all. This leads us to ask how many sending processes there are.

Architecture of the Hardware Interface

The number of sending processes depends greatly on the architecture of the security hardware, and its interface to the operating system. A typical building will have dozens, if not hundreds, of security-card readers, detectors, and alarms scattered about. It is inconceivable that each of these devices would have a separate interface to the computer. Many such

---

3. This presumes that the timers on the message buffers are not synchronized. If they are, then subsequent messages will all be delayed by the maximum delay time of 1 second. This would create a delay range of 1–2 seconds, with the average being 1.5 seconds.
4. This is not a hard-and-fast rule. Certainly IPC mechanisms that use low-speed communications links to communicate with remote machines will experience a very high correlation between throughput and message size. But in most IPC methods, where the communications channel is extremely fast, most of the time and effort are expended on securing the channel and then navigating the message through the channel. This time and effort is often roughly constant for messages whose sizes range from 1 byte to several K.

devices would probably be connected via some form of multi-drop circuit, which would interface to the computer as a single device. Such circuits may be able to support the entire building; however, prudence would dictate that several such circuits be used so that a single point failure does not take out the whole building.

The number of sending processes is therefore probably equivalent to the number of separate circuits connected to the computer. Each such process must manage all the devices attached to its corresponding circuit, along with the objects that control them, such as **Door**s, **Detector**s, and **SecurityCardReader**s. Thus, the process should probably be multithreaded (see Figure 7-4).

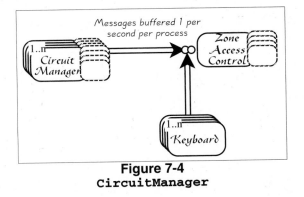

Figure 7-4
CircuitManager

By buffering the messages into one per process per second, we should also be able to separate the **ZoneAccess** process from the **SecurityControlCenter** process again, as shown in Figure 7-5.

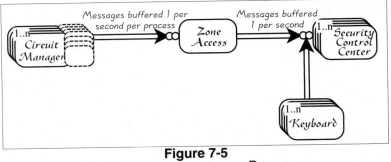

Figure 7-5
Separating **ZoneAccess** Process
from **SecurityControlCenter** Process

This decreases the complexity of the application by allowing us to eliminate a thread controller. It is also less cluttered; the two processes are different enough that they ought to be separate. I have kept the **Keyboard** processes separate, so that the **Security-**

ControlCenter process does not have to poll between its message queue and the keyboard device.

An examination of the class diagram in Figure 6-29 shows that the classes associated with the **ZoneAccess** process are used by the **OperatorTerminal** class. We should probably create a separate process, so that the **ZoneAccess** process does not have to poll between the operator terminal devices and its own message queue. Figure 7-6 shows this addition.

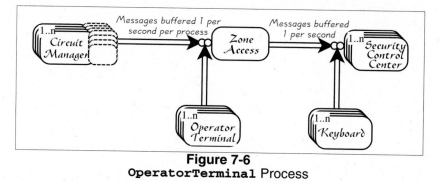

Figure 7-6
OperatorTerminal Process

Determining Parent/Child Relationships

An intimate relationship exists between the **Keyboard** processes and their respective **SecurityControlCenter** processes, because the **SecurityControlCenter** processes control the **Screen** objects that correspond to the **Keyboard** processes. It makes sense, therefore, to have the **SecurityControlCenter** process be the parent of the **Keyboard** process.

A similar relationship exists between the **ZoneAccess** process and its **Operator-Terminal** processes, although in this case the **ZoneAccess** process will be the parent of all the **OperatorTerminal** processes. Figure 7-7 shows these parent/child relationships.

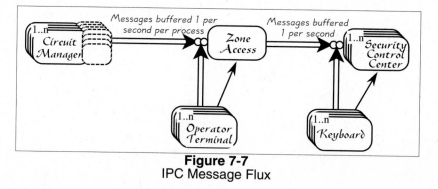

Figure 7-7
IPC Message Flux

Separating `CircuitManager` Input from Output

The devices controlled by the **CircuitManager** process are not limited to read-only access. Sirens must be turned on and off, and doors must be opened and locked. Thus, communications must go both ways through the security circuits.

We could satisfy this requirement by allowing the **ZoneAccess** process to send messages to the **CircuitManager** processes. However, that means that the **Circuit-Manager** processes will be forced to poll between the I/O hardware and their message queue. To avoid this, we have separated the **CircuitManager** process into a **CircuitSender** and a **CircuitReceiver** process, as shown in Figure 7-8. We have also arbitrarily made the **CircuitReceiver** process the parent of the **Circuit-Sender** process. This is expedient, since they must occur in pairs.

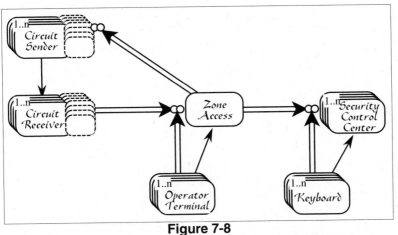

Figure 7-8
The `CircuitSender` and `CircuitReceiver` Processes

There is a problem with this structure: these processes must, together, manage objects such as **Door**, **SecurityCardReader**, and the **Detectors**, which have a single representation; they are not split into sending and receiving components. It would be very difficult to put half of a **Door** object into the **CircuitSender** process and the other half into the **CircuitReceiver** process. Thus, there is too much separation in the above model. We need a way to model the circuit and the corresponding devices that allows the circuit sender and receiver to remain separate, but does not require splitting up the object model of the devices.

Perhaps a better way to look at it, as shown in Figure 7-9, is to make the **Circuit-Receiver** and **CircuitSender** very stupid processes that simply communicate between the hardware and a **SecurityDevices** process that contains the representations of the objects.

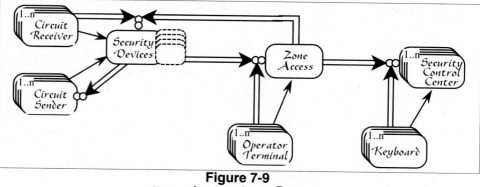

Figure 7-9
`SecurityDevices` Process

Although this solves our polling and splitting problems, it raises again the spectre of throughput and propagation delay. If we don't buffer the messages coming from the **CircuitReceiver**, the message flux into **SecurityDevices** will at times be very high. If we do buffer the messages, there will be two buffering delays between the reception of an event and the time that the **ZoneAccess** process is able to process it. Two buffering delays will increase the average response time from 1 second to more than 3 seconds.[5] This is pushing it; I believe the response time should be on the order of 1–2 seconds. A user who swipes a card should not have to wait more than 2 seconds for the door to open.

We can decrease the delay by shortening the buffering time, but doing so increases the message flux. This will require more CPU cycles to be expended on passing messages, which will leave fewer cycles for processing the content of those messages.

Adaptive Buffering

CPU cycles are precious when the demand on the system is high. When 5,000 people are hammering away at the system at the change of shifts, or at lunch hour, we want to reserve every possible CPU cycle for processing requests rather than transporting them. In the quiet times however, CPU cycles are very plentiful, and we could spare some to decrease response time during that period.

What we want to do is trade response time for throughput, so that during peak hours response time is longer than usual but throughput is high, while at other times response time is short but throughput is low. We can come up with an adaptive buffering scheme that increases buffering time when demand is high, but reduces it when demand is low. Thus, more time is spent gathering requests into messages when demand is high. This means fewer overall messages, at the expense of the time taken to gather the requests. We can accomplish this easily by counting the number of messages that a process sends dur-

---

5. Again, assuming synchronous buffering, all subsequent messages would suffer the full 1-second delay.

ing a buffer cycle. If the number is small, we can reduce the buffering time, but if the number is large, we should increase the buffering time.

Clearly we must set limits on both the minimum and maximum buffering times. If the buffering time were reduced to zero in a quiet system, then the process might sit and spin, uselessly burning CPU cycles and not sharing the system with other applications. On the other hand, if the buffering time were allowed to grow without bound, response times in busy systems could become needlessly long.

It is probably premature to assign realistic values to these limits right now; the values will need to be tuned once the system is operational, and we can measure performance. However, a reasonable guess for the initial values might be 100 ms minimum time, and 1 second maximum time.

By using adaptive buffering, we can guarantee that response time will remain a function of demand, and will not be arbitrarily lengthened by needless delays. This frees us from worrying about the problems of message throughput, and lets us concentrate on putting together a reasonable process structure.

Patrols

Now let's consider how the security patrols fit into the process model. This feature receives its inputs from **Checkpoint** objects, which certainly represent devices attached to the security circuits. The patrol feature sends its outputs to **Zone** objects that live in the **ZoneAccess** process. Thus, the architecture, as depicted in Figure 7-10, seems pretty obvious.

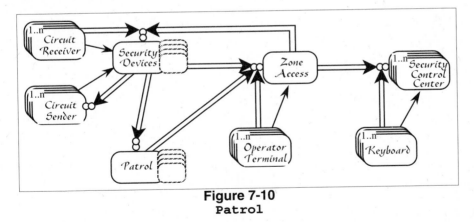

Figure 7-10
Patrol

The **Patrol** process is multithreaded because it needs to deal with many concurrent patrols. I have not separated those patrols into separate processes because each thread is contained within the **Patrol** class. Thus, processing an event for a particular patrol is simply a matter of finding the correct **Patrol** object and invoking the appropriate methods. We can handle this entirely within the context of a single process.

The Timer

One last element of the design needs to be placed into the execution model: the **Timer**. There are any number of ways to implement this part of the system. We could, for example, have a **Timer** process that sends trigger messages to the appropriate processes every second. Alternatively, we could use the facilities of the operating system to alert us once per second.

Where possible, I prefer the second approach. The main loop of each process contains a system call that either waits on a mailbox or on some physical device. If the operating system allows these calls to *time out*, then we can use this time-out indication as a way to derive timing triggers. Thus, each process waits at its message queue for a message, but the wait is set to time out after a second or so. Upon time-out, or upon receipt of a message, the process checks the current time to see if it ought to send **trigger** messages to the objects expecting them.

Communication Between the Processes

Having derived a likely[6] process model, we now turn to modeling the messages that flow between the processes, and their relative timings. This is done on a scenario-by-scenario basis, by examining the corresponding object diagrams and translating them into message-sequence charts.

Figure 7-11 shows the scenario for a card swipe opening a door. It includes some of the features shown in Figure 6-13, the object diagram for the same scenario. Any message that crosses a process boundary is shown. The messages on the object diagram that are not shown are wholly contained within a single process. Likewise, some of the messages on the message-sequence chart, such as **Event** and **Command**, are implementation artifacts and don't exist on the object diagram at all.

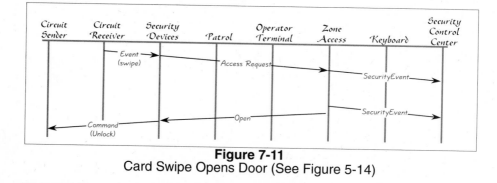

Figure 7-11
Card Swipe Opens Door (See Figure 5-14)

---

6. I use the word "likely" because we have not yet tested this structure. Such tests will undoubtedly uncover flaws.

The messages that come from the **CircuitReceiver** process are all named **Event**. They contain information that describes which kind of event was read from the security circuit. The **Event** message is decoded by the **SecurityDevices** process, which translates the event into the appropriate type of message, and sends it to the corresponding object. In the example above, a user swipes his card through a security-card reader, which causes the security circuit attached to that reader to generate an event. The event is received by the **CircuitReceiver** process and formatted into an **Event** message. The **Event** message is then sent to the **SecurityDevices** process, which decodes it as a card swipe, locates the appropriate **SecurityCardReader** object in its private data segment, and then invokes the **Swipe** method.

Similarly, when a **Lock** object within the **SecurityDevices** process receives an **Unlock** message, it creates a **Command** message that is sent to the **CircuitSender** process, which tells the hardware what to do.

Let's look at some more scenarios. Please compare the following charts with the corresponding object diagrams from the previous chapters.

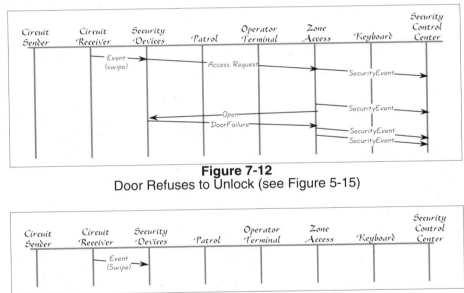

Figure 7-12
Door Refuses to Unlock (see Figure 5-15)

Figure 7-13
Door Already Unlocked When Swiped (see Figure 5-16)

Figures 7-12 through 7-17 are relatively simple, and agree well with their associated object diagrams. Figures 7-18 through 7-23 have to do with security patrols. Although the charts themselves are quite simple, the corresponding object diagrams are very complex. This disparity arises because almost all of the complexity within the object diagrams is contained within the **Patrol** process.

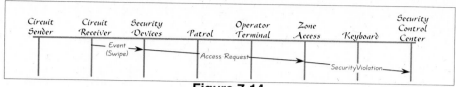

Figure 7-14
Exit Permission Denied (see Figure 5-17)

Figure 7-15
Entry Permission Denied (see Figure 5-18)

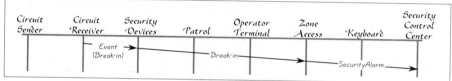

Figure 7-16
Break-in Detected (see Figure 5-26)

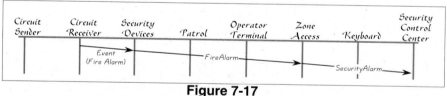

Figure 7-17
Fire or Smoke Detection (see Figure 5-28)

Some of the `PatrolSchedule` scenarios have no message activity at all, for example, "Trigger Doesn't Start a Patrol" and "Trigger Does Start a Patrol." Also, scenarios based on timer events seem to generate messages from nowhere, because we are modeling the timer as intrinsic to each process rather than as a process itself.

Figure 7-24 shows how the state of a zone can be set by the operator terminal. Some zone states cause the siren to sound.

Most of the scenarios that involve the internal workings of the `Security-ControlCenter` process do not involve IPC messages, so there are no message-

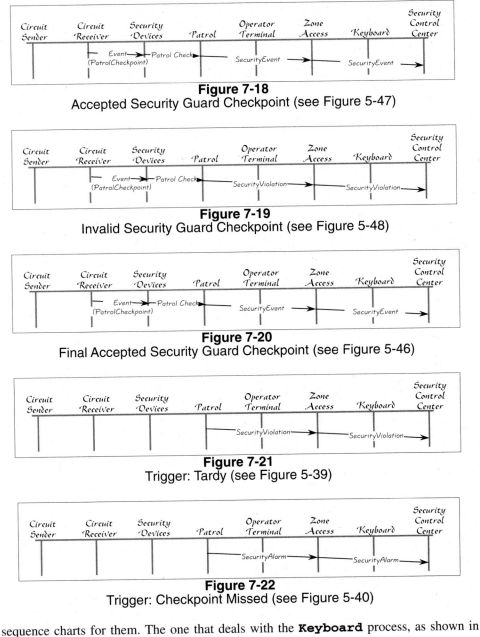

Figure 7-18
Accepted Security Guard Checkpoint (see Figure 5-47)

Figure 7-19
Invalid Security Guard Checkpoint (see Figure 5-48)

Figure 7-20
Final Accepted Security Guard Checkpoint (see Figure 5-46)

Figure 7-21
Trigger: Tardy (see Figure 5-39)

Figure 7-22
Trigger: Checkpoint Missed (see Figure 5-40)

sequence charts for them. The one that deals with the **Keyboard** process, as shown in Figure 7-25, is an exception, though not a very big one.

Finally, Figures 7-26 and 7-27 depict scenarios that involve asynchronous time-outs and events that involve doors.

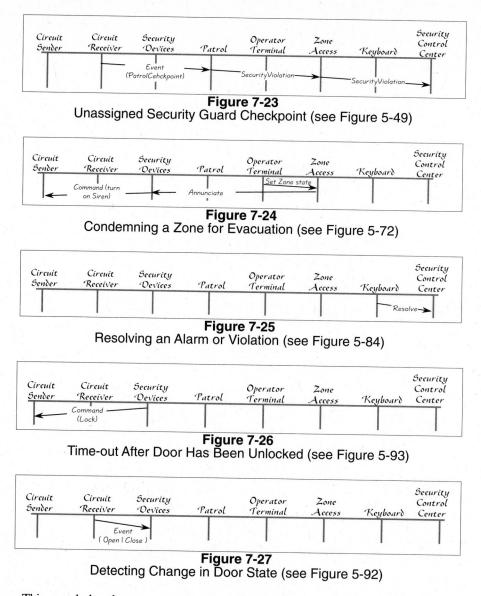

Figure 7-23
Unassigned Security Guard Checkpoint (see Figure 5-49)

Figure 7-24
Condemning a Zone for Evacuation (see Figure 5-72)

Figure 7-25
Resolving an Alarm or Violation (see Figure 5-84)

Figure 7-26
Time-out After Door Has Been Unlocked (see Figure 5-93)

Figure 7-27
Detecting Change in Door State (see Figure 5-92)

This concludes the message-sequence charts that we can derive directly from the object diagrams.

Designing the Messages

Now that we have mapped out the sequence of IPC messages that must exist in the system, it is time to describe the structure of those messages. This must be done, regardless of whether we use a lightweight or a heavyweight process model. If we use a lightweight model, we will encode the message structures into derivatives of some **Message** class (see Figure 4-14 and associated text). If we use a heavyweight process model, we will have to encode the structure of the messages in an external representation of some kind, and create the appropriate **Surrogates** and **Receivers** (see Figures 4-19 and 4-20 and associated text).

We derive the structure of the messages by examining the object diagrams and making sure that each IPC message contains the specified data. To describe the data, I will use standard data dictionary notation from structured analysis.

The first message we look at is **Event**, which comes in four varieties. Each includes the address of the device causing the event, and may also contain a user ID number.

```
• Event           ::= eventType + deviceAddress
  eventType       ::= [(Swipe + userID) | Break-in | FireAlarm
                      | (PatrolCheckpoint + userID) | Open | Closed]
  deviceAddress   ::= integer
  userID          ::= integer
```

Next we look at the structure of the **Command** message:

```
• Command         ::= commandType + deviceAddress
  commandType     ::= [Unlock | Lock | TurnOnSiren | TurnOffSiren]
```

The messages that travel from the **SecurityDevices** process to the **Zone-Access** process:

```
• AccessRequest  ::= userID
• DoorFailure    ::= doorID
  doorID         ::= integer
• Break-in       ::= detectorID
  detectorID     ::= integer
• FireAlarm      ::= detectorID
```

PatrolCheckpoint messages are sent from the **SecurityDevices** process to the **Patrol** process:

```
• PatrolCheck    ::= checkpointID
  checkpointID   ::= integer
```

The messages that travel from the **ZoneAccess** process to the **Security-Devices** process:

```
• Annunciate     ::= zoneID
• CancelAnnunciate
                 ::= zoneID
• Open           ::= doorID
• zoneID         ::= integer
```

The messages that travel from the **ZoneAccess** process to the **Security-ControlCenter** process:

- SecurityEvent::= authorizedExit + *doorID* + *userID*
                   | authorizedEntry + *doorID* + *userID*
                   | patrolCheckPoint + *checkPointID* + *guardID*
                   | doorWon'tUnlock + *doorID* + *userID*
                   | finalPatrolCheckPoint + *checkPointID* +
                     guardID
- SecurityViolation
                   ::= unauthorizedEntry + *doorID* + *userID*
                   | unauthorizedExit + *doorID* + *userID*
                   | patrolCheckPointLate + *checkPointID* + *guardID*
                   | doorHeldOpen + *doorID*
                   | unassignedPatrolCheckpoint
                       + *checkPointID*
                       + *guardID*
                   | invalidPatrolCheckpoint + *checkPointID*
                       + *guardID*
- SecurityAlarm ::=patrolCheckpointMissed + *checkPointID* + *guardID*
                   | doorBlockedOpen + *doorID*
                   | fireAlarm + *detectorID*
                   | break-in + *detectorID*
  guardID   ::= integer

The messages sent from the **Patrol** process to the **ZoneAccess** process:

- SecurityEvent ::= patrolCheckPoint + *checkPointID* + *guardID*
                   | finalPatrolCheckPoint + *checkPointID*
                       + *guardID*
- SecurityViolation
                   ::= unassignedPatrolCheckpoint
                       + *checkPointID* + *guardID*
                   | patrolCheckPointLate + *checkPointID* + *guardID*
                   | invalidPatrolCheckpoint + *heckPointID* + *guardID*
- SecurityAlarm ::= patrolCheckpointMissed + *checkPointID* + *guardID*

The messages from the **OperatorTerminal** process to the **ZoneAccess** process:

- SetZoneState ::= *zoneID* + *zoneState*
  zoneState   ::= [lockdown | noLockdown | evacuate |
                     noEvacuate]

The final message is sent from the **Keyboard** process to the **SecurityControl-Center** process:

- Resolve   ::= *screenItemID*
  screenItemID ::= integer

Routing Messages to the Correct Object

The packets we have just described are based on messages from object diagrams. Although they must physically move between processes, their true intent is simply to travel from one object to another. When one of these packets arrives at the recipient process, that process must then invoke the corresponding method in the appropriate object. How does the recipient process know which object to route the message to?

For example, consider Figure 7-28. Instances of **SecurityCardReader** run within the **SecurityDevices** process. **ZoneAccessController** runs in the **ZoneAccess** process. But where does **ZoneAccessSCRInterface** run? It runs in *both* processes by using the *Surrogate* mechanism from Chapter 4 (see Figures 4-19 and 4-20 and the associated text.)

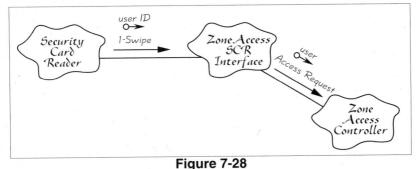

Figure 7-28
Card swipe generates access request

The static and dynamic models that adapt Figure 7-28 to the Surrogate mechanism are shown in Figures 7-29 and 7-30.

Upon receiving the **swipe** message, the surrogate formats an **Event** packet that includes the appropriate **userID**, and ships this packet through the IPC mechanism to the "Zone Access" process. Upon receiving this packet, the **ZoneAccess** process routes the packet to the **ZoneAccessSCRReceiver** object. This object unpacks it and invokes the swipe method upon the **RealZoneAccessSCRInterface**.

The advantage of this approach is that neither of our original objects has had to know anything at all about the IPC mechanism. All the packet building and routing is handled by separate objects. Thus, if we ever decide to change the way the processes are laid out, the application classes won't be affected very much. Only the classes involved in IPC surrogation and routing will be affected.

Managing Dependencies Between Processes

A glance at Figure 7-11 will show you that something is wrong. This diagram shows that the packet that travels between the **SecurityDevices** process and the **ZoneAccess**

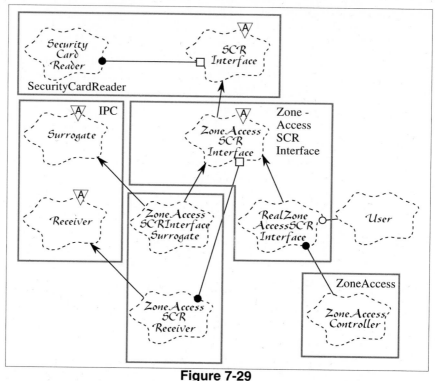

Figure 7-29
ZoneAccessSCRInterface Adapted to the Surrogate Mechanism

process is **AccessRequest**. Yet Figure 7-30 seems to be passing the **Swipe** message across the process boundary. Note that there is no difference in the data being transmitted; only the name of the packet is incorrect. We could ignore this, but it indicates an inconsistency in our thinking. Somewhere there must be an error.

One possible solution would be to change the name of the **Swipe** method of **Zone-AccessSCRInterface** to **AccessRequest**. However, it inherited **Swipe** from its abstract base class **SCRInterface**, which really ought to have a **Swipe** method, since it is the specific interface for a security card reader device.

Another possibility would be to change the name of the packet to **Swipe**. However this packet must be sent to the **ZoneAccess** process, which should not know anything about the details of security-card readers. This pinpoints a serious problem: The **Zone-Access** process has knowledge of security-card readers: we cannot reuse it with different kinds of security devices. The reason is that there is a dependency between **Zone-AccessSCRInterface** and **SecurityCardReader**. The **ZoneAccess-SCRInterface** class exists only to provide an interface between the **ZoneAccessController** class and the **SecurityCardReader** class. Thus,

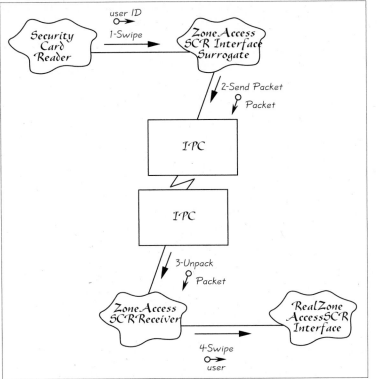

Figure 7-30
Dynamic Model of `ZoneAccessSCRInterface` surrogation

`ZoneAccessSCRInterface` belongs solely on the `SecurityDevices` side of the process boundary.

I have apparently chosen the wrong class to adapt to the surrogation mechanism. I should have chosen the `ZoneAccessController`. This would have left the `Zone-Access` process unpolluted by concepts that belong in the `SecurityDevices` process. It would appear that Figure 7-11 was correct after all, and that Figures 7-29 and 7-30 should be changed to show the adaptation of `ZoneAccessController` to the surrogation mechanism. I leave this adaptation as Exercise 1 at the end of this chapter.

Figure 7-31 shows an abbreviated category diagram with the process boundaries for the `ZoneAccess` and `SecurityDevices` processes drawn in. Note that my error was to move the `ZoneAccessSCRInterface` class into the process that contained the `ZoneAccess` category, creating processes whose dependencies were the opposite of the categories that they contained.

Thus, we can derive a rule for choosing which classes to adapt to surrogation: Always move surrogates *against* the flow of dependency between categories. For example, our solution to the above dilemma was to create a surrogate of the `ZoneAccessControl-`

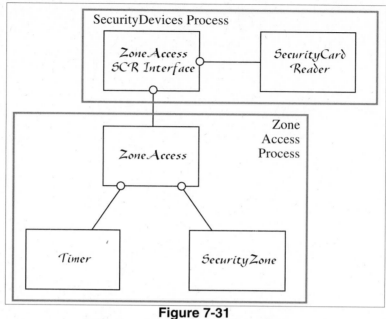

Figure 7-31
Process and Category Boundaries

ler class, and move it up into the **SecurityDevices** process. If this rule is followed, then the only dependencies that will exist between processes are those that already exist between the contained categories

Reflection

So far we have partitioned the design into an execution model consisting of several separate processes and the relationships between them. We have discussed throughput issues, and have invented a scheme of adaptive buffering that we think will address those issues. We have also chosen to employ the surrogation scheme, which allows objects within different processes to communicate without having to know that the communication is crossing a process boundary. We have found that dependency issues are important, even across process boundaries, and that exploring even the tiniest inconsistencies may lead us to discover serious design problems.

At this point in the design, I would strongly suggest some experiments. A simulation of the process model and the adaptive buffering scheme would be a good place to start. A good simulation would identify the actual bottlenecks in the system. It would also allow you to adjust the timings and delays in the system, so that you could see how sensitive it is to variations.

Keep in mind that what we have designed so far are "castles in the air." We have a nice theory for the way our execution model will operate, but such theories rarely survive exposure to reality unscathed. Experiments and simulations are valuable tools, and they will help us to refine the model and avoid disaster. However, they too are simply the expression of theories. In the end, reality will have its way.

Theories are the best way we have to predict the future. We attempt to develop a mathematical model that describes how our system will behave, but we must test the model with the best data at our disposal. For example, an actual study of the transaction rate of a security system would be invaluable. Such data should be applied to a simulation of the system to see if our design can truly handle the load. As the system evolves, more data about the actual performance of the individual processes will become available, and we should inject this data into the simulation model as soon as possible.

Designing the Processes

In what follows, we will study each process individually. Our goal is to derive the static and dynamic structure of each process, paying close attention to dependency issues.

The ZoneAccess Process

I begin with the **ZoneAccess** process because, in one sense, it is the highest-level process in the system. It is central to our process diagram. It is the sole point of communication between the left and right sides of the diagram, and it is involved in a majority of the message interactions. The classes within this process come almost entirely from the **ZoneAccess** and **SecurityZone** categories (see Figures 6-12 and 6-10).

Looking over the message-sequence charts, we find that several different types of messages are sent to the **ZoneAccess** process. The object diagrams in Chapter 5 show us to which classes these messages are being sent.

- **AccessRequest** is being sent to **ZoneAccessController**. (Figure 5-7 through 5-18)
- **Break-in** is being sent to **Portal**. (Figure 5-26)
- **FireAlarm** (5-28), **SecurityAlarm** (5-40), **SecurityViolation** (5-36), **SecurityEvent** (5-35), and **DoorFailure** (5-15) are being sent to **Zone**.
- **SetZoneState** (5-69 and 5-72) is being sent to **SecuritySystem** . . . or is it?

Certainly Figure 7-24 seems to imply that **OperatorTerminal** sends **Set-ZoneState** to **SecuritySystem** within the **ZoneAccess** process; however, Figure 5-69 tells a different story. It shows that the **OperatorTerminal** queries the **SecuritySystem** for the address of a **Zone** object by passing it something called a **ZoneID**.

Passing addresses of objects across process boundaries is generally invalid, since address spaces need not be shared by processes. The best that **SecuritySystem** could do would be to pass back some kind of token that represents the appropriate **Zone** object, but that's just what a **ZoneID** is, so we would just be trading one kind of token for another!

There is a flaw lurking here somewhere. We could fix it easily by returning the model to the form that it originally had in Figure 5-62 and changing the **LockDown** message to a **SetZoneState** message that passed a **ZoneID** instead of a **Zone**. However, this would make **SecuritySystem** aware of things like lockdown, Evacuation, and other concepts that are the domain of **SecureZone**. Is this a problem?

According to Figure 6-23 this is no problem at all. **SecuritySystem** is nicely entrenched within the **ZoneAccess** category, where all these detailed concepts belong. According to Figure 6-29, however, there is a deep problem, since this diagram puts **SecuritySystem** within the **SecuritySystem** category with **Operator-Terminal**. This is absurd; **SecuritySystem** should not be associated with **OperatorTerminal**. Its function is to relate **SecureZone** objects to **Access-Policy** objects. It belongs within the **ZoneAccess** category, as Figure 6-23 shows.

Thus, we will change the **SecuritySystem** category to the **Operator-Terminal** category and move the **SecuritySystem** class into the **ZoneAccess** category, as shown in Figure 7-32. This does not alter the metrics of Figure 6-30 significantly.

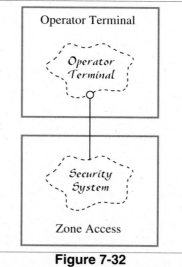

Figure 7-32
Move **SecuritySystem** Class
into **ZoneAccess** Category

We will also change the dynamic model in Figure 5-69 so that **Operator-Terminal** can pass the **SetState** message to **SecuritySystem**, as shown in Figure 7-33. Note that the issues of dynamic downcast mentioned in the text associated with Figure 5-69 are no longer relevant.[7] As described by the text associated with Figure 6-13, **SecuritySystem** contains **SecureZone** objects not **Zone** objects.

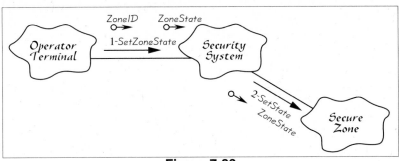

Figure 7-33
Passing **SetZoneState** to **SecuritySystem**

Receivers in the ZoneAccess Process

Since there are four different classes in the **ZoneAccess** process that can receive messages from other processes, we must have four receiver classes to catch and decode those messages. Figure 7-34 shows a tentative structure employing the pattern from Figure 4-20.

Notice that the **SecuritySystem** and **ZoneAccessController** classes have been split into abstract and real components, in support of the surrogation mechanisms. Remember that both the *Receiver* and the *Surrogate* must derive from the same abstract class (see Figures 4-19 and 4-20.) It is gratifying that the effort to integrate our design into a multiprocessing environment *increases* the level of abstraction within the categories. The higher the level of abstraction, the higher the potential for reuse.

The change in the level of abstraction leads us to reconsider the category architecture. Since we now have more abstract classes, we can probably put the concrete derivatives into their own category. Figure 7-35 shows how this might look.

Notice that we have placed all the classes that are polluted by multiprocessing concepts into the **ZoneAccessProcess** category. The **ZoneAccess** category still contains no evidence that a multiprocessing architecture is in use!

Surrogates in the ZoneAccess Process

The **ZoneAccess** process also sends messages to objects in other processes. Surrogates of those objects must therefore be present in the **ZoneAccess** process. By scanning the message-sequence charts, we can determine that the following messages are sent:

---

7.   This is not to say that such tactics can eliminate every instance of dynamic downcasting. In general they cannot. It just so happened that, in this case, the dynamic downcast was rendered unnecessary.

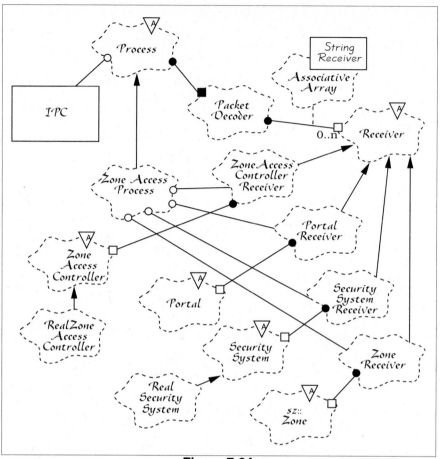

Figure 7-34
The `ZoneAccessProcess` Category

- **SecurityEvent**, **SecurityViolation**, and **SecurityAlarm** are sent to the **SecurityControlCenter** process (Figure 7-11 through 7-23).
- **Open** (7-11, 7-12) and **Annunciate** (7-24) are sent to the **SecurityDevices** processes.

The object diagrams tell us which classes should receive these messages. The **SecurityEvent**, **SecurityAlarm**, and **SecurityViolation** messages are meant for some derivative of the **SecurityControlCenter** class from the **SecurityZone** category. The **Open** message is meant for the **Door** class in the **Zone-Access** category. The **Annunciate** message is meant for some derivative of the **ZoneAnnunciator** in the **ZoneAccess** category.

This means that the **SecurityDevices** process will need a **DoorReceiver** class and a **ZoneAnnunciatorReceiver** class, and the **SecurityControl-**

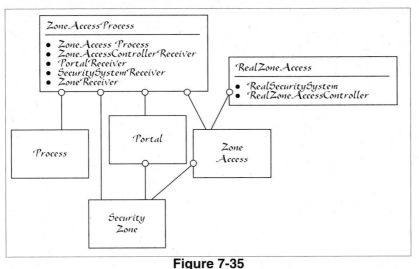

Figure 7-35
Changes to the Category Architecture

Center process will need a **SecurityControlCenterReceiver** class. This in turn means that the **ZoneAccess** process will need a **DoorSurrogate** class, a **ZoneAnnunciatorSurrogate** class, and a **SecurityControlCenter-Surrogate** class. Figure 7-36 shows the static model for the changes to the **Zone-Access** process. We will show the changes to the **SecurityDevices** process later.

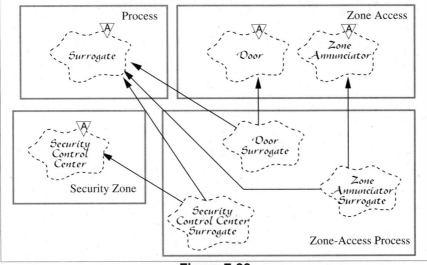

Figure 7-36
Adding the Surrogates to the **ZoneAccessProcess** Category

Identifying the Message and the Target Object

It is pretty easy to understand how a `ZoneAccessControllerSurrogate` can communicate with the `ZoneAccessControllerReceiver`. There is only one `Zone-AccessController` object in the system, so the receiver's job is pretty simple. However, the same is not true for `ZoneReceiver`s or `DoorReceiver`s.

When the `DoorSurrogate` in the `ZoneAccess` process receives an `Open` message, it must convert it to an `Open` packet and send it to the `SecurityDevices` process, which will then route it to the `DoorReceiver` object. The `DoorReceiver` has many different `Door` objects to choose from, so it must have some means of selecting a particular `Door` object as the target for the `Open` message. It must be that the `DoorSurrogate` object attaches some identifier to the Open packet that the `DoorReceiver` can use to select which `Door` object should receive the message.

Similarly, how does the `DoorReceiver` object know that the packet represents an `Open` message? Some kind of identifier must be built into the packet that specifies which message that the packet represents.

Thus, we must change the format for the `Open` packet to look like this:

- `Open`   `::=`   OPEN_ID + *doorID*

`OPEN_ID` is some numeric or alphanumeric code that uniquely specifies that this is an `Open` packet. Similar changes are required for all the packet definitions:

- `Event`   `::=`   EVENT_ID + *eventType* + *deviceAddress*
- `Command`   `::=`   COMMAND_ID + commandType + deviceAddress
- `AccessRequest` `::=`   ACCESS_REQUEST_ID + *userID*
- `DoorFailure`   `::=`   DOOR_FAILURE_ID + doorID
- `Break-in`   `::=`   BREAK-IN_ID + *portalID* + *detectorID•*
- `FireAlarm`   `::=`   FIRE_ALARM_ID + *zoneID* + *detectorID*
- `PatrolCheck`   `::=`   PATROL_CHECK_ID + *guardID* + *checkpointID*
- `Annunciate`   `::=`   ANNUNCIATE_ID + *zoneID*
- `CancelAnnunciate`

                   `::=`   CANCEL_ANNUNCIATE_ID + *zoneID*
- `SecurityEvent` `::=`   SECURITY_EVENT_ID + *zoneID* +
                          [
                          authorizedExit + *doorID* + *userID*
                          | authorizedEntry + *doorID* + *userID*
                          | patrolCheckPoint + *checkPointID* + *guardID*
                          | doorWon'tUnlock + *doorID* + *userID*
                          | finalPatrolCheckPoint + *checkPointID*
                          + *guardID*
                          | patrolCheckPoint + *checkPointID* + *guardID*
                          | finalPatrolCheckPoint
                          + *checkPointID* + *guardID*
                          ]

- SecurityViolation ::= SECURITY_VIOLATION_ID + *zoneID* +

  [

  unauthorizedEntry + *doorID* + *userID*

  | unauthorizedExit + *doorID* + *userID*

  | patrolCheckPointLate

  + *checkPointID* + *guardID*

  | doorHeldOpen + *doorID*

  | unassignedPatrolCheckpoint

  + *checkPointID* + *guardID*

  | invalidPatrolCheckpoint

  + *checkPointID* + *guardID*

  | unassignedPatrolCheckpoint

  + *checkPointID* + *guardID*

  | patrolCheckPointLate

  + *checkPointID* + *guardID*

  | invalidPatrolCheckpoint

  + *heckPointID* + *guardID*

  ]

- SecurityAlarm ::= SECURITY_ALARM + *zoneID* +

  [

  patrolCheckpointMissed

  + *checkPointID* + *guardID*

  | doorBlockedOpen + *doorID*

  | fireAlarm + *detectorID*

  | break-in + *detectorID*

  | patrolCheckpointMissed

  + *checkPointID* + *guardID*

  ]

- SetZoneState ::= SET_ZONE_STATE_ID + *zoneID* + *zoneState*
- Resolve ::= RESOLVE_ID + *controlCenterID* + *screenItemID*

Reflection

This was not too difficult. We have successfully integrated the **ZoneAccess** process with the surrogation mechanism for IPC. We made some changes to the original model in order to accomplish this integration, but the changes always involved the separation of a concrete class into an abstract base and a concrete derivative. It could be argued that these were oversights in the original design. In any case, the changes made do not force the original model to depend upon the IPC mechanisms in any way.

New categories have been added. Some, like **Process**, contain the generic multiprocessing abstractions. Others, like **ZoneAccessProcess**, contain the portions of the design that depend upon the multiprocessing mechanisms. Overall, the changes in the category structure will drive the categories closer to the main sequence.

We discovered an important flaw during this portion of the design. Two contradictory diagrams were found, and the contradiction was resolved. I always find it interesting that flaws are usually uncovered when you aren't looking for them, and the kind of the flaw generally has nothing to do with the kind of design activity you are performing.

I think that this points out the weakness of a phased design approach. No design is ever complete; we will continue to find errors in subsequent phases. Designers must be able to iterate quickly on those errors without losing track of what they are doing.

The `SecurityControlCenter` Process

The process shown in Figure 7-37 has only one kind of receiver: a **Security-ControlCenterReceiver**. Moreover, it sends no messages out, so it has no surrogates at all.

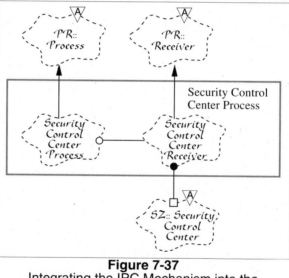

Figure 7-37
Integrating the IPC Mechanism into the
`SecurityControlCenter` Process

Figure 7-38 shows how the category structure is affected. This is very similar to the changes we made for the **ZoneAccess** process.

Reflection

They should all go so well . . . I think it is interesting that the **SecurityControl-CenterProcess** category does not depend upon the **GUIControlCenter** category.

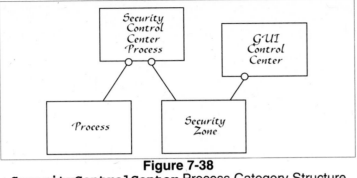

Figure 7-38
SecurityControlCenter Process Category Structure

This means that the GUI details have been kept completely separate from the multiprocessing details.

The **Keyboard** Process

The **Keyboard** process is very simple, as shown in Figure 7-39. It receives no messages, so it needs no receivers. This also means that we do not require a derivative of the class **Process**.

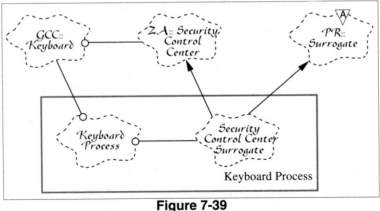

Figure 7-39
Keyboard Process Static Model

Figure 7-40 shows the category structure. Although the reasons for the dependencies are different, the structure of the dependencies is the same as for the other processes. It is interesting, in this case, that the **KeyboardProcess** category depends upon the **GUIControlCenter** category, because the keyboard itself is an artifact of the **GUI-**

ControlCenterCategory. The abstract **SecurityControlCenter** is ignorant of keyboards.

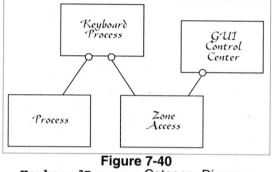

Figure 7-40
KeyboardProcess Category Diagram

The **OperatorTerminal** Process

The **OperatorTerminal** process is nearly identical to the **Keyboard** process (see Figure 7-41).

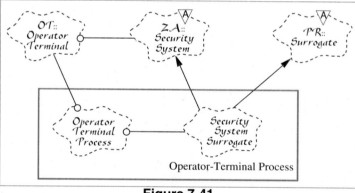

Figure 7-41
Static Structure of **OperatorTerminal** Process

A Slight Problem

There is something just a little bit flaky about this. Doesn't the **OperatorTerminal** process receive any messages? Aren't reports printed on it? Can't operators query the status of the system from the terminal? It seems likely that this would be the case, but our requirements do not seem to mention it. Moreover, our high-level design does not provide for it, and our process design specifically excludes it. According to the model above, and the process model derived in the previous sections, messages simply cannot be sent to the **OperatorTerminal** process. Perhaps a little re-analysis is in order.

This brings to mind a similar question. Can't the screens and keyboards in the security control centers be used as operator terminals? In our current model, the screen and keyboard in the security control center can only be used for resolving security alarms and violations. This seems wasteful. It requires that, even in smaller systems, we will always need at least two terminals: one for security control and one for evacuations and lockdowns.

It seems reasonable to assume that all the terminals connected to the system should be able to perform all the functions of the system. Certain functions can be restricted from certain users by using passwords or configuration data that denies certain functions to certain terminals.

For example, what if the security chief happens to find himself in the control room for Zone 7 when an emergency breaks out. We do not want to make him run back to the main control room where the operator terminal is in order to issue evacuation orders! He should be able to sign himself onto the terminal in that control room, and issue the evacuation orders from there.

Also, any terminal should be able request a report. For example, it should be possible for appropriately authorized users to request the list of outstanding alarms and violations for any particular zone, regardless of the terminal being used.

A moment's reflection about this reveals several problems with the current model. For example, if we want a report of the outstanding alarms and violations for Zone 6, who do we ask? The **Zone** 6 object does not keep them; it defers them to the **Security-ControlCenter** that is responsible for **Zone** 6. We could ask the **Security-ControlCenter** object, but how do we find it? Do we ask the **Zone**? That's kind of awkward. Worse, the **SecurityControlCenter** may serve many different **Zone** objects. Are we going to ask the **Zone** for the proper **SecurityControlCenter**, and then ask the **SecurityControlCenter** for the outstanding alarms and violations for just one particular **Zone**? (see Figure 7-42).

There is more ugliness to come. Report requests usually originate from a keyboard controlled by a **Keyboard** process. To query the **Zone** object, this process must send a message to the **SecuritySystemProcess**. Then, in order to query the appropriate **SecurityControlCenter** object, it must send a message to the appropriate **SecurityControlCenter** process (see Figures 7-43 and 7-44).

Oh what a tangled web we weave . . . .. Clearly, there is a problem with our model. How do we rearrange the model so that it can accept commands, alarm resolutions, and requests for reports from any terminal in the system? Actually, this begs a larger question. Why is it just terminals that we are worrying about? What if some larger management system wants to get reports from the security system. What if it wants to receive notification of alarms and resolve them, too? By generalizing the concept of a terminal, we have opened the can of worms named *interoperability*.

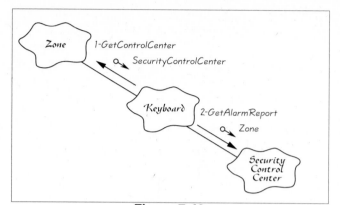

Figure 7-42
Awkward Query of Report by **Keyboard** Process

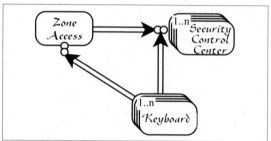

Figure 7-43
Additional Process Relationships Needed
for Keyboard Queries

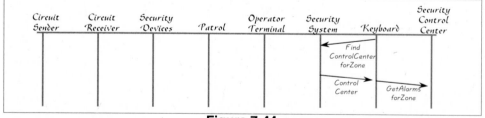

Figure 7-44
Very awkward Message-Sequence Chart, Showing Circuitous Message Flow

Reanalysis

Let's restate the problem. Our system includes clients that will want to exert control over the system's operation, as follows:

1. Asserting and canceling lockdown and evacuation

2. Resolving particular alarms and violations

3. Requesting immediate notification of alarms and violations for certain zones

4. Requesting alarm and violation summary reports by zone

These clients may be associated with terminals attached to the system, or with higher-level management systems in some kind of interoperability network.

We would like to isolate these client objects from the rest of our system. We don't want them to know too much about our internal makeup, because we want the freedom to change our internal makeup without forcing the clients to change. Thus, we want the clients to have a single point of contact. The message interactions that the client must participate in are shown in Figures 7-45 through 7-49.

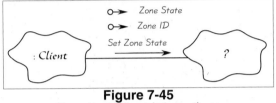

Figure 7-45
Required Client Interactions

Figure 7-45 is reminiscent of Figure 7-33, which showed an **OperatorTerminal** object sending the same message to the **SecuritySystem** object. This seems to support the idea that the single point of contact for the client object is the **SecuritySystem** object. However, let's reserve our judgment on that issue until later.

Next comes a trickier problem. How do clients resolve alarms and violations? More to the point, how do they identify which alarm or violation they are resolving? We solved this originally by passing a **ScreenItemID** in the **ResolveMessage** to the **SecurityControlCenter** object (see Figure 5-84). However, this assumed that each **SecurityControlCenter** had its own screen with which the **ScreenItemID** was associated. Now it seems that we must create a unique identifier for every alarm and violation in the system. The client will need to know this identifier if it is to resolve an alarm or violation; thus, it will have to be included in the alarm reports and immediate notifications (see Figure 7-46).

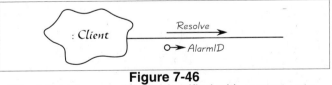

Figure 7-46
Client Resolves an Alarm Identified with an **AlarmID**.

A client can request immediate notification of the occurrence of an alarm or violation within a particular zone. From the client's point of view, this looks something like Figure 7-47.

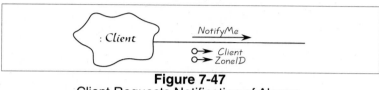

Figure 7-47
Client Requests Notification of Alarms.

The **Client** indicates that it wants to be notified of any alarm or violation that occurs in the specified **Zone**. The **ZoneID** is some unique code that identifies particular **Zone** objects. This implies that there must be a dictionary of **ZoneID** and **Zone** objects. Notice that the client must pass itself along with the **NotifyMe** message. Presumably, the recipient object will place the client in a list of clients to notify when alarms or violations are encountered. The inverse operation must also be supported, as shown in Figure 7-48.

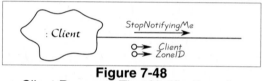

Figure 7-48
Client Requests That Notifications for
a Particular Zone Stop Being Sent.

This operation will remove the client from the list of clients to be notified of violations and alarms on the specified **Zone**.

The final requirement to deal with is the request for the currently unresolved violations and alarms for particular zones. To the client, this might look something like Figure 7-49.

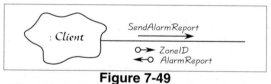

Figure 7-49
Client Requests that Alarm Report Be Sent.

What is an **AlarmReport**? Clearly, it is a list of the **SecurityMessage** objects that were received by a particular **Zone** (see Figure 7-50).

Remember that **SecurityMessage** is an abstract base class from which are derived all the possible alarms, violations, and events (see Figure 6-3a).

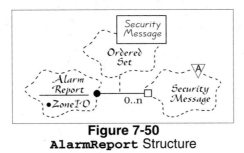

Figure 7-50
AlarmReport Structure

Figure 7-50 shows that an alarm report contains both a **ZoneID** and an **Ordered-Set** of **SecurityMessage** objects. The **OrderedSet** preserves the chronological order of the **SecurityMessage** objects.

Reconciling the Models

In our old model, the **SecurityControlCenter** objects remembered the security violations and alarms associated with the zones that they served. This is no longer acceptable. Now, **SecurityControlCenter** objects do not necessarily serve a particular set of zones. They have become one form of the general **Client** class we have been talking about. Moreover, we can eliminate the concept of **OperatorTerminal** as a separate entity, and merge its functionality with the **SecurityControlCenter**. Also, we can write other variations on **Client** to support networked access from other management systems.[8]

In the new way of doing things, **SecurityControlCenter** objects will be **Clients** that send **NotifyMe** messages, and receive notification of alarms and violations. They will also be responsible for resolving alarms and violations, and will request alarm reports.

Which objects or processes should **SecurityControlCenter** interact with in order to achieve these ends? The **SecuritySystem** process seems the most likely candidate. This process already knows which zones are locked down or being evacuated. It seems simple to extend it so that it also knows which zones have unresolved security violations and alarms, and which clients want to be notified when new alarms or violations occur. This implies the modification to the process diagram shown in Figure 7-51.

Notice that the **ZoneAccess** process has been renamed **SecuritySystem**. I did this because the new features of the **SecuritySystem** class make this process much more than an implementation of an access policy. We have maintained the original separation between the input and output sides of the **SecurityControlCenter**, but the input side has been renamed the **SecurityControlKeyboard** to represent its new

---

8. For example, we could create an SNMP agent, or even a CMIS agent that allowed remote access and management of the building security system. (If you aren't familiar with these terms, suffice it to say that they are protocols that allow remote management of many different kinds of systems.)

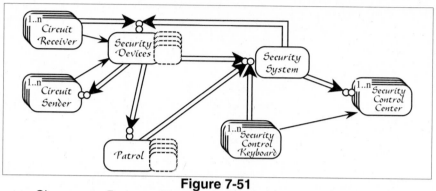

Figure 7-51
Changes to Process Diagram in Support of Client Mechanism

responsibilities. We have also obliterated the **OperatorTerminal** process; it will be up to the **SecurityControlCenter** and other similar clients to support its functions.

We seem to need three new entry points into the **SecuritySystem** process: (1) a **Registrar** object, which manages the **NotifyMe** and **StopNotifyingMe** messages; (2) a **ResolutionManager**, which knows how to find unresolved security events, and resolve them; and (3) some way to ask for reports. We could simply ask each **Zone** to collect all its outstanding **SecurityMessage** objects and gather them into an **AlarmReport**, but this lacks flexibility. We will probably want different ways to query the **SecurityMessage** database than simply by zone.

One solution is to create a **SecurityMessageManager**, which maintains the list of all the outstanding **SecurityMessage** objects. When a **Zone** object receives a **SecurityMessage**, it passes it along to the **SecurityMessageManager** to be stored. This structure allows one object to be responsible for all the **SecurityMessage** objects. It can also take the place of the **Registrar** and the **ResolutionManager** mentioned in the previous paragraph.

Since **Zone** objects simply pass the **SecurityMessage** objects through to the **SecurityMessageManager**, perhaps they should be bypassed altogether. Perhaps the objects that detect security alarms and violations should report them directly to the **SecurityMessageManager** instead of to their **Zone**. This might make sense from an efficiency standpoint, but there is something appropriate about giving the **Zone** a glimpse of the **SecurityMessage** before putting it in the general database. Varieties of **Zone** objects may want to massage or completely intercept certain varieties of **SecurityMessage** objects.

Thus, our structure for the **SecurityItemManager** is as shown in Figure 7-52.

This shows that the **SecurityMessageManager** maintains a **Bag** of **SecurityMessage** objects. A **Bag** is simply an unordered list that allows duplicates to be present. Since duplicate **SecurityItem** objects are a distinct possibility, the **Bag** is probably the most appropriate data structure. A **Queue** might also be appropriate, since it

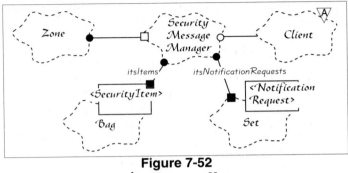

Figure 7-52
SecurityMessageManager

would store the **SecurityItem** objects in chronological order, as well as allowing duplicates, but I'll stick with the **Bag** for the moment.

The **SecurityMessageManager** also maintains a **Set** of objects called **NotificationRequest**s. These objects encapsulate the notion that a client can request notification of certain kinds of **SecurityMessage** objects, as they arrive. The idea is that there may be many different notification criteria. Thus, we might derive **ZoneNotificationRequest** from **NotificationRequest**, which would represent the request that all **SecurityMessages** from a particular zone be sent in a notification. Presumably, **NotificationRequest** has a pure interface, which allows a **SecurityMessage** to be passed in, and which returns a boolean result specifying whether or not the **SecurityMessage** satisfies the notification criteria. Figure 7-53 shows the dynamic model for the arrival and subsequent dispatch of a **Security-Message**. Completing the changes to the model is left as Exercises 2–5 at the end of the chapter.

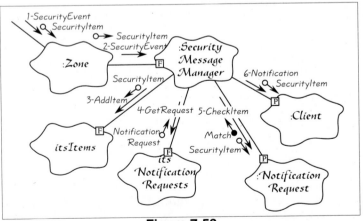

Figure 7-53
SecurityMessage Satisfies a **NotificationRequest**

Reflection

Quite a party—and all because of a slight problem that was nagging me at the beginning of this section of the **OperatorTerminal** process. One wayward thought, deep in the bowels of design, caused a major restructuring of the analysis of the project. This is typical of nearly all analysis and design efforts. The successful design and analysis of software is always punctuated with revolutions of thought and major upheavals of design strategy. This cannot, and should not, be avoided; these very upheavals cause the greatest improvements in our designs. Development environments that are not flexible enough to accept the inherent instability of the design process must consign themselves to mediocrity and failure.

The **Patrol** Process

The design of the **Patrol** process should be relatively straightforward. (Of course, I have said that before.) A glance at the **Patrol** class category diagram (Figure 6-24), and the associated object diagrams (Figures 5-44 ff) and message-sequence charts, shows that the **Checkpoint** object is the only object that receives IPC messages. According to our message-sequence charts, the messages received by **Checkpoint** are sent by the **CircuitReceiver** process, and represent "card swipes" by security guards when they arrive at a security checkpoint. Also, only one object, the **Zone** object, receives communication from the **Patrol** process. Thus, only the **Zone** surrogate must be modeled. Figure 7-54 shows the static model for the **PatrolProcess** category, and Figure 7–55 shows the category structure.

This pattern should look familiar by now. The **Checkpoint** class was abstracted, and the appropriate receivers and surrogates were created. Note again that the **Patrol** category is completely unaffected by the **PatrolProcess** category. Neither depends upon the other in any way.

The **SecurityDevices** Process

The **SecurityDevices** process contains all the device objects, and manages them independently. Each device object is a thread of control, and the thread controller is the **PacketDecoder - Receiver** complex used within the surrogation mechanism (see Figure 4-20).

Of all the processes so far, this one has the most receivers. It contains **Detector** objects, **Door** objects, **SecurityCardReader** objects, **Sensor** objects, and **ZoneAnnunciator** objects, all of which must receive IPC messages. It also requires surrogates for **Zone** objects, **Checkpoint** objects, and the **ZoneAccess-Controller** object.

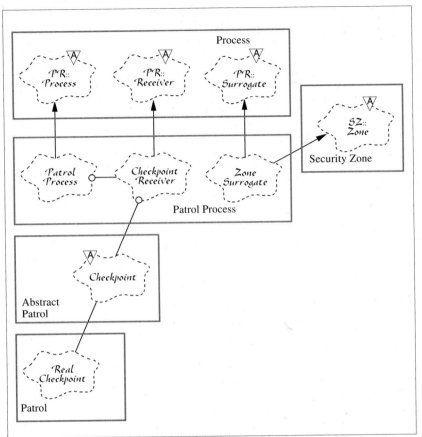

Figure 7-54
Patrol Process Static Model

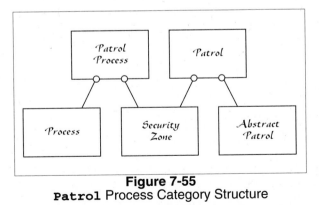

Figure 7-55
Patrol Process Category Structure

Figures 7-56, 7-57, and 7-58 show the static model that represents this process.

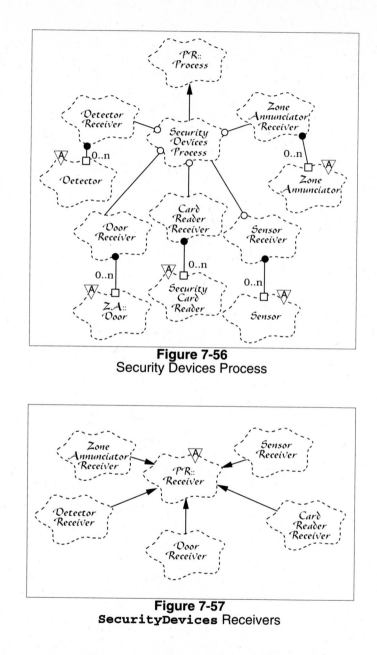

Figure 7-56
Security Devices Process

Figure 7-57
SecurityDevices Receivers

There are no surprises here. We have seen this same pattern of change in nearly every process so far. Figure 7-59 shows the corresponding category diagram.

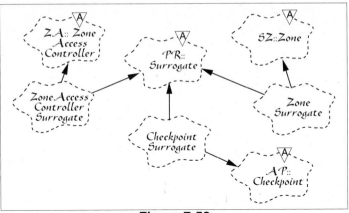

Figure 7-58
SecurityDevices Surrogates

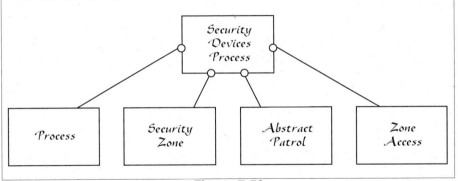

Figure 7-59
SecurityDevices Process Category Diagram

The **CircuitReceiver** Process

The **CircuitReceiver** process represents the afferent interface to the hardware. Through this process the hardware of the security system can influence the software system. Stimuli from the hardware are accepted by this process and translated into messages that are sent to the appropriate objects in the system.

How are the individual hardware devices identified? Probably by some kind of hardware address. It is not important at this time to know the format of the hardware address; it is enough to know that it exists. One of the primary functions of the **Circuit-Receiver** process is to translate the hardware address into the identity of an object that can handle reported stimuli.

Consider a particular stimulus: the swiping of a security card. When the card is swiped, the hardware will report the event. The **CircuitReceiver** process will accept that report and translate it into a message to be sent to the appropriate **Security-CardReader** object in the **SecurityDevices** process. In order to determine the identity of the appropriate **SecurityCardReader**, it must be able to look up the hardware address of the reporting card reader and find the identity of the corresponding **SecurityCardReader** object. Thus, we begin with a class structure that looks something like Figure 7-60.

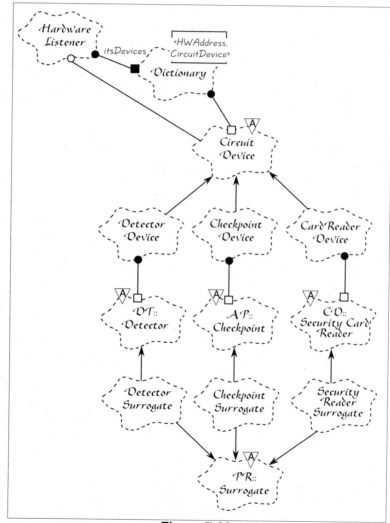

Figure 7-60
CircuitReceiver Process Static Model

The class **HardwareListener** is the lowest-level interface to the hardware. It "listens" to the security devices on the circuit to which this process is dedicated. If a stimulus is detected, the **HardwareListener** determines the hardware address of the device that sent the stimulus, looks that address up in the dictionary, and then forwards the stimulus on to the resulting **CircuitDevice**.

The class **CircuitDevice** provides a common interface for grouping the various device surrogates. Each derivative of **CircuitDevice** is responsible for decoding the information from the hardware and formatting it into an appropriate message to send through the surrogate. We might have accomplished this by letting the surrogate inherit from **CircuitDevice** rather than having **CircuitDevice** contain the surrogate. I felt that containment was a more proper model, since the surrogate should not need to know anything about the format of the information provided by the hardware. A typical scenario for this design is shown in Figure 7-61.

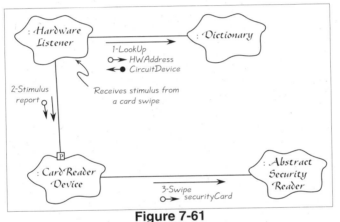

Figure 7-61
Scenario for **CircuitReceiver** Process

Note that the **CircuitDevice** that was looked up in the **Dictionary** was an instance of a **CardReaderDevice**. This object interprets the **Stimulus** message that contains the hardware-specific **report** data. All **CircuitDevice** subclasses must be able to respond to the **Stimulus** message, and be able to interpret the appropriate **report** data. It is vital that the **Dictionary** relate the hardware addresses with the appropriate subclasses of **CircuitDevice**, so that the **report** data will always be interpreted correctly. Again, the rest of the dynamic scenarios are left as an exercise.

The **CircuitSender** Process

By now it should be clear how to design the **CircuitSender** process. This process will need a thread controller in the form of a **PacketDecoder** - **Receiver** complex. Each device that needs to be controlled will require a subclass of **Receiver** that contains the real target class. The target class will then have to manipulate the hardware itself, or relegate that task to another (utility) class. The design of this process and all its dynamic behaviors is left as Exercise 7 at the end of the chapter.

Configuring the System

The system that we have designed so far depends upon a complex structure of dictionaries and pointers. For example, each of the **PacketDecoder** objects must have access to a dictionary that allows it to look up a name and get a reference to the appropriate receiver object. How does this dictionary get loaded? Each **Portal** object contains references to two **Zone** objects. How do these references get properly loaded, so that they point to the correct **Zone**s? Many other details of this nature must be addressed. This is the problem of *configuration*.

Configuration is a traditional problem in systems like this. The system is designed to work within the framework of a generalized data structure, but we must find some means for building that structure. This problem has several aspects that must be solved. First, how does the user communicate configuration decisions to the program? How are these decisions stored so that the system does not have to be reconfigured every time it reboots? How are these stored configurations read into the booting system and disseminated to the various extremities of the program structure?

Generally, the most effective way for the user to communicate configuration decisions is with some form of a graphic user interface, or a very intelligent forms package, or both. For our purposes, we could envision a GUI that allowed the user to draw a floor plan of the building, and then annotate it by outlining all the zones, naming all the appropriate doors and windows, and positioning all the card readers, checkpoints, break-in detectors, and fire and smoke detectors. The user would also have to draw each of the circuits connecting each device to a particular circuit receiver.

Although elegant, this solution is expensive to design and build. If the product is going to be very high-volume, or if the company is marketing it as a top-of-the-line system, the investment might be worth it. However, a forms package would probably come quite close to the effectiveness of a full-fledged GUI without being quite so expensive. Forms packages are usually much simpler to design and build than a GUI. The forms solution would pop up text forms that describe each element in the system—each zone, door, window, card reader, checkpoint, and so on. Each form would require that the element be named, and that the names of all associated elements be provided.

One acute problem that GUIs solve quite naturally, but with which forms systems must deal explicitly, is the problem of consistency. In a GUI, the data input by the user is usually self-consistent because it is being entered through a medium that naturally expresses the nature of the problem. For example, when a window is drawn on the floor plan, it is immediately obvious if that window separates two zones, and which two zones they are. With forms, however, the user may type in any name at all; thus, the form that describes a window might list two zones that are not related to the window in any way. With the forms package, therefore, some kind of intelligent consistency analysis must be performed. This can be quite expensive if the problem is complex enough.

Either of these techniques, the GUI or the forms package, will yield a description of the components of the security system and of their interconnections. The next problem is to find some way to store this information, so that it can be retrieved every time the system boots. Again, there are several solutions.

One interesting solution is to use an object-oriented database management system (OODBMS). An OODBMS allows the user to create objects and store them on disk. Other programs can then deal with those objects, just as though they were really in memory. The idea is that, at some level, the programmer does not need to know that the objects are on the disk. When objects stored in an OODBMS contain references to other objects, those references, from the programmer's point of view, are followed just as they would be if the object were stored in memory instead of on disk. Thus an object stored in an OODBMS is completely viable and maintains all its interconnections to other objects.

Our GUI or forms package could easily build the **Zone**, **Door**, **SecurityCard-Reader**, **Checkpoint**, and other objects and store them in an OODBMS. Then when the security system application runs, it will find its objects already built on the disk, and will be able to manipulate them directly.

While this may seem elegant, there are a few problems. First, our application requires a large amount of throughput. If we use an OODBMS to store the objects in the system, the throughput of that OODBMS must be a major consideration. Many OODBMSs have caching methods that allow the objects to remain in memory most of the time. Many such systems should be tried and careful experimentation and measurement performed. Also, at the time of this writing, OODBMS vendors have not come to a consensus regarding critical issues such as concurrency, locking, and transaction models. Careful scrutiny of the details of the OODBMS is therefore in order.

One of the benefits of using an OODBMS is that it eliminates the intermediate step that we are going to talk about now. If we cannot use an OODBMS, then we must use some other form of intermediate representation to store the configuration data. Most typically this is a *flat ASCII file*. This file would be written using a grammar that allowed the complete expression of the components of the security system and their interconnections. For example,

```
Window: W74, Zone[1]: Z5, Zone[2]: Z12;
BIDetector: BI22, Portals:(W74, W75, D21, D22, D23);
```

This trivial example shows two possible lines from such a grammar. The first line defines a window named **W74**, which separates zones **Z5** and **Z12** from each other. The second line describes the break-in detector named **BI22**. This detector protects five different portals whose names are listed in the parenthesis. Clearly we could extend this kind of grammar to describe the entire system.

One advantage of flat files is that we can write them with nothing more than a simple text editor. This allows us to configure the system without the benefit of a GUI or forms-based interface. It also allows us to modify existing configurations with nothing more than an ASCII terminal.

Upon boot, the file or files that describe the system must be read and parsed. The resulting information must then be disseminated, so that the corresponding components can be created and linked together. This final step, the step that builds and links the components together, will be a part of the system whether we use an OODBMS or not. If we use an OODBMS, then the GUI or forms package will invoke the building and linking of the components. If we use a flat ASCII file instead, then the boot-up procedure will invoke the building and linking of the components.

How are the components built and linked? This is an interesting problem indeed. Our system includes several processes. and each one must be made aware of the existence of components within the system. For some, we must build and link the components them-selves. For others, we need to build **surrogates**. For yet others, we need to build **receivers**. The names of all **receivers** must be placed in dictionaries that the **PacketDecoder** objects can access. The names of real objects must be loaded into all the **surrogates**. This is quite an undertaking.

Let's begin the design of this system by assuming that we are using a flat ASCII file. When the processes in our system boot, they each read this configuration file, and build their components accordingly. For example, the **SecuritySystem** process would build **Zone** objects for every zone described. It would also build the appropriate **ZoneRe-ceiver** objects and register them with the **PacketDecoder**. The process might look something like Figure 7-62.

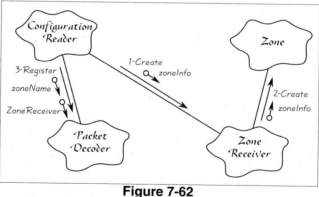

Figure 7-62
Dynamic Model of a Portion of Configuration

The **ConfigurationReader** is the object that reads the flat ASCII file and parses the information within it. It decides which objects need to be created for the current process and then creates them. Notice that the **ConfigurationReader** creates the **ZoneReceiver**, which in turn creates the **Zone**. This is a good paradigm. The **ZoneReceiver** that understands that the **Zone** is in a process separated from other objects by process boundaries. In general, the receiver processes should set up the process-dependent portions of the regular objects.

The **ConfigurationReader** class is probably an abstract class that encapsulates the ability to read and parse the flat ASCII file, but does not know what to do with the information once parsed. It should most likely have derivatives for each of the processes. Those derivatives would know what to do with the parsed data (see Figure 7-63).

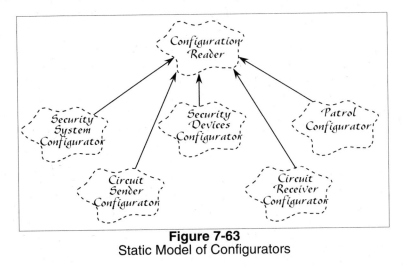

Figure 7-63
Static Model of Configurators

Many more details need to be dealt with in the subject of configuration, but the broad strokes have been made. I leave the development of the rest of the design as Exercise 8. You may find it quite interesting to finish the configuration model for just one process. You will probably be quite surprised at the complexity that remains to be addressed.

Summary

Details—that's what software design is all about. When we initially think about a program, we think about the required behaviors, not the horrible plethora of insidious details that will appear to haunt us. In our initial considerations of an application, we are often blind to those details. Thus, we may estimate the effort required based on the abstract view of required behaviors rather than the real-world view of the details necessary to support them.

In this chapter we have marched through a veritable army of such details, and after addressing the first phalanx or two, I began to delegate the solution of those details to exercises at the end of the chapter. Had I not done so, this chapter would have been many times larger. My intent has been to demonstrate the problems and solutions typical of design problems, but if I have simply communicated the enormity of the ranks of hidden details in any software project, then I have done half my job. Never underestimate the power of details to utterly ruin a design. A design that does not address the details will never see implementation.

Exercises

1   Change Figures 7-29 and 7-30 so that **ZoneAccessController** is the **Surrogate** rather than **ZoneAccessSCRInterface**.

2   Complete the dynamic model for the **SecurityMessageManager** (in Figure 7-53), including the following scenarios: Clients request notification, clients stop notification, clients request reports by zone, clients resolve an alarm or a violation, clients lock down a zone, clients evacuate a zone, and so on.

3   Try your hand at integrating the static model of the **SecurityMessage-Manager** (Figure 7-52) into the class diagram for the **SecuritySystem** process (Figure 7-34). Remember that it is the recipient of IPC messages, so it must be supported with a **Receiver** class. Also, remember that it must send messages to many different derivatives of the class **Client**, so there must be a dictionary in which **clientID** codes can be looked up to yield references to the appropriate surrogates.

4   Modify the descriptions of the IPC messages, and show how the new messages for the **SecurityMessageManager** flow by updating the message-sequence charts.

5   Refit the **SecurityControlCenter** process to the **Client** model. Remember that some class within this process must be derived from the class **Client**, so that it can register with the **SecuritySystem** process to receive immediate notification of alarm reports.

6   Complete the dynamic scenarios that were begun in Figure 7-61.

7   Complete the static, dynamic, and category models for the **CircuitSender** process.

8   Complete the design of the configuration system.

8

Epilogue

The art of programming is the art of organizing complexity"
—Edsger W. Dijkstra

We have come a long way. The first four chapters in this book discussed the various components of object-oriented design. The next three were devoted to the analysis, high-level logical design, physical design, and finally the low-level design of a building security system—a system whose requirements were specified on little more than one page. Moreover, those three chapters did not even come close to finishing the job. Chapter 5 completed the analysis and high-level design, and Chapter 6 pretty well covered the initial physical design. However, Chapter 7 only discussed part of the low-level logical and physical design, leaving much more as exercises.

What is wrong? Why does it take so much effort to convert one page of requirements into a computer system. If you think about it, the contrast is astounding! There is nothing particularly difficult about the requirements. They are pretty easy to understand. Why does it take so much energy and effort to analyze, design, and implement a system that can be described in so few words?

The answer is in ourselves. Each one of us has, encased within a protective vessel of sinew and bone, an instance of the most complex object known to man. These few pounds of material are made mostly of the common elements carbon, hydrogen, oxygen, nitrogen, and a few other trace elements. These elements, forged in the cores of stars and in the supreme violence of a supernova, are arranged with a complexity that far overshadows any other physical entity in the known universe. There are a trillion neurons in the human brain, and each neuron interacts with thousands or millions of others. The number of interconnections implied by those numbers is staggering, easily reaching quadrillions or even quintillions. The brain, which is defined by such numbers, cannot truly conceive of them.

How big is a quintillion: 1,000,000,000,000,000,000? It is roughly the number of grains of salt that could be put into a box 1 kilometer on a side. Think about that for a minute.

If the scale of the brain is impressive, think about the fact that those quintillion interconnections are organized in such a manner that *each one* serves a purpose. The raw processing power of this common organ is simply incredible. Consider the problem of recognizing speech. Computer scientists have been working on this problem for many decades now, and with only limited success. Yet our brains do it with amazing skill, as a secondary function that doesn't even begin to tax our processing powers. Consider the problem of recognizing faces, or of riding a bicycle through a town. These are problems that computers can barely even approach, yet they are child's play for the human brain.

It is the incredible power of this little organ to process data and to create abstraction that is at the root of our problem. Seemingly without effort, we can understand systems as complex as the building security example, with no more input than just a few descriptive words. That lack of apparent effort deceives us; our minds have abstracted the true complexity of the problem.

A system may be easy to understand in concept, but that does not mean it is not complex. As we have seen, systems that are easy to describe and understand can be very complex to analyze and design. The apparent simplicity fools us into thinking that the problem is simple. This leads us to underestimate the effort that will be required to analyze, design and implement the system.

When I first chose the building security system for the case study, I knew that I had four chapters to flesh out (I had been planning on a chapter that presented a skeleton implementation), and I knew, roughly, the structure of those chapters. My first thought was to describe a building management system, with security as only one component. The system would also have dealt with power management, elevator control, heating, and so on. I felt that this would be a worthy case study. During the initial analysis of this system, however, it became clear that the scope was far too broad, that it would not fit into the four chapters that I had planned. So I limited the scope to just the security portions of the project.

I felt that the building security system was just the right size. The requirements were easy to list, the functionality was respectable, but not overwhelming, and it looked like an interesting project to work with. I was, quite frankly, surprised and appalled when the analysis in Chapter 5 grew to be so plump. I had expected about half as many pages and diagrams. I was even more surprised when I had to skip over such large portions of the low-level design in Chapter 7. As always, I was amazed at the complexity that was uncovered as I examined the problem. This is the perversity of software. It is *always* more complex than you anticipate, even when you know this and compensate for it.

• • •

In this book, I have attempted to show how to use object-oriented design to manage the intrinsic complexity of software problems. We have explored the principles of OOD from its basics all the way through a reasonably complex case study. We have shown how to document software analysis and design decisions using the Booch notation, at every level of the process. We have shown how these decisions encompass not only the logical aspects of the design, but the physical nature of the development environment as well. We have shown how to document these decisions at the highest and lowest technical levels. And we have shown examples of how to implement these decisions in an object-oriented language such as C++.

I hope that the value of these techniques has somehow managed to come through. I hope that it is clear to you how you can apply these techniques to effectively analyze and design complex software systems, and to manage the complexity of the effort throughout the design and implementation process.

The problem of software complexity still looms before us. It is the biggest problem, the greatest challenge, that we face as software engineers. If we do not solve the problem, we will eventually (and probably soon), reach the limit of complexity. Beyond that limit are software systems that are too complex to write. Perhaps these are the systems that our civilization will desperately need in the decades to come. Already, in this country, experts have seriously recommended that the role of software be limited where public safety is a concern.[1] Such recommendations frighten me, because it is only through automation that our civilization can continue to grow and prosper. If we cannot conquer the problems of software complexity, then we may have reached the upper bounds of our civilization. If that is so, then what comes next?

I do not believe that we have reached such an upper bound, either in our civilization, or in the art of computer programming. Object-oriented design is just one advance in our battle against software complexity. To be sure, it is a very important advance. Its use will push back the limit of software complexity. And there will be other advances—advances in reliability, in efficiency, and in the management and expression of complexity.

Moreover, we have only begun to investigate the power of the object paradigm. New work in the area of *patterns* appears particularly promising. It may be that we can create catalogs of commonly used *patterns* and express the relationships between them so that we can handle complex design problems in a "cookbook" fashion.

The software industry is not even 50 years old. It is still in its infancy. I look forward to its centennial with anticipation. The years between now and then should prove to be very interesting.

---

1. "The Risks of Software", Scientific American, November, 1992.

Appendix A

C++ Coding Guidelines

"There always seems to be one or another Petty Bureaucrat on every project who insists that all is gone to hell in a hand basket unless every programmer dots every i and crosses every t the same way."

—Jim Adcock , 1992

This appendix presents the coding guidelines that I used in preparing the C++ code fragments in this book. The guidelines are simple and easy to remember. They do not place a great burden upon the programmer, and do not intrude on the programmer's use of the language (IMHO).

Introduction

Let's get one thing straight: Coding standards or guidelines will not make good programmers out of bad programmers. They have absolutely no effect at all on the correctness of the code that a programmer produces. *You cannot legislate good design.*

Having said that, why am I promoting a coding guideline by publishing this one? I do so because, even though it won't improve the correctness of the code produced, a decent guideline can facilitate the communications among the members of a development team.

Right. So, if communication is all we are after, our guideline should say nothing at all about the usage of language features. It should not restrict the use of **goto**s, nor define the maximum number of lines of code that are allowed within a function. It should not dictate that indenting levels must be kept to a maximum of four, nor restrict the depth or breadth of an inheritance hierarchy. It *should* talk about how to name variables and functions, and how to structure modules, classes, and functions. To that end, I present the following guidelines.

The Guidelines

I do not justify any of these guidelines, since there is little to justify. For the most part they represent arbitrary decisions that do not bear scrutiny.

Names

I never use underscores to separate words in names.[1] Instead I use the Smalltalk convention of capitalizing the first letter of every word in a name. I begin auto variables, enum tags, function arguments and member variables with a lowercase letter. I start functions and types with uppercase letters. I prefix a capital **G** to all global variables, and a capital **L** to all static variables. I prefix **its** to most member variables, **their** to most static member variables, and **the** to most arguments. I say *most* because this convention is not always useful. Sometimes an argument is better left simply as a single letter or word, such as **s** for strings or **i** for integers. At other times, however, it is far better to use a more descriptive name like **theColor** or **itsSpeed**.

```
class MyClass
{
  public:
    void MyMemberFunction(int theArgument);

  private:
    int itsMemberVariable;
    static int theirStaticMember;
};

enum Color {red, blue, green};

void MyClass::MyMemberFunction(int theArgument)
{
    int anArgument;
    static int LmyStaticVariable;
    extern int GmyGlobalVariable;
}
```

Header File Structure

Header files should begin and end with multiple-inclusion protection, as follows:

```
#ifndef symbol
#define symbol
<the rest of the module>
#endif
```

---

1. This has proven to be unfortunate, since the C++ Standards committee has (apparently) adopted the exact opposite style. Names of classes and keywords in the standard are almost always all lowercase with underscores separating words, e.g., **dynamic_cast** or **type_info** or **set_unexpected**.

This protects the module from multiple inclusion and circular references—problems that are extremely difficult to debug. The *symbol* used in the conditional compilation statement should be based on the name of the module. For example, if the module name is **myModule.h**, then the symbol name should be something like **MY_MODULE_H.** I generally prefix this symbol with the category name, thus: **MYCATEGORY_MYMODULE_H**.

Following the multiple-inclusion protection should be the **#include** statements that describe the interface dependencies of this module. An interface dependency is a dependency upon the interface of the included class. Typically such a dependency only occurs for base classes, classes that are contained by value, or classes whose member functions are called within inline functions.

Next come forward declarations of the classes involved in **uses** relationships and **contains** relationships. The value of preferring forward declarations to **#include** should not be underestimated. Woe to the beginning C++ programmer who heedlessly uses **#include** for every dependency. He will wind up changing them all eventually.

Next comes the class specification.

Class Declaration Structure

I like to arrange classes according to the *scissors rule*, which says that all **public** declarations come first, then all **protected** declarations, followed by all **private** declarations, and finally all **friend** declarations. I like to indent the **public:, protected:, private**, and **friend** specifiers by two spaces. I like to indent all the declarations four spaces. Thus:

```
class MyClass
{
  public:
    void PublicFunction();

  protected:
    int itsProtectedFunction();

  private:
    char* itsPrivateVariable;

  friend MyFriendClass;
};
```

Virtual Destructors

Unless it is absolutely obvious that a class *should not* have a virtual destructor, I will always supply one. Virtual destructors provide three pieces of information that the run-time system needs to properly destroy an object. Without this information, stacks and heaps tend to become silently corrupted, and program behavior becomes undefined.[2] The

---

2. Which means that it works —most of the time.

first piece of information is the identity of the appropriate destructor. The second is the actual size of the object, and the third is the address of the block of storage that was returned by **operator new** when the object was created.

If a virtual destructor is not declared in a class, then when a derivative of that object is destroyed, it may not call the correct destructor, it may not pass the correct size of the object to **operator delete(void*, size_t)**, and it may not pass the same address to **operator delete** that was returned by **operator new**. In any of these situations, the behavior of the program becomes undefined.

One Class Definition per Module

I generally adhere to the rule of having one class definition per module. Each class gets its own header file, and few if any header files define more than one class. I sometimes make exceptions if two classes are very tightly coupled, but this is rare. This rule allows me to include the classes I want, without automatically including a bunch of other classes just because they happen to be in the same module.

Comments in the Header File

I prefer to keep my comments minimal, especially within the definition of a class. I will usually provide a paragraph or two that describes the class at the top of the header file, before the class definition begins. Any particularly tricky member functions or usage paradigms will be described within these paragraphs.

Most member functions describe themselves by their names and argument types. If a particular member function requires more documentation, I will provide a line or two after the declaration of the member function. However, I consider the visibility of the structure of the class to be more important than individual comments for each member function. In my opinion, copious comments within a class clutter it and hide the structures that need to be seen.

Implementation Module Structure

Generally, I will place the definitions of all the member functions for one class within a single implementation module, and that module will not contain definitions for the member functions of any other class. Sometimes, if two classes are very tightly coupled, I will include the definitions of their member functions in the same module. On the other hand, sometimes there are so many member functions that a module becomes too big, so I split the implementation of the class into two or more modules. Both of these cases are rare.

Function Structure

In functions, I like my braces to be on their own lines and at the same indent level as the controlling statement. For example:

```
if (myCondition)
{
    // statements inside the if
}
```

This is hardly a critical rule, and I often violate it when the statements are simple enough. I do not consider brace placement to be particularly important.

Comments in the Implementation Module

Most member functions do not require any documentation at all, but some use algorithms that are tricky and must be explained. I will preface the definitions of such functions with a paragraph or two of comments that describe the algorithm used.

I may also put a short paragraph before a particularly difficult block within a function. I try to keep the comments within functions short, however, because they tend to hide the structure of the function.

Summary

That's all. Nothing spectacular—just a simple set of guidelines that are easy to follow and not very controversial. Although these guidelines are my favorites, they do not really stand on much substance. While they are useful as a communications aid, any other similar set of guidelines would do just as well. The important thing for a development team to do is to choose a set of guidelines and stick with them. It does not really matter much whose guidelines they are.

There are other rules of programming that I adhere to. They have to do with the use of copy constructors, assignment operators, **goto**s, **break**s, **continue**s, **return**s, and so on. I prefer that all my classes have copy constructors and assignment operators, so that I can properly copy them. I almost never use **goto**s. I avoid **break** and **continue**. I usually place one, and only one, **return** within each function, and so on. While these rules are important to me, and *do* have a positive effect upon the quality of *my* code, they are better left as the subject of another discussion. They are *not* guidelines that facilitate communications among team members; they are practices of a particular programming style. While it may be important in some organizations to legislate certain aspects of programming style, I don't think it is wise to mix such legislation with a document whose goal is to facilitate communication.

Appendix B

Multiprocessing: Concepts and Notation

The puppeteer stopped next to Louis and folded his legs under him.
One head fixed on Louis, the other head moved nervously,
circling, covering all angles of vision.

—Larry Niven, from *Ringworld*

The use of multiple processes in computer applications is an important technique that takes many forms. Most of us are familiar with the benefits (and the disadvantages) of multiuser operating systems. Each user creates one or more processes that run separate applications, either consecutively or concurrently. Engineers designing embedded systems often employ a different technique, in which several processes work together to perform a single job. Processes may run in separate data spaces, effectively isolated from each other. They may also execute together in the same data space, sharing their static and global variables.

This appendix presents the general concepts of multiprocessing, along with a convenient graphical notation for representing the multiprocessing structure of an application. There is a great deal of variety in multiprocessing models. Each operating system is different. This appendix does not try to describe them all; instead, it describes the most prevalent general concepts.

Introduction

The first few sections of this appendix provide a basic introduction to the subject of multiprocessing. We will discuss the definition of a process, how computers and operating systems handle multiple processes, and the various mechanisms used to switch control between processes. We also examine the different data models and the methods supporting communication between processes.

Multiprocessing is a complex subject. An in-depth study would require more than is covered here. This appendix is not an attempt to explain all the nuances of designing applications with multiple processes; it merely attempts to introduce the subject, and provide a basis of vocabulary and understanding.

I have used the notational conventions shown here for years. They have proven quite capable of representing both the statics and dynamics of applications with multiple processes.

What Is a Process?

The term *process* has many synonyms in the software industry. Among the more common are *task*, *job,* and *thread*. We will use these terms interchangeably throughout this appendix.

A process consists of three essential components: a program, a private data area, and a private thread of execution. The program component is a set of functions that operate together to perform a particular task. The private data area contains the variables that the program manipulates. The execution thread is the property of the operating system. It represents the association between the program and a specific private data area. It also represents an execution schedule.

Operating systems manage many threads of execution at the same time by sharing the computer among them. The operating system keeps a list of all the threads that are ready to run, and gives each thread its chance to execute. This sharing happens so fast that many processes may appear to be executing simultaneously. However, the maximum number of threads that can really be executing simultaneously is equal to the number of processors available to the operating system. Typically this number is one. With just one processor, only one thread can be executing at any given time.

In order to share the processor(s) among all the competing threads, the operating system determines which thread should run by checking the priority and status associated with each one. Higher-priority threads are allowed to execute before lower-priority threads. When a thread reaches a point where it must wait for something external to itself, an I/O operation for example, it must inform the operating system that it must wait, and exactly what it is waiting for. The operating system puts the thread on hold and allows other threads to execute. When the specified event occurs, the operating system reschedules the waiting thread for execution.

Context Switching

When the operating system must stop one thread and start another, it performs an operation known as a *context switch*, which is broken into two steps. In the first step, the complete context of the currently running thread is saved in the thread's private data area. This includes copies of all the machine registers, the stack, and a pointer to the next statement to be executed. The second step is to restore this same information from the private data area of the thread that is to start running. Once the context of this process is stored into the proper machine registers, the operating system allows that thread to execute.

The context of a process may be switched for one of two reasons. Either it gives up the processor voluntarily, or it is forced out by a higher-priority process. A process will give up the processor if it must wait for an external event. In that case, lower-priority processes are allowed to run until the event occurs. A process is forced out when a higher-priority process demands the processor.

Preemption

When a context switch is necessary, how does the operating system gain control from the executing thread? There are two primary mechanisms: preemption and cooperation. Preemption is based on the ability of the computer hardware to interrupt the normal execution of the computer when an external event occurs. Such an event might be the reception of a character from a modem, the completion of a disk operation, or even just the tick of an electronic clock. These interruptions return control of the computer to the operating system, which then saves the state of the previously running thread. The operating system attempts to discover if the interrupt was caused by an event that is awaited by one of the pending threads. If so, it restores the state of that thread and allows it to execute. This technique is called *preemption*, because it forcibly preempts the currently executing thread.

Another strategy, common in simple embedded systems, is based on cooperation. Instead of relying on the computer hardware to interrupt the running process, each running thread voluntarily relinquishes control of the computer as often as possible. This is usually done by calling a special operating-system service. When the operating system gains control in this manner, it searches its list of threads for the highest-priority process that isn't waiting for an event. If that process is not the one that just relinquished control, a context switch is performed; otherwise, control is simply handed back to the cooperating process.

There are advantages and disadvantages to both the preemptive and cooperative models. The preemptive model relieves the programmer from having to worry about sharing the processor, but it increases the likelihood of concurrent update problems. The cooperative model guarantees the programmer that he will not lose control of the processor unless he explicitly relinquishes it, but it increases the likelihood of timing-related problems. We will discuss these problems and their solutions later in this appendix.

Priority

The priority of a process thread determines whether it should have precedence over another process thread. When two or more processes are ready to run, the highest-priority process will gain the processor. High-priority tasks typically require very little computer time to run, but cannot tolerate long delays in processing their events. Low-priority tasks typically take lots of computer time, but can tolerate quick interruptions by higher-priority tasks.

As an example, let's consider a building management system. Assume that this system is responsible for monitoring the temperature in each room. If a room is too cold, the system opens a louver in the heating duct, allowing hot air into the room. If the room is too hot, the system closes that louver. The system is also responsible for responding to fire and burglar alarms. When an alarm goes off, the system flashes an alert on the security-management screen, rings a bell, and prints a report.

Now, let's assume that this system is installed in a building with several thousand rooms. The process that monitors the temperature in all the rooms takes a long time to execute, but it isn't in much of a hurry because the temperature in a room doesn't change very quickly. On the other hand, the system must respond very quickly to an alarm.

In this example, it is obvious that the alarm process should have a higher priority than the temperature monitoring process. Alarms rarely occur, so temperature monitoring will not normally be interrupted. If an alarm does occur, temperature monitoring will be suspended for a short time while the alarm is being processed.

Priority decisions are not always as clear-cut as this. We cannot always set the priority of a process simply on the basis of its importance or its need for quick response. For example, consider a computer bulletin-board system that has four 2400 bps modems and one 9600 bps modem. To prevent the computer from being overburdened, the designers have restricted the total throughput of the system to 14,400 bps. This is just enough for the 9600 bps port and two 2400 bps ports. Thus, if all five modems are connected, the users may notice communications delays. The system will refuse to transmit to all the users at the same time.

Now, how do we assign priorities to the communications processes of this system? If we want to maximize throughput, then perhaps we should give the 9600 bps process a higher priority than the others. This will guarantee that this process will always be able to transmit. Its higher priority will force the 2400 bps processes out of the way. However, this also means that very heavy traffic over the 9600 bps port will reduce all four 2400 modems to 50% efficiency, since they will have to vie for the 4800 bps throughput that remains to them. Is this fair to those users? They are already running at a slow rate; why should they be made to suffer for the benefit of the user who has a high-speed connection.

If we give priority to the 2400 bps modems, they can effectively shut the 9600 bps process down. If all four 2400 bps modems are working very hard, there will not be enough bandwidth remaining for the 9600 bps process. The high-speed user will be paying expensive connect charges while sitting at a dead terminal. This solution is also less than optimal.

What if all the priorities in the system are the same? Then, whenever three or four 2400 bps modems are running, any attempt to run the 9600 bps modem would raise the total throughput above 14,400. Thus, the 9600 bps modem will be locked out, and 4800 bps worth of bandwith will be wasted.

So, how do we maximize throughput and still treat all the users fairly? One possible solution would be to dynamically alter the priorities of the processes. Every time a process is given access to its port, we drop its priority by n priority units. Every 100ms or so we increment its priority by 1 unit. This juggles the priorities in a way that penalizes users for heavy traffic and rewards them for light traffic. The user that has been waiting the longest has priority. This is certainly fair, but if all ports are blasting away as fast as they can, this scheme gives us no better throughput than making all the priorities equal.

However, we can tip the scales in favor of the 9600 port by giving it a slightly higher reward for waiting. That is, we can raise its priority every 90ms instead of every 100ms, or decrease its priority by $n-1$ every time it is given access. Thus, the 9600 bps port will get a larger share of the processor than its 2400 bps brothers, but it will be unable to lock them out. Although this may not be entirely fair, it is an effective way to trade fairness off against throughput.

There are other perversities having to do with priorities. In later sections of this appendix we will see that priorities in nonpreemptive environments can have the opposite of the desired effect. We will also show that priorities and preemption must sometimes be disabled to avoid the problems of concurrent update.

Process Queues

Most operating systems manage their processes by moving them between three primary states as shown in Figure B-1. Processes that are waiting for some external event are placed in the *waiting* state. Processes that are ready to run and just waiting their turn to execute are placed in the *ready* state. The process or processes that are currently executing are said to be in the *running* state. These states are often represented by queues or lists within the operating system. Many processes may be queued up in the *ready* state, waiting for the processor. Their order in the queue is often dictated by their priority. Quite a few processes may also be sitting in one or more *wait* queues. There is usually no queue or list that represents the *running* state. The number of processes that can have that state at any time is no greater than the number of processors available to the operating system.

This explanation is very simplistic. Although most operating systems use more complex mechanisms, they are usually based on these simple principles.

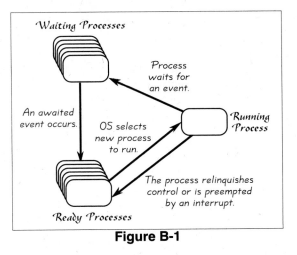

Figure B-1

What Is a Data Segment?

Data segment is a term that refers to the private area in memory where a program's variables are stored. Typically these variables are grouped together into a contiguous area. The address of the first byte of that area is considered the address of the data segment. Programs refer to their variables in terms of relative offsets from the beginning of the data segment. Thus, the data segment may be anywhere in memory. The program doesn't care where the data segment is, so long as it knows its address.

Data segments can also have a size. Some computers and operating systems can detect if a program attempts to access memory that is *outside* its data segment. This facility is usually called *memory protection*. Memory can be protected against modification, or against access of any kind. A violation of memory protection usually causes the violating process to be aborted.

What Is a Message?

In this appendix, the term *message* will refer to a stream of data that passes between two processes. Messages are sometimes referred to as *packets*. There are many different forms of messages, and many different ways to send them between processes. In general, however, a message is a discrete set of data representing a single semantic unit in the interactions between two processes.

The content of messages varies greatly. A message is often a command, a sort of function call, that contains a command code and any associated data. For example, a print-spooler process might be sent a message that contains the **print** command and the name of the file to be printed, or it might be sent a **delete** command, which specifies the name of the print job to delete from the spool queue.

Messages can also contain pure data, with no explicit command. It is up to the receiving process to decide what to do with such messages. For example, a monitor process may send an *alarm* message to an alarm-management process. No command is implied. It is up to the alarm-management process to decide what to do with the alarm. If the alarm is for a noncritical element, it may decide to ignore it, or just log it. If the alarm is for a critical subsystem, it may decide to turn that subsystem off, or notify a human via an emergency signal.

Multiprocessing Models

The operating system may manage its processes in several different ways. Processes can live in separate data areas, isolated from each other by the nearly impenetrable walls of memory protection, or they can live together in the same data area, and share the same global and static data. They can even be so intimate that they do not require any operating system facilities to manage their execution. We explore each of these process models in some depth below.

Heavyweight Processes with Separate Data Segments

Heavyweight processes are most commonly seen in workstation or large mainframe operating systems like UNIX or VMS. They run in data segments that are kept isolated from each other by memory-protection hardware. While a process is running, the computer hardware is set to disallow any access to the data segments of other processes. An attempt to access an address outside of its data segment will typically cause the process to abort. Communication between such processes requires explicit use of the operating system's facilities for interprocess communications (IPC).

Advantages of Isolation

The isolation in which heavyweight processes execute affords them a great deal of security. In general, malfunctions in one heavyweight process have no effect on other processes.[1] This means two things: you are pretty safe from other processes; and other processes are pretty safe from your malfunctions. These two reasons explain why this model of isolation is so prevalent in software development systems: developers can be

---

1. There are certainly exceptions to this rule. Some systems do not provide the kind of memory protection that would keep a "mad process" from corrupting the memory of another process. Also, subtle malfunctions may corrupt data files or messages, or even cause the computer to "hang."

reasonably sure that, no matter what the guy in the next "cubie" is doing, it won't have a major effect on them.

Another big advantage has to do with the convenience involved in building heavyweight processes, which are generally complete, executable programs that are compiled and linked. Two different heavyweight processes can be compiled and linked at separate times. A change to one process does not automatically force us to rebuild other processes in the system.

In very large projects, this can be a big advantage, because we can shorten the compile and test cycle for each process. In very large projects, the compile and link time can extend into hours and even days. When the project is split up into several small processes, we can test each process in isolation. Moreover, when a bug is found in a process, only that process need be rebuilt and reinstalled; the others can remain as they were.

Disadvantages of Isolation

Isolation is not without its costs. The very fact that the data segments of similar processes are separate means that it is very difficult to share common data. Although many operating systems provide mechanisms by which common data *can* be shared, these mechanisms usually bring along problems of their own. So the normal recourse is simply to copy the common data among all the processes that need it. This, of course, wastes a lot of space.

Any set of processes will include a lot of code that is common to all of them. This code includes support subroutines, common utility and interface classes, the standard C library, and so on. Often, no attempt is made to share this code between processes; each heavyweight process simply includes its own copy of the common code. This is clearly an inefficient use of memory. Some operating systems provide mechanisms that allow all processes to share this common code, but, as before, these mechanisms bring along problems of their own.

Another cost associated with heavyweight processes involves the cost of context switching. Operating systems are often very general and have lots of ancillary work to do. Context switching in such big environments can be expensive. Dozens, or even hundreds, of processes may be ready to run or waiting for an event. The cost of managing large process tables can be significant.

Notation

This icon presents a single instance of a process; however, a single program may be instantiated several times as separate processes.

The icon above shows four processes that are all instances of the same program. The actual number of processes can be shown as above, or we can insert a cardinality as follows:

Any number can be used as a static cardinality. Dynamic cardinalities are represented by 0..1 and 0..n. They indicate that the number of instances may change during the execution of the application.

Lightweight Processes Within a Data Segment

Lightweight processes share their data segment with other lightweight processes. There is typically no isolation at all between the processes; they are free to communicate with each other by using static or global variables. They often use the same heap for memory management, but almost always use separate stacks.

One variant is the run-to-completion (RTC) model. In this model, once a process gains control, it runs without interruption until it completes. Typically, an RTC process will schedule other RTC processes for execution. These schedule requests are held in a queue and sorted by priority. Thus, at any given time there will be one RTC executing and several waiting to begin. There will never be an RTC that has suspended its execution and is waiting for an event. This means that RTC processes can share a common stack. In fact, they can share the stack with the operating system.

Advantages and Disadvantages of Lightweight Processes

Lightweight processes are generally linked together into the same executable. As a result, they share the common data and code of the application, and they use memory very efficiently. Also, context switching is usually quicker, since the overhead in a lightweight OS is generally very small.

However, lightweight processes are completely vulnerable to each other. Usually, if one process crashes, they all do. One process can trample all over the private data of another, or even corrupt the stack of another. If the lightweight OS does not use preemption, then one process can steal the processor by refusing to share it. This means that other processes, even high priority processes, don't get to run.

Then there are problems of reentrancy. *Reentrancy* is a term used to describe concurrent use of resources. For example, when a global variable is updated by more than one process in an uncontrolled fashion, the results can be unexpected. Reentrancy problems occur in heavyweight processes too; however, the protection and isolation offered by heavyweight operating systems usually make reentrancy problems much less likely. Lightweight processes offer no protection at all, so the problem can become quite nasty. We will discuss this issue more in a later section.

Notation

```
.----------------.
: Lightweight :
:   Process   :
'----------------'
```

Sometimes we need to show a distinction between lightweight and heavyweight processes. We can use the above icon to represent a lightweight process.

Sharing the Processor

Since the context switching for a lightweight process is usually not preemptive, the processes must explicitly share the processor. This can be somewhat tricky. Improper sharing can lead to strange misbehavior and extreme sensitivity to external conditions.

Compute-bound tasks may run for a long time without waiting for any events. These processes must *explicitly* share the processor. What's more, this sharing must occur "often enough." This usually means calling a **share** function in an inner loop of the compute-bound algorithm. If such a task does not share the processor often enough, then high-priority processes may not be able to service their events in time. Care must be taken to measure the time spent in such inner loops and to call the **share** function more often than the maximum tolerable delay. For example, imagine a system containing a high-priority process, **X**, which collects input from a serial I/O device. Assume that this process must service the reception of data within 1 millisecond after its arrival. In such a system, no process must hold the processor for more than 1 millisecond; otherwise, **X** may miss some incoming data . If the inner loop of a compute-bound process in this system takes 100μs, then the **share** function must be called at least every ten times through the loop.

On the other hand, processes that spend less than the maximum tolerable delay between waiting for events have no need to share the processor. The very act of waiting for an event turns the processor back over to the OS so it can share it with other processes.

Since context switches are not driven directly by external events, but depend upon the state of the program, there is a certain *determinism* about when they occur. External stimuli that arrive at just the right frequency and in just the right order can set up *resonances* within the interplay of processes. These resonances can cause problems, such as preventing low-priority processes from running, or preventing high-priority processes from running often enough.

For example, in Figure B-2 the high-priority process **HR** collects readings from an input device and stores them in a buffer. This process must run before the arrival of the next item of data. Furthermore, the low-priority process **LA** reads all the available data from the buffer, massages it, and sends it to a message queue. No matter how much data **HR** has placed in the buffer, when **LA** runs, it processes all of it. Low-priority process **LB** reads all the messages from the queue and does some long-term processing on it. The priority of **LA** is set higher than the priority of **LB**, so that **HR**'s buffer won't fill up because of delays in **LB**.

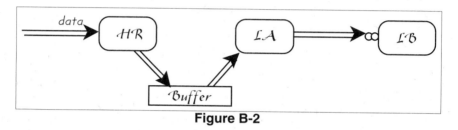

Figure B-2

HR requires 400 µs to run. **LA** requires 500 µs, regardless of the number of readings in the buffer. **LB** requires 300 µs to empty the queue, regardless of the number of messages in it.

In Figure B-3 we assume that data will be coming in bursts of only a few hundred readings at a time. If, during a burst, there is 1000 ms between readings, then after the first reading, **HR** and **LA** will run. Since 100 µs remain before the second reading is due, **LB** will get a chance to run. When it finishes, the second reading will have arrived, and will have been waiting for 200 µs. After **HR** and **LA** have processed that reading, the third datum will be present, and will have been waiting for only 100µs. **HR** and **LA** will again execute, and the fourth set of data will arrive just as **LA** finishes and **LB** begins. Thus, **LB** will run after every other reading. This is pleasantly appropriate and fits the model of priorities quite nicely.

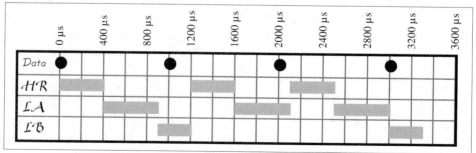

Figure B-3

However, if the frequency of readings increases to one every 900 μs, as shown in Figure B-4, then the behavior becomes perverse. **HR** executes, followed by **LA**. **LB** begins exactly at the same time that the next reading comes in, so **HR** executes 300 μs after the arrival of the data. **LA** follows 700 μs after the arrival of the data, and finishes 300 μs after the arrival of the next data. From then until the end of the burst of data, **LB** will be unable to run. This is perverse, because **LB** is being locked out by the fact that **LA** is able to run after every set of data. Yet **LA** does not need to run so often; it could run quite a bit less frequently. If it did, then **LB** would get a chance to run.

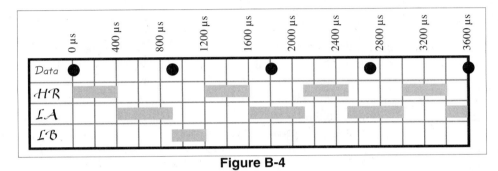

Figure B-4

A simple resonance has developed between the frequency of the incoming readings, and the execution period of the two highest-priority processes. This resonance blocks the lowest-priority process entirely.

A solution to this dilemma, shown in Figure B-5, is to make **LB** higher in priority than **LA**, so that **LB** will run after every execution of **LA**. However, this solution is strange. We had good reasons for making **LA** higher priority than **LB**: we didn't want **HR**'s buffer to fill up because **LA** was being blocked by unnecessary executions of **LB**. But because of the resonance set up by the frequency of data arrival, we must reverse the priority, so that **LA** is not executed more than is necessary.

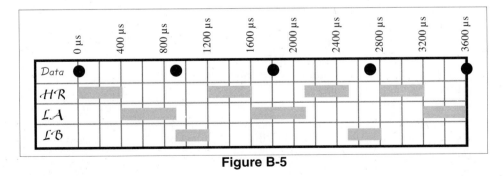

Figure B-5

The reversal of priority in Figure B-5, causes **LB** to be executed once after every execution of **LA**. In a sense, **LB** has become a part of **LA**. They can't actually be part of the same process, since their combined execution time is too long, but every execution of **LA** is followed by an execution of **LB**, with possible intervening executions of **HR**.

It might be possible to merge **LA** and **LB** into a single process by sharing the processor between the **LA** and **LB** parts. However, such mergers can only be accomplished where the execution of the various parts is guanteed to be sequential. When three or more processes vie for the processor, merging them is usually not an option.

Note that if the OS were preemptive, the resonance could not occur, since neither **LA** nor **LB** could delay the execution of the high-priority **HR**.

This has been a simple example of how nonpreemptive processes can resonate. Resonance problems can be quite complex, however, involving many processes. These problems are highly sensitive to input conditions and are very difficult to track down and repair. They are characterized by the apparent inability of a process to execute often enough, or by execution of a process that seems to occur too often.

Preemptive systems can also resonate, although it is a much rarer occurrence. The highest-priority processes within a preemptive system cannot be preempted; thus, when several of them are executing concurrently, they behave like a nonpreemptive system. Resonance between them and the external environment can cause them to overexecute and thereby lock out the lower-priority processes.

Resonances can sometimes be prevented by dynamically altering the priority of the processes involved. Their priorities can be dynamically lowered if they spend too much time executing, or they can be dynamically raised if they spend too much time waiting. This juggling of priorities tends to "damp" the resonances and keep a balance between the execution of the processes.

Heap Management

Quite often, lightweight processes share the same heap. This means that process **A** can allocate some storage from the heap, load it with data, and then pass its address to process **B**. Process **B** is then responsible for returning the allocated storage to the heap. This is a very common method of communication between lightweight processes. As a result, the heap is often heavily used for lots of small message blocks, which can lead to significant fragmentation.

A common strategy for reducing heap fragmentation is to provide *special-purpose allocators*.[2] Special-purpose allocators provide very efficient access to heap storage without causing excessive fragmentation. They can be modeled as lists of small memory blocks, all the same size. When a user wants a block of memory that is less than or equal to the size maintained in the allocator, the allocator just hands one of its blocks over. When the user is done he releases it back to the allocator, which simply inserts it back into its list.

---

2. See Bjarne Stroustrup, *The C++ Programming Language*, 2nd ed. (Addison Wesley, 1991), Section 13.10.3.

While this wastes a bit of memory, it is usually much faster than using **new** or **malloc**. Also, since all the blocks are the same size, no fragmentation can occur.

Several allocator objects can be instantiated, each one dealing with a different block size and a different amount of total memory. For example, you might want 1000 blocks of 20 bytes, 100 blocks of 256 bytes, and 10 blocks of 1000 bytes. The allocator objects will allocate this storage from the heap when the program starts up. Alternatively, you could provide the storage yourself from static arrays.

You can guarantee that the storage allocators are used to create certain objects by overloading the **new** and **delete** operator functions associated with those classes. Thus, whenever the user creates one of these objects with the **new** operator, it will be allocated from the appropriate allocator object instead of from the heap.

Stack Management

Each lightweight process needs a stack, but this stack is generally *not* located in the normal stack area. Instead, it often comes from the heap. One common strategy is for the main program to allocate the stacks for the lightweight processes before it starts the processes running. The fact that the lightweight processes do not share the normal stack space causes something of a problem. How much memory should you set aside for the stack of a lightweight process?

For some computers and operating systems, we can determine the answer by examining the function-calling tree of the process. For each leaf of the tree, we simply count the depth of the tree, the number of stack variables at each node, and the number of function arguments passed at each node. The leaf with the largest count represents the calling path that uses the largest stack. The number itself is proportional to the stack size needed. This may not be easy, but if done correctly, it will yield a workable stack size.

Some computers and operating systems force the current stack to bear the burden of any interrupt processing that may occur. This is typically a characteristic of the smaller operating systems found in embedded systems. When this is the case, the stack for *every* process must be able to cope with its own calling tree as well as the overhead of the interrupt routines.

These calculations are difficult. Moreover, they must be repeated, or at least reexamined after every change to the code. This process is highly error-prone. It is easy to forget, and it is easy to miscalculate. The result is a program that works *almost* all the time, but it fails under conditions of stress—and the failure mode is bizarre. When a process blows its stack, the process itself is not directly affected. The stack simply overruns some other portion of memory that some other process depends upon. Thus, there may be many millions of instructions between the cause and the symptom.

When processes follow the RTC model, these difficulties with the stack disappear. RTC processes use the same stack that the operating system uses; stacks do not need to be shared.

Run to Completion

Designing an application around the run-to-completion model is quite different from designing with processes that are allowed to wait for events or share the processor. For example, consider the problem of sorting an array of data. If we can use sharable processes, then the process can loop through the data, calling the **share** service from its inner loops.

In an RTC model, rather than looping through the data, the processes might make a single pass through the data, partially sorting it, schedule another RTC process to make the next pass, and then complete. Eventually the scheduled RTC process would run, and it would make the next pass through the data and then schedule yet another RTC process to continue the sort. Eventually, the sort would be completed, and the RTC process that completed it would schedule yet another to process the sorted data.

In an environment where processes can share the processor and wait for events, a great deal of information is stored on the stack. Consider that the stack contains all the automatic variables, function parameters, and function returns for the entire current calling hierarchy. This information must be saved while other processes are allowed to execute. In an RTC environment, this information must be specifically encoded by the processes and stored in memory that other RTC processes will examine in order to determine how to proceed.

Static Variables and Reentrancy

The problems of reentrancy are common to all applications that have more than one thread of execution. They may occur whenever a resource can be accessed by more than one process. If the processes involved do not follow some well-defined protocol for the access and manipulation of the resource, chaos will certainly result.

An everyday example of a shared resource, and of possible reentrancy problems, is a traffic intersection. Roads, in general, are not shared resources. Only one car may be using the piece of road that it occupies at any given time. Other cars may be on the same road, but they occupy a different piece. At an intersection, however, there is a small area that is common to both roads. Without some convention to follow, like stop signs or a stop light, two cars may attempt to use that common area of road at the same time. The intersection is entered by one car, but before that car exits, the intersection is *reentered* by another car. The result, of course, is unfortunate.

As a more germane example, consider Figure B-6. Suppose the shared resource is a static integer variable i, and assume it has a value of 6. There are two processes, **A** and **B**, that want to add 1 to i. **A** begins by reading the 6 out of i and adding 1 to get 7. However, before **A** can store the 7 back into i, process **B** gains control and also reads the 6 out of i. **B** then adds 1 and stores the 7 back into i. Finally **A** regains control and stores its 7 back into i. The end result is that the value of i is now 7 when it should be 8; the update made by **B** has been lost.

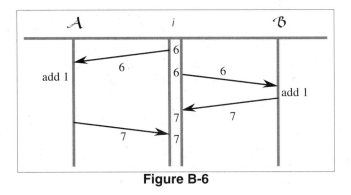

Figure B-6

Nonpreemptive processes have a built-in mechanism that helps to manage reentrancy problems. If a process does not release the processor while it is manipulating the shared resource, there can be no concurrent update. However, this technique is actually harder to manage than it seems. It is not always obvious which functions eventually share the processor and which do not. You may start a concurrent update on some resource **r**, call a function **f**, and then finish the update on **r**. This works well as long as **f** does not share the processor. If **f** *does* share the processor, or if **f** is changed at a later date so that it shares the processor, then a reentrancy problem will arise.

For preemptive processes, the problem is more difficult. The processor can be interrupted at any time and another process may context-switch in.

For either preemptive or nonpreemptive processes, we must use some protection mechanism to prevent reentrancy problems from occurring. The traditional mechanism for solving reentrancy problems, for both software and automobile traffic, is called a *semaphore*.

A semaphore, in its simplest form, is a binary flag whose two values are **inUse** and **available**. The flag is associated with the resource that needs protection. Normally, we can perform two operations on a semaphore: **seize** and **release**. The **seize** operation is performed by processes when they desire access to the resource. The **release** operation is performed by a process that has finished using the resource.

The **seize** operation has two possible outcomes. If the semaphore flag is **available**, then it is set to **inUse**, and the **seize** operation succeeds. Otherwise the flag is untouched and the operation fails. The **release** operation also has two possible outcomes. If the flag is **inUse**, then the flag is set to **available**, and the operation succeeds; otherwise the flag is untouched, and the operation fails.

Processes that need to use a resource protected by a semaphore cooperate by using the semaphore operations to coordinate their activity. When a process needs to use a resource, it must first **seize** the semaphore. If the **seize** operation succeeds, then the process may manipulate the associated resource as needed; otherwise it must wait and try again later. When the process is done with the resource, it must **release** the semaphore, so that other processes can use the resource.

The internal mechanism of the semaphore must be protected from concurrent update, too. After all, the flag inside a semaphore is really just a shared resource. Preemptive operating systems often offer semaphores as operating-system tools. If not, they at least offer a way to protect a small stretch of code from a context switch. Nonpreemptive systems simply code their semaphore operations without sharing the processor.

There are dozens of variations on the semaphore scheme. Some semaphores contain integers that count the number of allowed concurrent users of a resource. Other semaphores automatically wait for a resource to be released. There are database locks that protect database records from concurrent updates. Whatever the variation employed, the device is still a semaphore, and its purpose is to protect a shared resource from a concurrent update.

There are also many different types of shared resources: disk records, I/O devices, blocks of shared memory, and global variables shared by lightweight processes. Some resources are obviously shared; others are not. When designing an application that employs multiple threads of control, identification and protection of the shared resources is a very important concern.

"Rolling Your Own" Thread Controller

Another common technique for creating applications with multiple threads is to "roll your own" thread controller. This is typically done for simple applications that are event-driven and easily modeled as finite state machines. Each thread of control establishes a new state variable and must be associated with a discrete subset of the events that come into the application. These events are in turn associated with the transitions that drive the FSM from state to state. The behaviors of the FSM typically follow the run-to-completion model and are scheduled by the events incoming to the FSM.

Event Driven

An *event-driven* application waits for specific events to occur and then does a bit of processing based on the nature of the event and the current state of the application. The events can be I/O interrupts or messages from other processes within a larger application. If we want to establish multiple threads of control, we must have some method for divining which thread each event is associated with. This can be as simple as an I/O address for I/O events, or a thread ID for messages from other processes. A thread ID is simply an arbitrary number assigned to a particular thread when it is created. This ID must be used to label every message that qualifies as an event to the thread controller.

The Context Data Structure

Each thread of control should have a context data structure associated with it. At the very least, this data structure should contain the state variable for the finite state machine. However, it is typical for other thread-related data to be saved in the context. For example, the context data structure might contain the contents of the last message received for the thread, or the address of the I/O device that the thread serves.

Finite State Machine

A *finite state machine* (FSM) is a mechanism that can exist only in a discrete number of states. An event that causes the state of the mechanism to change is called a *transition*. Changing from state to state is governed by a set of rules, sometimes known as a *state map*. The rules are of the following form: *If the current state is A and event X is received, transition to state Y and perform action F.*

The control structures of many applications can be written as sequences of such rules.[3] We can code the rules directly into the application, or externalize them into data structures that a common driver interprets.

It is often useful to model the context data structure as a class. The class member variables contain the state of the FSM. The member functions represent the *actions* specified by the FSM. Thus, when the FSM wants to perform an action, it need only invoke the appropriate member function of the context.

Structure of the Thread Controller

The thread controller is the portion of the multithreaded application that receives events, associates them with the appropriate context structure, and sends the corresponding transition to the FSM. A simple pseudocode example follows:

```
while(1)
{
    Event* e = GetNextEvent();
    Context* c = FindContext(e);
    Transition t = ConvertEventToTransition(e);
    c->InvokeTransision(t);  // drive the FSM
}
```

---

3. In my opinion, far too few are. Burying the control structure of an application within the code of the application hides that structure. But designing that control structure as a set of rules for a finite state machine and then encoding those rules separately from the rest of the application code separates the function of the application from its control. Thus, either function or control can be changed independently.

Notation

This icon represents a single process that contains several threads of control. This may be a heavyweight process containing a set of lightweight or RTC processes, or it could be a process containing a "roll-your-own" thread controller. In either case, this icon typically requires a separate process diagram to describe its internal structure.

Hybrid Processes

We frequently see combinations of the different process types within the confines of a single application. The following paragraphs discuss some of the options.

Multithreaded FSMs Within a Heavyweight Process

It is very common for a single heavyweight process to contain its own thread controller and to instantiate multiple threads of control within itself. Typically such a process has a single mailbox or queue from which it receives messages from the rest of the system. Somewhere embedded in the incoming messages are codes that identify the thread to which the message pertains. The thread controller finds the appropriate context object and then calls its appropriate member functions.

For example, Figure B-7 shows a process that must control the dial-out sequence of three modems. This process receives commands from a client, instructing it to dial a certain phone number on a certain modem. The process then sends instructions to the appropriate modem server to accomplish the task.

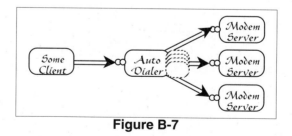

Figure B-7

The messages that pass between the **AutoDialer** and the **ModemServers** are depicted in Figure B-8.

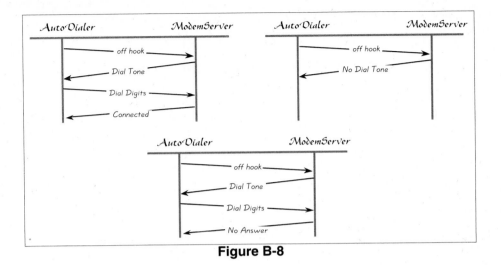

Figure B-8

There are three scenarios. In the first, the call is successful. In the second, no **Dial Tone** is received from the phone line. In the last, the call is not answered. This corresponds to the following finite state machine in Figure B-9.

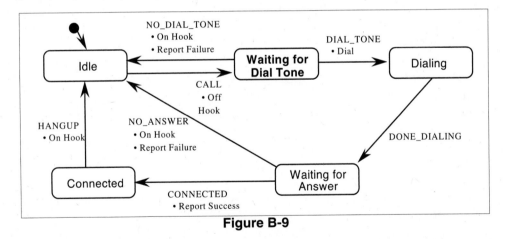

Figure B-9

The **AutoDialer** process maintains three context objects, one for each of the **ModemServer** processes. The messages that come in from either a client or one of the **ModemServer** processes contain the ID of a modem. The **AutoDialer** process finds the appropriate context for that modem, and then translates the message into a transition for the FSM. The action that results from the transition is translated into a message and sent to the appropriate **ModemServer** process.

Thus, there are three threads running within the **AutoDialer** process. Each thread has its own private data area, which is the context object. The thread controller is simply the code that receives the messages, figures out the appropriate context, and issues the transition.

Lightweight Processes Within a Heavyweight Process

Another way to mix process types is to bury some lightweight processes within a heavyweight process. Lightweight processes are especially useful for managing threads that must wait for external events or specific delays without stopping the other threads in the process.

For example, if any of the actions in our **AutoDialer** example had found it necessary to delay for a period of time, the entire process would have been delayed. All three threads would have frozen until the delay had passed. Lightweight processes, however, normally include special delay functions that only delay the lightweight processes that invoke them. The other lightweights continue to execute normally.

Another interesting application for lightweight processes occurs when we must control several devices over a single I/O channel. Consider a system that monitors communications problems in wide-area networks. Each node of the network includes a device that monitors the quality of the communications on each incoming circuit. The manufacturer of these devices has provided us a means of dialing into them using standard modems, so that we can extract the information that they contain. One receiving modem will serve as many as 16 of these devices. Thus, we must control 16 devices through one modem port. A lightweight process structure that supports this system might look like FIgure B-10.

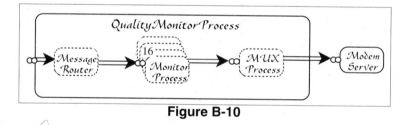

Figure B-10

In Figure B-10 we see two heavyweight processes. One is the familiar **Modem-Server**, but the other is a process that contains a set of lightweight processes. The outer, heavyweight process is the **QualityMonitorProcess**, which is responsible for establishing contact with the remote monitoring devices and directing their activities.

Inside this process are 18 lightweight processes. **MessageRouter** reads the messages that are sent to **QualityMonitorProcess**. It determines which monitoring device the messages are appropriate for, and then sends them to the appropriate instantiations of **MonitorProcess**. There are 16 instantiations of **MonitorProcess**. Each one controls one of the 16 monitoring devices that the modem is currently connected to. It models the state of the device, determines the commands that need to be sent to it, and sends them to the **MuxProcess**. The **MuxProcess** combines all the messages from the

MonitorProcesses and sends directions to the **ModemServer** heavyweight process in order to control the modem.

Interprocess Communication (IPC) Models

Any application involving multiple threads of control must include some means by which the threads can communicate with one another. Typically, this communication amounts to passing packets of data back and forth. A discussion of some of these communications methods follows.

Common O/S Resources

The use of O/S resources for interprocess communication is prevalent, especially for communications between heavyweight processes. Operating systems typically provide a range of communications methods, each with their own advantages and disadvantages. The examples below are generally taken from the UNIX operating system, but many of them are present, in one form or another, on other operating systems as well.

Disk Files

Processes that have access to a common file system can communicate by writing and reading files on disk. There are many different ways to use the file system to facilitate such communications. All of them have the benefit that the communications are saved on disk and thus survive the shutdown of the system. This could allow the state of the system to be reconstructed after a crash or a planned shutdown.

One very simple and prevalent technique is to use files as semaphores. Each semaphore is given a file name. The **seize** operation is simply an attempt to create the file. If the attempt fails because the file already exists, then the **seize** operation fails. If the file is created, then the **seize** operation succeeds. The **release** operation is simply the deletion of the file.

Processes can also use files as a way to send data to one another. For example, each process may have a special file that it reads its messages from. Sending processes simply append new messages to the end of the file. To keep the file from growing without bound, the reading process should delete it when it encounters the end. If the writing process cannot find the file to append to, then it should create it. Some file systems might allow two or more processes to write to the file at the same time. This could cause messages to be corrupted by interleaving their characters. To prevent this, the file can be opened using an *exclusive* mode that prevents other processes from opening it. If the operating system does not supply such exclusion, a semaphore can be used to protect the file.

Yet another technique is to write each message into its own file. The receiving process looks for such files in a preassigned directory. The sending process should build the file in a private directory and then move it to the receiver's directory. The **move** operation must either be an atomic operation at the file-system level, or it must be protected by a semaphore. This prevents the receiver from seeing the message before it is fully written.

This technique gets around the problem of multiple writers in the same file. No exclusive mode need be used to write the files, nor is any semaphore required during writing. However, there are other problems. We must find some method for giving the files unique names. This could be something as simple as blending the name of the sender and the sequence number of the message together. Also, if ordering is important, we must decide upon some means for preserving the sequence of the messages. Some file systems can keep track of this by remembering the order in which files are created within a directory. With file systems that do not keep track of this ordering, we must specify the ordering in the name of the file.

Using disk files for IPC is simple and general. It has the advantage that the code for writing and reading files can be extremely portable between systems. It has the disadvantage that it is likely to be slow.

Pipes and Sockets

Some operating systems, most notably UNIX, have elaborated on the above techniques by creating entities called *pipes*. Pipes appear as files to the applications, but are really queues into which the sending process can write, and from which the receiving process can read. Typically, pipes are used to make *specific* connections between two processes rather than as general mechanisms that allow many senders to talk to a receiver. Sockets are similar to pipes, but they are used to connect to processes that are running within the same network, possibly on different machines.

Signals

Some operating systems provide a mechanism called *signals* . This facility allows one process to send a simple stimulus to another process. Typically the stimulus contains no data, but can be characterized by a type. The execution thread of the receiving process is interrupted, and its *signal handler* is called. The signal handler identifies the type of the signal and then performs the necessary operation. It is then free to resume executing the interrupted thread.

Shared Memory

Another common mechanism that facilitates the communication between processes is *shared memory*. This is memory that the communicating processes have in common. In the case of lightweight processes, it can be any memory in their data segment. For heavy-weight processes, the operating system must provide special facilities. The following sections examine some of these facilities.

Semaphores

Remember that, in its simplest form, a semaphore is just a single bit. For lightweight processes, this bit can simply exist in the data segment that the processes share. However, when operating systems provide semaphores to heavyweight processes, the semaphore bit is kept in the working memory of the operating-system kernel. The amount of such memory to reserve for semaphores is often a configuration parameter.

Shared Memory Segments

Heavyweight processes may also be able to share blocks of memory. There are several ways to do this. A simple and common method is for the shared memory to exist *outside* of the control of the operating system. The communicating processes simply *know* where the memory is. They access it by using whatever facilities the operating system or machine provides for accessing memory outside of the normal data segment.

Some operating systems do not allow processes to access memory that is outside their data segment. Thus, if two or more processes are to share memory, the common memory must be brought into the data segment of all the sharing processes. This can be done if the computer hardware supports *memory management*, that can *map* portions of real memory into a *virtual* address space. All processes run within the same virtual address space. When the context of a process is switched to the running state, the specific portion of real memory that holds the program and private data are remapped into the virtual memory space, so that the process will find them where it expects them.

Shared memory is a chunk of real memory that has been set aside by the operating system. This chunk is mapped into the *virtual address space* of each process that shares it. (See Figure B-11.) Thus, each process will be able to manipulate the chunk of shared memory. However, the shared memory may not be mapped into the same virtual address for all the processes that share it. Thus, it is usually meaningless to store pointers to shared memory, *within* shared memory. Such pointers are usually only meaningful to one process; the other processes that share the memory would not be able to use them.

Messages & Mailboxes

Still another common technique by which processes communicate with each other is the use of message mailboxes. A process constructs a message within a block of memory called a *message buffer*. Then it moves the contents of that buffer into a mailbox. Another

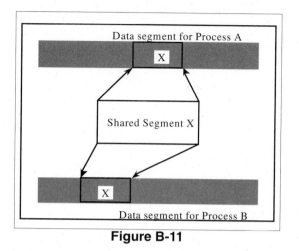

Figure B-11

process can then access the mailbox and move the data it contains into its own message buffer. Below are some of the various mailbox techniques.

Message Rendezvous

A rendezvous mailbox is able to pass only one message at a time between two processes. Both processes must meet at the mailbox before the data can change hands. Let's say that we have two processes, **A** and **B**. A has a message that it wants to send to **B**, so **A** prepares the message and posts it to **B**'s rendezvous mailbox. If **B** is already waiting for the message, then it happily takes it from the mailbox, and both processes continue from there. If, however, **B** is not dutifully waiting at the mailbox, **A** must wait. Once **B** decides to read its mail, it receives the message, and **A** is once again free to execute. If **B** wants to receive a message, but **A** has not yet posted it, then **B** must wait at the mailbox until **A** sends the message.

This technique is called *rendezvous* because both processes must *meet* at the mailbox. Neither can proceed unless the other does its job. An advantage of this technique is that the communicating processes remain closely in sync with each other. Neither can consume so much of the processor that the other cannot run, even if one has higher priority than the other. The act of sending messages to each other guarantees that they will release the processor if their partner is not ready, thus giving their partner the processor power it needs to complete its job.

On the down side, the two processes *must* wait for each other, even if they could be productively doing something else. This can cause the user to perceive needless delays.

Remote Procedure Call

Remote Procedure Call (RPC) is a special case of the rendezvous model. Using RPC, the sending process appears to call a function that exists within the receiving process. That function then returns a value to the sending process. In reality, the remote function call is translated into a special message by the RPC support code. This message is then sent to the receiving process and the sender waits. The receiving process decodes the message and then calls the appropriate function. The return value is encoded into yet another message, which is sent back to the calling process.

This technique has the advantage of providing a communications paradigm that is naturally familiar to all programmers. It has the disadvantage that the function call and return value must be encoded into messages, and the programmer must somehow direct this process. Typically, this is done by providing special encoding and decoding functions for each remote procedure.

Message-Queue Mailboxes

When using *message-queue mailboxes*, the sending process does not have to wait for the receiver; it can continue with its work. The mailbox remembers the message until the receiver is ready to get it. Many messages can be queued up in this fashion.

Sometimes the message queues are bounded, in that they can only hold a certain number of messages. When the limit is reached, the sending process must wait until the mailbox has room for more messages. Receiving processes typically wait if there are no messages in the queue, but sometimes they may simply poll the queue to see if any messages are present.

An advantage to using message queues is that senders do not have to wait. If sending processes must be able to send bursts of many messages faster than those messages can be processed by the receiver, then a message queue is appropriate. On the other hand, message queues can create substantial delays between the sending and reception of a message. If such delays are intolerable, then message queues may not be appropriate.

Sometimes the limits imposed upon message queues are system-wide. There may be a system-wide limit on the number of messages, or on the number of bytes that they consume. In this situation, a single misbehaving process can lock up the entire system by overloading that limit. Deadlock situations are not uncommon. Consider the scenario in Figure B-12 and Figure B-13.

A sends letters to **B**, which in turn sends letters to **C**. But **B** sometimes takes a long time to compose a letter. Let's say that **B** is working very hard on a letter that has just come in. Meanwhile, **A** is cranking out hordes of new letters and sending them to **B**. This continues until the system-wide limit on messages is reached. **A** is now blocked because the message system is overloaded. Furthermore, when **B** finishes working on its letter, it will attempt to send that letter to **C**. This attempt will fail because the message system is overloaded. The message system could be freed up if **B** would read some of the messages that

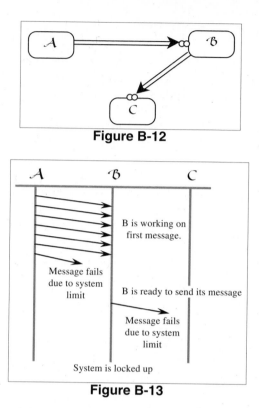

Figure B-12

Figure B-13

A sent, but **B** is frozen, attempting to send a message of its own. Thus, the system is deadlocked.

We will examine how to avoid these deadlock situations later in this appendix.

Notation

Mailboxes and queues are represented by the two icons above. The rendezvous mailbox should be used to represent RPC connections or any other form of synchronous connection. Message queues should be used to represent all forms of asynchronous connection, such as pipes, shared memory mailboxes, and so on. These icons can be dissociated from processes to represent a cooperative model in which many processes share a few mailboxes, or they may be closely associated to represent a client-server model in which every server has a dedicated mailbox.

To denote that one process communicates with another, we use a double-lined arrow. If the arrowhead is solid, the process relationship is permanent. If the arrowhead is hollow, the relationship is transient. Permanent relationships last as long as the application is running. Transient relationships come and go as needed.

Below are three forms of process communication. The first is *direct*. In this form, the processes communicate by very direct means: perhaps a signal, a direct hardware connection, or a direct software connection. This description is necessarily vague.

The second and third forms represent the *cooperative* and *client-server* process relationships, which we will describe in a later section. The hollow arrow below indicates that the relationship between the two processes is transient.

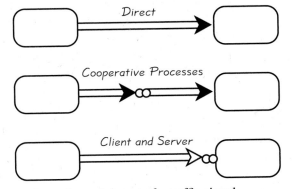

The icon for semaphores is reminiscent of a traffic signal.

It is often quite useful to depict storage areas such as files and buffers on a process diagram.

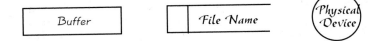

Machine-independent Messages

It is a fact of life in the computer industry that there are as many different ways to represent primitive data types as there are different types of computers. A string of bits that makes perfect sense on one machine will almost certainly be nonsense to another. A C **struct** on one kind of machine is represented by a particular bit sequence, but that same bit sequence on a different machine is not likely to represent the same C struct. When a set of processes running on the same machine want to exchange messages, they can simply pass C structs around.[4] If those processes are running on different types of machines, however, the messages must be translated into a form that is suitable for the receiving process. This is often accomplished by translating the message into a machine-independent form before sending it. When the message reaches the target machine, it is translated into a form suitable for that machine.

Several machine-independent data representations are popular in the industry. XDR is often employed in UNIX systems to facilitate RPC communications. X.409 is part of the electronic mail standard, and ASN.1/X.209 is used in the OSI seven-layer standard for computer communications. Although these schemes are all different in detail, they share the ability to represent complex data structures in a machine-independent form. A C struct of integers, floating-point numbers, and characters can be encoded into any of these forms, and decoded again into any other machine format.

The simplest type of machine-independent form simply represents each primitive data type in some canonical form. We can build complex data structures by concatenating these translated forms into a string of bits. The data structure may be reassembled on the other side *if the exact structure that was used to create the message is known.* So, the sender and receiver must agree on the precise structure and order of the data.

For example, consider the following data structure:

```
struct MyMessage
{
    int anInt;
    double aDouble;
    char aString[10];
};
```

If we have a canonical form for **int**, **double**, and **char**, we can easily convert each of the members of the structure into that form, and pack them all together into a nice string of bytes:

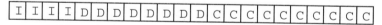

In order to decipher this string of bytes, we must know the exact form of the structure that was used to create it. Knowing this structure, we can determine that the first element is an **int**, the second is a **double**, and the next ten are **char**. If the sender and receiver do not agree on the form of the message, the receiver will decipher the message incorrectly. For example, the receiver might think that the structure looked like this:

```
struct MyMessage
{
    char aString[10];
    int anInt;
    double aDouble;
};
```

---

4. Beware, however, of passing pointers. Many operating systems remap the virtual address space between context switches. This makes pointers meaningless when passed between processes.

The receiver would therefore try to unpack `IIIIDDDDD` into the `char[10]`, `DDCC` into the `int`, and `CCCCCCCC` into the `double`. This is clearly undesirable.

Version-Independent Messages

There is a problem with expecting two processes to agree about the precise structure of the messages that they exchange: such processes are very difficult to upgrade if the message formats change. If the software for the receiver is upgraded before the software for the sender is upgraded, then the communications between them will probably break down.

For small systems, simultaneously updating all communicating processes is feasible, but for large systems, simultaneous update creates severe problems. If the system is very large, changing all its software is liable to take a long time. Users are not willing to tolerate long outages just for the purpose of software upgrade. Secondly, it is a fearsome thing to exchange software that *works* for software that has not yet been tried in your environment. Most users want to do limited trials of new software before doing a general upgrade. Such limited trials are nearly impossible if the new version of the software cannot interpret the messages it will receive from the older components of the system.

For example, consider a system for counting beans. Great sacks of beans are dumped into several hoppers on the plant floor. The hoppers accept the beans and attempt to sort them by size. The sorted beans are placed into bags of about 10 pounds each. For each bag, a message is sent to the main database processor. The message contains the ID number of the bag, its weight, and the average size of the beans it contains. The database processor then determines which production line the beans should be placed on. It sends a message back to the hopper directing it to place the bag on one of several conveyors.

Now let us say that modifications have been made to the bean-counting system. The users need to be able to track the color quality of the bags of beans as well as their size and weight. Hardware modifications are designed to allow the hoppers to measure color. Software changes are designed both for the hopper and the database system to deal with the new color measurement.

After months of hard work, the modifications are ready to be installed. However, the user does not want to do a "flash-cut" on this software. He does not want to risk the loss of his entire bean-counting operation, even for as much as an hour. So he dictates that the new modifications be tried out in the following manner:

(1) The hardware modifications will be made to a single hopper, and that hopper will be run with the old software for one week. This will prove that the hardware changes can be made one at a time, and that they do not interfere with the operation of the hopper.

(2) Once the first hopper has been tested, the new software will be run in that hopper for an additional week. All the other hoppers and the database system will continue to run the old software. This will ensure that the hopper software does not have any horrible bugs that might take the hoppers off line.

(3) Next, the new database software will be tried for yet another week. None of the other hoppers will be modified. This will prove that the color measurement and

analysis software is working as specified, and that the system is capable of running with both kinds of hopper installed.

(4) If the software and hardware work as predicted, then a new hopper will be converted every other day. This will allow management time to react if anything goes wrong with the system.

(5) At any time during the trial phase, and for one month after cut over, it must be possible to revert to the old software in any or all of the hoppers, or in the database system.

Clearly this strategy could not be followed if the database and hopper software had to agree on the exact format of their messages. The new hopper software will have to work with the old database software, and the new database software will have to work with the old hopper software.

Thus, the constraint that both sender and receiver must agree on the precise structure of their messages is too severe. It must be relaxed. If the *structure* of the data can be encoded in the message along with the data itself, then the receiving process can reconstruct the fields of the message that it needs. If some fields expected by the receiver are missing, the receiver may substitute default values. If other unexpected fields are present, they can be ignored. The sender and receiver do not have to agree on the exact format of the message; they only have to agree on the existence of a critical subset of the message fields.

For example, the new hopper software sends a **color** field in its messages to the database software. The old hopper software did not, but since the old database software doesn't look for the **color** field, its presence does no harm. Thus, the new hopper software would be compatible with the old database software. Also, if the new database software receives a message without a **color** field, it can be written to supply a default color, or a **NOCOLOR** value. Thus, the new database software remains compatible with the old hopper software.

To achieve this structural encoding, each field in the message must encode the *name and type* of the data, as well as the value. Moreover, we must have data fields that can be organized into arbitrarily complex structures. Thus a *named* field in a message may refer to a primitive value, or to a set of several dissimilar fields, or to an array of fields. For example,

```
Struct HopperMessage
{
    int hopperID;
    int bagID;
    int weight;
    struct
    {
        double meanSize;
        int percentileWeight[10];
    } sizeDistribution;
    int colorQuality;
};
```

This is an example of a possible format for the hopper message. It has a relatively complex structure. Both X.409 and ASN.1/X.209 are able to encode such arbitrarily complex data structures with named and typed fields.

Implementing Version-Independent Messages, Using Attributed Data Trees

Neither ASN.1/X.209 nor X.409 are convenient representations for messages. They are meant to be transmitted across a network, so they are optimized for density, not for ease of use in programming. Thus, they are not well suited for manipulating the data fields that they contain. For example, if you had an X.409 structure and you wanted to modify the value of a particular field, you would find the task somewhat daunting.

We need an intermediate form that is easy to manipulate and easy to convert to the chosen encoding scheme. Attributed Data Trees (**DTrees** or Soups) are such an intermediary.[5] Each node of a **DTree** represents a field name of the data to be encoded. Leaf nodes contain type and value information. Nonleaf nodes contain the links that tie all the nodes into a tree. (See Figure B-14.)

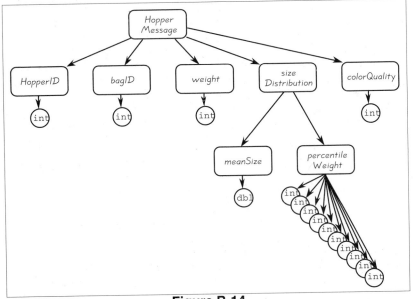

Figure B-14

DTrees are just simple trees. Although I have drawn them as *n*-way trees, I could just as easily represent them as binary trees. Managing them is as simple as managing any

---

5. Although the acronym for *attributed data tree* is ADT, this conflicts with another common OO term, *abstract data type*. So I commonly use the term *DTree* instead.

other kind of tree. **DTrees** can be built by calling functions that add name/value pairs into the tree. We can access the values within a **DTree** by functions that search the tree for a name and return the associated value. Such functions are relatively easy to use, and can be further abstracted to more convenient forms.

Once built, **DTrees** can be directly converted to a machine-independent format such as X.209. The X.209 stream of bits can then be transmitted to another machine, and reassembled into a logical copy of the original **DTree**. These operations are relatively straightforward and provide a convenient programming interface for version-independent messages.

Message Sequence Charts

Message-sequence charts (MSCs) are analogous to object diagrams in that they map out the dynamics of a particular scenario. As with Object Diagrams, we usually create many MSCs to test as many dynamic scenarios as possible. MSCs test the static structure of the process diagram to ensure that it can truly deal with the application.

However, there is a big difference between object dynamics and process dynamics. In an object diagram, the messages that are sent from one object to another are synchronous. For any given set of states and stimuli, there is only one way that the messages can flow through the objects. This is untrue for processes. A given stimulus will initiate one of many possible sequences of messages that may flow between processes. This ambiguity is a result of being unable to precisely predict when a process is going to execute. This imprecision gives way to situations called *race conditions,* in which the order of two or more events cannot be predicted.

To deal with the ambiguities of timing, MSCs take the form shown in Figure B-15, dedicating the vertical dimension to time:

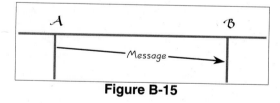

Figure B-15

Two processes are represented in this diagram. If more processes are involved with a single dynamic scenario, then we add more vertical lines to the MSC to represent them. In the example, we see that process **A** is sending a message to process **B**. The arrow denoting that message is angled downward to show that it takes *time* to send the message. Thus **B** receives the message some time after it was sent by **A**. This difference in time allows us to express race conditions. For example, consider a simple telephone call, which is depicted in Figure B-16.

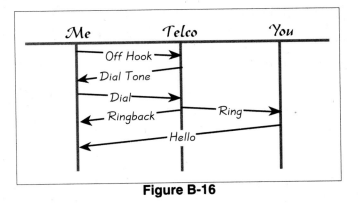

Figure B-16

This seems quite normal, and we might be tempted to think that this simple protocol is foolproof. However, sometimes **You** will pick up the phone just before it rings. That can lead to the sad, but familiar, state of affairs shown in Figure B-17.

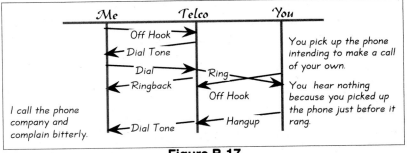

Figure B-17

The race condition in the example above is evidenced by the crossed lines. **You** and **Telco** were in a race to see who could get to the phone first. In this case **Telco** lost. In the time it took the **Telco** to decide to ring your phone, **You** were just picking it up to make a call of your own. Instead of the expected dial tone, all **You** hear is silence. If **You** are lucky, you might just hear **Me** breathing on the other end of the phone, but probably **You** will just hang up, leaving poor **Me** with the dial tone ringing in my ears.

The more complex a system becomes, the more significant is the potential for race conditions. Finding and fixing them is a major factor in the design of a multiprocessing system. Message-sequence charts are a simple mechanism for visualizing the flow of communications through a system, determining where race conditions may occur and diagnosing their effects.

Process Relationships

Beyond the simple message protocols that we have examined, lie issues of visibility and responsibility that have major effects on the architecture of a software project. These issues define the relationships between processes. We discuss several different types of process relationships below.

Independent Processes

Many processes are utterly unrelated. Such processes never communicate with each other in real time; they simply vie for the common system resources. Such processes include, for example, the *shell* processes running in a multiuser development environment. Each shell provides a command-line interface to its user, but shells do not usually communicate with one another.

Independent processes are very useful in most multiprocess applications. We can use them to monitor system activity and generate log files. They may be started up by a timer process to periodically delete files or purge logs. We may also use them to service particular pieces of hardware or to systematically reclaim lost system resources.

Client-Server

The client-server model is an asymmetric relationship: the two partners have very different roles. Server processes offer *services* to clients, and client processes direct server processes to perform those services. A pure server process does nothing of its own volition. It must wait for a client to tell it what to do. For this reason, this relationship is sometimes known as *master-slave*.

For example, imagine the software within an electronic organ. It might look like Figure B-18.

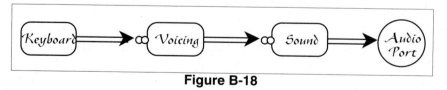

Figure B-18

Here we see three processes. The **Keyboard** process monitors the keyboard of the organ, and sends messages to the **Voicing** process whenever a key goes up or down. The **Voicing** process determines which voices should be played. It looks up the digitized voice in a database and then converts it to the proper frequency. Then it sends the converted voices to the **Sound** process. The **Sound** process accepts all the voices from the

Voicing process, mixes them, and sends them to the audio output hardware. The **Voicing** and **Sound** processes are perfect examples of server processes. They can do nothing until their particular client directs them to do so. The **Keyboard** process is a pure client. It receives no direction from any other process. Instead, it directs other processes on the basis of a change in the external state. The **Voicing** process is both a server and a client. It accepts commands from the **Keyboard** process, and gives commands to the **Sound** processes.

The mixture of roles experienced by the **Voicing** process is very common. It exists wherever there is a *chain of command*, with general orders being successively refined into more and more specific orders.

Parent-Child

When one process creates another, we say that the creating process is the *parent* of the new process. Such a creation establishes the *parent-child* relationship. This relationship is supported differently by different operating systems, but the majority of them share common traits. Child processes typically share some of the resources and restrictions of their parents. If the parent is restricted from using more than a certain amount of memory, that restriction usually includes the children of that process as well. Child processes are typically not allowed to exist in the absence of the parent; if the parent dies, the children are destroyed. Parents are typically notified of the actions of their children, so that they can manage them properly. Parents often have special privileges and authorities over their children; for example, parents may destroy their children.

The parent-child relationship is useful in situations where one process must ride herd over several others. For example, Figure B-19 shows an application that involves several modems. Each modem is supported by a **ModemDriver** process, and all the modems are managed by a single **ModemManager** process. The hardware that we are dealing with is *hot pluggable,* which simply means that existing modems can be unplugged and plugged back in while the system remains powered-on and running. Thus, **ModemDriver** processes must be created and killed as the modems appear in, and disappear from the system. Also, maintenance commands can enable and disable modems. A modem in the disabled state has no **ModemDriver** process.

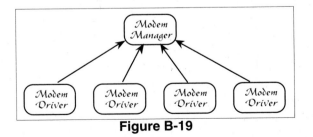

Figure B-19

The parent-child relationship between the **ModemManager** and the **ModemDriver** processes allows the **ModemManager** process to kill the **ModemDriver** processes whenever modems are disabled by the maintenance software. It also means that if a **ModemDriver** process dies because a modem was unplugged, the **ModemManager** process will know about it and properly manage the situation.

Cooperative Processes

In the *cooperative* model, processes do not necessarily know about each other. Instead, they receive processing requests from specific message queues, perform the requested operation and send the output to yet other message queues. This is different from the client-server and parent-child models since none of the cooperating processes know about the others. They only know about the queues they are supposed to read from, the tasks they are supposed to perform, and the queues to which they are supposed to send their output to.

In both the client-server and parent-child models, every interaction has a definite master. One process directs another to do something and typically receives a response. In the cooperative model, however, there are no masters and no slaves. No one process is in control of the application. Instead, all the processes cooperate to make the application work.

One of the hallmarks of this model is the sharing of single queues by multiple processes. For example, Figure B-20 depicts the modem example once again. Suppose that this system must be able to use the modems to place data calls to many different nodes in a dial-up network. The number of nodes in the network far exceeds the number of modems, so we have to share the modems in some reasonable manner.

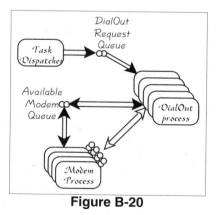

Figure B-20

When a **ModemProcess** is not being used, it leaves an identifying *token* in the **AvailableModemQueue**. If for some reason a **ModemProcess** becomes disabled or busy, it removes its token from the queue. Thus the **AvailableModemQueue** contains the tokens for all the modems that are currently available for use. A **DialOutProcess** manages data calls out to remote nodes. It performs all necessary communications with the remote nodes and then terminates the calls. All of the **DialOutProcess**es wait at the **DialOutRequestQueue**. Messages are placed in this queue by the **TaskDispatcher**, whose job is to decide which remote nodes must be talked to and when.

When the **TaskDispatcher** decides that a remote node must be talked to, its sends an appropriate message to the **DialOutRequestQueue**. A **DialOutProcess** gets the message (which one gets it is generally random). It then reads a token from the **AvailableModemQueue** that identifies an available **ModemProcess**. The **DialOutProcess** then communicates with the modem process, using it to place the data call and talk to the remote node. When it is done, it replaces the token on the **AvailableModemQueue**.

By controlling the number of **DialOutProcess**es that exist, we place a limit on the number of modems that can be simultaneously used for the dial-out task. Moreover, this limit is enforced without having to allocate specific modems as dial-out modems. All the modems can be used by the dial-out process, but never more than the limit at any given time. By having the **DialOutProcess** find available modems from the **AvailableModemQueue**, we provide a simple and secure method for resource allocation. It is also very easy to take a modem out of service; we simply remove it from the **AvailableModemQueue**.

Notice that none of the processes really know about any of the others. They know of certain queues, but not how those queues are serviced. The closest coupling exists between the **DialOutProcess** and the **ModemProcess**. When the **DialOutProcess** selects a modem, a client-server relationship is *temporarily* formed between them. This relationship is broken when the **DialOutProcess** completes its job.

Summary

This appendix has discussed some of the concepts and devices of multiprocessing. We have shown several different ways in which processes can switch context, pass messages, and protect themselves from the problems of concurrent update. We have examined schemes for constructing and passing messages, and for eliminating the machine and version dependencies within them. We have examined a notation for representing multiprocessing design decisions, and have seen several examples of how to use that notation.

I

Index

H

I

J

K

L

P